## PRAISE FOR YOUNG NEIL

*"Sharry Wilson's impeccably researched and written, beautifully illustrated* Young Neil *is the definitive chronicle of a Canadian icon's early years in his home and native land. Essential reading for diehard Neil Young fans, this book offers a lovingly detailed portrait of Canadian life in the middle of the 20th century, and of a sensitive young man who put his music above all else."*
— Kevin Chong, author of *Neil Young Nation* and *Northern Dancer*

*"A compelling look at the first 20 years of Neil Young's life as he sets out on his journey to find a heart of gold. Sharry Wilson not only takes us on Neil's voyage but also uncovers life in the '40s, '50s, and '60s in Ontario and Manitoba. A wonderful study of one the world's great artists written with passion and an obvious love for her subject."*
— Bernie Finkelstein, founder of True North Records and author of *True North: A Life in the Music Business*

*"Really enjoyed the book — especially the early years prior to Winnipeg — fun strolling down memory lane."*
— Ken Smyth, drummer, The Squires

# YOUNG NEIL
## THE SUGAR MOUNTAIN YEARS

**SHARRY WILSON**

ECW

Published by ECW Press
2120 Queen Street East, Suite 200
Toronto, Ontario, Canada, M4E 1E2
416-694-3348 / info@ecwpress.com

Library and Archives Canada Cataloguing in Publication
Wilson, Sharry, 1955–, author
Young Neil : the Sugar Mountain years / Sharry Wilson.
ISBN 978-1-77041-186-9 (pbk.).
Also issued as 978-1-77090-600-6 (pdf) and 978-1-77090-599-3 (epub)
1. Young, Neil, 1945–. 2. Rock musicians—Canada—Biography.
I. Title.
ML420.Y75W753 2014      782.42166092      C2014-902516-5
C2014-902517-3

Cover design: Gregg Kulick
Cover image: © QMI Agency / Harold Whyte
Every effort has been made to contact copyright holders and credit interior images appropriately
Type: Rachel Ironstone

A note on the type: Young Neil has been set in Sabon, a modern realization of the classic types of Claude Garamond and Robert Granjon, designed by Jan Tschichold circa 1967. The display font in use is Brandon Grotesque, designed by Hannes von Döhren circa 2009.

Printed and bound at United Graphics in the United States   5   4   3   2

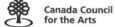

The publication of Young Neil has been generously supported by the Canada Council for the Arts, which last year invested $157 million to bring the arts to Canadians throughout the country. We acknowledge the support of the Ontario Arts Council (OAC), an agency of the Government of Ontario, which last year funded 1,793 individual artists and 1,076 organizations in 232 communities across Ontario, for a total of $52.1 million. We also acknowledge the financial support of the Government of Canada through the Canada Book Fund for our publishing activities, and the contribution of the Government of Ontario through the Ontario Book Publishing Tax Credit and the Ontario Media Development Corporation.

*For Scott Sandie,*
*who was there at the beginning*
*and saw the possibilities*

*When I get big I'm gonna get an electric guitar.*
*When I get* real *big.*
— Neil Young, *Live Rust* (1979)

# CONTENTS

Part Three ✱✱✱✱✱✱✱✱✱✱✱✱✱✱✱✱✱✱
## LEAVING SUGAR MOUNTAIN

## ⋆ PART ONE ⋆
# BORN IN ONTARIO

---

*I was born in Ontario*
*Where the black fly bites and the green grass grows.*
*That's where I learned most of what I know*
*'Cause you don't learn much when you start to grow old.*
*I left home at a tender young age*
*'Cause Mum and Daddy never seemed to stay*
*In any one place for very long*
*So we just kept moving, moving on.*

— Neil Young, "Born in Ontario"

---

## ✳ 1 ✳
## IN THE BEGINNING...

IT WAS A HARSH AND unwelcoming winter night — hardly unusual for early February in Toronto. A blizzard had rendered travel precarious. Only the hardiest souls ventured out.

On the morning of February 5, 1945, city residents woke to over 12 centimetres of fresh snow, bringing the total snowfall since November to more than 1.5 metres — more than would normally fall over an entire winter. And although the snow was not in itself overwhelming, it was accompanied by frigid, blinding winds.

Scott Young, then a sub-lieutenant in the Royal Canadian Naval Volunteer Reserve, was in Toronto on medical leave for fatigue, spending time with his wife, Rassy, and their nearly three-year-old son Bob. Scott was to undergo tests at a hospital in Ottawa, and Rassy and Bob planned to join him at the Lord Elgin Hotel during his recovery. But the snowstorm forced them to revise their travel plans.

3

They were invited to take refuge overnight in the home of good friends Ian and Lola Munro[1] at 361 Soudan Avenue, near the intersection of Eglinton Avenue East and Mount Pleasant Road in what was then a northern suburb of the city. The Youngs had been visiting the Munros as the day passed and weather conditions worsened.

Ian retrieved a spare mattress and put it on the dining-room floor as a makeshift bed for Scott and Rassy. The couple had been apart for a long period due to the demands of Scott's service. Happily reunited, they quietly made love as the snow sifted and deepened outside the darkened house. Scott Young writes:

> I know the exact time when Neil was conceived. I remember the street in Toronto, the wild February blizzard through which only the hardiest moved, on skis, sliding downtown through otherwise empty streets to otherwise empty offices. All trains were marooned or cancelled.[2]

NEIL YOUNG'S FATHER HAD ALREADY led a diverse and in some ways uniquely Canadian life. Born in Cypress River, Manitoba, in 1918, Scott's first job, at age 16, was manning the desk of a tobacco wholesaler in Winnipeg. He was a

---

CLOCKWISE FROM TOP: *361 Soudan Avenue.* [© 2010 Sharry Wilson]; *Scott Young in naval dress (circa 1945).* [Trent University Archives, Scott Young fonds (06-002 Box 1)]; *Scott Young,* Maclean's, *Articles Editor, 1945-48.* [Trent University Archives, Scott Young fonds (06-002 Box 1)]; *Aerial photo of Toronto General Hospital, 1951. Neil was born in the Private Patients' Pavilion, the T-shaped structure with the circular driveway in front.* [University Health Network Archives, Toronto]

hockey fan from an early age — in 1935 he lined up for hours to buy a $1 ticket to the Memorial Cup final between the Winnipeg Monarchs and the Sudbury Wolves. His literary career began in 1936, when he took a job as a copy boy at the *Winnipeg Free Press*.

In June 1940 Scott married Rassy. Born Edna Blow Ragland in 1918, Rassy was given her nickname — Rastus, later shortened to Rassy — by her father. She was the youngest of three daughters born to William N. Ragland[3] (a.k.a. Rags or Daddy to one and all) and his wife, Perle. Her two older sisters were Lavinia, known as Toots, and Virginia, nicknamed Snooky.

The marriage began on a troubled note, with Rassy facing an unwanted pregnancy. Neither she nor Scott was prepared to face the prospect of raising a child so soon and under their financial circumstances. Rassy told Scott she did not want him involved in what she decided should happen next. She tried various home remedies without success and eventually paid $15 for an illegal kitchen-table abortion that left her seriously ill. She recovered slowly, and according to Scott both of them regretted the decision.

Their relationship survived, and in November 1940 Scott left the *Winnipeg Free Press* to take a new job on the night rewrite desk with the Canadian Press in Toronto. Scott's uncle Jack Paterson,[4] then assistant editor at *Maclean's*, the iconic news and culture magazine, welcomed them to the city and found an apartment for them; Jack's wife, Ruth, helped them settle in.

Scott and Rassy's first son, Bob, was born on April 27, 1942. Five months later Scott was sent by CP to England, where for two years he wrote about the war. In 1944 he enlisted in the Royal Canadian Naval Volunteer Reserve as an ordinary seaman. Later that year he was commissioned and served in the landings in southern France and Greece, and with Royal Navy torpedo boats in the Adriatic.

Scott had come home suffering from chronic fatigue and weight loss. After the storm in Toronto, he completed the medical tests in Ottawa, but no serious problem was discovered, and following some rest and recovery he learned about a new position in the information branch of the navy. Scott was interested, and he secured the posting as assistant to Clyde Gilmour, lieutenant and chief public relations officer to the Flag Officer Newfoundland in St. John's. Gilmour would go on to achieve success as a print journalist and radio broadcaster and later enjoyed a half-century association with the Canadian Broadcasting Corporation (CBC), where his weekly music program, *Gilmour's Albums*, was a much-loved staple. Scott was soon promoted to lieutenant and succeeded Gilmour as chief public relations officer (CPRO-Newfoundland).

When the war in Europe ended a few months later, Scott had volunteered for duty in the Pacific. On leave for several weeks before reporting for duty, Scott met Rassy and Bob in Toronto in early August. They were staying with friends when the bombs were dropped on Hiroshima and Nagasaki. A few days later Scott received a telegram from Ottawa — he was to remain on leave until further notice. When the Japanese formally surrendered on September 2, 1945, Scott was released from the service.

A civilian again, he needed to find a full-time job and a place for his family to live — Scott and Rassy began to search for a new home in earnest. Bob was an active three-year-old, and by this time Rassy was at an advanced stage of her second pregnancy. Repeatedly rejected by landlords and rental agents who were reluctant to rent to families with young children, they decided to try and scrape together a minimum down payment on a home of their own.

Scott found work again at the Canadian Press. His manager, Gillis Purcell, had real-estate connections, and Gil's endorsement helped Scott and Rassy purchase a new three-bedroom bungalow in north Toronto, at 335 Brooke Avenue,[5] near the intersection of Lawrence Avenue and Avenue Road. Gil guaranteed their security for a $500 down payment and the builder agreed to reduce the price of the house by $500 to $6,500.

The Young family had barely settled into their new digs when Rassy went into labour. They didn't own a car, but a friendly next-door neighbour drove them to Toronto General Hospital, where Rassy was admitted to the Private Patients' Pavilion, later renamed the Thomas J. Bell Wing.[6] It was a plush environment in which to give birth. The ornate nine-storey, T-shaped structure, with a cut-stone entrance and Doric facade, was a complete hospital unto itself, accommodating more than 300 private and semi-private patients. It had officially opened on April 24, 1930, in an elaborate ceremony in which Ontario's Lieutenant-Governor W. D. Ross unlocked the door with a gold key, accompanied by the music of Romanelli's Orchestra. Mary L. Burcher, an executive member of the Canadian Hospital Association and a guest at the opening, said the new structure was "suggestive of a palatial and exclusive hotel."[7] *Construction*, the Canadian architectural and engineering journal of the day, glowingly wrote:

> Every unpleasant feature usually associated with hospitals has been most carefully eliminated from this building and a home-like atmosphere has been created. . . . The rotunda of dark panelled

treatment, the operating and anaesthesia rooms of mother-of-pearl finish, the gleaming nickelled monel metal fixtures, the wood finished metal beds and furniture, the chintz-covered chairs, the colourful curtains, the Persian rugs and the artistic lighting fixtures are all components in a well thought out and skilfully executed colour scheme.[8]

The Private Patients' Pavilion was also a source of controversy in the days before Canada's national health insurance program. Private patient facilities like this one brought into stark contrast the disparity in medical care between the poor and the more privileged classes.

It was in this environment that Neil Young first opened his eyes at 6:45 a.m. on Monday, November 12. Neil Percival Young[9] is the full name recorded on his birth certificate, according to his father. His first name paid homage to Rassy and Scott's brother-in-law, Neil Hoogstraten,[10] who married Rassy's sister Lavinia, and his middle name was likely a nod to Scott's father, Percy Andrew Young.[11]

Conceived during a time of war, Neil was born into a world more or less at peace. The war was over, though labour conflict continued. "Strike Settlement Hope Rises," proclaimed the headline of the November 12 issue of the *Toronto Daily Star* — workers at a Ford assembly plant in Windsor, Ontario, were still on strike but close to an agreement. In other news, Prime Minister Mackenzie King paid his respects to fallen soldiers during Armistice Day ceremonies at the Arlington National Cemetery, where he stood alongside U.S. president Harry Truman and Prime Minister Clement R. Attlee of Great Britain. The three leaders were in Washington to attend the first full working session of the U.S.-Canada-Britain conference on atomic power.

In Toronto, according to the paper's entertainment pages, the "Ice Capades of 1946" had an upcoming engagement at Maple Leaf Gardens, *The Hasty Heart* was playing at the Royal Alexandra Theatre, and a jazz concert featuring Charlie Parker was scheduled for November 14 at Massey Hall. Movies showing at cinemas across the city included *Kismet*, *The Devil and Miss Jones*, *Pennies from Heaven*, *Shanghai Cobra* and *House of Frankenstein*.

NEIL WAS SOON BROUGHT HOME to what was apparently a happy and successful Canadian family. Scott had been hired at *Maclean's*, and would retain his position as articles editor for the next three years. The magazine's editor, W. Arthur Irwin, gave Scott and many other notable Canadian writers their first solid start. He sent Scott to Vancouver with instructions to hire Pierre Berton,[12] then the world's youngest city editor at the *Sun*. Young was to entice him with an offer of $4,000 to $4,500 for the position of assignments editor. ("I'll take the $4,500," Berton said.)[13] Associate editor Ralph Allen, a good friend of Scott's from his early days in Winnipeg, would take over the editorship at *Maclean's* when Irwin left. A future who's who of Canadian literature passed through the portals of *Maclean's* during the 1940s and '50s, including June Callwood, Trent Frayne, John Clare, Robert Fulford, Peter

---

CLOCKWISE FROM TOP:
*Log cabin, Lake of Bays, summer 1948; Belmont Lake, September 1947; Rassy displaying a fine catch, Lake of Bays, summer 1948.* [Trent University Archives, Scott Young fonds (90-003 Box 26)]

Gzowski, W. O. Mitchell, Peter C. Newman and McKenzie Porter. This was the golden age at *Maclean's*, and Scott and Rassy befriended most of these writers.

It was customary for the *Maclean's* staff to get together for social occasions with their families and children. "We were all very close," recalls Janet Berton, Pierre's wife. One of the few *Maclean's* wives who did not have children yet, she was often recruited for babysitting duty; she began babysitting Neil and Bob in 1947, before her own children were born. Neil was "a sweet baby," she recalls, and they called him "little Neiler." On one occasion, according to the reminiscences of some of the "*Maclean's* kids," Pierre Berton consented to haul a hay wagon full of kids, including Neil, around the farm of *Maclean's* art editor Dave Battersby.

The salary for an assistant editor at *Maclean's* was modest, so Scott began to write short stories in his spare time to supplement his earnings. He wrote at a roll-top desk in the smallest of the three bedrooms, while Neil and Bob shared a bedroom. Rassy assisted Scott by typing and mailing his stories, which soon began selling to such major magazines as *Collier's*, *Argosy*, *Ladies' Home Journal*, *Women's Home Companion* and *Saturday Evening Post*. The Youngs were out of debt by 1947, and they celebrated by buying a well-used 1931 Willys-Knight automobile. Scott didn't yet have a driver's licence, so the duty of driving the temperamental old vehicle fell to Rassy.

---

CLOCKWISE FROM TOP-LEFT: *Lake of Bays, summer 1948;*
*Neil and Bob, Lake of Bays, June 1948; Neil, Bob and*
*two female friends. Lake of Bays, summer 1948; Neil and*
*Bob with some friends, Lake of Bays, summer 1948.*
[Trent University Archives, Scott Young fonds (90-003 Box 26)]

A friend had offered the Youngs the use of his cottage at Belmont Lake near Havelock, and they needed a car to get there. The oil-pressure gauge on the Willys-Knight didn't work, and between Toronto and Havelock it burned eight quarts of oil in billows of black smoke; nevertheless, the Youngs managed to have an enjoyable time — their first vacation as a family. Snapshots of the occasion include one of a 22-month-old Neil posed in the buff near the water's edge.

He was a plump and chubby-cheeked toddler. "Neil was funny as hell," remarks Rassy. "Great big eyes, yards of black hair and fat — my God, you could not fill him up. He ate and ate and ate. Wide as he was high."[14] He enjoyed pushing a toy wheelbarrow around the spacious backyard at 335 Brooke Avenue while Bob played ball with Scott. Neil would avidly point at whatever caught his attention and cryptically exclaim, "Dombeen!" — his first word as recalled by his father. Even at this early age Neil was known to dance a little jig in his playpen when music came on the radio or record player. Rassy recalls that he was especially fond of an old 78 recording of Pinetop Smith's "Boogie-Woogie." Scott wrote, "His whole body moved to the rhythm; it was his unconscious parlour trick."[15]

Neil's early life was not without some real health concerns. Scott remarked that Neil "used to get anything that came along. . . . [He] had pneumonia three times when he was a baby."[16] But he recovered well from these periodic setbacks and continued to enjoy a healthy appetite.

In June 1948 Scott quit his job at *Maclean's* to attempt a career as a full-time fiction writer. The Youngs disposed of their Willys-Knight after only eight months and bought a brand-new Monarch with $2,100 in cash from the proceeds of the sale of their house. Scott soon learned how to drive, and the family enjoyed the summer in a rustic rented waterfront log cabin on Lake of Bays in the Muskoka district, a couple hours' drive north of Toronto.

Neil and Bob spent much of their time fishing or swimming in a sandy cove that Scott had cleared of stones. A series of photos taken that summer shows Neil standing in shallow water playing happily with a wooden fruit basket, filling the basket with water, then watching in fascination as it dribbled out. The fruit baskets were more customarily used to collect wild strawberries, which Rassy would bake into pies. Scott wrote every day, though he failed to sell any of the stories he produced during this time. Friends often came to visit, usually other writers and editors. Scott recalled this time with his young family as his "best summer ever."

One family who visited the cabin on Lake of Bays was writer Max Braithwaite, his wife, Aileen, and their three children, Beryl, Sharon and Chris. Max had met Scott while serving in the Canadian navy. They shared an interest in writing, and both hailed from the prairie provinces — Scott from Manitoba, Max from Saskatchewan.

Eldest daughter Beryl,[17] then 12 and already well-known as the lead in the CBC radio program *Maggie Muggins*, recalls a day in Lake of Bays when the children were being "corralled" by their parents to come in for dinner. Neil, excited by all the activity, dashed past Beryl toward the dock and tumbled into the water. Beryl, a strong swimmer, instinctively jumped in fully clothed and pulled him out, perhaps averting a dire outcome.

Although Beryl was considerably older than the other children, she recalls that Bob and Neil were both "nice kids." Neil was a "chubby, funny little guy, lots of black spiky hair and big eyes."

Other visitors that summer included John and Lenore Clare; Ralph and Birdeen Allen; Trent Frayne and June Callwood, with their daughters Jesse and Jill; and Scott's brother Bob, his wife, Merle, and their daughters Penny, Marny and Stephanie. There was occasionally tension during these get-togethers. Rassy was uncomfortable with Birdeen and Merle, who had previously been emotionally involved with Scott, and she wasn't shy about sharing her concerns with him.

BY THE END OF SUMMER the cottage had grown uncomfortably chilly. The Youngs relocated to a rental house in Jackson's Point, a small resort town on Lake Simcoe north of Toronto. This large house also tended to be cold, the chill offset by the big cookstove in the kitchen. They shared the premises with their blue-grey cat Mary and Bob's dog Skippy, a cross between golden Labrador and Dalmatian. Scott had still not sold even one of the stories he wrote during the summer, so finances were tight.

Charlie Abbs, a boy who lived next door, was kind to Neil and often took him out to play. Charlie was about nine or ten, and every time Neil saw a boy around that age he called him "Chowlie."

Uncle Bob,[18] Aunt Merle and the "girl cousins"[19] were regular visitors at Jackson's Point. The three girls were about

---

CLOCKWISE FROM TOP: *Rassy, Neil and Bob playing with the family pets, Jackson's Point, 1948-49; Jackson's Point, 1948-49. Clockwise from top: Beryl Braithwaite, Sharon Braithwaite, Bob Young, Neil, Chris Braithwaite. Beryl rescued Neil from drowning when he was 2-1/2 years old.; Young family home, Jackson's Point, 1948-49.*
[Trent University Archives, Scott Young fonds (90-003 Box 26)]

the same age as Bob and Neil and enjoyed playing with the boys. The family pets also joined in on the fun and were well-loved by the children.

Writers June Callwood and Trent Frayne were frequent visitors. Frayne had met Scott when they shared lodgings in a ramshackle boarding house at 55 Donnell Street in Winnipeg in 1938. Scott was a columnist at the *Winnipeg Free Press* at the time and Frayne was a cub sportswriter at the *Winnipeg Tribune*. Ralph Allen, who also became a friend to Scott and Frayne, was a sports reporter at the *Tribune*. Scott and Allen were the first to make their moves to Toronto, and Frayne followed shortly. Frayne met June Callwood while both worked at the *Globe and Mail*, and they married in 1944.

Callwood contrasted the starkly different temperaments of the Young boys — Bob was outgoing and full of bluster, while Neil was much more reserved: "Neil was a sullen, fat, dark-eyed baby. Not a happy baby, not a smiler, not a joiner. Not getting much. Neil got good primary care, but he didn't get affection, hugs, from either of his parents. So he became a little watcher."[20] Rassy had her hands full with her two children and wrangled with them on a regular basis; Scott's attempts to smooth things over only further infuriated her.

IN THE SUMMER OF 1949 Scott took the family to visit Rassy's parents at their cottage on Lake Brereton in the Whiteshell Forest Reserve in eastern Manitoba. It was a memorable drive. Neil and Bob shared the back seat with their dog and five felines — Mary had recently had four kittens, sired by a neighbour's male cat named Charlie. Mary didn't like travelling: every time the family stopped, she would take one of her kittens from the basket and bolt out of the door. Scott "fielded kittens on the first bounce"[21] during the entire long drive. The Youngs and their pets arrived intact on Friday, July 1, the start of the Canada Day long weekend, and the family soon found homes for the thriving kittens.

Other guests at the cottage that summer were Neil and Toots Hoogstraten and their children, Bill and Janis. Bill remembers sleeping in a tent in the backyard with Bob Young, since all the beds in the cottage had been taken. Toots, writing under the name Vinia Hoogstraten, composed a humorous short story about the family's experiences that summer. It was Bill who provided the title for the piece — "Sleeps Twelve."

One day Bill was hiking along the path from the lake to the cottage when he noticed Neil — a "chubby, happy kid" at four years old — walking a short distance ahead, singing to himself. As he caught up he heard Neil belting out "I got a bloodsucker on my leg" in several verses. (Perhaps Neil's first musical composition, Bill has speculated.) Sure enough, it turned out there was a well-fed leech clinging to his ankle. At the cottage, the traditional treatment of table salt was administered and the leech was successfully disengaged.

During the winter and spring of 1948-49, Scott had been hunting for a home to buy, this time with the assistance of a government land-settlement plan for ex-servicemen called the Veterans' Land Act. He had discovered an ideal house in a small Ontario town called Omemee, and in mid-August the family left Manitoba and enrolled Bob for the fall school term. (A kennel shipped Skippy and Mary back east in September.)

Omemee would prove an idyllic home for Neil during the next five years. But it was impossible to ignore the shadows that had begun to fall over the family. It was in Omemee that the first cracks appeared in Scott and Rassy's relationship.

And to add to the tension, these were the days before the Salk vaccine, when every family with young children feared the spectre of a polio epidemic.

---

## ☆ 2 ☆
## OMEMEE AND BEYOND

*I am a child*
*I'll last a while*
*You can't conceive*
*Of the pleasure in my smile.*

— Neil Young, "I Am a Child"

IN OMEMEE, THE YOUNG FAMILY lived in a detached red-brick two-storey (plus attic) turn-of-the-century home at 33 King Street West. Located on five acres of land on the town's main thoroughfare, the property included a large barn-like structure and a few apple trees out back. The Youngs purchased the house for $5,400 from its former owner, an elderly woman named Mrs. Haygarth.

A large and welcoming front porch opened into an entryway and then into a spacious kitchen in the middle of the home. Some smaller family rooms were located off to the side and a more intimate "summer kitchen" was situated at the back. A stairway led up to the second floor, where there were three bedrooms — a large master bedroom and two smaller ones, one of which was Neil's.

Scott Young did his writing on a big Underwood typewriter in the house's attic, a warm, generous space with a peaked ceiling and small windows at either end. In a fax sent to Scott and his third wife, Maggie, in 1992, Neil writes, "As I pound this out I can't help but think about Daddy typing in the attic in Omemee."[22] And in an interview with Jimmy McDonough, he recalls, "I can still remember goin' up the steps, up into the attic. He'd be on the typewriter and I'd just walk up and stand there looking at him — my head was just a little bit higher than his desk. He never, never got mad at me. It was always 'Nice to see you.'"[23]

Many years later Neil was asked if the process of writing his memoir, *Waging Heavy Peace*, made him feel more connected to his father. "I always remember that my dad used to call me Windy," he said. "That was what he called me because I always had ideas. . . . He had a big old Underwood and it was on the third floor of our house up in the attic with little windows and the peaked ceilings and everything. He had a couple of doors that he put on sawhorses up there and he had his study up there. That's where he wrote his books. He was up there every day. . . . It was a rule that no one could go up and talk to him while he was writing, so I went right up. I would ask, 'What are you writing about?' He said, 'Well, I don't know . . . I found that if you just sit down and start writing that all kinds of things happen.'"[24]

Omemee is a bucolic village on the banks of the Pigeon River, about 140 kilometres east of Toronto, situated between

---

CLOCKWISE FROM TOP: *Pastoral Omemee welcome, circa 1950.* [Courtesy of Joan Rehill. From the September 9, 1950, issue of the *Toronto Telegram.* © 1950 QMI Agency / Harold Whyte.]; *33 King Street West.* [© 2009 Sharry Wilson]; *Santa Claus Parade, Omemee, December 1949.* [Trent University Archives, Scott Young fonds (90-003 Box 26)]

the cities of Lindsay and Peterborough. Founded in 1820, the town took its name from the Algonquin word *omimi*, which echoed the sound pigeons made. King Street crosses the Pigeon River on what is locally known as the White Bridge (or Highway Bridge), a cement structure built in 1933. The population was approximately 460 when the Youngs moved to Omemee in 1949.

Neil and Bob often indulged in the simple pleasures of a small-town boyhood, including swimming, fishing off the ledge under the Mill Bridge, and catching turtles and frogs in the muddy shallows. Scott took Neil and Bob for long drives in the country, singing old songs to entertain them, often accompanied by the family dog Skippy. (Neil and Skippy were inseparable, seemingly attached at the hip.)[25] Early television programs were another part of Neil's nostalgic memories of Omemee. Saturday-morning favourites included *The Lone Ranger* and *Hopalong Cassidy*, and the family passed companionable evenings with *The Honeymooners, Jack Benny, The Perry Como Show, Dragnet, This Is Your Life* and *The $64,000 Question*. Bedtime stories consisted of one chapter per evening from the popular Thornton W. Burgess children's series with characters such as Reddy Fox, Jimmy Skunk, Chatterer the Red Squirrel and Blacky the Crow. Rassy and Scott had read their older son the same stories a few years earlier. "I think Neil would probably agree." Bob Young remarks, "if there's anywhere either of us would point to as home, it would be Omemee."[26]

---

*Four-year-old Neil fishing on a bridge over the Pigeon River.*
[Trent University Archives, Scott Young fonds (90-003 Box 26).
© 1950 QMI Agency / Harold Whyte]

Neil's nostalgic memories of Omemee are suggested in the lyrics to "Helpless" (*There is a town in north Ontario / With dream comfort memory to spare / And in my mind I still need a place to go / All my changes were there*), although he has stated that the "town in north Ontario" celebrated in the song is actually an amalgamation of several places he recalls fondly from his childhood: "Omemee's a nice little town. Sleepy little place. . . . Life was real basic and simple in that town. Walk to school, walk back. Everybody knew who you were. Everybody knew everybody."[27]

The September 9, 1950, edition of the *Toronto Telegram* devoted an entire page to the delights of life in Omemee. An article titled "Omemee Kids Like School" remarked on the fact that Omemee schoolchildren had nature at their doorstep. Another such article included a photo of a smiling four-year-old Neil proudly holding a 20-pound muskie. (The photo was faked: the fish was frozen.)

Long-time Omemee resident Joan Rehill recalls that Neil would sometimes pay a visit to the convenience store where her husband, Willard, sold fishing tackle and supplies. Willard was a talented muskie fisherman, and Neil often asked for his help putting a fishhook on the end of his crude fishing pole — a stick with a string on the end of it. Willard thought Neil looked more like "a Zeke," and called him by that nickname whenever he saw him. (Neil would eventually name his firstborn son Zeke, perhaps a nod to Willard Rehill's affectionate nickname.)

---

*Neil holding a 20 lb. frozen muskie, August 1950.*
[From the September 9, 1950, issue of the *Toronto Telegram*.
© 1950 QMI Agency / Harold Whyte]

As a budding fisherman, Neil ran into more difficulties with fishhooks, occasionally embedding them in his skin: "God," Rassy remarked, "Neiler had little pinprick scars all over his stomach for years."[28] On one memorable occasion when he was five, Neil hooked himself in the abdomen and sought assistance from Austin Hayes, whose family home was close to the Mill Bridge and who, after raising four sons, was well-versed in the removal of fishhooks. Mr. Hayes retrieved a pair of pliers and carefully worked out the hook, then disinfected the wound with iodine and applied a Band-Aid. Neil went back to his fishing.

The Hayes family were good friends of the Youngs; Jay Hayes, son of patriarch Austin, often hunted ducks with Scott in the surrounding countryside. Bob also enjoyed hunting and sometimes joined his father, but Neil refused to have anything to do with the activity. (He didn't object to eating the ducks, however, once Rassy had cleaned and cooked them.)

The Youngs also befriended another family, the Allens. Writer Robert Thomas Allen was a professional colleague of Scott and lived with his family in Omemee for three years starting in 1951. Robert, with his wife, Helen, and their daughters, Jane and Mary, lived just north of town on a rental property called Glen Farm. It was a working farm: the Allens lived in the gorgeous farmhouse while a farmer from the community planted and harvested. The Allen family had free reign over the rest of the property, and the children enjoyed roaming over it. There were interesting outbuildings to explore, including a summer kitchen where the family's cats lived and gave birth, an abandoned silo and a shady barn where an old horse carriage had endured for countless seasons. Townspeople enjoyed skating on Finnegan's Pond, a short distance north of Glen Farm. The pond was also a popular destination during summer months.

The Young and Allen families often traded visits. Jane recalls that Scott and Rassy were guests at a corn roast her parents held in the fields behind their house one summer evening. It was an "adults only" party, so Jane and Mary had to peer through their bedroom windows to catch glimpses of the festivities. An old pump organ had been moved from the farmhouse to the field for the occasion, and the sisters heard "happy voices coming across the hedge into the night" as they drifted toward sleep.

WHEN HE WAS FIVE, NEIL received his first toy train set from his parents, the beginning of what would become a lifetime hobby. That first set was a Marx Santa Fe diesel rig, purchased through the Eaton's department store mail-order catalogue. With his father's help, Neil assembled the L-shaped layout on a table Scott had built. "The couplers were flat and fit together in a way that made them stay together," Neil recalls, "but if you tilted them one way the cars would come apart and disconnect. I still remember the layout well, so it made quite an impression on me."[29] The layout was situated across from his bed in the corner of the room, and at bedtime Neil would turn off his light, switch on the train and watch it make its rounds through the darkness.

Real-life railroad tracks located about 300 metres from the backyard afforded Neil the opportunity to see real trains up close. A railroad bridge spanned the river, and he enjoyed watching the big steam trains with their passenger or freight cars rumble by. He relished placing copper pennies on the railroad track and picking them up after they had been flattened. "I would put my ear down on the rail so I could hear the train coming before I could see it," he recalls. "Once we heard the train, we would carefully place the coin on the rail and then wait for the big moment to arrive."[30] Train imagery figures in several of his songs, including "Southern Pacific" and "Box Car." "I liked the smell of the track," Neil says. "I liked the railroad bridge — which is still there. . . . Trains. I find their sounds inspirational."[31] Neil would remain an ardent admirer of trains all his life and would share his love of trains with his own children.

A CONSTANT FEATURE OF FAMILY meals was Scott Young's spaghetti. "We had spaghetti a lot," Neil remembers. "It was really good with my dad's special sauce. [H]e would add hamburger meat and let it simmer for hours, covered. Al dente was his preferred way to cook the noodles. . . ."[32] The smell was intoxicating.

Scott's spaghetti recipe achieved an almost cult-like status among friends and relatives.[33] He began including it on occasion in his *Globe and Mail* columns when he worked at that newspaper in the late 1950s and '60s. The readership clamoured for repeat printings.

A copy of his original typed recipe[34] reads:

SCOTT YOUNG'S SPAGHETTI RECIPE

Start with two pounds of lean minced beef, the best you can afford. Place this in a large pot with the contents of a large can of stewed tomatoes and one 4-ounce can or two (depending on taste) of tomato paste. Add a tablespoon of salt, a half-teaspoon of black pepper, a tablespoon of curry powder, a tablespoon of sugar, a pinch of rosemary, a tablespoon of oregano or pre-mixed

Italian seasoning, a teaspoon of cayenne pepper. Crush two to four cloves of garlic in a garlic press over the pot, and then scrape the crushed buds into the sauce along with the juice.

Stir well with a long fork to make the meat break up into a sauce without lumps.

Cut five medium-sized onions (red Italian or Bermuda preferred but cooking onions okay) into the pot. Wash a pound of mushrooms and add without browning, unless you happen to be a nut on browning mushrooms. Cut a green pepper or two into long strips and hold ready to add later.

When the mixture begins to simmer boldly, let it cook for a minimum of one hour, a maximum of two. About 30-35 minutes before you plan to serve, add the green pepper strips and one six or eight-ounce (or so) smoked sausage for every intended serving (these only need time to heat through; I use Schneider's).

Cook the spaghetti itself (I use Lancia), about one-quarter pound per person, about 15 minutes after it begins to boil. Drain and place on plates. On top of each mound of spaghetti, place one sausage and generous portions of the meat sauce. Your table also should have grated parmesan or romano cheese; cold celery, radishes and dill pickles; the small dish of ground red peppers for customers who like the sauce hotter.

Neil keeps a framed copy of his dad's recipe in the kitchen at Broken Arrow Ranch. "It is so faded," he says, "that I can hardly read it anymore, but it does have his [Scott's] original handwriting. Pegi [Neil's wife] has made it a few times, and it's great when she does. At least someone is making it, and that feels good to me. I would like to taste that again."[35]

LIFE WAS TRANQUIL FOR THE Young family during their earliest days in Omemee, apart from a bout with scarlet fever Neil suffered when he was four.[36] That crisis passed, but during the late summer of 1951, when Neil was five and a half and preparing to enter Grade 1 at Omemee Public School, his health would be in jeopardy once again.

Late summer and early fall were polio season, and this year was no exception. Daily newspaper headlines recounted the toll of the latest victims of the disease. During 1951 a total of 2,568 cases were recorded nationwide, 1,701 of them in Ontario.[37] Most of the victims were under 15 years of age. The worst cases resulted in death, while nearly half of those afflicted suffered paralysis or muscle loss. The public was warned to stay away from crowds and avoid public transportation. Even

---

CLOCKWISE FROM TOP: *Willard Rehill.* [Courtesy of Marlyne Fisher-Heasman with assistance from Joan Rehill]; *The Swimming Hole, Pigeon River.* [Courtesy of Marlyne Fisher-Heasman. © *Hamilton Spectator*, August 1961]; *The Hospital for Sick Children, 1951, the same year the new building was finished and Neil was admitted for treatment of poliomyelitis.* [Reproduced by permission of the Hospital Archives, The Hospital for Sick Children, Toronto]

a simple sore back or sore throat provoked anxiety, as these could be the first symptoms of infection.

The disease was spread primarily through contamination of the hands by fecal matter and the resulting contact with food and the mouth. Water in pools, ponds or other swimming areas was an especially common vector of infection. Omemee had so far been spared, but the possibility of an outbreak was on everyone's mind.

During the afternoon of August 30, Scott took Neil to the local swimming hole at a bend on the east side of the Pigeon River in between the White Bridge and the Mill Bridge. They spent a pleasant afternoon in the water and then returned home. Around 1 a.m. that night Scott heard groans coming from Neil's room. He went in and asked what was wrong. Neil complained of a sore right shoulder blade, and Scott also noticed that his forehead seemed a little warm. He gave Neil an aspirin with water and Neil sat up gingerly to swallow it. He was quiet for the rest of the night.

Scott was the first one up the next day, and he headed downstairs to start breakfast. He called out to Bob and Neil to come down, but Neil didn't want breakfast — his back was still sore and he was feverish. The family doctor, Bill Earle, arrived shortly before noon and began performing manual tests. Neil couldn't touch his chin to his chest and cried out in pain when his knees were bent upward toward his chest. The doctor diagnosed the possibility of polio, gave Neil a shot of penicillin and promised to return at 4 p.m., when his office hours were finished. Neil slept through the rest of the afternoon while his family fretted.

On his return, the doctor sensed that Neil's condition had worsened. He recommended taking Neil to the Hospital for Sick Children in Toronto, where a lumbar puncture could be performed — and where an ample supply of iron lungs was available, should Neil's condition take a turn for the worse.

Dr. Earle advised the hospital that the Youngs were on their way and provided a surgical mask for Neil to wear on the trip. He told the Youngs they were under quarantine and instructed them not to stay the night in Toronto.

It was Friday evening of the Labour Day long weekend. The drive to Toronto meant negotiating not only heavy traffic but gusty rain and lightning. Neil, laid out on a board on the floor in the back seat of their early-1950s Mercury Monarch, wore his surgical mask and clutched a toy train his father had bought for him that morning. The train made clacking noises when the wheels turned, but Neil was too weak to spin them. He wasn't happy about having to wear the surgical mask either. Bob sat with Neil in the back while Rassy sat up front, leaning back from time to time to offer soothing words. They pulled up to the entrance of the hospital at 8:30 p.m.

The most trying time for the family came when Neil was given tests for pain and stiffness. He refused sedation before his lumbar puncture and his screams echoed down the hallway beyond the closed room where he was being treated. Neil remembers "this big table and the biggest needle I had ever seen. It turns out I was getting a lumbar puncture. That hurt like hell and scared me to death. I really think that was my first big trauma."[38] After the procedure, Scott and Rassy were called in to calm Neil down. The doctor returned about 15 minutes later to tell them Neil's spinal fluid had tested positive for poliomyelitis. He would have to stay in isolation for seven days while the hospital monitored his condition. With fever, there was always a chance that paralysis would ensue. After a week's time the temperature usually abated, the Youngs were told, and if any paralysis or weakness did develop, Neil would be moved to a surgical ward for therapy. In the meantime they would have to wait and hope for the best. At the back of their minds, of course, was the uneasy knowledge that they had been exposed to the disease as well.

The family spent the next week at home, in quarantine. Only Scott was allowed to go out to buy groceries. Bob Young recalls, "I spent a lot of time as a child in Omemee being quarantined because of diseases that caught Neil. There was polio, diphtheria, measles and others."[39] The family called the hospital every day for updates. Neil retains a strong memory of his hospital bed and "a nurse who always sang 'Beautiful Brown Eyes' to me."[40] He had had a rough start, but by Wednesday there was a noticeable improvement, and he was allowed to return home after the sixth day. His parents came to retrieve him from the hospital: "I was trying to walk across the floor to my mommy and daddy in a little room. My mommy had her hands open and said, 'Come on, Neil!' So I went over to her in stiff little steps and everyone was happy."[41]

"I didn't die, did I?" Neil asked his family.[42] He hadn't died, but the disease had left him weak, and the family prepared a downstairs bed where he could recuperate. "When he came home he had to learn to walk again," Bob Young recalls. "I remember him trying to get from one part of the living room to another by hanging on to furniture to keep his balance."[43] The family gathered round and dedicated time to talking with him and keeping him company. "Walking was hard for a while, and my back hurt," Neil says. "We had a quarantine sign on our house that said Poliomyelitis on it and warned people about not entering. . . . No one wanted to be near me for a while."[44] It was during this period that Neil confided to his father, "Polio is the worst cold there is."[45]

By his sixth birthday Neil had become something of a

celebrity — the first polio case in Omemee. Since then another local boy had contracted the disease and had died. Neil, a survivor, was one of the so-called "lucky polios."

Luck is relative, of course. During the 1980s Neil would suffer post-polio syndrome. As an adult he battled the physical symptoms of muscle weakness with a routine of vigorous exercise, contrary to energy-budgeting advice advocated by some health-care experts at the time. "It affected me particularly in the mid-'80s," he recalls, "when I couldn't even pick up my guitar. My body was starting to fall apart on me. That's when I started 'working out.' It's proven to be my salvation too. Lifting weights and exercising have completely changed everything for me, with regard to my health."[46] Neil adds in a later interview, "I started working out when I did *Landing on Water*. I didn't have enough strength to lift my guitar up over my shoulder — it was all fucked up, pain up and down my arm, pain in my back, pain in my leg. That was like post-polio syndrome or something. But I've been able to beat it by weightlifting. That was the beginning of my physical reconstruction."[47] Asked in 2005 if anything good had come of his having polio, he responded, "Yes, there was something good that came out of having polio as a kid. Walking."[48]

NEIL CONVALESCED AT HOME DURING the fall of 1951. He amused himself by drawing, especially pictures of trains, and Rassy noted that he was ambidextrous when he drew. "Polio," Neil remarks, "affected my left side, and I think I was left-handed when I was born. What I have done is use the weak side as the dominant one because the strong side was injured."[49]

During this time Neil often sat on the front stoop of the house and watched the other children walk home from school. Some of the kids would stop to chat with him, but as soon as something else caught their attention they would scurry away. Neil occasionally tried to follow them, but would fall when he went to take a first step too quickly. Because he was too frail to walk far, some of the other children took him for wagon rides. Shirley Black recalls that she and her older brother Al used to pull Neil around the village in his wagon so he could get some fresh air and join in some fun with the other children. Even before he was stricken with polio he was known for taking his wagon everywhere with him. Scott remarked, "If he became tired away from home, he'd hail the first passerby and have himself pulled home."[50]

Neil entered Grade 1 at Omemee Public School sometime later in the fall. The school was housed in the same brick building as the high school; younger children attended class on the main floor while high school students were taught on the second floor. Omemee Public School was located on the southeast corner of Rutland and George streets, diagonally opposite the Orange Hall and next to Cap's Place and the Mill Pond, upstream from the dam. The water-powered mill was still in use at the time. The gently sloping, grassy schoolyard ended in a marsh on the shore of the pond.

One of the peculiarities of Omemee's history is that its schoolhouses often suffered destructive fires, and the "Brick School" (as Omemee P.S. was called in its later years) was no exception: it was destroyed by fire in 1964. An earlier school had burned down in January 1904, and classes were held in temporary quarters for almost a full year before the new school (the one Neil would eventually attend) was ready in January 1905.

Jessie Lamb was Neil's Grade 1 teacher. Classmate David Finney recalls that Miss Lamb was a "wonderful teacher." One of Neil's earliest school memories is of his Grade 1 teacher holding him off the ground by his chin — he says he was being punished for making faces in class and that this incident set the tone for the rest of his academic career.[51] Neil's "partner in crime" was Henry Mason.[52] "He and I laughed a lot at the funny faces we would all make behind Miss Lamb's back," Neil says. "He was hysterical, as I remember."[53] Jessie Lamb's portrait now hangs proudly on the wall of Scott Young Public School in Omemee; the resource centre at the school is named after her, a commemorative plaque is displayed by the door, and the school presents an annual literary award in her honour. Teacher and student were amicably reunited during the opening ceremonies at Scott Young Public School on November 4, 1993.

Every morning students stood at attention to sing "God Save the King," the national anthem. (This would become "God Save the Queen" on February 6, 1952, when Princess Elizabeth ascended to the throne upon the death of her father, King George VI.) The song was an important ritual of the school day, and it left a strong impression on Neil: in 2012 he recorded a version of it for the album *Americana*. He commented to Terry Gross during an interview on the "Fresh Air" segment of NPR on June 6, 2012, "I woke up one morning a couple months ago, and I was hearing 'God Save the Queen' in my head, and I thought, 'That's probably because when I was little, I went to school and sang "God Save the Queen." That's what happened.' So I kind of had this thing driven into my head, so it randomly came back, and I just happened to be recording *Americana* and I thought, 'I'll just do "God Save the Queen" today and see how that works.'"

A Grade 1 classmate, Morag Gray, recalls that Neil had a reputation for being "a bit mischievous and naughty." Miss Lamb regularly asked if any of her students happened to be celebrating birthdays on that particular day. Neil stood up one day and declared that it was his birthday. The ruse failed — Miss Lamb had a list provided by the school — and she gently admonished Neil: "It's not your birthday. You've already had your birthday so you may sit down, Neil."

At the risk of being caught and sent to the principal, Neil also took part in the students' favourite illicit thrill — taking rides down the tube-shaped fire escape that ran from the third floor to ground level.

When he wasn't causing mischief in the public school system, Neil attended Sunday school at one of the churches in town. "When I was six," Neil says, "I really didn't know what God was. But I did know about Sunday school. I was reading a lot about God, but I was bored. I couldn't wait to get out of Sunday school."[54]

Sports were difficult for Neil, who was still suffering lingering effects from his bout with polio. "I remember not being very good at sports," he recalls, "and my back hurt when I was skating and leaning over, so my position as a goalie was in jeopardy on the rink. I couldn't skate that well, and the puck scared the hell out of me. I was not meant to play hockey. . . ."[55]

---

CLOCKWISE FROM TOP: *Omemee Public School, Grade 1, 1951-52.* [Courtesy of Don Weir with assistance from Ellie (Munnings) Lavery]; *Neil and his Grade 1 teacher, Jessie Lamb, at the opening ceremonies of Scott Young Public School in Omemee, November 4, 1993.* [© 1993 Joan Rehill]; *Henry Mason, age 10. Neil's best friend from Omeee Public School.* [Courtesy of the Youngtown Museum with assistance from Henry Mason]; *Neil's drawing of Rassy.* [Trent University Archives, Scott Young fonds (90-003 Box 26)]; *Omemee Public School/High School.* [Courtesy of Marlyne Fisher-Heasman]

Mrs young
drawn by Neil Young

It was around this time that Scott and Rassy instituted an incentive-reward system for their sons based on the child-rearing philosophy of esteemed Canadian child psychologist Dr. William Emet Blatz. Bob was 10 then, Neil six. Scott briefed the boys on the details of the new plan. "This column," Scott said, pointing to a ruled sheet of paper tacked to the back of the kitchen door, "is for Bob, the other for Neil. That one is for the days of the week. This amount up here is the basic allowance for the week (25 cents for Bob, 15 for Neil). Each day, you will be credited with amounts for extra work, such as doing dishes, weeding the garden and running errands, except when these are routine, in which case there will be no extra pay.

"Each day, also, you will be credited with two cents for having clean fingernails when challenged, which may be at any time of the day. Same goes for carrying a handkerchief. You will have deducted two cents for every time you don't hang up the towel. There will also be two-cent deductions for being bad in a minor way, five cents for majors. Just like in hockey."[56]

The plan worked for a while but, as Scott discovered, it required a lot of bookkeeping. If his records were incomplete or there was anything short of a thorough explanation of why he had trimmed Bob's or Neil's allowance, he would be challenged at the family's Saturday board meetings. Eventually this incentive system was abandoned when the "crime sheet" and its penalties became a subject of ridicule among Scott and Rassy's friends. "Exposure to public view," Scott wrote, "has the effect of making ridiculous things look at least as ridiculous as they really are."[57]

DURING THE 1951 CHRISTMAS SEASON, Neil was still in a weakened condition, and Scott and Rassy[58] decided the sun and warmth of Florida might hasten his recovery. Their friends from Toronto and Omemee, the Allens, had spent a few winters in the central-east coast town of New Smyrna Beach, and it sounded to the Youngs like an ideal location. They left Omemee on December 26 in their 1951 Monarch, and on New Year's Day of 1952 they arrived in New Smyrna Beach, where the weather was a sunny 82 degrees Fahrenheit. Neil and Bob immediately headed for the beach.

The family settled into a small cottage (two bedrooms, fully furnished, for $100 per month, with two picture windows in the living room and an interior panelled in Ponderosa pine), one of a group of three similar cottages on South Atlantic Avenue.[59] Since this was a beachside residence, only a small door faced west on the South Atlantic Avenue side, while a more welcoming porch entryway fronted on the ocean. A sloping sand dune separated the homes from the beach in front of Buenos Aires Street, an unpaved road. The beach was basically at their doorstep. And they had friends in the neighbourhood: the Allen family had returned to New Smyrna Beach that winter and lived nearby.[60]

Decades later Neil referenced their time in New Smyrna Beach in the song "Born in Ontario": *One cold winter we went down south / With Daddy's typewriter for a couple of months*.[61] Scott tried to work when he was not busy with the family or social activities with the other adults.

The neighbourhood on the east side of the barrier island, Coronado Beach, had been incorporated with New Smyrna Beach in 1947. Coronado Beach had been founded in the Hill Street area, between Seventh and Ninth avenues, in the late 1800s, but the centre of population moved to Flagler Avenue after the North Bridge was built across the Indian River in the early 1900s. The water between the barrier island and the mainland is part of Florida's Intracoastal Waterway. Ocean breezes made Coronado Beach cooler and more pleasant than the mainland.

Local families socialized at the Coronado Civic Center on Flagler Avenue on the island's west side. The popular city shuffleboard courts were next door to the Civic Center, and the old post office, where the Youngs picked up their mail, was in front. The centre was used mostly by adults during the winter months for all sorts of activities, including "card game night." Children were allowed to participate at bingo and were included in the weekend community dances, but the shuffleboard courts were sacred ground for the adults — children and teens were strictly forbidden.

Flagler Avenue's other attractions included a small grocery store, a drugstore with a soda fountain, another civic building known as the Beach Club, a Methodist church, the Riverview Hotel at the foot of the North Bridge and the "very modern" Ward Motel.[62]

Neil and Bob had to take a bus to school on the mainland. The school bus picked them up in front of Pop Thornal's gas station[63] on the southeast corner of Flagler and South Atlantic. Children who joined them on the walk to the bus stop included Martha Cleland and Sandra Ezell, two of Neil's classmates. Martha lived with her family on nearby Cedar Avenue, while Sandra lived with her mother in a garage apartment on the Ward family's property on the southeast corner of Columbus at South Atlantic. Pat and Earl "Bucky" Beeman, neighbours of the Cleland family on Cedar Avenue, were part of the same group of children. Pat, eldest in the group, shepherded the younger children and made sure no one strayed. It wasn't always a comfortable walk: Martha remembers "wiping away hordes of mosquitoes." (The county had once been called Mosquito County, for good reason.) The school bus normally followed a route over the North Bridge, but during 1951-52 the wooden bridge was being replaced by a cement structure and the bus took an alternate route over the narrower South Bridge.

Neil joined the Grade 1 class at Faulkner Street Elementary School, where his teacher was Cathy Gatliff, a recent graduate from Stetson University. This was her first year of teaching. Martha Cleland recalls that Miss Gatliff was "an excellent teacher and a lovely person." The principal was Philip Jones, who lived in quarters at the Riverview Hotel. He was "a lot of fun, but kept a paddle handy." Neil impressed Martha as "one of the nicest boys I knew at that time." The school itself, which taught grades 1 through 6, had been constructed in 1916 and was originally a segregated school for white students. Located at 401 Faulkner Street, the building was a large grey two-storey stone structure with *Faulkner St. School* inscribed in stern capital letters on a lintel above the main doors. It occupied an entire block, from Murray Street in the south to Mary Avenue in the north. A large playground at the back of the property bordered the river. The school's wooden floors and stairs creaked with age; the large classroom windows were propped open to let in fresh air; and the basement often flooded in the wake of heavy rains.

Former student Kathy Hughes remembers Faulkner Street Elementary as "a lovely Old South school." It was officially closed in June 1986 and torn down a few years later, but the school bell was retrieved by former Faulkner teacher Jane (Chapman) Gould and remains on display in the New Smyrna Museum of History.

Hygiene standards at the school were apparently quite high: on one occasion Neil was sent home for having dirty

64
10

Neil Young
    Cat Kin
I have a little pussy,
And her coat is silver gray;
S (S)he lives in a great wide
meadow And she never
runs away. she'll never
be a cat Because—shes a
pussy willow!
Now what do you think
of that!


Baby Rabbits Name
Baby Rabbits was ten
days old, and he did
not have a name.
Let's call him Bunny
siad his father.

SCHOOL DAYS
1951 – 52

ears. A furious Rassy considered the offence trivial and made sure her opinion on the subject was well-known.

Outside of school the children had the run of the streets and kept themselves busy with the customary pastimes of the era: cowboys and Indians, hide-and-seek. They often encountered skunks, possums and other creatures on the beach, while the woods just west of Cedar Avenue invited exploration.

Neil especially enjoyed the beach. In the February 1952 issue of *Saturday Night* magazine, Scott wrote an article extolling the virtues of their winter home, "[Neil] seems just plain born for sun and sand instead of cold and snow." Neil continued to be an avid fisherman: "His Grandpa gave him a new fishing outfit for Christmas and he hangs over the edge of the bridge with the rest of the tourists, hoping for that big bite." The sunny climate also improved Neil's health. "He's rapidly losing the last visible effects of the polio he had last September; lighter clothes help."[64]

Neil enjoyed building elaborate sandcastles on the beach and playing with blocks while indoors. Even at this age, Rassy thought, he had the makings of an architect. "I know you're going to be an architect," Neil recalls her saying. "I know that's what you are because when you were just a kid, all you would do was build things." Neil himself confirms, "I got my building blocks, got so many building blocks and

---

CLOCKWISE FROM TOP: *Faulkner Street Elementary School, First Grade, 1952.* [Courtesy of Shalaine (Crain) Solomon with assistance from Sandi (Ezell) Blackmer]; *Solo photo of Neil taken at Faulkner Street Elementary School, New Smyrna Beach, Florida, 1952.* [Trent University Archives, Scott Young fonds (90-003 Box 26)]; *The poem "Cat Kin," transcribed by Neil for a school assignment. Signed by Rassy at top.* [Trent University Archives, Scott Young fonds (90-003 Box 26)]

I was building all these structures, and ways you get in and out, and then building big sandcastles on the beach. Trying to figure out how to catch the water, and make the water stay. Then try to make the water do things."[65]

He adds, "I never gave it a lot of thought growin' up, but I think if I'd had the dedication, architecture would've been like fallin' off a fuckin' log for me. . . . I always liked building things."[66]

Neil's fondness for architecture would surface in the song "Like an Inca" from *Trans* (1982), and was echoed more recently in "The Hitchhiker" from *Le Noise* (2010). Both songs share the same verse: *I thought I was an Aztec / or a runner in Peru / I could build such beautiful buildings / to house the chosen few / like an Inca from Peru*. "I like Frank Lloyd Wright and Gaudí . . ." Neil sums up, "ancient things in architecture like Aztec architecture. . . . Architecture is a reflection not of the one person, but of a time and place where civilization is at. The architecture is more important than the artist. . . ."[67]

THE YOUNG FAMILY RETURNED TO Omemee in May 1952 and Neil finished Grade 1 back at Omemee Public School. Classes were dismissed for the year at the end of June.

During the summer months Neil spent more time at the swimming hole. Old boathouses sheltered by groves of trees lined both sides of the Pigeon River. Scott would sometimes swim across a deep part of the river with Neil riding on his stomach. The Mill Pond, another favourite swimming spot, was located upstream near Cap's Place. Built by Captain Fred Evans shortly after World War I, Cap's Place consisted of a half-dozen outfitted rental cabins. Swimmers were charged five cents for admittance to the pond by the wooden pier, though children often tried to sneak in.

The Mill Bridge, 90 metres south of the White Bridge, was an ideal place to fish. The abundance of logs and stumps under the water attracted a thriving fish population. Neil often came home with large catches of muskie, perch, bass or pickerel, which he had washed off at the town pump. Neil's best friend from his Grade 1 class, Henry Mason, often accompanied him on these excursions. The two boys would clamber around the timbers below the bridge to retrieve their hung-up fishing lines. On one outing Neil and Henry pulled in a broken fishing line to find a 60-pound snapping turtle hooked on the other end. They spent all afternoon loading the creature onto Neil's wagon, where its legs dangled awkwardly over the sides. A passerby spotted the boys with their catch and offered to take the turtle off their hands, presumably for dinner. Neil agreed, reasoning that it was too big for the sandbox where he kept a collection of smaller turtles.

Another friend was Garfield "Goof" Whitney,[68] who lived a few doors away from the Youngs. Goof was five years older than Neil and enjoyed teasing his naive and gullible young friend. One of the Youngs' neighbours was a woman named Olive Lloyd, who was often the victim of children's pranks and who had been known to retaliate by chasing the offending youngsters with a butcher knife. Goof told Neil that Mrs. Lloyd would give him candy if he called her "Mrs. Peeniehammer," and Neil figured this was a good idea, with the inevitable result: "Holy Jesus, she come right out chasin' Neil," Goof recalls. "Every time he walked to school he'd have to cross the street. He was scared to walk by the place."[69]

In the Jonathan Demme film *Neil Young Journeys* (2011), Neil points out Goof's home to Demme and remarks, "Goof was older than me and he used to give me, like, he'd give me a nickel to go up and say, you know, 'You have a fat ass,' or something, to an old lady, ya know. . . . Give me a nickel, I'd do anything. [He] also convinced me that eating tar was a good idea. I should try it. It's a lot like chocolate. So I tried to eat some tar off the road. That was the beginning of my close relationship with cars, I think."[70, 71]

OUT-OF-TOWN FRIENDS WHO VISITED THE Young family in Omemee during this time were almost all writers or journalists, including Farley Mowat and his first wife, Fran; Thomas J. Allen, an editorial writer from Peterborough; and Robertson Davies, who was editing the *Peterborough Examiner* at the time. If Neil was listening to the adults' conversation, much of what he heard would have been about writing. "A group of writers in our living room smoking their pipes and talking into the night was not uncommon to me growing up," he recalls. "Books have always been close to my life, with my father being an author and our family knowing so many writers as family friends."[72] Scott Young was making his living entirely as a writer of fiction now, and two juvenile novels were published during his residence in Omemee: *Scrubs on Skates* in 1952, followed by *Boy on Defense* in 1953.

The Youngs visited Pierre and Janet Berton at their sprawling home in rural Kleinburg on occasional summer weekends. A small gully separated the Berton home on one side from that of their good friends Lister Sinclair and his then-wife, Alice Mather, on the other. Sinclair had purchased a 1.2 hectare parcel of land on the banks of the Humber River, intending it to be part of an idyllic co-operative for writers. Neil enjoyed splashing in the water there and playing with the other kids. The Berton family would eventually include seven children, all of whose names started with the letter *P*: Penny, Pamela, Patsy, Peter, Paul, Peggy Anne and adopted daughter Perri.[73]

Uncle Bob, Aunt Merle and the girl cousins often visited the Youngs, as did Granny Jean — Scott's mother — on occasion. Granny Jean had a musical bent: she enjoyed singing and playing the piano and organ, putting on spontaneous performances and entertaining people with lively renditions of such standards as "Pack Up Your Troubles" or "Bicycle Built for Two." Uncle Bob had famously large hands and could play almost any stringed instrument, in addition to piano. Astrid — Neil's half-sister — would later remark, "Uncle Bob could play anything on the piano, mostly in the key of F-sharp (all the black ones), but man, could he boogie."[74] He often played the foot-pedal organ the Youngs had purchased from Mrs. Haygarth along with the house. Neil displayed only a cursory interest in the organ; when he tried to play it, he discovered his legs were too short to reach the pedals.

Usually Uncle Bob selected a song and his daughters joined in on three-part harmony. They sometimes performed as a travelling singing group. Neil fondly references them in "Far from Home" on *Prairie Wind* (2005): *Uncle Bob sat at the piano / My girl cousins sang harmony / Those were the good old family times / They left a big mark on me.* Uncle Bob was the one who first showed Neil a few rudimentary chords on the ukulele. A few years later Neil would acquire as his own first instrument — a plastic ukulele.

In early August, Neil and Bob attended Camp Kandalore, "A Summer Camp for Boys," located at Halls Lake near Minden, Ontario. Both boys sent letters home during their three-week stay. One such letter,[75] apparently written by Neil's counsellor and signed by Neil, reported that he had passed his 25-yard swim test, that he was having lots of fun on hikes (where he saw a bird's nest in the woods and a beaver dam) and that the camp food was good and he was getting a good tan. An archival photo from the camp shows Neil dressed as a stereotypical "Indian," standing alone in the woods and facing the camera. He's wearing a headband with a large feather in it and war paint on his naked chest. Dave Graham, a former director of the camp, reports that the campers were taking part in "Indian Day."[76]

One memento that survived from Neil's time at the camp is a piece of birchbark in the shape of an arrow, inscribed *Kandalore Banquet 1952. Neil Young*.[77] The occasion was a farewell banquet with a dude-ranch theme. A photo that later appeared in *Toronto Life* magazine shows Neil and Bob with suitcases in hand boarding a bus: "Neil and Bob off to camp, 1952." Scott writes, "Crazy place for a country kid. At the dinner table a few months later when we said they could go back to camp next summer, both burst into tears."[78]

IN EARLY SEPTEMBER 1952, NEIL entered Grade 2 at Omemee Public School, where his teacher was Doris Jones. Classmate Don Weir recalls that Miss Jones was an often stern teacher who demanded strict obedience from her students as well as good results on their schoolwork. On February 10, 1953,

---

FROM TOP: *"Indian Day" at Camp Kandalore, August 1952.* [Camp Kandalore Archives]; *New Smyrna Beach, April 1953. Neil is in the centre and Bob is on the right.* [Trent University Archives, Scott Young fonds (90-003 Box 26)]; *Boathouses along the Pigeon River.* [Courtesy of Marlyne Fisher-Heasman with assistance from Gladys Goodin]

Principal Leslie M. Curtis[79] sent a note to Rassy about Neil's less than stellar behaviour in Miss Jones's class:

> This small person has been causing Miss Jones a very great deal of trouble over a long period, so I asked her to send him to me when necessary. I am sending him to you for the remainder of the day — to be kept in durance — or what have you. Perhaps we could discuss with Miss Jones this afternoon and gain some ground? Would 3:45 here be convenient? Or early evening at our house? I am sending Bob along to see that you receive both packages.[80]

THE YOUNG FAMILY MADE A second trip to New Smyrna Beach over the Christmas break in December 1952. "I remember drivin' down to Florida," Neil remarks. "Seein' all the new cars. Going down in the winter of '52, seein' a new '53 Pontiac. . . . I could name any car, who made it, what year it was, what model, if it was the big one or not. I knew every car on the fuckin' road."[81] Neil adds, "I love old cars. Forties, fifties. Big cars. Heavy metal. I even love new cars. 'Cause they get me where I wanna go. I love travel. I got hooked on those trips when I was five, six years old. I think it was my dad. The highway bug. I've always loved it."[82]

This time the family stayed in a small, old, green-roofed rental cottage[83] on the southeast corner of Ninth Avenue and Hill Street, an unpaved road that faced the beach and ran parallel to South Atlantic. Front and back porches with broad roofs helped shelter the home and capture stray breezes. A ramp led up to the cottage from Hill Street, while the beach and ocean were accessible by a short walk over the rolling dunes. This southern part of Coronado Beach was much less densely populated than the busy area around Flagler Avenue to the north.

The family of Neil's schoolmate Martha Cleland had moved to a nearby home on the corner of Eighth Avenue and South Atlantic during the summer of 1952. Their home, almost directly across the street from the San Marino Motel, was the only house on their side of the street between Third and Eighth avenues.

Old friends the Allens lived close to the Youngs in a two-storey pink cottage on the southeast corner of Ninth and South Atlantic. The families had socialized in Omemee and continued to do so in New Smyrna Beach. Neighbours on Hill Street running south from the Youngs included the Finneys, the Shepards and the Radimers. The Joergs lived in the house just north of the Youngs', on the other side of a sandy path that led to the beach.

Ted and Frieda Shepard were also "snowbirds," and lived the rest of the year in Skaneateles, New York. The Shepard children were Barbara, Katherine ("Kay") and Norman.[84] Frieda was fond of the Young family, especially Rassy, and Kay recalls that Rassy had "a deep voice, was a constant smoker and was very funny."

Racial segregation was a matter of course in Florida in that decade. African-American bathers were restricted to Bethune Beach, just south of New Smyrna Beach and accessible by a single road. Jane Allen recalls bicycling there on Saturdays, through long stretches of palmetto scrub with shimmering water on either side.

Mary Allen played occasional ball games with Neil on Hill Street, while Jane — closer in age to Bob[85] — socialized with him more often. Neil spent much of his free time in a swimsuit that showcased his slender frame and skinny legs. A popular activity among the children was "squeezing oranges," as Jane recalls, "till we could suck the juice out of them through straws." Kay Shepard thought Bob and Neil were "very nice kids" who always seemed to be together, Neil following Bob wherever he went.

It's unclear whether the family extended their time in New Smyrna Beach after the traditional two-week Christmas-break period. Neil recalls, "I went to school there for a couple of months for a few years in a row."[86] Nevertheless, the Young family returned to Omemee and Neil was back at school by the beginning of February.[87] They returned to New Smyrna Beach for the last time during the Easter break period in April, staying in the same cottage on Hill Street. A photo[88] bearing the processing date of "Week of April 27, 1953" shows a happily grinning Neil, Bob and playmate buried to their necks in the Florida sand.

NEIL'S OUTDOOR ACTIVITIES DURING the winter were traditionally Canadian: building snow forts and snowmen, sledding and tobogganing. Scott Young recalls that Neil once went tobogganing with Robertson Davies (future winner of the Governor General's Literary Award and author of such Canadian classics as *Fifth Business* and *The Manticore*), who lived with his family in Peterborough. The Youngs spent many companionable winter evenings at the Davies' family home. Both adults and children enjoyed playing word games, and the children were fond of turning off the lights and playing hide-and-seek. Neil recalls, "[We] used to go to his house every Christmas and play charades at a party. He had a bunch of daughters. Very exciting."[89]

Something else that caught Neil's attention at Robertson

Davies' home was his Buick. "It was brand-new and made a large impression on me," says Neil, "with its beautifully designed grille, taillights and an overall shape that featured a kind of bump or ripple in the lines at about the midpoint, accentuated by a chrome strip that mirrored it. The ripple emanated from the rear wheel's circular well and was unique to Buicks."[90, 91]

NEIL FINISHED HIS SECOND SCHOOL year in Omemee. Classes were dismissed at the end of June. During a time when most children were preoccupied with playing baseball, Neil preferred fishing, the family dog Skippy always close by his side. He was inherently shy: "I never took part in anything. If there was some sort of group thing, I always just sort of stood and watched."[92] Neil entered Grade 3 at Omemee Public School in September 1953. The year would pass uneventfully for him, but personal problems were beginning to surface between Scott and Rassy. The magazine market for short fiction was less robust than it had been, which was stressful both for Scott and for the marriage. *Sports Illustrated*, then just gearing up to begin publication, offered Scott a full-time position in New York City. He turned the opportunity down — he saw himself more as a fiction writer — but agreed to accept freelance assignments from the magazine.

After the end of the school year the family moved to Winnipeg for the summer.[93, 94] They rented a compact stucco-and-wood one-and-a-half-storey home at 95 Hillcrest Avenue[95] in Norwood East, a neighbourhood in the southeast part of the city.

Rassy's sister Lavinia (known affectionately as "Toots") lived with her husband, commercial and fine artist Neil Hoogstraten, at 14 Beechwood Place in nearby Norwood

Flats. Toots was a popular local writer and radio personality. Her short stories and articles appeared in such publications as *McCall's*, *Good Housekeeping*, *Maclean's* and *Chatelaine*. She would go on to write and broadcast scripts for the CBC and was later the president of the Winnipeg branch of the Canadian Authors Association and national president from 1966 to 1968. (Rassy's other sister, Virginia, or "Snooky," had married Brandt Ridgway and moved to Corpus Christi, Texas, where she ran a successful public relations firm.)[96]

Rassy knew the Winnipeg neighbourhood. When she was growing up, the Ragland family had lived in a sprawling home at 145 Monck Avenue,[97] a mere seven streets east of Hillcrest. Bill and Perle Ragland had since moved to a spacious apartment in the DeBary Apartments at 626 Wardlaw Avenue, also nearby, and Neil recalled visiting them:

> [Perle] was very old. They lived in an apartment, and we went there and saw them a couple of times with my dad and my brother. We'd all get dressed up. That's one thing I remember. "What the hell am I having to get dressed up so nice. . . ." What a head space. It's not like, "Wow, we're gonna go over and see Grandma and Grandpa and hang out." No — we're gonna get dressed up. I don't know why my mother had to do that. I'm sure my father was much looser in the dress code.[98]

THE YOUNGS RETURNED TO THEIR home in Omemee at the end of August so the boys would be settled for the start of the new school year.

Near the end of October, Scott accepted an assignment from *Sports Illustrated* to report on duck hunting in Manitoba and Saskatchewan. His article, "Where Ducks Cloud the Sky," appeared in the November 15, 1954, issue as part of an 11-page feature on duck hunting. During this time he met, and fell hard for, another woman. Scott travelled to James Bay on the fringe of the Arctic for another *Sports Illustrated* item on hunting geese, and over the course of this trip he weighed his choices. His marriage was in trouble, he was looking for a way out, and in the end he composed a long letter to Rassy asking for a divorce.

The couple briefly separated, but after a two-week interlude there was a tearful reunion. The Youngs had originally planned to spend another winter in New Smyrna Beach after Scott's James Bay assignment — they had already rented their home to the Phillips family — but now those plans were up in the air. Scott and Rassy's personal relationship was still fragile, and spending a winter in New Smyrna Beach was simply not feasible.

They decided instead to rent a place in Toronto for the six months the Phillips family would be occupying their home in Omemee. It was under these less than ideal circumstances that the family arrived in the city for the start of a new, uncertain year.

## ★ 3 ★
## AN UNEASY TIME IN TORONTO

THE LOWER FLOOR OF A duplex at 133 Rose Park Drive[99] in the upper-middle-class Toronto neighbourhood of Moore Park was the Young family's next home. This very desirable central residential area of the city was originally settled in the late 1880s, when it was subdivided by founder John Thomas Moore. Rose Park Drive originally served as the driveway for the mansion of Moore, who was also president of the Rose Society, a horticultural club. Number 133 is a solid red-brick two-storey detached home built in 1922. Originally owned by two maiden aunts, the house was designed as a duplex, with each of the sisters occupying one floor. When the sisters died, the house was sold to schoolteacher Ada Purvis, who rented out both floors and was the Young family's landlady when they lived there.

The interior still retains its old-world charm. Wood wainscotting and polished hardwood floors, a large bright front bay window and a welcoming fireplace with built-in shelving on either side all contribute to the ambiance of the large front living room. A separate dining room, behind the living room, is attached to the kitchen in the back via a solid wood entry door. Wood wainscotting and a ceiling medallion complement this room. There are two bedrooms; the slightly larger master bedroom is located at the rear, while the second bedroom is next to it. Neil most likely shared the smaller second bedroom with Bob. The house is set well back from the street and the curb, and has spacious front and back gardens with many mature trees.

Neil was enrolled for the start of the second term of Grade 4 at Whitney School, east of MacLennan Avenue on Rosedale Heights Drive. The main entrance faced west into the "senior" schoolyard, and a concrete wall bound the property where the MacLennan hill sloped downward. A gate opened onto a wide sidewalk leading to the main steps. A high steel fence surrounded the property, with two breaks in the fencing on Rosedale Heights near the school. There were two additional entrances on the east side of the building, one for boys and one for girls. The playground was well-stocked for sporting activities, with three baseball diamonds, a pole-vault pit and sandpit. The older children congregated on the west side of the school on a black-cinder-covered playground while the younger children's concrete-covered play area was on the east side. The narrow "girls' hill" was just south of the school, dropping off steeply toward the Old Bridle Path. Boys were prohibited from venturing into the girls' play area — trespassing was punishable by a trip to the principal's office and a black mark against the student's record.

Named in honour of Sir James Pliny Whitney, long-time leader of the Conservative Party and the sixth premier of Ontario, the school first opened its doors in September 1926.

Students from both Moore Park (north of the nearby CPR tracks) and North Rosedale (south of the tracks) attended the school. Rosedale, one of the city's oldest suburbs, held a more prestigious air than neighbouring Moore Park. Long-established families with "old money" ties, as well as other wealthy families and famous individuals, called this part of the city home. Moore Park was considered to be "on the other side of the tracks," less socially and economically advantaged than Rosedale to the south.

An elevated steel and concrete pedestrian bridge known as "the ramp" allowed safe passage for students travelling to school from south of the tracks. The north side of the ramp, entered at the bottom of the MacLennan Avenue hill, led straight over the tracks while the south side consisted of a few jogs down the escarpment, eventually exiting at the junction of Summerhill Avenue and the continuation of MacLennan.

The school sits on the escarpment of the old shoreline of Glacial Lake Iroquois, which runs east-west, and the CPR line skirts the bottom of the escarpment. Steam locomotives still pulled trains along the tracks during the 1950s. Children made a game of hurrying onto the ramp when a locomotive passed under so they could experience the thundering vibrations and chug-a-chug noise of the engine as it spewed billowing smoke and steam.

Whitney's student population was drawn from some of

---

CLOCKWISE FROM TOP: *Whitney School, Grade 4, 1954-55.* [Courtesy of Bain Myers]; *"The Flood" by Scott Young. Front cover illustration by Neil Hoogstraten.* [Courtesy of Mike Salisbury, Nessa Books]; *Rosedale Park, Mayfair, May 1955.* [© 1955 Mary Ellen Blanch]; *133 Rose Park Drive. The Young family lived in the lower duplex.* [© 2009 Sharry Wilson]

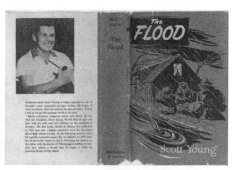

the most established, prominent and influential families in Toronto. There were two classes in each grade level, from kindergarten up to Grade 8. At the end of Grade 6 or Grade 8, some of the privileged students would transfer to the private school system. The girls would be enrolled at Branksome Hall, Havergal or Bishop Strachan, while the boys would attend Upper Canada College, Ridley College, Trinity College School or Lakefield College. During the 1953-54 academic year, two portable classrooms were installed on the eastern side of the younger children's playground. More were erected on the senior playground in the following few years. The last Grade 7 and 8 students graduated in 1962 and the new building soon opened on the northeast corner of the school property at MacLennan and Rosedale Heights.

Margaret Powell was Neil's teacher, and classes were held in Room 9. The principal at this time was J. H. C. Vanderburgh. In the class photo Neil sits at the front desk in the third row from the viewer's right, nattily attired in a dark shirt and dark blazer. Sitting three desks directly behind him is Mary Ellen Blanch,[100] his first close female school friend.

Mary Ellen, now a retired schoolteacher, recalls that Miss Powell had an authoritarian manner and was often angry. She was notorious for cracking her ruler on a desktop to get the class's attention and raising her voice so that it terrorized the more sensitive students. On one occasion the students brought their lunches to school, anticipating an afternoon walk to nearby Deer Park Public Library for a "book talk" session; the class was more exuberant than usual, and Miss Powell suddenly bellowed for the children to settle down. Neil reacted by grabbing a Coke bottle[101] from his lunch bag and pitching it at the chalkboard, where it smashed and left foamy brown liquid dripping over the chalkboard ledge. He was sent into the hall as punishment. Miss Powell's scare tactics had upset everyone, especially Neil, but his rebellion may have had a laudatory effect: Mary Ellen recalls that after this incident the class atmosphere improved slightly. Classmate Eddie Wingay confirms that "Miss Powell was quite crabby at times. Neil didn't like that."

Neil displayed a mischievous streak when, as classmate Forbes Pritchard recalls, he dipped a girl's pigtail into a nearby inkwell. It was a trait he would demonstrate increasingly often in his school career.

STUDENTS FROM WHITNEY often congregated in Moorevale Park (referred to as Moore Park by locals), Rosedale Park or Chorely Park (known to the children as Charley Park). The Moore Park Ravine offered enticing rambles with its interesting and varied landscape. The Vale of Avoca, with its rolling hills and reservoir, was located just west of Mount Pleasant Road. This generous green space gave the children a rich natural playground to explore.

A small strip of commercial stores was located just east of the ramp on Summerhill Avenue, south of the CPR tracks. Whitney students, especially those who lived south of the school, patronized a confectionery/smoke shop named Dot's, where they would buy penny candy such as black balls (three for a penny), sponge toffee, red wax lips, licorice cigars and bubble gum packaged with trading cards. Not as conveniently located was a deep, narrow store called Robinson's (also known as Quinn's, after the previous owners), about a kilometre north of the school on St. Clair just cast of Welland Avenue. It was a very different place than Dot's, more like a conventional grocer's with a butcher section in the back. The main attraction was a cooler well-stocked with Popsicles

and Fudgsicles. An empty field west of the store afforded a convenient place for the children to play ball, while the store's east side had a small parking lot and a loading area where trucks could pull up at the back. A laneway ran behind the store between St. Clair and Rose Park Drive.

Neil often spent time after school and on weekends with fellow student Bain Myers. Bain, Neil, John Simmons and Bertram Hulbig sometimes went over as a group to Mary Ellen's house on Astley Avenue. She lived south of the tracks, so a trip over the ramp was necessary to get to her place. Forbes Pritchard, who lived on Heath Street East at the south end of Moore Park, remembers the shortcut he took to Neil's place via his backyard, a hop over the wire fence and a trespass through the backyard of the house opposite Neil's on Rose Park. Another chum was Eric Hennessey, who often played with Neil in the unfinished basement of 133 Rose Park Drive. He remembers Neil as "highly organized, using three-by-five cards with notes on them," a memory aid Neil might have learned from his dad.

Each year, over the Mother's Day weekend in May, the Mooredale Community Association held a fair in Rosedale Park called the Mayfair. The fair traditionally opened with a parade featuring the Boy Scouts, Girl Guides and Brownies, and Mary Ellen Blanch took part in May 1955. Onlookers, including Neil, followed the parade on its journey from the sidewalk into the park. Children on brightly decorated bicycles also took part, and a team of judges, behind the tarpaulin-covered wire fences of the tennis courts, evaluated their vehicles for awards to be presented later in the day. The

---

*Neil, age 9.* [Trent University Archives, Scott Young fonds, (90-003 Box 26)]

fair featured games, fund-raising bake sales and an evening dance with live entertainment on the tennis courts. A popular game was the coin toss, in which the player had to land a coin on one of the many plates displayed on a table. Neil won a prize at the coin toss that day: a chain dog collar with miniature medallions dangling from it. After winning this prize, Neil went with John Simmons to knock on the door of Mary Ellen's house on Astley Avenue, but she wasn't home; her mother answered, and Neil left the gift with her. Mary Ellen thinks Neil must have imagined it was a "golden necklace," not just a fancy dog collar. She appreciated his "sweet" gesture but passed on the gift to Bonnie, their pet boxer.[102] Mary Ellen took a photo with her Kodak Brownie camera of Neil at the Mayfair festival, a wonderful study of the nine-year-old on a summer's day in Toronto in 1955. Wearing a plaid shirt and jeans, his hair neatly combed, Neil Young gazes at the camera with an earnest, almost solemn expression. Mary Ellen believes one of the items he is holding is a Boy Scout sheath knife with the handle pointed downward, most likely won at the Mayfair. He also appears to be clutching a notepad (upside down, it seems, since the pages are falling open). Mary Ellen wonders whether Neil, even at this age, was making notes about his thoughts and experiences.

Neil's time at Whitney wasn't especially happy, she believes; he seemed like an "outsider looking in" who preferred one-on-one interactions to large groups and crowds. At the time she was probably unaware that Neil's parents were going through a rough patch in their marriage.

It was during this time that Scott Young wrote *The Flood*, a novel based in part on his experiences working on the Norwood dike during the Winnipeg flood in early May 1950.

Eight dikes had given way and flooded much of the city — the Norwood dike was the largest. Four of 11 bridges had been destroyed and almost 70,000 residents had to be evacuated. Scott had wrangled a railroad pass and left his family in Omemee to help emplace sandbags against the rising tide of flood waters along the Red River. Working for the *Winnipeg Free Press,* he filed front-page stories about the disaster and then the early days of recovery.[103] The protagonist in *The Flood* is a widower with two sons, torn by his love for two women. Scott has admitted that the characters of Don and Mac were based on his own two sons. (The outgoing Mac was inspired by Neil.) The widower, Martin, loves Mac "deeply and without reservation. Sometimes he thought it a little silly for a man to feel that he could tell everything to a nine-year-old and it would be understood, or that it would be understood without telling, but that was how he felt about Mac."[104] Brother-in-law Neil Hoogstraten[105] supplied the cover illustration for the hardcover first edition.

Scott wrote the novel "in a twenty-five-dollar-a-month room I rented on Dundonald Street,[106] where I could work better than at home. It sold in Canada and England but didn't make much money. The year was full of tears and recriminations and separations again."[107] Scott dedicated the book to Rassy because of all the hurt he had put her through, but the gesture was lost. Rassy saw herself in Martin's wife, Fay, who had died in a car crash. She took this to mean that Scott wanted her out of the way. He was often travelling, and when he was home there was friction in the family. Like the hero of his novel, Scott had been seeing another woman — even staying with her for a while and returning home for brief periods — and the family knew. The inevitable arguments must have been difficult for Neil and Bob to either ignore or endure.

The marriage was wounded, perhaps mortally, but Scott believed it might yet survive. His prescription for renewed happiness was another move — away from the city, to a rural crossroads outside of Pickering, Ontario.

# 4

# BROCK ROAD:
# A RURAL IDYLL

THE YOUNG FAMILY SPENT THE first month of the summer of 1955 in one of the cabins at Cap's Place.[108] In August they rented a cottage in Cedarville Park on the Pigeon River just north of Omemee. Neil and Bob thrived in this environment. Neil contented himself with swimming, fishing and collecting turtles. Scott gave him a dime-sized turtle he found near its egg, and Neil christened it Fearless Freddie. Dirty Ernie was a larger turtle he gave away earlier on.

One evening the family went for a drive along a back-country gravel road, "scouting wild apple trees for something sharp enough and juicy enough for the first green apple pie of the season."[109] On the way back, Scott spotted a bird sitting on the road ahead. He swerved and slammed on the brakes. Bob recognized the bird as a domesticated budgie and quickly got out of the car to approach it. As he moved his hand gently toward the bird, it hopped onto his finger and stayed there as he came back to the car. The "blue and tired-looking"

71

creature nestled onto Bob's shoulder, and now the family had to decide what to do with it. They drove to a farmhouse they had spotted a kilometre back and asked whether the family had recently lost a budgie. No: they already had a budgie — a green one — and it was safe at home. Calls were made to other families nearby, but no one was missing a budgie.

Bob knew where they might be able to borrow a cage — a nearby family had owned a budgie that had died. Bob contacted the family and arranged to borrow the cage and buy some birdseed and other necessities, and Rassy drove to a pet store 50 kilometres away to purchase a "Budgie Starting Kit." Neil happily volunteered to be the budgie's main caregiver, but Bob asserted his authority on all things budgie-related. The family thought of various funny things to teach the budgie to say, but the bird already had a vocabulary of its own: "Kiss me, cutie. Don't shoot. That's okay, skipper. Don't shoot. Kiss me, cutie." He would then make kissing noises, give a wolf whistle and ding his bell twice.[110]

Shortly before it was time to leave the cottage, Bob suggested they offer the bird to the family whose budgie had died — they had to return the cage anyway, and he thought it might be a welcome gesture. "So," writes Scott Young, "with a single mild dissent from Neil, who had never met a living thing he didn't love and want to own, we gave away the bird. Easy come, easy go."[111]

THE PHILLIPS FAMILY CONTINUED TO rent the Young family home in Omemee over the summer, but in August the Youngs sold the property to Gordon and Barbara Bocock to finance their move to Pickering.

With the proceeds from the sale, Scott and Rassy bought a three-bedroom white clapboard bungalow on an acre and a half in the hamlet of Brock Road within the Township of Pickering, 40 kilometres east of Toronto. As with their Omemee home, this property was purchased through the assistance of the Veterans' Land Act. The house, with its generous lawn, was located on the west side of Brock Road. There was no official street number; their postal address was simply R.R. #1, Pickering. Some old poultry houses at the back of the property had been used to keep chickens when the land was a farm.

The home was directly across the road from the Pickering Golf Club, an 18-hole course that had opened two years earlier and would exercise a particular attraction for Neil and his family. (The house no longer exists; it burned down a number of years ago. All that remains is a vacant lot.)

The hamlet of Brock Road began to take root during the 1860s when a sawmill, a school and a blacksmith shop were erected at the crossroads of the original Fourth Concession Road and Brock Road, northwest of Pickering Village (now part of the City of Ajax). The former hamlet is now included within the City of Pickering and is located northeast of the city centre. The residents of Brock Road were a tightly knit community during the years when the Young family lived there — all the neighbours knew each other. Brothers, sisters and cousins shared classes at school, and interrelated families were commonplace.

The best way to stabilize his marriage, Scott had decided, was to take a steady job, which he found in the public relations department at Orenda Engines Limited in Malton near the Toronto airport. The position was not ideal, and Scott never felt entirely comfortable working there. Nevertheless, it provided a steady income until something more suitable materialized.

Scott and Rassy's relationship had improved sufficiently that they enjoyed travelling west to Manitoba and Saskatchewan for annual autumn duck-hunting trips. They would stay briefly with the Raglands — Rassy usually flew out a week early to visit her extended family — then Scott, Rassy and her father would leave on a two-week hunting expedition to western Manitoba and Saskatchewan. They travelled in Bill Ragland's car, a Ford supplied by his employer, Barrett Roofing, where he was the manager of operations in western Canada. Neil fondly recalls, "My granddaddy . . . used to go duck hunting with my mom and dad. And then he'd come back and my mom would cook the ducks and, you know, make them with the wild greens or with the wild rice. And we'd have roast duck with wild rice . . . They'd come back and maybe have 50 birds or something, and get us through the winter . . . Maybe once, couple of times a month, we'd have a big roast-duck dinner and everything. It was really cool. And there were a lot of pictures of my dad in *Sports Illustrated* magazine with my grandpa. And, you know, they did articles on duck hunting in northern Manitoba. . . . If you went at the right time, you actually couldn't see the sun, there were so many birds in the sky. I mean, it was just black when they'd all take off at once. It got dark."[112] Neil would later reference his parents' duck-hunting activities in "No Wonder" from *Prairie Wind* (2005): *Back when I was young / The birds blocked out the sun / Before the great migration stopped / We only shot a few, they last the winter through / Mother cooked them good and served them up.*

Scott and Rassy enrolled Neil in Grade 5 at a humble, two-room brick schoolhouse called Brock Road School (formally known as School Section Number 6 West). The school had been built in 1868, replacing a log-and-frame structure on the same site. It was originally fashioned as a large one-room schoolhouse, heated by a wood-burning pot-bellied stove with long stovepipes running to the chimney at the end of the room. In the 1890s a small anteroom was partitioned, through which students passed to reach the classroom at the back of the building. In the early 1950s the smaller front room was converted into a second classroom for use by the younger children. It had its own pot-bellied stove to heat the immediate area. The wooden entrance door to the school was on the south side of the building, and the children played in a small area in front of the school.

"We used to play baseball there," Neil recalls, "and home plate was right in front of the main door of the old schoolhouse."[113] To the north, a small slope ran down to Duffins Creek. A wooden janitor's shed projected from the east side of the school and served as an entrance to the cellar where the janitor kept his supplies. The school's west side faced Brock Road. Children were summoned to classes by a bell mounted atop the peaked roof. "That schoolhouse was like something out of a history book," Neil remarks, "and it was about a hundred years old when I was there as a kid in the mid-1950s."[114]

The school sat on the east side of Brock Road, just north of the point at which the Fourth Concession Road met Brock and took a jog north for 150 metres and then carried on in an easterly direction. (The continuation of the original Fourth Concession Road on the east side of Brock Road is today called Forbrock Street. During the 1950s when the Young family lived there, everyone referred to it simply as the Fourth Concession Road.) The road then wound around, crossing the railway tracks over an old humped wooden rumble bridge

just about where Taunton Road now crosses the railway. The Young family home was located in the Third Concession, and children who lived in the Third and Fourth concessions within a kilometre or two of Brock Road customarily attended Brock Road School.

Neil retained vivid memories of his daily walks to and from school: "I have this one image that keeps coming to mind with that song ['The Wayward Wind'] — where I used to live in Pickering, there's the Brock Road Public School. Just a two-room school and it's still there. I'd walk there every day from our house, and that song was on the radio at the time. The railroad track used to go right behind the school, and the trains would go by, and there's somethin' about that song — I always think about that one area. There was a little shack back there, a tool shed or something . . . I see it when I hear 'The Wayward Wind.'"[115, 116] (Neil remembered this song many years later and in 1985 included it on *Old Ways*.)

Susan Wilson, a classmate from Brock Road School, thinks the "little shack" Neil is referring to was the Grundy family home, a small two- or three-room house on the east side of Brock Road just south of the tracks. Another local landmark was a dog kennel owned by Owen Bretts, just north of the tracks.

In a class photo taken in June of 1956, Neil stands grinning in the front row, fifth from the viewer's left. This

---

FROM TOP: *Brock Road School, senior class, 1955-56.* [Courtesy of Susan (Wilson) Hill with assistance from Shirley (Cargill) Cloar]; *Brock Road School, 1960. The two-room schoolhouse was originally built in 1868.* [Courtesy of the Pickering Public Library]

was the senior class, which included students from grades 4 to 8. Margaret Rowe, the teacher, is cut off in the photo at the extreme left. Among the other students, Ivan Kring, standing in the middle of the front row, was something of a pariah because his mother, Jean Kring, taught the junior class at Brock Road School. Susan Wilson is also in the front row, two students to the right of Neil. Susan was in Grade 4 — a year behind Neil — and her father, Len Wilson, was chair of the school board at the time. Susan, her father and her mother, Clara, lived on the south side of the Fourth Concession Road about a kilometre west of Brock Road. Marilyn LaBrie is standing in between Susan and Neil. She and Neil would share some special time together during the next few years. Fair-haired classmate Reggie Taylor (second from the right in the front row) was one of Neil's best friends; they often roamed the nearby fields and wandered home at night, hungry and tired from their long outings. Reggie's family lived on the south side of the Fifth Concession Road — also known as Whitevale Road — in the first house east of Brock Road. Birthday parties at the Taylors' were always fun because Reggie's mom baked cakes with coins hidden in them.

Another good friend of Neil's, dark-haired Doug Suter, stands in the front row next to Reggie. The Suters lived in a solid old stone house on an acre and a half of land on the west side of Brock Road about a kilometre south of the Third Concession Road, an area known as Barrett's Hill. The Third Concession Road was located at the top of the hill and the Suters' home was at the bottom of the hill just south of a creek. Peter McMurtrie recalls that Doug's parents were "wonderful people. Like June and Ward Cleaver." Doug owned a large and much-envied Dinky Toy collection. Neil and Doug would construct airfields, roads, stores and garages and run the Dinky Toys through their courses in an old sandbox in the Suters' yard.

Neil and Doug also enjoyed bike-riding. It was the habit of the senior-class students to ride their bikes during recess: they would circle the schoolyard, manically picking up speed. Younger children had to be careful not to be clipped by one of the fast-moving bicycles.

Doug's younger brother Terry tagged along on a day when Neil and Doug were biking home from school along Brock Road. All three had pumped up the tire pressure on their one-speed coasters, to create a satisfying squeal when the boys stepped hard on the brakes or, even better, long black skid marks on the pavement (achieved at the expense of bald back tires). Terry was riding directly behind Neil as they approached the railway tracks at full speed. When Neil's bike crossed the rails there was a loud pop and bang as the pressure shredded his stressed back tire. Neil managed to keep his balance but looked back at Terry with a startled expression, as if to say, "What the heck just happened?" The tire couldn't be repaired on the spot, and Neil resigned himself to pushing his bike the rest of the way home.

The Suter brothers enjoyed playing with Neil's massive Lionel train layout,[117] set up on a four-by-eight-foot piece of plywood in the Youngs' basement. (Lionel was the prestige brand: the Suters also owned a Lionel set.) This was an upgrade from Neil's old Marx Sante Fe diesel set in Omemee. Neil recalls, "I think I was 12 or 13 when I finally got my first Lionel locomotive, a no. 2035. Until then, it was those hook-and-loop couplers all the way."[118] The basement had a tendency to flood, so Neil grew accustomed to mild electrical shocks whenever he ran the trains.

Neil and his male classmates also enjoyed catching

minnows, frogs and crayfish in the river flats of Duffins Creek behind the school. "[M]e and my buddies would set traps in the morning," Neil recalls, "and then at recess we'd see if we could catch any crayfish. Then we'd get the crayfish and scare the hell out of the girls. . . . Fantastic!"[119] On some days he would take the crayfish home in a pail: "Then I would store them in a little makeshift water scene I had created in one of my mother's old roasting pans with some water, sand, and rocks placed very carefully to give a natural look. I used to stick little green plants in the sand and make believe they were trees."[120]

Students at Brock Road School were at the mercy of a few older bullies — "flunkies just waiting to turn 16 and get out," according to Ross James, an older classmate of Neil's and now a respected Canadian ornithologist. "They basically ran the school. You did what they said or you were bullied and harassed." Ross believes most of these offenders were gone by the 1955-56 academic year, but the school was still notorious for being unruly. Tackle football on the bare gravel of the schoolyard was mandatory because "that is what the bullies wanted." Students were often coerced into riding their bikes to neighbouring schools — Cherrywood, Brougham, Whitevale, Green River and Audley — for after-school baseball matches. "You weren't allowed to go home and do something else or there would be hell to pay later." The same crowd of toughs thought nothing of going into the barn of a farmer, stealing an old buggy and joyriding it down hills until it plunged into a ditch or was otherwise wrecked. Slingshot fights were started for the sake of "something to do."

At recess and lunch, students in the senior grades tormented the younger ones by holding their arms down and kneeing them in their legs until they dropped to the ground.

This was all done, of course, when the two teachers weren't there to witness anything.

Neil was occasionally the victim of these tactics. Once, when he was targeted by two school bullies, his brother Bob came to the rescue. After being dropped off by the Pickering District High School[121] bus at Middleton's — the general store located where the Fourth Concession Road hit Brock Road and took a jog north — Bob caught sight of Neil being pummelled by a pair of bigger kids. Bob, compact and athletic, quickly cornered Neil's attackers and was punching them repeatedly when Scott Young happened past. Scott put a stop to the fighting, but after Bob's display, Neil found he was picked on less often. Confrontations with bullies — and with injustice in general — would be a continuing theme, both in Neil's later school career and in his music. His sympathy was always with the victim.

The school held its annual bazaar in the fall, a Halloween party for the children on Friday, November 2, and a Christmas party as the season approached.

Scott wondered what he would get Neil as a special gift that year. It was easier to shop for Bob, who played hockey all winter and golf all summer and seemed to have an insatiable appetite for sporting equipment. (This Christmas he was hoping for new hockey pants and a golf bag.) One day, as Scott drove along Jarvis Street in Toronto, he spotted a sign for a tentmaker and thought a tent might be just the thing to interest Neil. His intuition proved correct: Neil was "delighted and astonished" by the gift. It turned out that he had "wanted a tent for years, more than anything else in the world, but he hadn't realized it until he received this one." Gratifyingly, he had it "pitched and in full use in their basement by noon."

"I guess that's the perfect gift," Scott remarked, "the wonderful thing that you didn't even know you wanted until it was yours."[122]

THE OLD BROCK ROAD SCHOOL closed in November of 1956. (The Ratepayers' Association had voted and approved the building of a new school on December 14, 1955. The population was growing rapidly and a new and larger school was sorely needed.) After several metamorphoses — including a stint as a Red Cross station — the building was demolished in 1993 and the school sign donated to the Local History Room at the Pickering Public Library.

The November 23, 1956, edition of the *Pickering News* reports that 62 pupils began classes for the first time at the new Brock Road Public School on Monday, November 19, 1956. The new school, "modern and up-to-date in every way," was located on the south side of the Fourth Concession Road, just west of Brock Road. "The boards are green and each room has a different colour scheme," according to the *Pickering News*. Len Wilson, chair of the school board, presided over the official opening ceremonies. Teaching staff included Miss L. Bouck, Miss K. Gostick, and Mr. W. A. Bush (music).

Miss Gostick taught the children in grades 1 to 4, and those in grades 5 to 8 were taught by Miss Bouck. This meant only two of the three classrooms at the school were used for teaching. The third was for storage and for special occasions such as dances and the annual school bazaar. Children could also play there during bad weather. All in all, the new school was roomier than the old one, and there was plenty of outdoor space for baseball and other activities. Students learned to avoid a patch of wild bush on the southwest corner of the property, which was infested with poison ivy. Other dangers lurked elsewhere. Neil recalls, "I went there when it was still brand-new, ran right into the glass door leaving class one day and got a concussion."[123]

A Halloween party was held for the children on October 31, and a school bazaar on November 2 in conjunction with a "grocery shower," so parents would have an opportunity to meet the new staff. The school's Christmas pageant and concert took place shortly before the Christmas break.

Neil had a bad fall right around this time. It's not clear if it occurred at school, at home or elsewhere. "Neil Young of Brock Road had a nasty fall on Monday," the December 21 edition of the *Pickering News* reported: "Hope he is not badly hurt." Apparently he wasn't.

A Victoria Day fireworks display was held on May 25 on the property of Mr. and Mrs. Bill Sowerby, a large 10-acre lot just north of the golf club. Over a hundred people, no doubt including Neil and family, attended and enjoyed the fireworks, bonfire and refreshments.

Swimming in the "pit pond" on the Fourth Concession Road was a popular summertime activity among the children. On June 15, 1956, the *Pickering News* reported, "Two boys had their pants stolen Tuesday while they were swimming at the pit pond on the 4th conc. — a sneaky trick." Other favourite spots for swimming were in Duffins Creek at the foot of Church Street and near the old dam site. On June 22 the *Pickering News* issued a warning from Dr. W. W. Tomlinson, the minister of health for Pickering Village: "The creek is dirty and not fit for the children to be in. . . . I would ask every parent in the village to take the caution of seeing that their children stay away from it."

APART FROM BULLYING AND OTHER nuisances, the time Neil spent in Pickering was another idyllic interlude in his childhood. And, at least for now, all was well on the home front. His parents were making a reasonably successful effort to get along, and rural life suited Neil. He was beginning to entertain some ideas about where his life might be headed and what he wanted to accomplish. His embryonic entrepreneurial skills flourished in this setting. Neil embarked on a number of different cash-generating enterprises, including selling freshly picked wild raspberries at a roadside stand under a sign marked *"Raspberries . . . THEY'RE WILD!"*

But it was his chicken-farming business that proved most successful. Neil already had some raw material close at hand, beginning with the decrepit poultry house at the back of their property. Neil was 10 when he approached his father in May 1956 with his proposal. "Say, Dad," Neil said, "how be I get into the chicken business?"[124] Neil had presented his father with various other moneymaking schemes in the past, but Scott thought this one had particular merit.

Scott told Neil he could use one acre of damp open meadow, a comfortable distance behind the family's home. This was where the old chicken coops were located, close to the property line of the red-brick house just to the south. Neighbour Howard Bath and his friend Albert Watson helped clean out the old chicken coops, which were overgrown with weeds and had been colonized by rats. Scott offered to provide a small advance in start-up funds, but Neil had other plans. Not wanting to incur a debt, he sought donations from neighbours instead. Next-door neighbour Don Scott made a generous donation of 30 fertilized chicken eggs. Neil then persuaded Howard Bath to allow him free use of one of his incubators. From this set, Neil was rewarded with 24 chicks.

He arranged to borrow a brooder lamp, an automatic water supply, a non-automatic feed trough and a long extension cord.

The frame of the old poultry house was still in useable condition, but the roof had long since rotted away. Don Scott, who owned the Scott Glass Company in Toronto, offered some surplus tin sheets from his business, and one Saturday he and Neil re-roofed the coop, with Neil operating mainly in a supervisory capacity.

There was a brief delay when the would-be entrepreneur found a family of rabbits living in the long grass under the unfloored poultry house. Neil kept his 24 chicks in a crowded enclosure for an additional week, the time it took for the baby rabbits to mature and make a graceful exit. By this point the chicks were about six weeks old and almost fully feathered. Neil piled them into cardboard boxes and proudly carried them out to their new home.

Neil and his friends spent hours at the poultry house watching the chicks grow. He already had big plans for his business: he would use his profits to buy more chickens, make more money, buy a new bike, a baseball glove and a car when he turned 16. He pitched a pup tent — the same one he had received from his parents as a Christmas gift the year before — near the range house so he could sleep on a cot there and look after the chicks without disturbing the rest of the family. Scott would call out to Neil from the back door in the morning with a shrill whistle to make sure he was up, and Neil would wave an arm at his father through the slit in the tent to signal that he was awake.

All was well for about a week. Then tragedy struck. One morning Neil ran into the house crying. He had headed out to the poultry house that morning as usual, but discovered some stray feathers on the path. Realizing that at least one of his chickens had escaped the shelter, he quickened his pace, only to discover that all of the chicks were missing. Scott was at work, so Neil recruited his mother, grandmother, brother and John and Ruth Pearson (along with their two Labrador dogs) to scour some 20 acres of meadowland for any sign of survivors. Much to their horror, they found dead chickens strewn in a line from the poultry house to a valley in the woods. They concluded that a fox — or perhaps some raccoons — had invaded the coop. Ten dead chickens[125] were ultimately recovered, all killed by a single snap from a set of sharp teeth.

Neil, perhaps surprisingly, had an enterprising thought as he gazed at the pile of dead chickens. "Just about frying size," he said. "Should be worth 75 cents each. Ten at 75 cents each, that would be $7.50. With that I could buy some more."[126, 127]

Incredibly, later that afternoon, one small, dirty white chicken struggled out from under a clump of weeds, having somehow escaped the massacre. Neil had named all his chicks, and the survivor was Petunia. "Petunia — now there was a chicken," Neil recalls. "She was one of the original batch. One of the only survivors of the great attack."[128] This gave Neil hope that his business could be revived. His expressed opinion that Petunia would be lonesome produced an immediate gift of two chickens from sympathetic neighbours Howard Bath and Don Scott. Neil worked two days at the Pickering Golf Course and made $2.50 to go with the $7.50 he got for the fryers. With these funds in his pocket he biked along a gravel road to T. L. Wilson & Sons, a gristmill in the hamlet of Whitevale, where he placed an order for 25[129] four-week-old chicks from Hillside Poultry Farm at New Dundee, Ontario.

Neil's brother stood guard at the chicken coop with a shotgun immediately after the attack and during the following few days, but the fox never returned. Apart from an owl attack that took two of the new young chicks, things went well through the rest of the summer and fall of 1956. Neil did more occasional work at the golf course, turning his meagre salary into, literally, chickenfeed. His father helped by constructing a wire-fenced chicken run, with Neil again acting in a supervisory capacity. When the cold weather came, Neil helped where he could as his father and Don Scott put together a more elaborate chicken house. It was Neil's idea to use a set of wooden crates from Don's glass company as prefabricated sides for the chicken house. The wooden panels were each eight by twelve feet. Don added a salvaged seven-by-three-foot piece of plate glass, and the chicken house soon had a large picture window overlooking the endless field behind it. "Those lucky chickens had a great view,"[130] Neil says.

December 3[131] was a momentous date: Neil and Scott discovered that, for the first time, one of the hens had laid an egg. "An egg! An egg!" Neil shouted, dancing around with his father on the straw-covered floor.[132] By Christmas the chickens were producing 20 eggs a day on average. On two memorable days during the winter, the 26 hens produced 26 eggs — a 100 per cent effort!

Soon Neil was averaging about 11 or 12 dozen eggs per week. His first regular customers were neighbours, including the Vernoy, McMurtrie and Summers families. Neil found he could now clear about $10 a week. He made small but regular deposits to his bank account and eventually saved enough to buy new bicycle tires, birthday and Christmas gifts, a baseball glove and a new breeder lamp. He knew he would need to increase production to make enough money to purchase a car in five years' time, so he ordered 50 more day-old chicks. This meant he was now at the point where his hens reliably laid enough eggs to pay for their own feed and that of the new chicks, and he was doubling his profit margin. In a later school presentation about his chicken-farming enterprise, Neil said, "When I finish school I plan to go to OAC [Ontario Agricultural College] and perhaps learn to be a scientific farmer."[133]

Neil's chickens were all given whimsical names. Three roosters from one of his later purchases were Ike, George and Hoiman.[134, 135] A note in an outline for the oral composition Neil presented at school a few years later reads bluntly, "Hoiman for dinner."[136]

Neil kept detailed financial records of Neil Eggs[137] on pages tacked to the back of his clothes-closet door. The four columns on each page are headed *Eggs, Income, Expenses* and *Date*. On one of these pages, dated November 1957, Neil typed the name of the company as if it were a corporate logo:

N
EGGS
I
L

---

CLOCKWISE FROM TOP: *Building used for storage at T. L. Wilson & Sons.* [© 2011 Sharry Wilson]; *Neil Eggs, financial record dated November 1957, and financial record showing Neil's signature.* [Trent University Archives, Scott Young fonds (90-003 Box 26)]

## Egg List

Neil Young *Neil Young*

| Date | Eggs | Income | Expenses |
|---|---|---|---|
| March 1 | 23 + 7 over | $1.00 | $5.90 (feed) |
| 2 | 19 + 2 over | 1.00 | |
| 3 | 18 + 8 over | 50¢ | |
| 4 | 23 + 7 over | 1.00 | |
| 5 | 18 + 7 over | 1.00 | |
| 6 | 20 + 9 over | 50¢ | |
| 7 | 20 + 9 over | 100 | |
| 8 | 16 + 9 over | 50¢ | |
| 9 | 17 + 2 over | 1.00 | |
| 10 | 14 + 7 over | 50¢ | |
| 11 | 22 + 7 over | $1.00 | |
| 12 | 16 + 11 " | .50 | |
| 13 | 21 + 8 " | 1.00 | |
| 14 | 19 + 3 " | 1.00 | |
| 15 | 18 + 6 " | 50¢ | |
| 16 | 21 + 6 " | 1.00 | $1.00 (wire) |
| 17 | 19 + 1 " | 1.00 | $2.95 (chick) |
| 18 | 19 + 3 " | 50¢ | |
| 19 | 19 + 2 " | 1.00 | |
| 20 | 20 + 11 " | .50 | |
| 21 | 18 + 15 " | 1.00 | |
| 22 | 19 + 0 " | 1.00 | feed $11.30 |
| 23 | 34 + 9 " | 100 | |
| 24 | 24 + 8 " | 50¢ | |
| 25 | 22 + 7 " | 1.00 | |
| 26 | 19 + 2 " | 1.00 | lamp $3.95 |
| 27 | 22 — " | 1.00 | repair 1.25 |
| 28 | 18 + 6 " | 1.00 | |
| 29 | 22 + 4 " | 100 | |
| 30 | 19 + 11 " | 50¢ | |
| 31 | 22 + 9 " | 1.00 | |

## November '57

| Eggs | Income | Expenses | Date | N EGGS T L |
|---|---|---|---|---|
| 28 - 8 | 100 | | 1 | |
| 26 - 10 | 100 | | 2 | |
| 23 - 9 | 100 | | 3 | |
| 20 - 5 | 100 | | 4 | |
| 24 - 5 | 100 | | 5 | |
| 18 - 11 | 50 | | 6 | |
| 19 - 6 | 100 | | 7 | |
| 15 - 9 | 50 | | 8 | |
| 17 - 2 | 100 | | 9 | |
| 18 - 8 | 50 | | 10 | |
| 12 - 1 | 100 | 25.80 | 11 | |
| 22 - 11 | 50 | 16.20 feed | 12 | |
| 16 - 3 | 100 | | 13 | |
| 19 - 10 | 50 | | 14 | |
| 20 - 8 | 100 | | 15 | |
| 15 - 9 | 150 | | 16 | |
| 22 - 7 | 100 | | 17 | |
| 19 - 2 | 100 | $1.00 fire | 18 | |
| 17 - 7 | 50 | | 19 | |
| 24 - 7 | 100 | | 20 | |
| 26 - 9 | 100 | | 21 | |
| 21 - 9 | 100 | | 22 | |
| 19 - 1 | 100 | | 23 | |
| 33 - 10 | 100 | | 24 | |
| 22 - 8 | 100 | | 25 | |
| 26 - 10 | 100 | | 26 | |
| 23 - 9 | 100 | | 27 | |
| 26 - 11 | 100 | | 28 | |
| 26 - 1 | 150 | | 29 | |
| 37 - 4 | 100 | feed $17.20 | 30 | |

# LOCK

# UP

# CHICKENS

*Nate is a good boy.*

Just to be sure he didn't forget one key aspect of the business, his dad made a sign to remind him to lock up the chicken house each night (presumably to avoid a repeat of the previous year's massacre). In bold black letters, with one word on each line, Scott printed *LOCK UP CHICKENS!* Below this, Neil added a handwritten response — *Neil is a good boy*.[138]

Although Neil was dedicated to his new enterprise, his father occasionally felt obliged to provide written reminders. One such note[139] read:

> Neil:
> after school, BEFORE YOU DO ANYTHING ELSE, do the following:
>
> 1. Remove dead chicken from the hen house.
> 2. Gather eggs.
> 3. See whether six chickens will go into one of those crates under the apple tree.
> 4. Take a dozen eggs to Mrs. Vernoyes [sic].[140] She picked up one dozen and will pay you for two.
> 5. Have fun.
>
> Love, Dad

Neil often visited the Cargill family to look at their chickens. John and May Cargill and their four children — Shirley, Bill

---

*"Lock Up Chickens!" sign made by Scott Young with a comment added by Neil at bottom.*
[Trent University Archives, Scott Young fonds (90-003 Box 26)]

(who was in Neil's class at old Brock Road School), Bob and Mary Anne — lived on the south side of the Fourth Concession Road, a couple of kilometres west of Brock Road and the new school. Bob Cargill remembers going on a long walk with Neil to the mill in Whitevale to check the price of chickenfeed. Bob was never sure whether Neil came to the house because he liked him or because he wanted to see the chickens. "Neil was quite obsessed with chickens,"[141] Shirley Cargill says.

"Maybe you can imagine the thrill of watching young chicks grow into husky, healthy chicks," Neil wrote in his English presentation a few years later. "I'm sure that none of you could ever describe a half-grown chicken. They have more body than feathers, more feet than body, and more pep and energy than their odd bodies are capable of. It is very easy to become attached to these abnormal birds. I did."[142]

Neil's egg business brought him into close contact with his neighbours. His usual first stop was at the home of the McMurtries, who were regular customers. Joyce and Gil McMurtrie rented an old red-brick farmhouse directly south of the Young family on the west side of Brock Road, where they lived while waiting for the completion of their new home seven houses to the south. Their son Peter was six years younger than Neil, but often helped him with his chickens and tagged along on other adventures. Neil was a lunch and dinner guest at their home a few times, and Peter recalls that he and Neil "crashed our train sets together." Peter got in his way occasionally, but Neil took it in his stride. "Neil," says Peter, "was a good-natured geeky kid with a kind heart; kinda like Beaver Cleaver but skinny."

Neil arrived at the McMurtries' farmhouse with an egg delivery one day in 1957, only to discover that the family cat had recently given birth to a litter of kittens. Neil was fascinated by the kittens, and he and Peter "stroked the kittens, slid them along the polished wood floors and argued about their names," until Peter's mother gently reminded Neil to get back to delivering his eggs.

Neil tried to sell his eggs to anyone who might be interested. He routinely stood at the entrance to the Pickering Golf Club, hoping prospective customers would drive by. This was the same golf course where Neil occasionally worked for money to buy more chickens. "I figured out how to get more chickens by selling golf balls," Neil remarks. "Go out and find balls in the rough and sell 'em to the golfers. A lotta kids I knew did that to make money. I'd find golf balls, sell 'em, save the money up and go get the chickens."[143] The sums of money involved were not exactly large. Doug Suter recalls that he, Neil and Reggie Taylor were collecting stray golf balls one day. After some negotiating, Doug sold a ball for three cents to Wilson Paterson, the assistant pro at the time. Reggie promptly topped him by selling a ball for five cents to someone else.

As the egg business expanded, Neil's father sometimes helped with the deliveries. When production hit four or five dozen eggs a day, Scott began to deliver some in his VW Bug on his way to work in Malton.

Neil enjoyed visiting the homes of various neighbours on Brock Road. There was an open-door policy at all of the homes, and children came and went with carefree abandon. Howard and Ruby Bath and their children lived in a farmhouse on three acres of land, three houses north of the Young family home. Don and Alyson Scott lived immediately north of the Youngs, and Sam and Isa Kaiser lived in between the Scotts and the Baths.

Howard, who worked at General Motors in Oshawa, kept

two incubators in the basement of their home and operated them as a hobby, hatching eggs for the Bath family or their neighbours — Neil had put one of the incubators to good use with his original set of 30 fertilized eggs, donated by Don. There were five children in the Bath family; from oldest to youngest: Karen, Marlene, Robert, Randy and Kevin. Marlene[144] recalls how she and Karen would regularly check the eggs in the incubators first thing in the morning, anxious to see whether any had hatched overnight. The Baths kept a number of animals on their property, including chickens, horses, geese, dogs, cats and rabbits, and neighbouring children enjoyed visiting. One of these eager visitors was Neil. He ostensibly came to see the chickens, but was often distracted by the other animals. Children liked to climb the trees on the Baths' property to look at birds' nests, and on one spring day Neil spotted several nests with new hatchlings in them. He found a basket nearby and began to collect baby birds, then suddenly remembered it was dinnertime and left abruptly to hurry home; Ruby Bath was left to sort out the abandoned birds and put them back in their proper nests.

As TIME PASSED, SCOTT FELT increasingly unhappy with his work at Orenda. In February 1957 he was offered — and accepted — a vastly more satisfying position at the *Globe and Mail*. Long-time columnist Bruce West had recently moved on to the promotions department, and Scott replaced him at a starting salary of $170 weekly. Neil remarks, "Daddy had a daily column on the first page of the second section where he wrote human-interest stories. Every day he would write about a different subject, and I think he was very happy doing this job."[145]

Shortly after Scott began working at the *Globe and Mail*,

Neil took on the added responsibility of a delivery route for the same paper. Neil recalls his routine: "[M]y dad and I used to get up at six every Sunday morning and drive about five miles down Brock Road to the intersection with Highway 2, where the newspapers for my paper route were dropped."[146] Neil and his father retrieved the papers and loaded them into the car. Then Scott would drive home and Neil would carry on with his duties. "I would then take my bike," Neil recalls, "and deliver them once we got home and my dad would stay at home while I delivered and make a pancake breakfast with a different twist (bananas, oranges, berries) every week. That was a really good time."[147] Neil adds, "Every week was a surprise to get home and find out what he was creating. We would sit at the table and enjoy the pancakes together, just my dad and me — nobody else was up yet."[148]

Before enjoying a special pancake breakfast with his father, Neil first had to complete his hour-and-a-half news-paper route and feed his chickens. Since the Youngs lived in a rural area, the houses were spaced far apart and Neil needed to cover a lot of territory. He would pedal north on Brock Road, dropping off papers at about 10 homes that were clustered close together. "Every one [of the houses] had a long driveway," he says, "and a dog was usually present. I would carefully survey the situation and move in for the delivery, trying not to wake the dogs or the customers. I was pretty darn good at it."[149] After the first part of his route was completed, Neil would arrive at the old Brock Road School at the Fourth Concession Road. He would turn left, heading west, and pedal past the new schoolhouse to where four more customers lived.

Neil's classmate Marilyn LaBrie lived with her family in one of the houses nearby. Neil's classmate for the past few years, Marilyn had an engaging smile, and Neil enjoyed being around her. His interest had first been piqued in Grade 5, and she continued to hold his attention when they made the move to the new school.

Neil remembers exactly where Marilyn used to live: "There was a bridge[150] crossing a creek at the bottom of the canyon near her house, and I crossed it on my bike every Sunday morning delivering the route."[151] Classmate Susan Wilson's family lived nearby, and Susan recalls that Marilyn's father taught law at the University of Toronto and that her parents were very strict with her.

The LaBrie family home was on the south side of what is now Taunton Road, just past where the Wilsons and Cargills lived on the south side of the Old Fourth Concession Road. (The two roads now merge over that same creek where the bridge was located.) The LaBrie home was distinguished by the many trees Marilyn's father had planted on the family's property leading out to the road.

An opening in the brush led down a steep hill that bottomed at a narrow concrete bridge at the Fourth Concession Road. A creek — part of the West Duffins Creek system — ran underneath the bridge. Susan Wilson adds some further detail: "There was bush on both sides of the creek. At the top of the hill, on the south side, there was a lane going south. There was a white house on the left, and Marilyn lived in a small house to the right of the lane."

Neil had become friendlier with Marilyn and sometimes walked her home after school. One afternoon while carrying

---

*Car-themed birthday card made by Neil for Bob's 15th birthday.*
[Trent University Archives, Scott Young fonds (90-003 Box 26)]

her books for her, Neil decided to demonstrate his affection. "I kissed Marilyn on the bridge," Neil reveals. "I think that was the first time I ever kissed a girl. What a thrill!"[152]

OTHER INTERESTS THAT WOULD LAST a lifetime began to emerge when Neil lived on Brock Road. One of these would become his career. According to Scott Young, "Neil, then ten or eleven, had two main pursuits — listening to pop music on CHUM on a radio under his pillow and raising chickens to sell the eggs."[153]

Neil confirms that his love for music first took root during this period. "When I first really started focusing on rock and roll was in Pickering," he says. "Brock Road. . . . That's when music started getting through to me. Early rock and roll."[154] He recalls, "It was about 1955, I guess, when I really became aware of what was going on in music. I knew that I wanted to play, that I was into it."[155] At night, Neil often listened to the transistor radio concealed under his pillow: it was "a little cream-coloured one, with a little chrome thing on the front. . . . Transistor radios are fuckin' great. The original boom box. Just the fact that you could have your tunes with you. That was amazing."[156] He paid rapt attention to the early rock and roll that dominated the airwaves during 1955-56 — Elvis Presley, Fats Domino, Chuck Berry and Little Richard, among many others. "When I was a kid," he says, "I thought Elvis was pretty hot. . . . I just dug it. 'All Shook Up' was a really good record. When it came out, it just had this beat that made you feel good."[157] Neil kept his transistor tuned to 1050 CHUM AM[158] in Toronto, and it fed him a constant stream of rock and roll, rockabilly, doo-wop, R&B and country music. During May 1957 the station made a major programming change, introducing the Top 50 format that had already proved popular in the U.S. The first song played in the new format was Presley's "All Shook Up," which was also the first No. 1 hit on the newly introduced CHUM Chart.[159]

Neil recalls, "Mom and Dad used to listen to the old big bands, Lena Horne, Della Reese, Tommy Dorsey, Glenn Miller Orchestra, Cab Calloway . . ."[160] Even though Scott and Rassy's music collection was an odd assortment, Neil found some records he enjoyed playing on their old Seabreeze portable record player. Whenever his parents went out for the evening and he was left alone, the Seabreeze would be cranked up to maximum volume. Neil played his records and danced, indulging the fantasy that he was first-place winner at a dance competition. The place where he won these fantasy dance contests was the Legion Hall in Omemee, likely the only hall he knew at the time.

Neil had been playing records the day his parents bought him his first musical instrument — a plastic Arthur Godfrey ukulele[161] that Neil had spotted in a Pickering store window. "I loved music," Neil remarks. "I used to buy records and I grooved on that. I'd save up my money and go to the store every week and buy a 45. There was a ukulele for sale there, and it was cheap — two bucks, maybe three-fifty, and that was kind of within my range, you know? Actually, I had only about 25 cents, but at least I *knew* people who had that much money. But my dad went with me to the store one day, and he must have seen me looking at that ukulele because he brought it home a couple days later."[162]

Neil recalls some further details: "It had a picture of Arthur Godfrey on it, was a plastic little ukulele. . . . And then he picked it up and started playing it. And I never heard him play before. He never said he played. And then he sang this song to me, and I'm going, my god, look at that. . . . And he's sitting there playing this thing. The sounds are coming out, and he's laughing away and singing a silly sad song to me, and I was just — you know, blew my mind."[163]

Scott showed Neil how to finger a few simple chords, and the ukulele came with a songbook containing a few sheets of "cowboy songs," including "She'll Be Comin' 'Round the Mountain," "Clementine" and "Oh Susannah."

Although Neil's father got him started on the ukulele, it was his musically talented uncle Bob who broadened his knowledge of the instrument. The simple plastic ukulele helped steer Neil toward a career in music, and the traditional folk songs he learned would prove to be a lasting influence.

NEIL'S FRIENDS PETER MCMURTRIE AND Doug Suter often visited the Young home. Rassy made a big impression on both of them, and Peter allows that even at his youthful age he knew something about Rassy was "different." Doug remembers her as being "a bit of a loose cannon." Scott usually seemed to be absent: out of town on assignment, or "perhaps tucked away somewhere committed to his writing," according to Peter.

Another good friend was Brian Boys, a year younger than Neil. The Boys family lived on the north side of the Fourth Concession Road east of Brock Road, part of a small enclave of interrelated families. Neil enjoyed going over to Brian's house to use his sister Beverley's trampoline. Beverley, who used the trampoline for training, would later go on to compete in diving, representing Canada in three consecutive Summer Olympics games. The Boys family also kept chickens and an incubator, a big draw for Neil.

Ross and Bob James, classmates of Neil at Brock Road School, lived on the east side of Brock just north of the Fourth

Concession Road (now Forbrock Street), at the junction of what is now Taunton Road. The property included an apple orchard and two ponds surrounded by willow trees. Ross remembers learning to swim in "the bottom of old gravel pits where there were water pools, complete with all manner of giant water beetles. It was kind of 'sink or swim,' and the faster the better." In winter, these same gravel-pit pools became natural hockey rinks. Ross and his friends "played hockey with newspapers stuffed down our pants to act as shin pads. That was the only padding anywhere. And we came home with freezing feet all too often and were in agony as they thawed out."

Middleton's store, at Fourth Concession and Brock, was a popular gathering place for local children, though non-paying customers were "generally not welcomed." Peter McMurtrie remembers grey-haired Mrs. Middleton as "sort of a kindly old aunt from Mayberry, but not as nice as Aunt Bea." The store sold "all sorts of old candy, pop and food stuff," though Neil was probably saving most of his hard-earned money for chicken-related paraphernalia. Children who did have spare change most likely spent it on grab bags (small brown paper bags filled with a variety of mysterious candies and whatever else wasn't selling very well) and black balls, which were popular items at the time.

ANOTHER FOCAL POINT FOR THE Brock Road community was the Pickering Golf Club, which had opened in 1953 — the Youngs lived right across the road, just north of the fourth tee. Mr. Knopf, the greenskeeper, lived with his wife and three daughters[164] in a small house on the grounds of the golf course directly across from the Youngs. The course was owned and operated by Bruce and Gwen Summers, whose modern but

101

traditional grey brick house was located along the treeline at the midpoint of the 16th fairway. (The Summers family were regular customers on Neil's egg delivery route, and one day he decided to play a joke on them by putting one of his chickens in their mailbox. The family's eldest daughter Susan was gratifyingly startled when the chicken flew out, and Neil thought it was hilarious — at least until Gwen came roaring out of the house to give him a piece of her mind.)

The golf club's new swimming pool was perhaps its biggest attraction for local children: Ross James recalls swimming there during the summer and even into September, when "the nights were getting cold, but the water was still warm. Nice to swim in, but not so nice to get out of." Bill Sowerby sold five acres of his 10-acre property abutting the north end of the golf club to use for building the swimming pool. Although the Youngs certainly made good use of the swimming pool, they also used the course for its traditional purpose.

Bob had already displayed a talent for golf, and he would go on to become one of Ontario's top junior golfers. Rassy had been an avid golfer since her days at the Winnipeg Canoe Club, and when she and Scott felt it was time for Neil to learn the game they enlisted Wilson Paterson, the assistant golf pro at the course, to teach him the basics. Wilson recalls giving Neil three private lessons.

Two of Neil's old scorecards from the Pickering Golf Club, dated June 7 and 8 (year unknown, but presumed to be in the mid- to late-'50s), show Neil playing golf with "Ian and Ken."

---

FROM TOP: *Snack bar beside the swimming pool, Picking Golf Club.* [© 2011 Sharry Wilson]; *Ad for Pickering Golf Club, dated 1961.* [Courtesy of the Pickering Public Library]

# PICKERING GOLF CLUB

FOR THE BEST IN GOLFING AND SWIMMING
**VISiT PICKERING GOLF CLUB**

1 Mile North of No. 2 Highway on Brock Road
**For Information Call**

**BRUCE   SUMMERS**
## WH. 2-4977

Fortunately for the other boys, Neil's score was unimpressive on both days.[165] The golf lessons weren't wasted, however: a July 5, 1958, article in the sports section of the *Globe and Mail* notes that Neil was selected as one of the starters in the Bantam category of the qualifying rounds for the Ontario Junior Golf Championship Finals. In the same article, Bob is listed as a starter in the qualifying rounds for the Juniors. Bob was a more skilled golfer than Neil and would participate in many junior golfing tournaments and championships over the coming years.

Neil still enjoys the occasional game with friends and family. Most notably, he played in the 2003 AT&T Pebble Beach National Pro/Am Golf Classic; his official handicap at the time was 18.6.[166]

JUST BEFORE NEIL BEGAN CLASSES in September 1957, Scott had a chat with Ray Doble, the principal at the newly opened six-room Lincoln Avenue Public School. Scott was concerned that Neil's education at Brock Road School lacked discipline and structure. William Bush, the music teacher at both Brock Road and Lincoln Avenue, had introduced him to Mr. Doble, who had a reputation as an effective disciplinarian. Scott felt that Neil would benefit from a school with a more organized structure. Scott and Ray got along well and respected each other.

The Youngs lived in the catchment area for Brock Road Public School, so strings must have been pulled to enable Neil to attend Lincoln Avenue. It's unclear whether the Youngs paid a fee to the school board, but an arrangement was somehow contrived.

In addition to his duties as principal, Mr. Doble taught the Grade 8 class part-time, assisted by Mabel Barkey. Mr.

Doble's class also included some overflow Grade 7 students, and Neil was part of this group.

No buses were used to transport students to elementary school, so Scott had to drive Neil to school and pick him up on his way back from work at the *Globe and Mail* in Toronto. Because Scott often worked late, he arranged for Neil to meet him at the home of the Maurers, who were friends of the Youngs. The Maurers lived at 9 Sherwood Road, just north of Highway 2 and a short walk north from the school. Waiting for his father, Neil would pass time watching television. If Scott was running especially late, the Maurers' son, Murray, would walk Neil partway home. It was during one of these walks that Neil confided to Murray that he wanted to be a musician when he grew up. Neil said he was anxious to get home so he could listen to his transistor radio or listen to music on his parents' record player.

It's unclear how long Neil attended Lincoln Avenue Public School, but it seems to have become increasingly difficult for Scott to pick him up after school. Murray Maurer recalls that Neil attended Lincoln Avenue very briefly: "He was there one day and gone the next." Presumably, he went back to Brock Road to finish the year.

IN DECEMBER 1957, WHEN NEIL was 12, he was chosen for a speaking role as a shepherd in the school Christmas concert. Rassy threw herself into the task of putting together a professional-looking costume, only to discover that the other parents hadn't been so inventive. The disparity didn't seem to bother Neil in the slightest: "I'm a rich shepherd,"[167] he announced. For the following year's Christmas concert, Neil and a classmate were assigned to work the curtains, which unfortunately collapsed during the performance.

One of the junior-class students was Mike "Shorty" Shanley, whose family lived on the Fourth Concession west of Brock Road. Mike, who was in Grade 1 or 2 at the time, recalls standing on his tiptoes trying to drink from the water fountain in the hallway of the school — a risky endeavour, since students drinking from the fountain often received a slap on the back of the head from passing classmates, a "joke" that usually resulted in the victim getting water all over his face. Neil spotted Mike at the water fountain and gave him the customary slap to his head, but he slapped a bit too hard and Mike's front teeth connected with the chrome water spout. Mike realized something was wrong when he found part of his tooth lying in the basin. He looked around and spotted Neil retreating down the hall. "That's the new kid that did it," Mike thought to himself, "that Neil Young guy!"

Trains often rumbled past on the tracks that skirted the southern edge of the school property. Susan Wilson recalls that she and her classmates made a game of counting the cars as the trains went by, comparing numbers once they were gone. Peter McMurtrie remembers an incident that took place at the new school at a time when Neil may have been in attendance. It was "during the winter sometime, and there was lots of packing snow on the ground. A jigger, a four-seater mini-working vehicle, electric-powered, that would carry railway workers from one work site to another, came into view during recess. Everyone — what seemed like half the school — ran toward the fence and peppered these four guys with snowballs as they slowly passed along the railway tracks." Peter was close enough that he saw "a few direct

*At home on Brock Road, circa 1957-58.*
[Trent University Archives, Scott Young fonds (90-003 Box 26)]

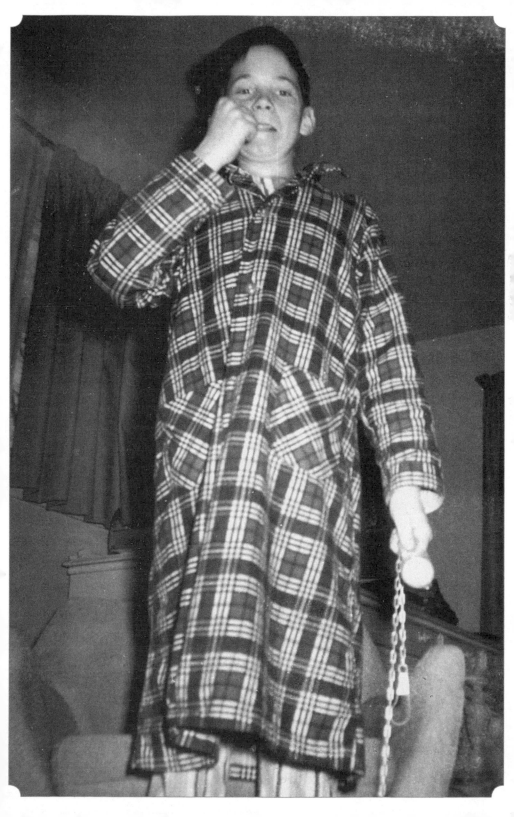

hits." The school's response was swift. The same day, there was an "inquisition and about 20 people got the strap. That was a new record by a mile!"

DURING A DRAB, OVERCAST DAY one weekend in early March, Neil paid a visit to the Wingay family in his old neighbourhood of Moore Park in Toronto. He had come into the city with his parents, but they were busy elsewhere for the day.

Eldon Wingay[168] had recently convinced his parents to cash in some of his Canada Savings Bonds so he could buy an acoustic Stella guitar. He was anxious to install a new electric pickup, and Neil displayed a keen interest in the process. Youngest brother Elvin — almost 10 at the time — remembers Neil "watching intently" as his brother strummed chords while sitting with his back to the fireplace at their home on Moore Avenue.

After Eldon had practised, he, Neil and Elvin decided to make their way across the street to Moore Park to "mess around on the natural ice rinks." A chill drizzle had set in, however, and the boys were forced to take cover in the change room at the clubhouse, where Neil found a single beat-up, abandoned skate. He sat down on a bench, put the skate on one foot and tied what remained of the lace. Carrying one boot while wearing the other boot and the skate, Neil headed to the hockey rink in the park. Elvin remembers Neil running headlong down Kingsmere Road, gliding where the patches of spring ice were still intact, stopping and stumbling whenever he hit bare pavement, his winter coat undone and flapping behind him like the wings of a bird.

THE YOUNGS LIVED ON BROCK Road in a time that now seems both innocent and irretrievably lost. "It really was a beautiful field of dreams," Peter McMurtrie observes. "It was Huck Finn's Mississippi, full of adventure and a real hub of activity and excitement, centred around the school, the golf course and the swimming pool."

But Scott's work at the *Globe and Mail* now necessitated a tedious daily drive. He had recently switched to writing a daily sports column. Editor Jim Vipond had been writing the column, but his editorial duties made it hard for him to keep up, and Scott was more than willing to take his place. That commute, coupled with the offer of work as an intermission host on the Saturday-night telecasts of CBC's *Hockey Night in Canada*, finally drew him back to the city.

In the late spring of 1958 the Youngs decided to lease their Brock Road bungalow to the McPhail family and buy a house in Toronto. After the boys finished the school year, the family would make their move to the big city.[169] The Youngs took possession of their Toronto home in early June, but still had their Brock Road property to look after until they moved at the end of the month. "It takes five hours to cut the home lawn," Scott remarked. "Then we load the equipment in a car and drive 25 miles to cut the other one."[170]

"My father told me not to be surprised if we moved," Neil wrote in a composition for his Grade 8 English class in Toronto. "I didn't really think we ever would move, anyway, so I thought nothing of it then. But one day it happened. We were forced to move to Toronto because of my father's work. I was asked to sell my chickens to my neighbours."[171]

The rural idyll was over.

# ✸ 5 ✸
## SAD MOVIES

*Sad movies, they make you cry.*
*Sad movies make you wonder why you ever came.*

— Neil Young, "Sad Movies"

THE YOUNG FAMILY HAD BOUGHT a solid two-storey brick detached house at 49 Old Orchard Grove[172] in North Toronto. The Bedford Park neighbourhood, located just north of the more economically and socially advantaged Lawrence Park, was originally conceived as a middle-class housing development, and most of the houses had been built between 1890 and 1946.

Neil had the summer to spend as he pleased. Music was becoming an increasingly important part of his life, and Scott grew accustomed to hearing his son practise his plastic ukulele in his upstairs bedroom. Neil "would close the door of his room at the top of the stairs and we would hear *plunk*, pause while he moved his fingers to the next chord, *plunk*, pause while he moved again, *plunk* . . ."[173] In a 1968 interview with Judith Sims for *Teen Set* magazine, Neil mentioned his ukulele: "I learned three chords on it: really went wild and learned 'Blueberry Hill' and 'On Top of Old Smokey' . . . all those neat songs." Other songs he remembers playing included "Billy Boy," "Rachel, Rachel" and "Bury Me Not on the Lone Prairie." "I went from a ukulele to a better ukulele[174] to a banjo ukulele to a baritone ukulele — everything but a guitar," he recalled. "I was getting into music."[175, 176]

IN THE FALL NEIL WAS enrolled at John Wanless Public School at 250 Brookdale Avenue,[177] between Yonge Street and Avenue Road, north of Lawrence. The school began its existence on February 15, 1926, when it opened as a temporary annex of Bedford Park Public School. John Wanless[178] — a jeweller who later served as a Toronto alderman and school board trustee — placed the cornerstone on January 18, 1927, and the new brick building was ready for occupation that September. The building originally housed nine classrooms on the Fairlawn side of the current-day structure; the Brookdale section (housing the kindergarten) was added in 1929. The separation of the two halves of the building can still be seen in the hallway today. An extension of six rooms on the northern Fairlawn side was constructed during 1935-36. At the time Neil attended, the school offered classes from kindergarten to Grade 8.

As he passed through the boys' playground just outside the east-facing main entrance doors, Neil would have seen students shooting marbles and trading sports cards. A popular game in the fall was "conkers." The conker was a horse chestnut with a string attached; players used them as flails, the object being to crack an opponent's conker. The school's two cinder-covered baseball diamonds were also put to good use, even outside of regular school hours, as were the three ice rinks during the winter months. Popular winter games included King of the Hill and Red Rover, which often escalated to aggressive battles in the snow. During the late spring, a yo-yo expert might visit the playground to show the boys tricks they could perform, such as "rock the baby" and "around the world." The more sedate girls' playground was on the west side of the school property, where a staff parking lot now stands.

Neil began Grade 8 in early September 1958, and again he was thrust into an unenviable spotlight as the new kid in class: "I think back on my childhood and I remember moving around a lot, from school to school. I was always breaking in."[179]

He was assigned to Ethel M. MacKay's class in Room 16. Classmate Marilyn Mutch remarked that Miss MacKay was "the best teacher I ever had. She brought out the best in her students and had won awards for her teaching." Neil was "a class clown and very funny."

Many of the students — especially the boys — knew that Neil was Scott Young's son. Scott's sports reporting on radio and TV broadcasts for *Hockey Night in Canada* had already brought him a degree of national recognition. He had appeared on *The Hot Stove League*, which began in 1939 as a radio broadcast during intermission periods. The popular segment, which brought together well-known hockey writers in a small studio to air their opinions, eventually made the move to television, but it proved less successful in that medium and was finally shelved in 1957. It was then that Scott became

---

CLOCKWISE FROM TOP: 49 *Old Orchard Grove*. [© 2011 Sharry Wilson]; *Golf-themed birthday card made by Neil for Bob's 17th birthday.* [Trent University Archives, Scott Young fonds (90-003 Box 26)]; *Glendale Theatre*. [City of Toronto Archives, Series 249, File 771, Item 1]

YOU'RE A HOLE
SEVENTEEN YEAR
OLE

Love, from
Dad
mum
and.

one of the on-air hosts who interviewed players during intermissions of the now nationally broadcast games. "Now that was a really big deal," Neil remarks, "because, as you may have heard, hockey is the national game in Canada."[180]

Neil's classmates were also aware of Scott from his columns and articles in the *Globe and Mail,* and some of the boys would have read his hockey-oriented juvenile novels, *Scrubs on Skates* and *Boy on Defense.* Neil was soon befriended by students in the popular athletic crowd, including Brian "Bunny" Stuart,[181] a skilled player for both the school and church hockey teams.

Outside of school, Neil continued to enjoy playing golf as long as the season lasted. He was joined on some of these outings by Bunny and another boy, Ricky Wardell, who had skipped a grade and was a year ahead of them. Ricky's family lived one block south of the Youngs on Deloraine Avenue, while Bunny lived on Yonge Boulevard, a block north of Neil's place. (Bunny lived with his father, aunt and cousin; his mother lived elsewhere.) Bunny most likely got his nickname from family members, Ricky believes; he was short and compact and had a "cherubic" face with prominent front teeth. The three of them would sometimes play golf at the Don Valley Golf Course nearby. ("Very cheap summer kids' rates," according to Ricky.) Ricky recalls Neil "as an enthusiastic brush-cut kid," proud of his older brother Bob's prowess in golf and hockey. Ricky himself had only recently taken up the sport and was impressed with Neil's ability: "Neil was already an accomplished player who knew the game."

JOHN WANLESS WAS A TYPICAL Canadian school of the era. Its fundraising activities have a nostalgic ring nowadays: every autumn students collected empty wooden fruit baskets from their families and neighbours, to be stored in the school basement until they were purchased and picked up by a neighbourhood supermarket. The student who collected the most baskets received a prize.

According to classmate Mike Foulds, the school's principal, H. Lloyd Matthews, was "a fairly serious fellow who rarely visited the classroom. When he did, one of his favourite lessons was the spelling of three words: *omission, occasion* and *occurrence.*" Ricky Wardell recalls, "Mr. Matthews was a very stern, tall, imposing disciplinarian. Because of his receding hairline and high, shiny forehead, he was referred to as 'old marblehead' — quietly, of course." Gordon A. Crutcher, a well-liked and popular teacher, served as vice-principal.

But there was a darker side to John Wanless Public School. "John Wanless? You had to go at the right time," Neil later said. "If I got there a little early, I could get the shit beaten out of me, so I made sure I arrived right on time. And when you got outta that school, you got fuckin' out. Got away. People used to be assholes. You know how they pick on you in school."[182] Although Neil's continuing friendship with members of the athletic crowd helped to insulate him from school bullies, on one occasion he was obliged to defend himself in class. Neil later remarked to Cameron Crowe:

Once, I'd become a victim of a series of chimp attacks by some of the bullies in my room. I looked up and three guys were staring at me, mouthing, "You low-life prick." Then the guy who sat in front of me turned around and hit my books off the desk with his elbow. He did this a few times. I guess I wore the wrong color of clothes or something. Maybe I looked too much like a mamma's boy for them.

Anyway, I went up to the teacher and asked if I could have the dictionary. This was the first time I'd broken the ice and put my hand up to ask for anything since I got to the fucking place. Everybody thought I didn't speak. So I got the dictionary, this big Webster's with little indentations for your thumb under every letter. I took it back to my desk, thumbed through it a little bit. Then I just sort of stood up in my seat, raised it up above my head as far as I could and hit the guy in front of me over the head with it. Knocked him out.

Yeah, I got expelled for a day and a half, but I let those people know just where I was at. That's the way I fight. If you're going to fight, you may as well fight to wipe who or whatever it is out. Or don't fight at all.[183, 184]

Neil recalled the same incident to Jimmy McDonough many years later: "It wasn't like literally 'KILL!' But I did hit this person over the head with the dictionary as hard as I could, and it felt great. I don't advise it, but it sure opens ya up. I could feel good about myself."[185]

Sports were an important element in the pecking order among male students, and Neil was fortunate that his father's status lent him a certain cachet. During Minor Hockey Week, Scott arranged for Bunny Stuart to be interviewed about his enthusiasm for hockey during an intermission on *Hockey Night in Canada*, transforming his friend into an instant schoolyard celebrity.

The school's three ice rinks were dedicated to distinct

purposes — one was a competitive hockey rink, one was for pleasure skating and the smallest was reserved for shinny, informal hockey without strict rules. Although Neil had been befriended by the athletic crowd, his skating skills were no match for his friends' — they preferred the hockey rink while Neil spent more ice time on the shinny rink. Classmate Owen Charlesworth remembers playing some companionable games of shinny with Neil after school, which suited Owen fine; he wasn't a particularly skilled skater either.

The boys were also fond of street shinny, a favourite after-school game. There were fewer automobiles on the road in the late 1950s, making residential streets available for informal games of shinny and street football. Whenever a vehicle was sighted, the iconic Canadian childhood cry of "Car!" rang out in the wintry air, and play would be suspended until the intruder had safely passed.

THIS WAS ALSO THE YEAR Neil gave his oral presentation on chicken farming to Miss MacKay's class. It started with a written outline:

Introduction — how I got the Idea.
Purchase of Chicks.
Description of half-grown chicken.
Becoming attached to them.
Tell about disaster — Find nine dead chicks from shock.
Find one chicken alive in afternoon — Petunia.
Sell chickens for 75¢ each — $6.75.
Buy 26 more chicks with proceeds.
Chickens lay first egg on Dec. 27, 1956.
Proceeds each week amount to about $10.

Double proceeds by buying more chicks.
Profits doubled & redoubled by purchase of
more hens.
Roosters in third group — Ike, George & Hoiman
— Hoiman for dinner.
Had to move to Toronto so sold entire flock and
three henhouses.
When I finish school I plan a course at OAC to
learn more about poultry.[186]

During the actual presentation, as Owen Charlesworth recalls,
"Neil lacked a lot of self-confidence. He spoke hesitantly with
a lot of pauses." "He spoke only from notes," according to
Scott Young, "but seems to have written it out to see how it
would sound."[187]

"Miss McKay & Class," Neil wrote (all spelling and
punctuation verbatim),

> the subject of my oral to-day is a personal
> experience. In July '55[188] I came up the stairs
> of our bungalow home and stumbled into my
> father. Smiling, he asked me "Well Neil, what
> hair brained scheme have you worked up in your
> head now? Well dad," I said, "I was thinking
> about that old range shelter in the back field,
> and well, I'm going into the chicken business.
> O.K." he said Good Luck." It was a simple plain

---

FROM TOP: *John Wanless Public School, Grade 8, 1958-59.*
[Courtesy of Michael Foulds]; *John Wanless Public School.
Main entrance, east side of school.* [© 2011 Sharry Wilson]

answer showing that he thought nothing would ever come of my "just another idea." I set out to prove that I was once going in business for myself. This is the story of what I did to prove my sincerity.

In less than one weekend I had finished a shelter for the chicks. I received the chicks from a friend a few doors down the road who had an incubator. Maybe you can imagine the thrill of watching young chicks grow into husky healthy chickens. I'm sure none of you could ever describe a half grown chicken. They have more body than feathers, more feet than body, and more pep and energy than their odd bodies are capable of. It is very easy to become attached to these abnormal birds. I did.

Every morning I would go out to our back field, feed, water, and set free my chickens and return home for breakfast. One morning I went ambling out to do the work and spotted some feathers on the path. At least one of my chickens had escaped the shelter. I ran anxiously to the pen to find out how many chickens were left if any. Around the pen were nine dead chickens, apparently dead from shock. Many other traces of a fox or coon were found. In the afternoon I went out to the pen, I don't know why, and just looked, without a hope for even trying to raise chickens again. Then a dirty white chicken popped it's head out from under a clump of weeds. Everything seemed to change and I knew I wasn't finished yet.

Then everything seemed to go well, I purchased 26 female chicks from a hatchery, raised them the same way as before. On Dec 27, 1956 I got my first egg. From then to summer I made around ten dollars clearance per week. In the mid summer I got more chickens and doubled my profits.

My father had told me not to be surprised if we moved. I didn't really think we ever would move anyway, so I thought nothing of it then. But one day it happened, we were forced to moved to Toronto because of my father's work. I was asked to sell my chickens to my neighbour. When I finish school I plan to go to OAC and perhaps learn to be a scientific farmer.[189]

OUTSIDE OF SCHOOL, NEIL KEPT busy with a full-time *Globe and Mail* route. ("I know the newspaper business," he would remark to Cameron Crowe in his February 1979 interview for *Rolling Stone*.)[190] Neil took responsibility for the paper route and handled it without assistance from Scott or Rassy, except once when he was sick. His alarm rang at 6 a.m. every morning and he would deliver his newspapers and be home in time for breakfast before school, no matter how hellish the weather. The deliveries were made easier by the bicycle his father gave him for his 13th birthday. (It was a men's roadster with 28-inch wheels, front and rear carriers, kickstand and lock, from Art's Cycle & Sports. The bill came to a not inconsiderable $56.60.)[191] Neil enjoyed riding along the sparsely occupied early-morning streets. "There are other paper boys I don't even know," he told his father, "but we wave at each other from a block or two away, and it's company."[192]

Daniel Lanois, the acclaimed Canadian record producer, guitarist and songwriter who produced Neil's album *Le Noise* (2010), remarks on the fact that both he and Neil were paper boys in their youth: "We laugh about it. We attribute our work ethic to having delivered the morning *Globe and Mail* newspaper."[193]

ON WEEKENDS NEIL ENJOYED SATURDAY matinees at the Glendale Theatre,[194] located near the corner of Avenue Road and Cranbrooke Avenue. His memories of those afternoons would eventually be immortalized in a song. During his Chrome Dreams Continental Tour in 2007 Neil introduced his performance of "Sad Movies" by noting it was about the old Glendale Theatre in Toronto. (The lyrics describe the theatre's "velvet chairs" and "popcorn boxes flyin' through the air.")

Another favourite gathering spot for young people was Shea's Bowl,[195] a bowling alley on the west side of Avenue Road, just south of the Glendale. And the same crowd often adjourned to Hall's Pure Milk Dairy Store[196] on Yonge Street for malted milkshakes and ice cream. The proprietors at Hall's were the well-liked Mr. and Mrs. Bob Jones. "They made the best milkshakes!" according to John Flower.

BACK IN CLASS AFTER THE New Year, Neil wrote an English composition titled "Resolutions — Do we keep them?"[197] It took a humorous tone and is an early example of Neil's wit (again, all spelling and punctuation verbatim):

> With 1959 here now we should be happy, but some of us aren't. The most popular reason for unhappy children is that mother made their

resolutions. This can be disasterous, so my advice to all children is to make a resolution before your mother finds out you haven't. Make up an easy one for you to keep and keep it. If you don't, mother will make one up like washing dishes, waxing floors, taking out garbage, or worst of all, making your bed. Mothers can be nice, but don't let them get your resolution before you. My resolution this year was to wear my shoes in the house, not my guloshes.

The school's ice rinks were still busy. Forbes Pritchard — Neil's classmate from Whitney School, who was playing a practice hockey game against John Wanless as part of the Whitney Senior Hockey Team — caught sight of Neil one cold February day by the hockey rink on the school property. Forbes recalls that "snow was piled up to the top of the boards and Neil was standing on the snowbank, I guess because he'd gone to Whitney and knew some of us from a few years before. From that chance meeting, even as a young boy, I sensed a loneliness [in Neil]. And what keeps coming back, and has done so for all these years, is a feeling of melancholy about him." Forbes and Neil chatted a bit until the game started, then parted company. The next time Forbes heard about Neil would be when Neil performed at Carnegie Hall in New York City. "Not bad for a lonely kid on the fringe of his peer group," he says.

By June, the Grade 8 students were preparing for their graduation. The ceremony was held in the basement of Fairlawn United Church on a sweleteringly hot day. Doug Maxwell — a notable hockey broadcaster/writer — was the keynote speaker. He mentioned that it was nice to see a familiar face in the crowd when he spotted Scott Young in the audience. Owen Charlesworth gave the valedictory address to the Class of 1959. The front cover of the program booklet[198] shows a bouquet of seven roses. Neil's name is listed with the other Room 16 students in Miss MacKay's class.

THE SUMMER OF 1959 WAS a memorable one for the Young family, for all the wrong reasons. For Rassy and Scott, 19 years of bickering and petty arguments had eroded their relationship, and the conflict intensified as the summer progressed.

Rassy's drinking had been a long-simmering issue, and it compounded and underscored the problems the couple were experiencing. Her beverage of choice was rye whisky and water.[199] Neil would later say of his mother's drinking, "It's quite possible that during the entire time she was bringing me up, she was a raving alcoholic. Now, I still don't know if it's true, but now I think it's possible. And that I just didn't recognize it."[200]

In any event, Scott began to look elsewhere for companionship and love. The tipping point came when the *Globe and Mail* assigned him to cover a 45-day royal tour across Canada (June 18–August 1, 1959). Queen Elizabeth II, accompanied by Prince Philip, was scheduled to visit every province and territory in the country, in the longest royal tour to date in Canadian history.

It was during this assignment that Scott met Astrid Mead, to whom he took an immediate liking. Astrid, 29 years old, worked in public relations and was a divorcee with an eight-year-old daughter. For the six days the royal tour moved through British Columbia, Scott and Astrid were thrown together in a close working relationship. She ran the press room, and they began to share lunches, dinners and coffee.

During a late-night walk in a park near the hotel, they shared something more intimate — a kiss. It went no further than that, but by the time Scott returned home a few weeks later he knew he had fallen in love.

Scott and Astrid exchanged daily letters throughout August and September.[201] Astrid sent her letters to Scott's brother Bob, who forwarded them to Scott at work. This arrangement worked until Bob's wife, Merle, who had an antagonistic relationship with Rassy, intercepted two of these letters and redirected them to 49 Old Orchard Grove.

Rassy, immediately suspicious upon seeing a woman's handwriting, opened the letters and read them. The already-stressed relationship between Scott and Rassy had received its final blow. Their marriage was effectively over.

---

## ✴ 6 ✴
## IT MIGHT HAVE BEEN

*The saddest words / Of tongue or pen*
*Are these four words / It might have been*
*We had big dreams / We made big plans*
*How could they slip / Right through our hands.*[202]

— Kane and Green, "It Might Have Been"

IN THE MIDST OF HIS family's crisis, Neil began his first year of high school at Lawrence Park Collegiate Institute.[203]

Residents of the Lawrence Park neighbourhood were a mixture of well-to-do "old money" families and middle-class arrivistes. Those who aspired to climb the social ladder often met resistance from established families or were hindered by the cost of keeping up appearances. Families on the receiving end often resented the subtle, and sometimes not-so-subtle, snobbery they encountered. Students from Lawrence Park Collegiate — a publicly funded high school — commonly socialized with students from upper-echelon private schools such as Upper Canada College, University of Toronto Schools, Trinity College, Bishop Strachan and Havergal College. It was expected that Lawrence Park students would go on to attend university, and academic studies were yoked to this overriding goal. It was into this challenging social and academic milieu that Neil was thrust.

On the family front, all hell broke loose in early October. Scott and Rassy had "a major, name-calling fight"[204] over a golf game Rassy had played in a tournament Scott had watched. She had played reasonably well but still ended up with a poor score. When Scott asked why, Rassy confessed she was playing in another tournament the following week and didn't want her handicap to be too low. Scott felt this was dishonest, bordering on cheating; Rassy thought it was trivial, and Scott defended his position. The ultimate outcome was that Scott packed a couple of bags and took a taxi to a hotel.

Rassy cried for days afterward. She felt Scott's desertion was yet another major betrayal of their marriage vows, which she took very seriously. Both of her sisters — Toots and Snooky — came to comfort Rassy and lend a hand where they could. They found the household in chaos, with Bob and Neil largely fending for themselves. Rassy was emotionally unavailable, too wrapped up in her own sorrow to care about much else.

A day or two later, Scott took Neil and Bob to Ciccone's[205] on King Street West. The restaurant was a family favourite, and Scott thought it would be a good place to break the news to the boys. He told his sons that he loved them but couldn't live with their mother anymore. After what must have been an excruciatingly uncomfortable dinner, the three walked east along King Street to the *Globe and Mail* building at King and York. The boys then parted ways with Scott, but not before Neil reached over and patted his father on the shoulder in a show of sympathy.

By the middle of October, Scott was living in a studio apartment in the City Park Apartments, overlooking the parking lot of the Torontonian Hotel in downtown Toronto.

He sent a telegram[206] to Astrid on October 17, giving his new address as 31 Alexander Street, Apt. 820. He felt guilty about leaving Rassy after the years of support and trust she had devoted to him, and thought it best to let the boys continue living with their mother.

The stormy breakup coloured Neil's memories of his time at 49 Old Orchard Grove. "It hadn't been very happy around the house," he recalls. "The vibes had been pretty heavy. I don't have the best remembrance of that place on Old Orchard. I remember not spending a lotta time there, spending time at other people's houses."[207] If Neil's life to this point had been like the "Sugar Mountain" he later celebrated in the song of the same name (*But all your friends are there . . . and your mother and your dad*), his parents' separation was his introduction to the harsher realities of life.

At the end of the summer, shortly before he began Grade 9 at Lawrence Park Collegiate, Neil encountered a boy named Comrie Smith. "I was walking up Old Orchard one Sunday afternoon," Comrie recalls, "and out in front of one of the houses, No. 49, there was this kid playing with a little airplane, a yellow one. I thought, 'There's another guy interested in model airplanes.' I used to save up like crazy for gasoline to fly them down at the Loblaws [grocery store] parking lot."[208] The parking lot at the A&P grocers was also a favoured spot for this activity. The boys discovered a shared interest in cars and music that cemented the friendship. Comrie remembers that Neil was deeply affected by his parents' split: "Neil was very twitchy about the breakup. He talked about it a lot. His face would usually be bright red by the time he finished."[209]

COMRIE AND NEIL ATTENDED LAWRENCE Park Collegiate at 125 Chatsworth Drive, near Avenue Road, just south of

Lawrence. Built in 1936, the school held classes for students in grades 9 through 13 during the time Neil attended. The school has changed little in its physical appearance over the years. The "new" auditorium and music rooms located at the north end, the library at the back, and the large art room and swimming pool at the south end were all in place by 1959. An unusual feature was the basement rifle range, used by the Cadets for after-school target shooting.

The principal was the much-vilified William K. Bailey. He was given the nickname "Ace" (or "the Ace") by students as an ironic reference to beloved hockey player Irvine Wallace "Ace" Bailey, a leading goal scorer for the Toronto Maple Leafs from 1926 to 1933. (The hockey player was much admired by the students; the principal was not.) Principal Bailey ruled the school with an iron fist and was notorious for his rigid discipline. He had the uncanny ability to remember the names of all 1,200 of his students and could greet (or more likely admonish) any of them by name. Bob McConnell, who also attended Lawrence Park and would be introduced to Neil by Comrie Smith, was struck by the principal's face: "His eyes were always red-rimmed and I don't recall ever seeing him smile. Thinking back, I have to wonder if he even liked his job. He ran a school full of university-bound students, whether they wanted it or not, whether they could [achieve it] or not. Because he was so intolerant and strict, students tended to hate him first and fear him second." Principal Bailey, who had a nervous habit of playing with the ring on his left hand, habitually demanded that students walk on the right side of hallways and staircases. Lawrence Park student Harold Greer, who would also meet Neil through his friendship with Comrie, recalls that the principal once sent him home with one dollar and strict orders to get a haircut.

He came back suitably shorn but was obliged to refund Principal Bailey's dollar.

All students entering Grade 9 in the fall of 1959 were herded into the large auditorium, where they were given a standardized IQ test. Those who scored highest were offered a spot in a special gifted class, then seen as "experimental" and progressive. Students in the gifted class would stay together for an accelerated program that compressed the normal five years of study into four. Perhaps predictably, Neil was not included in this select group.

Neil was placed in class 9B, Pat Smith's homeroom English class. He displayed a keen wit and was popular with the girls because he was so funny. "He had a habit of flicking his fingers forward at such velocity as to cause a loud snapping of [his] fingernails,"[210] Comrie recalls. Neil would do this behind the heads of his classmates. He also took great joy in shooting elastic bands at unsuspecting victims, often female classmates. And he occasionally handed in lyrics from such songs as "Blueberry Hill" and "Framed" rather than the memory work Miss Smith assigned to the class.

These and other antics garnered Neil a semi-permanent seat at a desk in the hall outside Vice-Principal Vern Baker's office. "I remember the odd firecracker soaring past the classroom window," Comrie writes, "Neil rushing back past the room . . . Miss Smith rocketing out the front classroom door to apprehend him . . . the class breaking up [with laughter]. Miss Smith was a kind, softly-spoken, encouraging

---

FROM TOP: *Lawrence Park Collegiate Institute, Class 9B, 1959-60.*
[Courtesy of Keith C. Cowan]; *Lawrence Park Collegiate Institute.*
[© 2009 Sharry Wilson]

person, who had her hands full — Neil usually did something on entering the classroom to gain everyone's attention."[211]

Bob McConnell,[212] who met Comrie in Mr. Watts's Grade 6 class at Bedford Park Public School and remained a lifelong friend, recalls that "Comrie was always attracted to eccentrics. He certainly enjoyed being one himself. And among teenagers, as you know, being known as an eccentric is a curse of derision or general exclusion, at least until everybody grows up and gets some life experience. Neil was, if nothing else, a teenage eccentric, and for that reason people — including teachers — found him either interesting and refreshing, or foolish and irritating. A few years after Neil had become famous and successful, I went back to Lawrence Park one day with the single purpose of asking Miss Smith what she thought of Neil. (She was very approachable.) I went to her especially because at least some of us knew that she had a soft spot for misfits. The way she smiled at my question and the way she said, 'I'm happy for him and wish him well,' convinced me that even if he'd been a pain in the classroom, she liked and sympathized with him."

Comrie had been a gifted elementary school student and had skipped ahead a grade, but his high school work declined as he pursued an extracurricular interest in music, cars and motorcycles. Originally a year ahead of Neil, though the boys were the same age, Comrie had failed Grade 9 math and was placed in Mr. Butterill's class with Neil the following September. He continued for a time at a Grade 10 level in his other subjects, but from the results of his Christmas exams it was obvious that Comrie was having serious difficulties. "At Christmas, it was decided that I should go back to Grade 9," he recalls, "and complete that year as a success with my contemporary age group."[213]

Comrie was placed in 9B and joined Neil in his other classes for the rest of that year.

Neil and Comrie had a daily routine. On weekday mornings they met in front of the Dominion grocery store on the northwest corner of Yonge and St. Germain to walk to school — often to attend "early detention" for infractions they had committed in class.[214] The main topic of discussion almost every day was their mutual love of rock and roll. "Neil would have his transistor radio blaring and we would talk music all the way down to Lawrence."[215] Comrie recalls that Neil often shouted out, "Hey Comrie, listen to this one!"[216] "Mule Skinner Blues" by the Fendermen was a particular favourite of Neil's at the time.

Comrie was also impressed by Neil's sense of style: "Neil bopped down Yonge Street. Very thin, very tall, with a greased-back DA on the sides but a crew cut on top. He had a transistor radio, white bucks, a nice sweater, black pants. Very slick-lookin' guy."[217]

Before Neil began wearing his iconic plaid flannel shirts in the late 1960s/early 1970s, he was better known for wearing sweaters. Although Rassy could ill afford extravagant clothing, she indulged Neil's fondness for "sporty sweaters" from Halpern's,[218] an upscale men's and boys' clothing store. Neil's love of sweaters would continue unabated for a decade, up to and including his tenure in the Buffalo Springfield. Comrie confirms that "Neil was well-dressed in this era."[219]

Neil was also known for having a transistor radio glued to his ear, even during class time at school. He received a new transistor from his father as a birthday gift in November 1959. In a thank-you note[220] Neil wrote:

Dear Dad,

Thank you very much for the Portable radio. I have been playing it quite a lot and the kids all like to sit around and listen with me. Thanks.

Love, Neil

Neil would famously make reference to his white bucks in his autobiographical song "Don't Be Denied."[221] (*I wore white bucks on my feet / When I learned the golden rule.*) "I was always about two or three years behind everybody," Neil remarks. "There was nothin' new about white bucks by the time I started wearin' white bucks. They were, like, out. *No one* was wearing them. That's when I got mine. They were enough of a statement to piss people off. They set me apart." Remarking on his fondness for his white bucks Neil adds, "I liked the fact that your feet were light and you could move around. I had this Sani-White stuff I used to clean 'em — this white stuff in a bottle with this sponge thing on the end — you *paint* them. It's like whitewashing your feet."[222]

Neil used his white bucks to advantage when it came to the school's Cadet program. The boys' phys. ed. courses from grades 9 to 11 included marching drill, and the climax was Cadet Day, when the boys would parade around the football field under the command of the most senior member of the group. The uniform code called for polished black shoes, but Neil contrived to avoid "cadet inspection" by wearing his bucks. According to Comrie, "It was a very hot day in May. I remember chewing an elastic to keep from passing out on the football field as we stood at attention for what seemed like hours. Standing still was a torture for both of us, so when the final inspection day arrived [and] having rehearsed a day early, we knew what to expect. Neil figured they wouldn't allow him on the field if he modified his wardrobe, and he was right."[223] Neil was thrown out of the ceremony, as he had hoped. He laughed as he left the group, knowing they would be standing at attention for the next hour.

ANOTHER CLASSMATE IN NEIL'S HOMEROOM form was Gary Renzetti. Gary and Comrie were both enrolled in Grade 9 classes the year before Neil arrived and were already well-acquainted with each other: their separate homeroom classes met together for phys. ed. — both gym and swim. Like Comrie, Gary had failed his year and was held back. Comrie admits he "scuffed regularly with Gary Renzetti, a street-wise kid with brains and no money." He adds, "Neil always 'dug' Renzetti."[224] Neil confirms as much: "I never really got to know him very much, but I liked him."[225]

"Neil and I always had an amicable relationship," Gary says, "and I am fairly certain we never exchanged a harsh word. . . . Neil's total focus was music even then. He had a pocket transistor radio he used to wear under his sweater, with the wire to the earphone concealed in his sleeve. One of his favourite songs of the period was 'Shimmy, Shimmy Ko-Ko-Bop' by Little Anthony and the Imperials. He listened to this contraption whenever he thought the teacher wouldn't catch him. Miss Smith never did." About Neil's relationship with Comrie, Gary notes, "He lived for three-twenty, at which time he and Comrie Smith would make a beeline to Smith's place where they would jam until suppertime." Gary refers to Neil and Comrie as "pickers," the students who were most intensely interested in playing their guitars and creating music. He considered Neil a loner in many ways:

"If you were a musician, he was interested, but otherwise not really. Not that he was ostracized or unpopular, he just wasn't interested."

Mr. Butterill's math class in Room 215 was the scene of a lot of classroom hijinks involving Neil, Comrie and Gary. Comrie recalls:

> Mr. Butterill [who was] also a patient, gentle man, had left the room briefly. Gary Renzetti turned in his seat to borrow a book and once received (snatched from the desk behind his) a scuffle ensued. Neil's history book landed abruptly on R's head — a playful clobbering. A series of clobberings ensued. . . . Actually I rose to the occasion as Renzetti had let me down on a hubcap deal which turned out to be serious trouble. With Neil, Renzetti and myself pushing and shoving each other at the rear of the classroom, Mr. Butterill returned, his head thermometer-red as he sentenced us to appear downstairs in Room 112. Shaking with frustration and anger we three appeared at Mr. Baker's desk.[226]

Punishment detentions were duly meted out by Vice-Principal Baker. Because they didn't want to reveal the details of their hubcap deal, Gary and Comrie fabricated a story to cover it up. What really happened was that Gary bragged in math class that he had two Cadillac hubcaps at home and would be willing to sell them for $5 each. (He had been using them as ashtrays.) Comrie said he wanted a set of four, and gave Gary $20 in advance. Gary was a no-show with the hubcaps, and there was a scuffle when Comrie demanded his money back. Gary had been arrested while attempting to procure the additional hubcaps and had been taken to juvenile detention, which is why he wasn't available to give Comrie the merchandise. ("Neither I nor they were available," Gary remarks.) Comrie's parents got wind of what had happened and were understandably displeased. Gary and Comrie blamed each other for their misfortune, and the incident amplified the antagonism between them. "We certainly had no love lost between us," Gary recalls. "We detested each other and avoided one another as much as possible."

But they did eventually cross paths again. When Neil returned to Toronto five years later, he and Comrie were driving down Yonge Street one evening when Neil spotted Gary walking by. Neil shouted from the back seat, "*Look, there's Renzetti! Stop!*" To get Gary's attention, Neil yelled out the window, "Renzetti, you *old fart!*"[227] "I made a rapid stop," Comrie recalls, "and Neil ran out to shake his hand and say hello. Renzetti was taken completely by surprise."[228] Asked if he remembers the episode, Gary says, "Indeed, I do! He jumped out of the car and gave me a big hug. Since I had seen him previously he had grown a huge mop of unkempt hair and I didn't realize who it was until he was back in the car and gone. He took me completely by surprise." Gary adds, "I've always considered Neil a decent bloke and am delighted that he became a musical success."

PETER BRODERICK WAS ANOTHER OF Neil's classmates. Neil sat behind Peter and often inflicted his "warped sense of humour" on him. On one occasion Neil grabbed Peter's hand and twisted it behind his back until he begged for mercy. Peter recalls that Neil was a particular trial for the balding and moustachioed math teacher, Mr. Butterill: one of Neil's tests came back with the remarkable score of 3 out of 150, a result so strikingly bad that the other students gasped in astonishment.

Latin was another troublesome class for Neil and Comrie. Vernon Cunningham, a stern and serious teacher who did not take kindly to the two boys' classroom antics, often called them into his class on the third floor to serve after-school detentions. Comrie refers to Mr. Cunningham as the "Smiling Executioner." Bob McConnell recalls, "He was a tall, dark-haired, cadaverous-looking man who came from the 'Ace' Bailey school of teaching. Like 'Ace,' he never smiled and was intolerant of any student who did not demonstrate serious scholarly ambitions. . . . If 'Ace' was hated more than Cunningham, it was only because the latter only exercised power in the classroom while the former exercised it everywhere." Gary Renzetti concurs: Mr. Cunningham was "[a] big guy, stickler for decorum, very loud voice. Quite an intimidating character who most of the junior boys tended to give a wide berth." It was Mr. Cunningham who sent Gary to Vice-Principal Baker's office for wearing the "dreaded blue jeans."

NEIL MAINTAINED HIS FRIENDSHIP WITH Bunny Stuart, his close friend from John Wanless. Bunny was in form 9F, Miss Leonard's homeroom class at Lawrence Park Collegiate. Outside of school, he occasionally joined Neil in collecting stray golf balls at two golf courses in the nearby Don Valley: the Metropolitan Golf Course and the Rosedale Golf Club. They resold the used golf balls for pocket money, a practice Neil had picked up when he lived on Brock Road.

Bunny also joined Neil for impromptu jam sessions at the

homes of mutual friends, pounding out a beat on a garbage pail while Neil played his baritone ukulele. It was at these sessions that Neil occasionally strapped on one of his friends' guitars, though he didn't yet know how to play the instrument.

NEIL SELECTED ART AS HIS optional class at Lawrence Park. The subject was taught in a large basement room at the south end of the school by Dr. Dickinson, a bespectacled gentleman with grey hair and a moustache. "Dr. D," as the students called him, was a "one-man art department." It may seem puzzling that Neil selected the art option instead of music, but as Bob McConnell remarks, "When I was in high school, a student's love of music had little to do with choosing the music option. Rock and roll was (and still is, for some people) the music of rebellion. You couldn't be a serious rebel and study music in a traditional way." Gary Renzetti seemed to think art classes suited Neil: "I know Neil liked drawing and sketching, so I can see him selecting art as his option." Comrie also took Dr. D's class with Neil. Bob McConnell says, "Comrie . . . often talked about Dr. Dickinson . . . with a mixture of genuine admiration for some things and teenage contempt for others."

Neil and Comrie spent many hours at the Smith family home at 46 Golfdale Road, listening to records on Comrie's father's new Philips hi-fi system. They loved to play 78 rpm singles, including songs by Buddy Holly, Duane Eddy, Bill Haley, the Kingston Trio, Elvis Presley, Danny and the Juniors, Jerry Lee Lewis, Link Wray, Little Richard and Ritchie Valens. Comrie recalls listening to one of Gene Vincent's B-sides — "Yes, I Love You Baby" — which featured a unique guitar sound for the time. Neil and Comrie played the song repeatedly during afternoon visits in 1960. Another favourite was "Crackin' Up" by Bo Diddley.

Although the boys spent a lot of time together, Comrie's parents did not entirely approve of their son's close friendship with Neil. This was a time when divorce was still uncommon, and there was a stigma attached to a child from what was then called "a broken home." "My parents couldn't really accept Neil," Comrie recalls, "always feeling that it would be better for me to hang out with more balanced people."[229] Comrie, on the other hand, envied the freedom Neil's mother gave him. "[Rassy] was really nice and open with us. She had a kidlike feel to her. I thought it would be so nice to have a mom like Rassy — 'Go ahead, do it,'"[230] he says. "Neil's mother has a very special place in my memory as one of the few grown-ups I ever knew who laughed and encouraged young people to pursue their talents."[231]

Comrie's older sister Sheila remembers Comrie coming home from school one day with Neil in tow. "Look who's here!" Comrie excitedly announced to his sister. Sheila saw Neil sitting in the sunroom off of the kitchen, presenting "a larger than life persona." He was a "joyful and jolly person with a solid head of black hair." She was aware that neither Neil nor Comrie had not the slightest interest in school. "Their pursuits and interests were decidedly non-academic in nature," she says.

The pair made frequent trips to Robinson's Radio Service,[232] where one counter was devoted to the sale of records, mainly 78s on the Decca and Columbia labels. Neil remarks, "I

---

FROM TOP: *Comrie Smith, 1962.* [© 1962 Robert J. McConnell]; *46 Golfdale Road, Smith family home. Comrie Smith and Neil recorded some songs on a tape recorder in the attic in the fall of 1965.* [© 2009 Sharry Wilson]

started buyin' 78s. Larry Williams, 'Bony Maronie.' Hank Ballard and the Midnighters. 'Rawhide' by Link Wray . . . Phil Phillips, 'Sea of Love.' . . . I used to really love Floyd Cramer, 'Last Date.' . . . I bought the 78s as soon as I could."[233]

First issued in 1898, 78 rpm records were popular until the late 1950s. The discs came in a variety of sizes, the most common being the 10- and 12-inch diameter size. Because the records were made of a brittle shellac compound, they were fragile and easily broken — like china plates, they had to be handled with care. The 10-inch discs held roughly three minutes of music per side, while the 12-inch format extended that to four or five minutes of music. (Lengthier pieces of music such as classical symphonies were sold in compilation "albums" of several records.) Records in the 78 rpm format continued to be produced and sold in North America in the 1950s but were gradually displaced by more modern formats (the 45 rpm vinyl single and the 33-1/3 rpm album).

The elderly Mrs. Robinson ran the store. "Robinson's was like an appliance store," Neil recalls, "and there was this nice lady that we used to talk to all the time. . . . I loved Roy Orbison from the beginning — 'Only the Lonely,' that was big when we were visiting that lady at the record store."[234]

Records were stocked in a large wooden stand behind the counter. No browsing was allowed, Bob McConnell recalls. "You asked if she [Mrs. Robinson] had a title and, if she did, she usually went straight to it. It was a narrow store that shared a wall with the laundry on the south side. A set of stairs, inaccessible from inside, was located behind a door in between the two stores and led to an apartment above. Presumably Mr. and Mrs. [Robinson] lived there, and I expect the Mister had a day job because Missus ran the store and he appeared only on rare occasions — perhaps weekends. The modest window display changed occasionally, but I don't recall ever seeing anything much of interest there. The store itself was dimly lit, and the Robinsons made little attempt to modernize it. The back one-third of the room had a few radios on bookshelves, not that anyone ever bought them, and a soft chair or two, suggesting to me that locals (adults) might pass some time there. If a customer wanted a small appliance repaired, a 'man' came in on Thursdays to do the jobs. Most of the business was conducted at the counter just inside the front door. It was definitely a nickel-and-dime, mom-and-pop enterprise."

Records that had fallen off the hit parade were generally reduced to a sale price of 39 cents at Robinson's. Neil and Comrie listened to these singles religiously, the B-sides as well as the A-sides.

Another popular source for records was Danforth Radio, on the east side of Yonge, midway between Golfdale Road and Teddington Park Avenue. The split-level store included a larger white room on the upper floor where appliances, record players and radios were sold. An eclectic assortment of records — with a modest section devoted to rock and roll — was stocked in the smaller room downstairs.

Comrie and Neil fantasized about forming a band of their own, amusing themselves by making up wild names for the group. "We spent the entire year listening to music and wanting to have a successful band," Comrie recalls. "Most of our adolescent hours were spent devoted to this cause."[235] Neil has confirmed that Comrie is the friend referred to in the lyrics of "Don't Be Denied"[236] (*We used to sit on the steps at school / And dream of being stars*).

At first it was just the two of them. Their instruments were less than stellar. Comrie[237] bought a set of $12 bongo drums at Neil's urging, and Neil had his baritone ukulele. They both played along to "Bongo Rock" by Preston Epps, a big hit at the time. Neil also paid some attention to Rassy, who told him he should play in a lyrical, Kingston Trio–like style. Comrie remarks, "She was a great mom for us in that teenage time . . . very supportive of our musical interests."[238]

But Comrie and Neil soon realized they would need a few additional members to make it a proper band, so they asked Comrie's friends Bob McConnell and Harold Greer[239] to join. (Comrie, Bob and Harold had all attended Bedford Park Public School together.) Bob's first impression of Neil was that he was "a bit of a flake" who laughed and giggled a lot and always had a transistor radio pressed to his ear. He also thought Neil's ukulele was not very cool; you had to play a guitar to be hip. Bob played acoustic guitar, while Harold played a stand-up bass from his music class[240] at Lawrence Park Collegiate. They practiced on the main floor at 46 Golfdale Road when Comrie's parents were out of the house. A consensus was reached to play along to "Let's Go to the Hop" by Danny and the Juniors, and they eventually tried a run-through on their own. Bob notes, "The emphasis is on 'try' because, as I recall, none of us could play anything more than a few chords." Harold remembers that in addition to the baritone ukulele, Neil occasionally played a harmonica.

Comrie and Neil became regulars at dances for teenagers at St. Leonard's Anglican Church[241] and St. Timothy's Anglican Church.[242] St. Leonard's held dances on Friday nights, while St. Timothy's occasionally held dances on Saturday nights. Bob McConnell recalls that St. Leonard's Friday-night dances were the "big draw." Comrie Smith admits, "I could never dance fast, so Neil and I would stand by the stage and drool at the musicians." Every now and then a local group would appear. One time it was the Sultans,[243] and Comrie happened to know one of the band members; Carl Scharfe had been in his homeroom class the year before. "We got (somehow) to go to a practice of [the Sultans] on a Saturday afternoon," he recalls. "It was at Ian Stewart's house on Brooke Avenue. Ian Stewart sang lead, Carl Scharfe[244] was rhythm guitar, Terry Bush — lead [guitar]. We glued ourselves to the working out of a whole bunch of tunes, such as 'Baby Jean' and 'Bo Diddley.' All of these songs were done in the Ronnie Hawkins style."[245, 246] Comrie and Neil were excited about seeing the Sultans rehearse. They were impressed with the chords Carl and Terry knew. They were still trying to learn the simplest ones, while Carl and Terry seemed to move effortlessly through much more complex changes. Bob McConnell recalls Comrie commenting on "the large number of songs the band knew and how they just kept playing on and on."

It was at one of these church dances that Neil first heard "It Might Have Been," Joe London's 1959 cover of the popular country waltz. "It was a big hit in Canada," he recalls, "though it didn't mean anything in the United States. Great record. Real, real soulful rendition."[247] The song impressed him, and he would record his own version many years later.

Introducing the song at a Toronto show in 1984, Neil described it as

> an old tune that I, uh, what I learned at a church in, uh — actually it was down there near, uh, what street was that now? Lawrence Park, I think it was — I used to go to these school dances down there, and I heard this song, I never forgot it — maybe some of you heard it before. I don't think anybody else has, though.[248]

ALWAYS A SNAPPY DRESSER — at least during his time at Lawrence Park — Neil one day noticed a boat-necked jersey with three-quarter-length sleeves in the window at Franklin Men's Wear,[249] a small upscale clothing store on the west side of Yonge opposite Glenforest Road. The shirt was an army olive/khaki green, with an overlay of black stripes running at right angles. Neil convinced Comrie and Bob McConnell that they should each purchase one. All three boys wore their matching shirts to school one day, but Comrie was embarrassed and elected to keep his coat on. Bob says that he and Neil attracted some attention when they walked around the auditorium at lunch. The shirts were "distinctive and glaringly unfashionable," according to Bob, and Comrie recalls being compared to the Bobbsey Twins by one of the students. Bob liked the shirt well enough that he continued to wear it even after a firecracker burned a small hole in it. And, says Bob, Neil loved the shirt so much that "he wore it till it fell off his body." He was especially fond of "wearing tops that hung down loose," as that one did.

The routine at school carried on, but the academic monotony was broken up by Athletic Nights (or A-Nights), which were scheduled a few times throughout the year. Students would sign up for one or two events, such as volleyball, badminton, floor hockey, swimming, basketball or so-called "murderball" in the pool. The events began in the early evening and concluded with dances in both of the gyms (girls' and boys').

The first A-Night of the school year was held on November 13, beginning at 7:30 p.m. The boys cross-dressed for a fashion show in the girls' gym, followed by a speedball match between the grades 9 and 10 girls. Lawrence Park vanquished their Royal York Collegiate rivals in a volleyball game. A mixed swim meet was held in the pool, with Grade 9 students competing against those in Grade 10.

A dance featuring Top 60 tunes from CKEY radio attracted younger students, while a more mature group enjoyed slow songs played in the girls' gym. Both gyms were decorated in a Halloween theme, with yellow-and-black streamers and paper cut-outs of witches and cats. Colourful balloons filled the basketball nets.

Another memorable occasion was the Rugby Dance, staged on November 20 in the boys' gym. Johnny Allison and his band supplied the music. The Panthers were the school's football team, and one of the highlights of the evening was the coronation of Miss Panther of 1959. The gym was decorated with caricatures of the faces of teachers perched atop gigantic blue-and-gold football uniforms, looking down on the festivities from various parts of the gym. Refreshments were served in the cafeteria.

The second A-Night was held on February 19, this time with a St. Valentine's Day theme. There were demonstrations of Interform Basketball, Old Boys' Basketball and Gymnastic Exhibitions in the boys' gym, while the girls' gym featured Grade 11 Basketball, Old Girls' Basketball, a volleyball match between staff and students and a tumbling demonstration. A four-way swim meet between Lawrence Park, Upper Canada College, Trinity College School and University of Toronto Schools was held in the pool. Other events included "clown diving" and Girls' Ornamental Swimming.

The Heart Beat Hop commenced in both gyms at 9:10 p.m. Once again the more energetic students danced to the hits in the boys' gym, while slower music was featured in the girls' gym. Streamers and balloons added to the festive air.

Special "Junior Noon-Hours" were held in the auditorium

for students in grades 9 and 10, who tapped their feet in time to music from CKEY and CHUM. At one of these events, boys from a Grade 10 class dressed in women's clothing for a comedy fashion show — "in a variety of poses the boys showed their version of female apparel today," the Lawrence Park yearbook declared, "but were glad to become boys again for the afternoon classes." Cross-dressing aside, the gender barrier was strictly enforced: at lunch, male and female students ate in separate halves of the cafeteria, while a teacher patrolled the border between them.

Neil and Bill Purkis, a Lawrence Park footballer, had become good friends during the school year and garnered a reputation as the two troublemakers in class. Based on their past behaviour it was no surprise when they were both suspended, on an especially hot June day, for wearing shorts to school — strictly forbidden and a punishable offence at the time.

Unsurprisingly, girls were also a major topic of discussion among Neil's school buddies. Clive Merritt and Chris Begg, who used to hang out with Neil during lunch periods, sometimes hopped the back fence at Havergal College, a private school, to stir up trouble and chase the girls. They were inevitably caught by the school security guards and escorted off the property.

Neil, meanwhile, took some of his first baby steps at dating. Sheila Lilly went out with Neil on a blind date. She recalls having "one short embarrassing date. . . . We went to the Dairy Queen." Neil had called for her at home on Ardrossan Place, where Sheila's mother noticed that Neil's sweater had a snag and offered to stitch it.

Christine Bryan, a girl in Mr. Penny's homeroom class (9C), attracted Neil's attention. She was considered quite demure and not a likely match for Neil, but his individuality and sense of humour won her over. They dated occasionally, but nothing serious ever developed.

ACADEMICALLY, 1958-59 WAS A BAD year for Neil. In fact, it was disastrous. Scott Young arrived at school one day with Neil and Bob in tow for a meeting with Principal Bailey, most likely to confer about Neil's poor marks. Since Scott was well-known among the students, the visit to the principal's office caused considerable speculation. The conference may have alerted Scott to Neil's academic problems, but it didn't resolve them — Neil failed his Grade 9 year.

Things weren't going well at home, either. Rassy decided to pursue a divorce on the grounds of adultery, naming Astrid as the correspondent in the case. The divorce would not be finalized until May 1961, but in the meantime Rassy resolved to make a new start in Winnipeg. Scott had expected that both of his sons would go to Winnipeg with their mother, but Bob chose to stay in Toronto at the last minute. Tired of the family's frequent moves, and increasingly focused on amateur golf, he hated the idea of once more finding himself in an unfamiliar environment without friends. He went to live with his father in a small apartment downtown, but the arrangement proved unsatisfactory and Bob soon moved out on his own. "At the time I did not know that Bob would soon be coming to live with me," Scott writes. "If I had I would have chosen something larger than the downtown bachelor apartment I rented. Bob stayed with me part time while going to school in Pickering." [250, 251]

At the beginning of August, Rassy and Neil began the long drive from Toronto to Winnipeg. The move had a direct and powerful impact on Neil. In many ways Winnipeg would provide a fostering environment for him — a place where he could grow and thrive both musically and personally. But his family was permanently fractured, and his academic career would never recover.

---

## PART TWO

# WINNIPEG...
# FIELD OF OPPORTUNITY

*When I was a young boy*
*My mama said to me*
*Your daddy's leavin' home today*
*I think he's gone to stay*
*We packed up all our bags*
*And drove out to Winnipeg.*

— Neil Young, "Don't Be Denied"

## ☆ 7 ☆
# EARL GREY JUNIOR HIGH SCHOOL:
## The Jades, The Esquires

*When we got to Winnipeg*
*I checked in to school.*
*I wore white bucks on my feet*
*When I learned the golden rule.*
*The punches came fast and hard*
*Lying on my back in the schoolyard.*

— Neil Young, "Don't Be Denied"

IF THERE IS SUCH A thing as a gene for musical talent, Neil Young was blessed with it. He arrived in Winnipeg trailing a rich and diverse musical heritage. Both of his great-grandfathers on the Young side of the family boasted musical ability. Robert Paterson was a "better-than-average church tenor," while John Young was "one of the great country fiddlers of his time and place."[1]

The succeeding generation on both sides of Scott's family produced an assortment of banjo players and country fiddlers, and Scott's mother, Jean, played the piano and organ to much acclaim. After moving to Flin Flon in 1937 with her 11-year-old daughter Dorothy, Jean Young[2] found work in the machine shop at Hudson Bay Mining and Smelting, a copper mine 901 kilometres north of Winnipeg, where she entertained the miners by playing piano and singing in the Legion Hall on Saturday nights.[3] According to Neil, her duties at the mine included "handing out the metal ID tags to the miners before they descended and collecting them back, hanging them on nails in the wall of a little shack, when they finished their shift, thereby becoming the first to learn of a missing soul in the mine."[4] Neil recalls, "She was a valued member of the community, but more than that, she played a helluva honky-tonk piano."[5] She had committed to memory a wide-ranging repertoire of songs and would ask people to "just hum a few bars" of any request. After a long day at the mine, Granny Jean was known for "partying into the night, singing and playing a barroom piano or producing and playing in the local theatre productions she created."[6]

Jean's daughter Dorothy — Neil's Aunt Dot — received formal voice training and often performed as a contralto soloist. Handel's *Messiah* was one well-remembered performance. She came to be a popular figure in the thriving arts community in Flin Flon, where she joined various choirs and amateur musical productions, all while raising six children with her husband, Stanley Liss. Her signature song was "My Man" (from the Broadway production of *Funny Girl*), which she enjoyed belting out to her mother's piano accompaniment.

Scott's younger brother Bob could play virtually any stringed instrument in addition to clarinet and piano, while other relatives had mastered an eclectic assortment of musical instruments, including banjo, guitar, harmonica, ukulele, mandolin, violin and Jew's harp.

Neil had been surrounded by music and music-makers all his life, and by the time he left Ontario, rock and roll and the guitar had already become central interests. But Winnipeg would offer him something new and important: the opportunity to play with other like-minded young musicians, for audiences that shared his fascination with this new youth-oriented music.

NEIL AND RASSY ARRIVED IN Winnipeg at a propitious time, although neither could have foreseen the significance of the move. Inadvertently, Rassy had given Neil access to a fast-track, real-world musical education. And she supported him all the way.

Winnipeg is situated more than 2,000 kilometres west of Toronto in the prairie province of Manitoba, near the longitudinal centre of North America. The city's location at the confluence of the Red and Assiniboine rivers, commonly called "the Forks," was for thousands of years a crossroads for native peoples travelling by canoe from the Great Plains to the west and from the rugged Canadian Shield to the east and north. French fur trader Pierre de la Vérendrye built the first trading post on the site in 1738 and named it Fort Rouge. Generations of fur traders and voyageurs were drawn there by the lucrative trade in beaver pelts and buffalo hides. Many of the fur traders — first the French, then the British — married First Nations women, and their mixed-race offspring became known as Métis. The city's population grew with the addition of United Empire Loyalists fleeing the newly created United States at the end of the American Revolutionary War, and grew again as settlers from Ontario arrived in search of land and opportunity. The coming of the Canadian Pacific Railway in 1881 cemented Winnipeg's status as a transportation hub, an important way station for trade between eastern and western Canada. Later, an influx of Eastern European immigrants joined the expanding population, leaving a unique mark on the city, not least in the creation of distinctive ethnic neighbourhoods.

In the midst of the dog days of summer — the city is notorious for its sweltering, mosquito-ridden summers and frigid, windy winters — Neil and Rassy settled into their new home at the Gray Apartments. Her mother had found them the apartment in the working-class neighbourhood of Fort Rouge. They lived in apartment number 5 on the second floor of a three-story building at 250 Hugo Street at Corydon Avenue, modest accommodations that were a significant step down from 49 Old Orchard Grove in Toronto. In effect, Rassy had returned to her childhood home, where her sister Toots still resided with her family and where Rassy's parents still lived. (Toots's family lived at 14 Beechwood Place in Norwood; Bill and Perle Ragland remained a few blocks away in their spacious accommodations at the DeBary Apartments.) Rassy's old and dear friends Chris and Howard Wood Jr. lived on Harrow Street, across from Kelvin High School in nearby Crescentwood.

Uppermost in Neil's thoughts at the time was the purchase of his first guitar. "I got a Harmony with a DeArmond pickup in it,"[7, 8] he recalls. More specifically, it was a used archtop Harmony Monterey with a DeArmond pickup. Although Neil doesn't mention the exact model number, it was probably an H950. The H950 Monterey Leader — the most popular guitar in the line, low-priced and very appealing as a beginner guitar — was produced from 1938 to 1972. It was made completely of birch, with a reinforced steel-rod neck that wasn't adjustable, meaning it was harder to keep in tune than higher-priced models. It had open tuning pegs, a simple nickel-plated trapeze tailpiece, an adjustable bridge made of ebony and a celluloid pickguard. The body was finished in a black polish with contrasting reddish highlights, a style called the Redburst pattern. The H950 was not equipped with a DeArmond as standard; the previous owner must have installed the pickup. The price Neil paid for his used guitar and pickup is in line with the price for a new Harmony Monterey H950 at the time:[9] "I think I bought it at the little music store in Winnipeg that had Fender equipment and old stuff. . . . I might've gotten it in a pawnshop. Thirty bucks."[10, 11]

Neil knew he would need a source of income for pocket money and music-related materials, and he soon secured a newspaper route with the *Winnipeg Tribune*. His route (#F-3, along Corydon Avenue) was a highly prized one. Approximately a hundred newspapers were distributed within only two city blocks — this meant there were several apartment blocks in the designated delivery area, offering a shivering paper boy a chance to warm up for a few moments during bitter winter weather.

As for Rassy, sports continued to be an important part of her life. She had always enjoyed hunting trips with her father and his cronies — witnesses claim she could drink and swear with the best of them. She joined Winnipeg's Granite Curling Club and enjoyed curling with the "Granite Ladies" during the winter months. Golf remained a passion, one she shared with Neil. They became members of the Niakwa Golf and Country Club and the Winnipeg Canoe Club. Rassy was also a proficient tennis player, and often played on the courts at the Canoe Club, one of her old stomping grounds.

Neil remained an avid golfer. "I almost was a professional golfer," he later remarked to deejay Tony Pig. "I used to wear alpaca sweaters. I was on a whole trip."[12] The August 17, 1960, issue of the *Winnipeg Free Press* reports that Canoe Club member Neil Young tied for second in the rankings in the "14-and-unders" in the Manitoba Golf Association's sponsored Junior Tournament and Championship. Neil would continue to play golf over the next few years, participating as a team member from Niakwa at a Junior Inter-Club event during early August 1962.

The family celebrated a happy occasion toward the end of August. Neil's cousin William Neil Hoogstraten married Esther Lillian McClements on August 27 at Regents Park United Church in St. Vital, and Neil was one of the ushers. A reception was held at the Marion Hotel. Bill Hoogstraten remembers 14-year-old Neil as a "gawky and naive kid."

NEIL ENROLLED AT EARL GREY Junior High School, where classes commenced in early September. The school had a dicey reputation, and the more affluent residents of nearby Crescentwood and River Heights regarded its students as working-class toughs.

"The school did not have a good reputation, at least from the students' perspective," recalls Barry Brazier, another Grade 9 student at Earl Grey. "You were mocked by others if you mentioned you went to Earl Grey, and I remember being quite nervous entering Grade 7. Of course, there were tough guys, but there are tough guys in every school, and it didn't take long to realize that the majority of kids were really nice."

The imposing school building, dating from 1914, was located at 340 Cockburn Street North at Fleet, south of Corydon Avenue, Fort Rouge's main thoroughfare. Designed by architect J. B. Mitchell, the building is a mix of Romanesque Revival and Neo-Georgian architecture and was named in honour of Sir Albert Henry Grey, the 4th Earl Grey and Canada's ninth Governor General. (Canadian football's Grey Cup also takes his name.) The school's motto is *Honour, Truth and Duty*, and carved above one of the main entry doors are the words *God save our gracious King*. During Neil's time there the building housed both an elementary school and the junior high, each operating distinctly and independently. Earl Grey Junior High occupied the north end, Earl Grey Elementary occupied the south, and each had a separate entrance.

There were three Grade 9 homeroom classes at Earl Grey — Mr. Yarmie's (Room 10), Mr. White's (Room 11) and Mr. Stark's (Room 13). Homeroom students stuck together throughout the day, moving from class to class for different subjects. There were separate phys. ed. classes for the boys and girls; the boys walked to Kelvin High School "shops class," where they were instructed in wood- and metal-working, while the girls remained at Earl Grey for home economics.

Neil's homeroom was the math class of Mr. White. The tall and balding World War II vet, who walked with a limp, had taught at Earl Grey for many years.

Neil came to school looking much the same as he had the year before in Toronto: he sported a short haircut and favoured preppy sweaters. Classmate, friend and future bandmate Ken Koblun remarks on first meeting Neil, "I didn't think he was cool in the greasy-haircut sort of way. Neil was different. He had a brush-cut. He was about the only guy in the class who wore a sweater."[13, 14] Fellow Earl Grey student Erwin Ploner never saw Neil wear his white bucks at school, although he does recall Neil occasionally wearing them to weekend teen dances. Ken Koblun doesn't recall seeing Neil's white bucks at all: "That's something I would have noticed since they're very distinctive-looking."

From the beginning, Neil's status as the new kid — as well as being from a "broken home" — marked him as different from most of his classmates. The jocks in class didn't know what to make of him. He didn't seem to have a talent for sports, but his classmates were aware of his father's lofty status in the sports world. He was labelled a "weak guy" by some of the more testosterone-charged boys in the class. Neil was never directly involved in any physical fights and was most certainly not to be found "lying on his back in the schoolyard," as the song lyric has it. It was classmate Ken who got into a scuffle with one of the jocks in the class, defending Neil's honour when an unkind remark was made about him.

After a rough start at the beginning of the school year, Neil learned to use his sense of humour defensively, and he soon attracted some friendly attention from his classmates.

JOHN DANIEL, ONE OF NEIL'S classmates, would play an important role in Neil's musical development. A former Earl Grey student named Barry Carther was instrumental in bringing them together.

Barry had attended Earl Grey the year before, when he participated as a deejay at the Friday-night canteen dances for teens at the Earl Grey Community Club. He also worked part-time at Eaton's department store as a "carrier," collecting deliveries from departments on different floors — one of them being the record department — and taking them down to dispatch. Barry thus had access to the latest records, which he would spin at the Friday-night dances. He recalls meeting Neil shortly after Neil moved to Winnipeg, when Barry was living in a corner house at Jessie Avenue and Hugo, close to the Gray Apartments. He and Neil met before the school year started, and their common interest was a love of music. Barry remembers Neil as being "a bit exotic" because he came from Toronto and because his parents were divorced. With his short hair and skinny stature, Neil struck Barry as a "string-bean type" who was "a little more literate than most of the guys." Neil sometimes joined Barry and mutual friend Gary Fowler in their activities. Neither Barry nor Gary played an instrument, but they did enjoy music and listening to records. Gary's nickname for Neil was "Neily Posturepedic."[15]

Neil asked Barry, "Do you know anyone who plays guitar? Do you think you could ask them to teach me?" Barry immediately thought of John Daniel from Earl Grey Junior High. (John was in Grade 8 when Barry was in Grade 9.) Barry had heard John play guitar and was impressed by his skill, and he told Neil he thought John might be open to some kind of arrangement.

Toward the end of August, Barry took Neil over to John's house for a visit. Neil recalls that the house was located "right in front of his dad's business 'Dot Transfer' [a hauling, cartage and courier service]. *Dial Dot and Dot Dashes* was written on a few trucks parked behind the building."[16] Half of the large three-storey house on Corydon just east of Lilac Street was devoted to John's father's business, while the other half served as the family's residence. Barry recalls, "The company was run out of the back of the house and they had five or six trucks always parked at the back and in an open lot next door. The trucks were different sizes from a half ton to five tons, with staked sides and canvas tops. The cab part was painted yellow with black letters."

John invited Neil and Barry down to his bedroom in the basement, where John and Neil discussed their mutual interests and got to know each other. Neil admitted he was keen to learn how to play the guitar. When he mentioned that he belonged to the Niakwa Golf and County Club and was an avid golfer, John proposed a deal: he would show Neil some chords on the guitar if Neil taught him the basics of golf.

During that first visit, Barry recalls, John demonstrated for Neil how to finger some elementary chords. John subsequently set him up with his guitar teacher Jack Riddell, but Neil lasted only one formal lesson. "I was basically self-taught," he recalls. "I took one guitar lesson but I don't really remember anything from it. I do remember that I didn't want to play whatever it was the guy was trying to teach me. It was obvious he was good, and I was impressed with all the chords he knew. But what he was doing didn't seem like fun to me, so that was it."[17]

Once school began, Neil found himself sharing his homeroom class with John Daniel. John and another classmate, Bill "Beetle" Pawlyk, sometimes got together with Neil for jam sessions at John's house. John was "the smartest kid I knew," Bill recalls. "He was good at everything he did — calligraphy, stamp and coin collecting, comic collecting and guitar playing." Bill usually joined these jam sessions as a percussionist, pounding enthusiastically on the bottoms of five-gallon cardboard ice-cream drums.

John was also good at hockey. He and classmate Garry Bowles played on the school team, where John was the goalie even though he wasn't especially big for his age. For boys growing up in Canada in the 1960s, playing hockey was more than a national pastime — it was almost an instinctual act. They contented themselves with playing street hockey in the fall while they waited impatiently for outdoor rinks to freeze; in winter they willingly endured temperatures that plunged into double-negative figures. Unusually, Neil was less enthusiastic about hockey than his classmates.

Garry Bowles sometimes joined John and Neil. He remembers Neil as "very likeable. Polite, soft-spoken, well-mannered, but private. He kept things to himself unless he had something important to say. He was gangly and skinny and a bit of a loner."

Neil and classmate Ken Koblun also became friendly, although they would become much closer the following year. Both Ken and Neil came from broken homes. Ken was living with the Claytons, his foster family, in a duplex at 501 Hay Street — across the road from Churchill High School, which he attended the following year while Neil went to Kelvin High. Problems with Ken's biological family had led to his placement in a foster home, seen as a temporary solution that would provide him with a more secure environment.

Ken was unusually tall and lanky — at over six-foot-five he towered over his other classmates. Quiet and soft-spoken, he was known by the nickname "Kooby," which he had acquired in Grade 4 when the class was studying Genghis Khan and Kublai Khan. Ken's insularity, literal-mindedness and close attention to detail would become defining hallmarks of his character over the years. "I knew Neil played the guitar and I thought that was interesting," Ken says. He wanted to get to know him better but was timid about approaching Neil about his guitar playing, since he didn't have a guitar himself. For the time being he remained in the background of Neil's life, content to be strictly a school friend. Ken would become a mainstay in some of Neil's earliest bands over the next few years, but that was still ahead of him.

Neil felt an intuitive kinship with students who were considered different or unusual, and his friendship with Ken certainly qualified. One of those who appreciated his empathy was Erwin Ploner,[18] who was in Mr. Stark's homeroom class. Erwin had come to Canada from Austria in 1958, when his family settled into a home on Stradbrook Avenue near Corydon, just a block from Neil's place. Erwin was enrolled in an English course for immigrants at Earl Grey. He recalls, "With my horrific accent, I was, as you can imagine, a target for ridicule. Neil was different and we became friends."

Erwin, who did not play an instrument or sing, was slightly jealous of Neil's ability to command attention with music. "I do remember that we kids used to hang out together and it always turned into a jam session," he says. "There was great talent and I could never figure out why they hung out with me since I can't carry a note if my life depended on it." Erwin adds, "From the beginning I was impressed with his musical talents. We stayed friends all through the Earl Grey and Kelvin High days." Since Erwin had a car, he was often the one who drove Neil to gigs and stayed to watch him perform in whatever band he was with at the time. (One snowy evening Erwin had a minor accident while Neil was in the car — "I had a 1957 yellow-and-black Mercury Meteor. It was snowing like crazy." — but no major damage was done.)

Harold Westdal, also in Mr. White's homeroom class, was another friend of Neil's who had a reputation as an outsider. He lived at the corner of Hugo and Warsaw streets. Harold's family had moved to Winnipeg from a rural area and he was also a "new kid" at Earl Grey. Although Harold did not have a musical background or know how to play an instrument, Neil tried to persuade him to buy a set of second-hand drums for sale in the neighbourhood — the vendor was anxious to get rid of them, but Harold wasn't interested. An attempt to convince Harold to take up golf was similarly unsuccessful.

Neil continued to enjoy stirring up trouble and playing practical jokes. There was a cloakroom with a window at the back of one classroom, and when the teacher was out of the room Neil enlisted Harold to help him collect some of the students' coats and sweaters. Harold tied the clothing together, and Neil opened the window and dangled the long line down the side of the building. Alas, the principal happened to be walking outside and saw what was happening; he had a word with the teacher, and Neil and Harold were duly reprimanded.

Mr. Yarmie, Earl Grey's "dedicated and patient" science teacher, was well-liked by students. A compulsive tobacco addict, he was known to leave class at around 11 every morning for a cigarette break. On one of these occasions Neil launched a paper airplane that somehow managed to strike the returning Mr. Yarmie in the head. Neil was rewarded with a detention.

In many ways, the school's teachers were as colourful as its students. Mr. Stark, the geography teacher, was of imposing physical stature and would break into song at the least provocation. Earl Grey student Susan Kelso remembers Mr. Stark as a talented singer: "He had a fabulous voice. He sang for years in the Winnipeg Philharmonic Choir." One day, as the class took the usual minute or two to settle down, Mr. Stark stood silently for 10 seconds and then launched into an a cappella version of the French national anthem. "Today," he announced at the end of this startling performance, "we start studying France."

Mr. Stark was also known for his habit of doling out "stingers" to misbehaving students. He carried a ruler that he'd taped at one end, and if he believed you deserved a stinger he would stroll down the aisle between desks, grab your hand and administer a slap to the palm that left it stinging for a good 15 minutes. (Corporal punishment in school was commonplace and relatively uncontroversial in that era.) Neil's favourite pastime was hiding the stinger stick, and he went to great lengths to do this. He would take it off the desk when Mr. Stark was out of the room and hide it in various places — behind the portrait of the Queen, on a high window ledge, under the cushion on Mr. Stark's chair. Whenever Mr. Stark looked for the stick and failed to find it he would immediately ask, "Okay, Neil, where is it?" Neil would ultimately confess — usually getting a stinger of his own in return — and Mr. Stark would then proceed to deliver the punishment to its intended recipient.

As a study in chivalry, Mr. Stark usually asked for a boy to volunteer to receive a stinger whenever a girl misbehaved and was singled out for punishment. Wayne "Smitty" Smith was one of the volunteers — on multiple occasions. The write-up beside Wayne's photo in the yearbook observes that he is "kind enough to take the strap for the girls." One hopes the girls appreciated his generous spirit.

Erwin Ploner confirms that receiving one of Mr. Stark's stingers left a firm impression: "All I remember is that it hurt like hell, and when he was finished, you had to face the strap again with the principal." The principal used a two-by-eighteen-inch piece of leather — a "school board certified strap."[19]

At noon, students typically headed to the corner store to stock up on penny candy. The challenge was to keep the bag in your pocket and extract the candy without creating enough noise to attract attention, especially in Mr. Stark's class, where the penalty for being discovered was the inevitable stinger.

Neil formed a lasting friendship with Jim Atkin, who was in Mr. Stark's homeroom class. Jim was well-liked and served as class president. "Jim is always seen laughing and talking," according to the caption accompanying his photo in the 1959-60 yearbook. "He is quite active in organizing the Grade 9 Coke Dances this year. 'Beatniks' are one of his favourite topics of conversation." Neil and Jim had much in common. Like Neil, Jim was repeating his Grade 9 year. Both had experienced the trauma of early childhood illness; Jim had contracted tuberculosis as a child and walked with a slight limp. He played percussion instruments and xylophone and would participate in many of Neil's earliest bands. Neil and Jim had already combined forces to act as emcees/deejays at the Earl Grey Community Club's Friday-night canteen dances for teens, which lent them a cachet among school friends.

As the year progressed, Neil's friend and classmate Susan Kelso convinced him to join the yearbook staff. Neil became co-editor, along with Susan and Laurelle Hughes. Ken Koblun, Ken's foster brother Richard Clayton and Jim Atkin were also members, and Neil developed a close friendship with the picture editor, Shirley Lord. Neil was attracted to the yearbook project because his friends were members, but he also seems to have developed an interest in English and writing. The behind-the-scenes experience of journalism he had picked up from his father made him a useful presence.

The yearbook staff met during regular school hours in the library room, where a selection of stuffed birds was on display. One day, in a larkish mood, the group decided to take a photo with Neil by the open window with a stuffed owl posed to look like it was attacking him. Unfortunately Mr. Yarmie walked in on them and took exception to the disrespectful treatment of the bird. From then on, he declared, the yearbook meetings would take place after school, since valuable time was obviously being wasted. The students remained unrepentant: "It was a hoot!" Shirley Lord remarks jokingly.

Susan recalls that Neil loved practical jokes and fun. "He was always very kind and I felt comfortable around him. He made me laugh." She added, "He never spoke down to people or argued. He was good to people. It was in his nature.

He was always upbeat, funny and positive." Susan felt that Neil was "very tight" with Jim Atkin. "They were very much alike — both very kind-hearted."

The 1960-61 Earl Grey yearbook included an editorial page from the three co-editors. One of Neil's short English compositions, "Why I Chew Gum," was prominently featured:

> Some people like to chew gum. I am one of them. Chewing gum, in my opinion, is something to do when I'm nervous, playing golf or just doing nothing.
>
> This makes me proud. You see, I'm never caught doing nothing. When I might be caught doing nothing, I'm chewing gum. That's why I chew gum. — Neil Young, Room 11.

Shirley Lord's photos of Neil are scattered throughout the yearbook. In one photo Neil sits with his feet propped on a desk and an upside-down Latin textbook obscuring his face. In another, Neil is seen from behind, walking with a friend, wearing a traditional Bavarian-style trenker hat and a white sweatshirt with *Canadian Freeloaders Society* printed on it in black capital letters. A third photo shows Neil with three of his friends — Harold Westdal, Erwin Ploner and Richard

---

CLOCKWISE FROM TOP: *Field Day, Earl Grey Junior High School, June 1961. Left to right: Harold Westdal, Erwin Ploner, Neil, Richard Huska.* [© 1961 Shirley Lord]; *Yearbook Staff, 1960-61, Earl Grey Junior High School.* [Courtesy of Shirley Lord]; *Earl Grey Junior High School.* [© 2005 Stephen Cross]; *Neil walking away from the camera and wearing a white sweatshirt with* Canadian Freeloaders Society *printed on it.* [© 1961 Shirley Lord]

TEAR BOOK STAFF

Seated: Jim Arkin, Joann Hagyford, Susan Kehr, Neil Young, Laurelle Hayfar, Jane Hagyford, Kes Kahler, Standing: Mrs. Quinn, Richard Charles, Garry Searle, Shirley Lord, Mr. Patterson, Ruth Harris, Joe Vent, Mrs. Mills.

## YEAR BOOK
## STAFF

| | |
|---|---|
| Co-Editor | Laurelle Hayfar |
| Co-Editor | Susan Kehr |
| Co-Editor | Neil Young |
| Literary Editor | Richard Charles |
| Special Events | Kes Kahler |
| Art Editor | Garry Searle |
| Music Editor | Joe Vent |
| Little Sports Editor | Joann Hagyford |
| Boys' Sports Editor | Jane Hagyford |
| Candid Camera | Jim Arkin |
| Picture Editor | Shirley Lord |
| Elementary Editor | Ruth Harris |

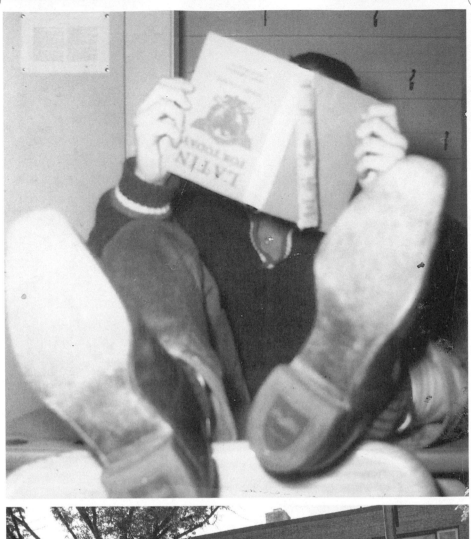

Huska — sitting casually by the school fence. All three photographs were taken in June 1961.

SCOTT INVITED NEIL TO VISIT him in Toronto that summer, but Neil turned down his father's request in an undated letter[20] that appears to have been written at the end of June or beginning of July. Neil's deepening involvement in the Winnipeg music scene held far more attraction for him than a visit to his father and stepmother in Toronto.

> Dear Daddy,
>
> I am glad to hear Bob's marks and would like to thank you for your invitation to Toronto but I don't want to come this summer. There are too many important things for me to do around here. This is my own decision. Mummy has no objection to my coming.
> I will let you know when I want to come. Thanks again for your invitation. I think I did well in my finals.
>
> Love, Neil.

MANY GENRES OF MUSIC WERE represented in the thriving local music scene. Country-and-western was still popular in the mid-to-late-1950s, as was "hit parade music," rockabilly

---

FROM TOP: *Neil holding a Latin textbook upside down and masking his face.* [© 1961 Shirley Lord]; *250 Hugo Street, the Gray Apartments. Neil and Rassy lived in Apt. #5 on the second floor.* [© 2009 Sharry Wilson]

and the harmonies of vocal groups. It was during this time that famed Winnipeg jazz guitarist Lenny Breau began his professional career, playing a rockabilly/country show with his parents — Hal "Lone Pine" Breau and Betty Cody — when he was just 12. (Lenny was occasionally billed as Lone Pine Jr.) There were only a couple of rock-and-roll bands in the city, but an abundance of vocal groups. Because instrumental music was gaining popularity, some of these groups began to introduce guitars and adopt riffs from hits by such bands as the Ventures, the Fireballs, Johnny and the Hurricanes, and Duane Eddy.

Most of the city's neighbourhoods featured a community club, originally designed as an adjunct to the outdoor rinks that were an essential part of the city's mania for hockey, but offering a variety of other organized sports, as well as social clubs, summer activities for children, a snack bar and — critically for Neil — teen dances. A proliferation of such community clubs during the 1960s served to anchor the developing music scene and catered to a generation of baby boomers, now entering their teens. The tendency for young people to stay indoors playing rock and roll was enhanced — one might even say enforced — by extreme winter temperatures. (*Growing up in a prairie town / Learning to drive in the snow / Not much to do so you start a band*, Randy Bachman wrote in "Prairie Town.")

During the early 1960s a teen council was established at each community club. These councils took on the responsibility of organizing dances — keeping administrative records, booking bands and attending to logistics. Dances prior to this time had usually been informal "record hops," haphazardly organized by enthusiastic parent volunteers. But things were beginning to change as more live bands were offered chances to perform.

Bands typically began locally. Students from a given school would get together to explore their musical interests. Embryonic bands rehearsed in basements and garages, often to the irritation of neighbours. Skill at playing an instrument was not necessarily a prerequisite; owning decent equipment and/or a car was often all that was needed to become a member in a band. (Amplifiers in particular were expensive and hard to come by; owning one was a sure ticket to membership.) Garnering a booking at the neighbourhood community club was a sign of success, and friends and supporters of the band supplied a ready-made audience. Clubs with a good reputation were generally those with strong and active teen councils. A gig at the River Heights Community Club was considered top tier.

Bands were closely associated with particular neighbourhoods and community clubs, and territorial rivalries were often heated. Some of the Winnipeg bands held in high regard circa 1960-61 were Carmine La Rosa and the Thunderstorms (Fort Rouge); Mickey Brown and the Velvetones (West Kildonan); the Silvertones (East Kildonan); Wayne Walker and the Strollers, the Chord U Roys, Roy Miki and the Downbeats (the North End); and the Jaywalkers (St. Vital). This would soon change, however, as the more serious band members sought out others with similar aspirations and territorial boundaries began to blur.

The Galaxies were another hugely popular band. Formed in 1958 by Bill Jacques, Jim Ackroyd and Don Maloney, they specialized in instrumental covers by the Ventures and the Fireballs, two of Neil's major influences during his earliest years. They became the "Club 63" Galaxies after the band became affiliated with radio station CKRC. Anyone who called the radio station to request a particular deejay for a dance would be informed that the "Club 63" Galaxies were free that night. The deejay would come along with the band. Guitarist Jacques was highly regarded by young musicians just starting out, including Neil who recalls, "They [the Galaxies] had three huge Fenders, two Showmans, and a Band-Master. They were the coolest band as far as equipment went."[21]

Neil also paid particular attention to the Silvertones. His musical development would be influenced by this band, and two of its members would become important as early heroes.

Allan Peter Stanley Kowbel, later known as Chad Allan,[22] was the spearhead of the group. He started out playing lead guitar and was the principal singer. The band took its name from the guitars its members played — the popular Silvertone model made for Sears by various manufacturers, including Harmony, Danelectro, National, Kay and Teisco. Silvertone guitars, well-made and budget-priced, were an ideal choice for young musicians just starting out. Chad Allan was known for playing a Harmony Stratotone guitar sold by Sears as Silvertone model 1423 during his early years. The Silvertones boasted a British-based repertoire, playing hits from bands that were part of the pre-Beatles British wave.

Allan Kowbel, Jon Glowa and Ralph Lavalley comprised the earliest lineup of the Silvertones. Drummer Brian "Ducky" Donald would be the next musician to join the band. Skilled and admired musicians from other popular bands throughout Winnipeg were recruited to the Silvertones as others left. The pattern would persist for years to come as the band underwent many personnel and name changes. The same dynamic governed bands all over the city.

ONE OF THE WINNIPEG BANDS with which the Silvertones were friendly was a vocal group called the Escorts. Two members of the Escorts would eventually found a group called the Esquires, for which they would recruit a rhythm guitarist named Neil Young.

The Escorts suffered a massive onstage meltdown one night at St. Ignatius church in the late fall of 1960. Ken Johnson, one of the vocalists, had asked drummer Don Marshall — a workmate at the Canadian Wheat Board — and guitarist Jon Glowa from the Silvertones to provide backup. (Don did not yet have his own drum kit and remembers borrowing a set.) Glowa's friend and fellow Silvertone Allan Kowbel was in the audience when an intense argument broke out among the members of the Escorts, resulting in an on-the-spot breakup: only Ken, Jon and Don were left onstage. Jon invited Allan to come up for the remainder of the show. He agreed, and joined the trio to finish the evening. The Escorts would never play another gig.

Later, Allan asked Ken and Don if they knew a good piano player who might like to join the Silvertones. They thought of Bob Ashley, a classically trained pianist who worked with them at the Canadian Wheat Board. Bob auditioned for the band and was immediately hired.

Bass player Ralph Lavalley soon departed, and Jim Kale — another friend from the Canadian Wheat Board — was urged by Ken and Don to follow in his friend Bob's footsteps. Jim was a natural fit: he had been playing his Silvertone six-string as a bass — an effect he achieved by tuning down the bottom four strings — in the Jaywalkers, a group based in St. Vital. He was soon taken on as bass player in the Silvertones, having acquired a Danelectro bass in the meantime.

Jon Glowa left the Silvertones at the end of August 1961 to concentrate on his studies at high school, and Larry Wah replaced him on guitar, staying in the band for the next six months. Larry and drummer Ducky Donald departed at this point and were replaced by Randy Bachman and Garry Peterson (from the Jurymen and — earlier on — Mickey Brown and the Velvetones). Jim Kale had suggested bringing Randy on board, since he was doing very well locally. Allan took on the position of rhythm guitarist and promoted Randy to lead guitar. Randy, who was also an admirer of the latest sounds from the U.K., impressed him as a strong guitarist who could play both lead and rhythm and learned quickly — he passed his Shadows-oriented audition with flying colours. Randy, in turn, suggested Garry Peterson, who was playing drums in the Winnipeg Junior Symphony in addition to his work with the Jurymen.

The band's name, altered to Allan and the Silvertones shortly before Randy and Garry joined, became Chad Allan and the Reflections in late 1962, when their first single, "Tribute to Buddy Holly," was recorded. There was yet another name change in 1964-65, when they became Chad Allan and the Expressions. The name they took in early 1965, when Quality Records released their Canadian hit single "Shakin' All Over," was the one that would stick: the Guess Who. Bob Ashley left the band near the end of that year, weary of the constant touring, and a 17-year-old Burton Cummings, from the popular North End band the Deverons, replaced him as vocalist/pianist.

---

CLOCKWISE FROM TOP: *Don Marshall's Slingerland drum kit from the Esquires.* [© 1961 Don Marshall]; *Esquires business card.* [Courtesy of Garry and Yvonne Reid]; *250 Hugo Street, Earl Grey Junior High, Graduation Day, June 1961. Left to right: Harold Westdal, Shirley Lord, Neil, Susan Kelso.* [© 1961 Shirley Lord]

AUG • 61

E
The Esquires

FINE MUSIC AND ENTERTAINMENT

*************

KEN JOHNSON
DON MARSHALL

INSTRUMENTAL AND VOCAL STYLING

GL 2-9051
338-0335

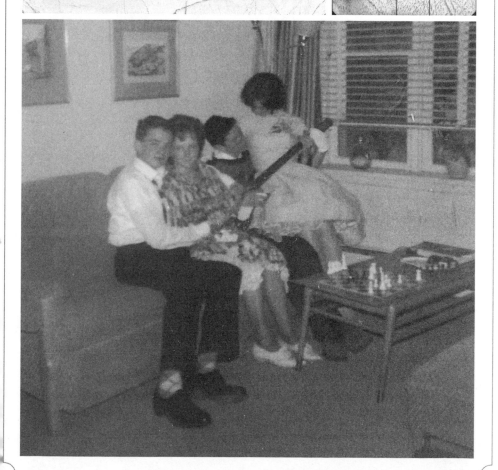

# DANCE

———————

———————

———————

## WITH THE

# ESQUIRES

## ONE OF WINNIPEG'S FINEST
## ROCK & ROLL GROUPS

Neil would cross paths with many of these musicians as his own musical identity began to emerge.

NEIL AND JOHN DANIEL DECIDED to start a band of their own in the late fall of 1960. It was Neil who came up with the name — the Jades. Jim Atkin was recruited to play conga drums, vibes and xylophone, while David Gregg played a set of bongos loaned to him by Jim. Neil played rhythm guitar and John played lead, and John also provided a small amplifier that he shared with Neil. David, already in Grade 10 at Kelvin High, recalls that John was "quite a skilled player."

Neil's burgeoning interest in music and the guitar is highlighted in one of the letters Rassy sent to Scott in November 1960:

> Please do not send Neil Bongo Drums [for his 15th birthday] — he doesn't want them. What he really craves is an amplifier for his electric guitar which I cannot afford. Otherwise a sweater would be his second choice. Perhaps the amplifier would be better at Christmas. You can suit yourself. He is about 5'9-1/2" now and quite big.[23]

Scott went for the sweater, not the amplifier, and Neil added his own note to another of Rassy's letters to Scott:

> Thanks for the sweater. It's just what I wanted. I am playing guitar in the Jades, a rock and roll

*Esquires poster.* [Courtesy of Garry and Yvonne Reid]

group here and am doing quite well. As far as my part goes, I play in a quite simple pattern. I really want a second-hand electric amplifier for Christmas as I am having trouble getting good tone from my friend's.[24]

The Jades rehearsed at David Gregg's house on Dudley Avenue, at John Daniel's house and in Shirley Lord's basement on Garwood Avenue. They did most of their practising over the Christmas holidays. It was during this period that David first met Rassy at the Gray Apartments on Hugo Street. "She was a different brand of cat," he recalls. "A little unusual."

Friday-night canteen dances at the Earl Grey Community Club were overseen by a teen council, and a booking for the Jades was easily secured: Jim Atkin happened to be council president. The band was booked for a Friday evening early in the New Year.

The dance's customary record-spinning stopped so the Jades could take the stage for a half-hour. "Fried Eggs" — an instrumental by the Intruders — was their big crowd-pleaser, but they included other popular instrumentals and a few vocal numbers. According to John Daniel they played "Walk Don't Run," "Sorrento," Pat Boone's "Why Baby" and "I'm Confessin'." They also performed "Perfidia" by the Ventures; John Daniel missed a note, but Neil was quick to cover up.[25] He had already acquired some skill at the guitar and enjoyed the risk and challenge of performing live.

Neil was eager for the band to practise and increase its repertoire (and thus its bookings), but John's hockey schedule conflicted with rehearsals. Neil asked him to choose one or the other — a classic Canadian dilemma — and hockey won out. "There really wasn't anything more important in my life than playing music," Neil remarks, "and you had to really want to do it and you had to make music first in your life."[26] The Jades folded shortly thereafter. Their gig at the Earl Grey Community Club was their one and only public appearance.

NEIL'S PREOCCUPATION WITH MUSIC WAS beginning to have a negative impact on his schoolwork. Scott stressed the importance of Neil's academic career and insisted on being informed of all his grades. Often, the news was bad. Neil's mid-term marks for the fall were Science 44, History 54, English (Literature) 52, Math 68, Music 60, English (Composition) 69, Latin 77, Spelling 96.[27] Rassy felt Neil had done well, given the differences in curricula between the Ontario and Manitoba school systems. His best marks were in English (Composition), Spelling and Latin. Perhaps exposure to his father's craft as well as some natural talent in this area worked in his favour. Ken Koblun confirms, "He wasn't good at school, except for English."[28]

But Neil's attention had drifted far from his studies; there were more important matters on his mind. Once the Jades disbanded, his goal was to get himself into another band as quickly as possible. Neil also decided to retire his paper route, which was interfering with his music. He resolved to make money playing in a band in his spare time, all the while honing his skills as a musician.

Brian Klym, a year behind Neil at Earl Grey, heard that Neil was thinking of relinquishing his much-prized paper route and wanted to take it over. Neil told him he intended to hang on to the job until after Christmas, a tactical manoeuvre to take advantage of holiday tips from customers. After that, as far as Neil was concerned, Brian would be free to take over.

The changeover took place in the schoolyard at Earl Grey. Once again Neil proved his mettle as a quick-thinking entrepreneur. Brian had agreed to kick back a nominal fee to compensate Neil for the company bag as well as the "ring" used to cut the binding from the bundled papers that were dropped off every day. Neil showed Brian what to do and explained some of the finer points of the job.

Local paper boys generally gathered in "the depot," an old building at the corner of Lorette Avenue and Wentworth Street about the size of a single-car garage and heated by a woodstove during the frigid winter months. This was where the paper boys handed over cash collected from customers. David Gregg, the Jades' bongo player, worked as a "depot helper" at the time. Brian later found out through David that another boy had already been pegged to take over Neil's route — the other boy was understandably upset by Neil's unauthorized side deal, but Brian was allowed to keep the route.

In any event, Neil was now free to secure a position with a band. Vocalist Ken Johnson and drummer Don Marshall, both formerly of the Escorts, had formed a band called the Esquires and placed an ad in the *Winnipeg Free Press* seeking guitarists. Neil expressed his interest, and a date was set up for an audition. Ken suggested holding the audition at Neil's place, close to where he lived in the Wentworth Apartments on Corydon Avenue. Garry Reid had also answered the ad and was told to meet them at Neil's apartment as well.

Don remembers that Neil had "a really cheap guitar, and he didn't have an amp," so he plugged into a console record player/radio in the living room opposite the bay window. Garry pulled up to the apartment in a 1957 red-and-white Olds 88. He had brought along his father's guitar

— a sunburst archtop model — and knew five or six songs, so he and Neil played together for the first time. Because Garry played more solidly — and smoothly — than Neil, it was decided he would play lead guitar and Neil would play rhythm. Garry's car was a welcome bonus, a solution to the band's transportation problems — no one else in the band had a car, or even a driver's licence, at the time.

Ed Klym also answered the ad; he auditioned and was hired as the band's second rhythm guitarist about a week later. One thing working in Ed's favour was that he owned good equipment — a 1959 blond Gibson Les Paul Special and a Silvertone amp (purchased from Sears) with four inputs, reverb and two 12-inch speakers. Another attraction was that his younger brother Brian — the same boy who took over Neil's paper route — also had a new gold-flake basic drum kit Don could use until he got his own set. "All I had," Don recalls, "were a pair of drumsticks that I used to bang on everything."

Jim Atkin was soon hired on Neil's recommendation. He was "a phenomenal bongo/conga player," Don recalls. "[He] played a song called 'Bongo, Bongo, Bongo' that I couldn't keep up with, so I just laid down the basic beat and he carried the show."

Shortly after Garry joined the band, he went to Winnipeg Piano on Portage Avenue at Edmonton Street to buy a guitar and amp — a late 1959/60 rosewood-neck Stratocaster with a three-tone sunburst finish and a Harmony H305 amp. Winnipeg Piano's "pay as you can" schedule was well-suited to the shaky finances of a youthful clientele, and the store did much to midwife the birth of Winnipeg's rock-and-roll scene.

The Esquires began rehearsals, first at St. Ignatius church and then in the basement of Ed Klym's house at 807 Dudley Avenue, where they could avail themselves of Ed's brother's drum set. Don owned a copy of the first album by the Ventures, and Garry scrupulously worked out chord changes for the various songs and shared them. Each song as they learned it became a kind of theme song for the band; first it was "Walk, Don't Run," then "Perfidia," then "No Trespassing" and so forth. When Garry auditioned, he knew only half a dozen songs, but by the time rehearsals began he had 10 or so under his belt. (The learning curve was steep, and the other band members had to work hard to keep up with Garry's pace.) Most of the songs from the Fireballs' first album soon followed, including "Torquay," "Bulldog," "Vaquero," "Foot Patter," "Yacky Doo," "Rik-a-Tik" and "Quite a Party."

The band had been holding practices for about three weeks when Brian's drum set suffered an injury. Ken, trying to show Don when to come in on "Dizzy Miss Lizzy," accidentally tore the delicate calfskin drumhead. Brian was there when the accident happened. "My dad got mad," he remembers. "It [the drumhead] was replaced with a plastic one, not another calfskin." Ed's father forced him to quit the band, and he never had an opportunity to play onstage with the Esquires.

Neil was now the band's only rhythm guitarist, even though he was, as Ken Johnson described him, a "skinny kid with [a] brush cut who didn't quite look the part of a hip musician."[29] Don used to say to Neil, "You have more hair on your sweater than you do on your head."

It was at this point that Don arranged to buy a second-hand Slingerland snare and bass. (The drumheads on the snare and bass were made of calfskin. He switched to Mylar as soon as he was able.) The set cost $80, borrowed from his mom. He then purchased Zildjian cymbals at Lowe's Music on Kennedy Street. Don recalls that the cymbals cost more than the drum set. His mother once again covered expenses, and he eventually paid her back with what he earned from the band's bookings.

Rehearsals switched to Don's home at 385 Jamieson Avenue in East Kildonan. Ken was now the de facto leader of the band, but he and Don shared management duties. Don arranged bookings, since he was the one with useful connections. The band printed up business cards — *The Esquires. Instrumental and Vocal Styling. Fine Music and Entertainment* — and included contact information for Ken and Don. Garry and Neil did their part by collaborating on instrumentals. Don purchased albums by the Ventures and Fireballs, and Garry worked out which songs they would cover. Don and Neil might suggest a few other songs, but it was ultimately Garry's choice. Ken picked all the vocals he wanted to do.

The Esquires booked their first gig at Churchill High School. They were to play after a provincial basketball tournament. When the band arrived, the game was just finishing. Don Marshall recalls, "It looked like there was only a dozen or so people there at the time. We set up behind the curtain, started playing 'Bony Moronie' with the appropriate kick dance steps and then Ken started singing it and got as far as 'I've got a girl named Bony Moronie' as they opened the curtain. We were in shock that the hall was crowded, packed in fact. It looked like 500 pairs of eyeballs staring at us. We were so startled that we actually stopped playing for a millisecond and I think I accidentally hit the snare and we continued on to finish the song and the rest of the show."

Thanks to Don's father, the band secured a steady two-month gig at Patterson's Ranch House, at 120 Keewatin Street just off Logan Avenue.[30] Mr. Marshall had worked as the head of security at Patterson's in the late 1940s and '50s. He had maintained friendly contact with Andy Patterson, the owner of the establishment, and introduced his son Don to him. Country music was Patterson's bread and butter on Friday and Saturday nights, but Saturday afternoons from 2 to 5 p.m. were set aside for rock and roll. The building was a converted barn with a restaurant and lounge downstairs, a small stage for dancing upstairs. The dance floor had been so finely polished by years of hay bales that it was considered one of the best in the city. Linda Woodhall and Tom Abbott were premier fans and dancers there, doing a dance called the Savoy that was widely imitated.

The arrangement wasn't without its bumps — the band dickered with Andy Patterson over their earnings. "We were to get 50 per cent of the gate," Don recalls. "The biggest crowd we ever got was maybe 14 people, but it was a good place to practise!" But it was at Patterson's that Neil learned his basic instrumental chops, as well as how to play collaboratively as a member in a band.

Neil's guitar playing was still rudimentary, but Don and Garry recall that he was a "quick study." Because Garry incorporated so many new songs into their repertoire, and because they had so little time to rehearse, the Esquires learned many songs on the fly. This meant Garry often had to yell out chord changes to Neil while the band was onstage. They were able to get away with this because most of the stages they played were small — most weren't more than a few metres across. Neil's usual position was stage right, with Garry stage left so Neil could follow the changes.

A rare photo captures the Esquires playing at Patterson's Ranch House on a Saturday afternoon in February 1961. This is likely the earliest photo of Neil playing with a band, predating any known photo with the Squires by almost two years. Neil stands stage left (not his usual position, according to Don), staring intently at the neck of his guitar[31] to ensure that his fingering is correct. All four band members wear standard-issue outfits: dark slacks, long-sleeve white button-down shirts and skinny ties. Garry is playing his Strat and appears to be scrutinizing Neil to make sure he's playing the right chords. Jim Atkin sits on the edge of a riser, bongos braced between his legs. (A conga drum can be seen behind one of the twin Harmony H305 amps.) A bespectacled Don Marshall perches on the seat of his Slingerland drum set while Ken Johnson sings.

Their biggest gig at Patterson's by far was a B'nai Brith[32] dance that attracted a full house, about 300 people, according to Don. Ken invited his good friend Jim Kale, bass player in the Silvertones, to sit in with them, since Jim didn't have a gig scheduled for that night. (Jim would join them on a few other occasions as well.) It was the first time the Esquires had a bass player. Garry recalls that Jim sang "Cry Baby" by the Fireballs as well as a few others. The band started the show with instrumental numbers before Ken came on to sing a few songs — he recalls singing numbers by Buddy Holly and Ronnie Hawkins — and they finished with a few more instrumentals. Their appearance at the B'nai Brith dance was captured on 8 mm film — without sound — by Paul Letain, but the only copy of the film that ever surfaced was lost many years later.

When the band members were not onstage, they circulated through the crowd, handing out the business cards Don and Ken had printed up, generating several new bookings for the band. They made relatively good money for the gig. "I think we got paid the astronomical sum of $25 that night," Don

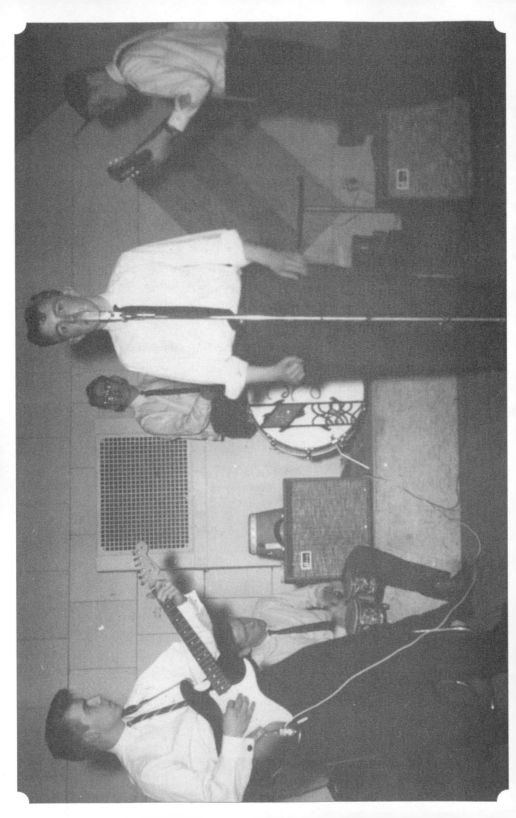

recalls, "a whole five bucks each. We spent it at the Salisbury House restaurant on the way home."

Susan Kelso and Shirley Lord remember going to Patterson's on Saturday afternoons to see Neil play. The Esquires' regular set list included instrumentals by the Ventures and Fireballs (both major influences), as well as vocals by Ken, such as "To the Aisle," "Scarlet Ribbons" and "Johnny B. Goode." Ken had a "choirboy's tenor voice," according to Don and Garry, "but couldn't hit the falsetto notes in 'Runaway'" — Neil and Garry cringed whenever he sang that part. He had a "beautiful, soft, sweet rounded voice" for the ballads, but had trouble belting out rockers for which "all-out screaming" was required.

Often Neil would get home late after weeknight gigs when he had classes to attend early the next morning. Rassy expressed her displeasure to Ken Johnson once when he picked up Neil for a gig: "She really lit into me one time that Neil shouldn't even be in a band, that I was keepin' him out way late for someone his age, he's not even sixteen, he's gotta be in school. She was very tough. It scared the shit outta me."[33] Ken had to promise to get Neil home by 11 p.m. at the latest on school nights. The other band members learned that Rassy was a force to be reckoned with when she was in a foul mood; they steered clear of her whenever possible.

Don Marshall visited Neil at the Gray Apartments and got the distinct impression that Neil was often left to fend for himself. "Looking back on it," he recalls, "I think he

_____

*The Esquires, Patterson's Ranch House, February 1961. Left to right: Garry Reid (lead guitar), Jim Atkin (bongos), Don Marshall (drums), Ken Johnson (vocals), Neil (rhythm guitar).* [Courtesy of Garry and Yvonne Reid]

was alone more than he shoulda been."[34] Rassy had recently begun to appear as a regular panellist on a stump-the-panel game show called *Twenty Questions*. The show premiered on CJAY-TV at 10 p.m. on Friday, March 10, 1961, and Rassy appeared under her maiden name; other regular co-panelists included Nola Macdonald and Bill Trebilcoe. Rassy was a wild card on the show, always entertaining to watch. The three panellists soon became close friends, and Rassy eventually began to date Bill. "He was her last flame, I think," Neil recalls. "Big, tall, bald guy, horn-rimmed glasses and polka-dot shirts. Great guy. Real gentle."[35] Rassy was often busy with her commitment to show tapings in addition to her active social life and sporting activities.

This meant Neil was frequently left on his own. He survived on a diet of peanut butter sandwiches and macaroni and cheese when dining at home. Typically, he invited friends over to talk about music, eat peanut-butter sandwiches and watch Rassy on television. Neil remarks, "Rassy was pretty funny on TV. That was pretty out-there."[36] Ultimately, Rassy found she didn't need to keep a firm rein on Neil; he was independent-minded, determined and focused enough to take care of his basic needs himself. Many of his friends were jealous of the freedom he enjoyed. Rassy's hands-off parenting served to foster his independence and created a space in which he could pursue his music — if not necessarily his school work.

One evening toward the end of April, Neil and Don decided to hitchhike to Portage la Prairie — a distance of over 80 kilometres — to see a band called the Fendermen[37] perform. They were lucky enough to get a lift from someone driving a brown Corvair station wagon. According to Don, the Fendermen's gig took place just south of town in a school auditorium along a country road on an Indian reserve. Don recalls that the band played their big hit, "Mule Skinner Blues" — one of Neil's favourites — along with "Don't You Just Know It," as well as some others. After the show Neil and Don tried to hitchhike back to Winnipeg. It was a cold evening, and they were wearing regular street shoes and clothes. They were picked up by a drunk who told them he couldn't drive anymore, and they asked politely if *they* could take *him* home. Don took the wheel, though he didn't have his driver's licence and had never driven a car. As they reached the town limits, the car's owner revived sufficiently to entertain second thoughts; Neil and Don were left shivering by the side of the road. They hiked to Fortier, a small town 27 kilometres outside Portage la Prairie, where they found a house with a light on and knocked at the door. From there they telephoned virtually everyone they knew, without success, and were finally forced to contact Rassy. She drove out to pick them up, but she wasn't pleased — Don suspected that Neil hadn't told her where they were going. The atmosphere in the car was as icy as the air outside, and they endured the ride back to Winnipeg in a stone-cold silence. Don got the idea that Rassy felt Neil was being led astray and that nothing good would come of Neil's involvement in the band. She forced him to quit the Esquires not long after this incident.

Decades later, Don met Neil backstage after his April 15, 1991, show with Crazy Horse at the Northlands Coliseum in Edmonton. Don remarked, "You've come a long way, my friend." Neil replied, "It's just a bigger barn."

IN MAY 1961, NOT LONG after Neil's parents' divorce, Scott visited Winnipeg on his way to Victoria to wed Astrid Mead.[38]

He met Neil at a dim sum restaurant in the late afternoon, after school, and Neil talked about his interest in music. Scott, who had missed recent developments, couldn't quite fathom the depth of Neil's involvement and commitment. As he dropped his son off at home, Scott mentioned that he was heading to Victoria to marry Astrid, and that Neil would soon have a 10-year-old stepsister named Deirdre. Scott recalls, "He smiled at me a little bleakly but self-possessed, and said 'Corn-grad-ulations.'"[39]

EARL GREY JUNIOR HIGH SCHOOL held its closing exercises at the Crescent–Fort Rouge Church on Wednesday, May 31, at 2:15 p.m. Neil managed to pass his year, but received no awards or notice at the graduation ceremony. The church was located at 525 Wardlaw Avenue — close to the Gray Apartments — so Neil and a small group of friends adjourned to Neil's place between the graduation ceremony and an evening gathering at Shirley's home at 982 Garwood Avenue. Shirley had brought her Brownie camera along, and Rassy took a photo of the group of close friends — Harold Westdal, Shirley, Neil and Susan Kelso — sitting on the sofa. In the photograph, Neil is holding a guitar[40] and showing Susan — perched beside him on the arm of the sofa — how to finger a chord. Susan, one white-gloved hand on the neck of the guitar, pays rapt attention. (She and Neil were close friends, but the relationship never went any further.) Harold has his arm around Shirley as they both gaze at the camera. The after-party was held in the basement "rumpus room" at Shirley's home. Noticeably absent was Ken Koblun, who was not part of the close circle of friends that Shirley invited to the party. In fact, Ken had yet to visit Neil at his apartment.

It was a bittersweet time for the classmates and friends. They would all be heading off to Grade 10 — their first year in high school — in September, but not necessarily to the same school. Neil would be attending Kelvin High School, the school his father had attended nearly three decades earlier.

---

# ★ 8 ★
## KELVIN HIGH SCHOOL (YEAR ONE):
### The Stardusters/Twilighters/Teen Tones
### (and Others)

NEIL BEGAN GRADE 10 AT Kelvin High in September 1961. The school was located in the northeast section of affluent River Heights and drew its student population from that neighbourhood, as well as Crescentwood and Fort Rouge. At the time, Neil was still living with Rassy in their apartment at 250 Hugo Street in Fort Rouge, which set him apart from the more wealthy students in the school. There were invisible but powerful social barriers at Kelvin, and Neil had the continuing disadvantage of being a child of divorced parents. He failed to distinguish himself as a scholar or jock, his physique was on the skinny side, and he was already a year older than most of his classmates. His interest in music was his saving grace, along with a lively sense of humour and an amiable manner.

Kelvin Technical High School was built in 1912. During Neil's tenure it was known simply as Kelvin High School, and the front doors were located at 55 Harrow Street. Two additions in 1963 and 1964 replaced the original school building, which was demolished in 1965-66. (Construction began during the fall of 1962. The new gymnasium and cafeteria were in place by 1964. Neil would see a great deal of ongoing construction during his time at Kelvin.) The front doors of the new school fronted Kingsway Avenue, and the address changed to reflect this new orientation.

The school celebrated its 50th "golden" anniversary during the 1961-62 academic year. Compared to the majestic-looking older building, the new school was arguably more modern but architecturally sterile and nondescript. Kelvin alumni include author, philosopher, scholar and media theorist Marshall McLuhan (class of 1928); lawyer, business leader and Global Television founder Izzy Asper (class of 1950); writer, director, actor and filmmaker Ken Finkelman (class of 1964); and children's entertainer Fred Penner (class of 1965). The school motto is *Courage, Truth and Right.*

Many of Neil's classmates from Earl Grey had moved to Kelvin with him. Harold Westdal was one. Harold typically walked along Hugo to Corydon on his way to school, picking up Neil along the way. He noticed that Neil and Rassy did things differently than his family did: Rassy was usually still in bed when Harold knocked, while Neil would be eating his standard breakfast of peanut butter on toast. Harold, accustomed to a breakfast of hot oatmeal unfailingly served by his mother, thought this was odd. He concluded that Rassy was "exotic," in part because of her television appearances.

Neil's Grade 10 homeroom teacher was Mr. March, who taught English. His math teacher was Clarence Kerr, a legendary presence in the school. (A younger Clarence Kerr had taught math to Scott Young when he attended Kelvin.) Classmate Jean Truman recalls that Mr. Kerr, always impeccable in a blue suit and white shirt, was liable to shout at students who neglected their homework and throw chalk and chalkboard erasers at students whose attention lapsed. He was nevertheless considered an excellent math teacher who ruled his classroom with strict military discipline and drilled lessons into his pupils by sheer force of will.

Richard Koreen, who would become Neil's first bass player in his next band, the Stardusters, had "Clancy" Kerr[41] as his Grade 12 homeroom teacher. "Former military, present math sergeant" is how Richard referred to him at the time. Mr. Kerr unexpectedly walked into the boys' washroom one day when Richard was grabbing a quick smoke. "Your name?" Mr. Kerr asked with pencil poised over a detention form, even though he knew Richard's name. "Trouper Koreen H804200, sir," Richard replied, and received a smirk in return. Mr. Kerr then stared pointedly at the toilet, inviting Richard to extinguish his cigarette butt. The infraction was deemed to be worth 10 detentions.

Garry Bowles, who lived in Fort Rouge and had attended Earl Grey with Neil, was also enrolled at Kelvin. Garry was impressed by how little time Neil devoted to his schoolwork and how much he devoted to his music — as soon as the bell rang at the end of the day, Neil headed for his guitar. Garry remembers Neil as a loner, polite and soft-spoken, not saying much unless he had something to say. "He blended in with the other students — at least until he got near his guitar," Garry says. "Then he was a different person entirely, outgoing and confident."

The school's annual Freshie Dance, on Friday, September 22, proved to be a popular event. At intermission the crowd jammed into the auditorium for the crowning of the 1961-62 Freshie Queen. The yearbook observes (under the heading *Kelvin Kapers*) that "although the large attendance made it almost impossible to move on the dance floor, people met people, boys met girls, girls met boys . . ." Music was a social catalyst for Neil's cohort. He was undoubtedly paying attention.

IT WAS IN MRS. BROWN'S music class that Neil first met Ross F. "Clancy" Smith.[42] Neil noticed Clancy, not vice versa. Clancy recalls that two "all-boys" classes were combined in this particular music class — Neil being from the other class. Clancy wasn't aware of Neil's existence until a few years later.

Clancy was a bit of an odd duck, as Neil almost certainly noticed, and he would later serve as partial inspiration for the song "Nowadays Clancy Can't Even Sing," written during Neil's sojourn in Toronto in the fall of 1965. Neil has said that Clancy is only peripherally the subject of the song and that the lyrics are better understood as describing Neil himself and his hang-ups with an old girlfriend in Winnipeg; nevertheless it was Clancy's name Neil chose for the title.

In a KSAN radio interview on November 12, 1969, Neil was asked about the song and its relation to Clancy. "The song isn't about him," Neil replied. "The song is about me. He's a cat who used to ride to school on a bicycle. Not too cool. Freaky-looking guy. Early Canadian Jewish."[43] Neil added that Clancy was scruffy and often in need of a shave, wore horn-rimmed glasses, carried his books in a knapsack and was known to sing "Valerie, Valera"[44] while walking down the hallways at school. Clancy was "pretty spaced out, people put him down and he didn't have any friends." Neil added, "You know, if you're different, you don't have any friends at school. It's *Lord of the Flies*."[45]

In a 1967 interview with Los Angeles reporter Jeffrey C. Alexander, Neil remarked, "Many people, I know, tell me they don't understand 'Clancy.' They can't figure out all the symbols and stuff. Well, I don't think it's possible at all for them to know who he really is. For listeners, Clancy is just an image, a guy who gets come down on all the time. He was a strange cat, beautiful. Kids in school called him a 'weirdo' 'cause he would whistle and sing 'Valerie, Valera' in the halls. After a while, he got so self-conscious he couldn't do his thing anymore. When someone as beautiful as that and as different as that is actually killed by his fellow men — you know what I mean — like taken and sorta chopped down — all the other things are nothing compared to this."[46]

Clancy himself failed to notice Neil when they were in music class together in Grade 10. He thinks they first met at a party held by his stepbrother Tim Henry[47] at their family home at 366 Oxford Street in River Heights in the mid-1960s. Clancy finds it odd that Neil remembers him riding a bike to school — he recalls that his bicycle was stolen in Grade 9 and he never got a new one. In fact, Clancy preferred walking to school. He's also amused that Neil called the song "Nowadays Clancy Can't Even Sing," given that Clancy by his own admission is a terrible singer. Nor can he recall singing "Valerie, Valera" in the hallways at school.

Clancy first learned of his connection with the song while attending the University of Winnipeg, when some friends

---

FROM TOP: *Ross F. "Clancy" Smith.* [Courtesy of Joe Barnsley]; *Pages 1 and 2 of original manuscript with lyrics and chords for "Nowadays Clancy Can't Even Sing."* [Lyrics © 1965 Broken Arrow Music Corporation (BMI), manuscript © 1965 Neil Young, courtesy of Ken Koblun]; *Kelvin Technical High School, circa 1910.* [Photo Archive (Communications Department), Winnipeg School Division]

Baby, That Don't Mean a Thing,
Cause Even, Clancy can't sing.

Who's that stompin' all over my face   A C F G
Who's that silhouette in tiger colace
Who's puttin' scrooge the bells honeswing
Who's takin' my gypsy before she's begun   
To singin' the meanin' of what's in my mind   Am 7 - Dm 7
Before i can take home what is in there   Dm 7 - Dm
For givin' and distrin' on talkin' in sleeves   Am 7 - Dm
For stoppin' the bells to wait for the time   Am 7 - Dm 7
And who's sayin' baby that doesn't mean a thing   F   G 7
Cause nowadays Clancy can't even sing   A m C G F (F 7)

And who's all screwed up if happiness thing
And trys to turn all the bells to harmonize
And who's in the corner in down on the floor
With pencil and paper just drawin' the scene
And who's tryin' to act like he's faster to lose
the night an' to doubt if you know what is true
And don't bother' ... lookin' wise too blind to see
And who's comin' on like he wanted to be
And who's sayin' baby that doesn't mean a thing
Cause Nowadays Clancy can't even sing

silhouette
silouette

And who's comin' along an' old nights fears
and who's got the brain to keep in alive

And who's seein' eye through a crack in the floor
There it is baby don't twist your memory
And why should he stay, but twist the song
And where's he is that he was remembered
And who's sayin' baby that don't mean a thing
Cause Nowadays Clancy can't even sing

And who's gone away to the place she once   A m
went      G 7   steppd
all the time are sittin' eat food to come around   Am
One more small thread he has to add   D 7
Nowadays Clancy can't even sing down   B m F F
             D 7   G

But here's sharin' an' it's quite the same
It ain't no old niggerd you can't lay a claim

mentioned that Neil Young had used his name in a song. It was news to Clancy, who didn't follow popular music and still doesn't. "The genre itself is the problem," he remarks. "Most rock-and-roll music bores me to tears. It's to music what chewing gum is to nutrition." He adds, "My connection to Neil Young is peripheral and accidental, and it's amusingly ironic that most rock music bores me." In 2010, after reading the lyrics and listening to two different recorded versions of the song,[48] Clancy wrote:

> 1. Neil must have felt the proverbial square peg in a round hole. The conformist mind-set of the times would likely have made him all the more aware of his not "fitting in."
> 2. The lyrics are not belligerent like those of so many protest-era songs (Bruce Cockburn comes to mind). Rather, he seems bewildered by, or at most, slightly put off with those who don't see how vital being true to one's own vision is.

Neil would probably agree.

Ken Koblun, who kept Neil's original lyric sheets for "Clancy" in a cardboard box under his bed along with other memorabilia from his music career, told *Broken Arrow* editor Scott Sandie how he came to have them:

> Back in the old days in Toronto in 1965 Neil was feeling tired and lonely so he wrote a song called "Nowadays Clancy Can't Even Sing." The day after he wrote it I visited him in his room [at 88 Isabella Street] and he told me about the new song and fished the lyric sheets out of the trash in

his room and showed me the words. I cottoned on to the fact that he had thrown away the first and only manuscript to the song and asked him about it. He told me that he had the song memorised and didn't need the bit [of] paper. He said that he had the ability to remember all of the words to all of his songs after he had written them. So I said to him "since you have this ability and the paper is in the garbage could I have it?" And he said yes.[49]

Ken still thinks of the lyric sheets as Neil's — he's only "holding them for safekeeping."[50]

The lyric sheets are revealing. The original name of the song was "Baby, That Don't Mean a Thing, Cause Even Clancy Can't Sing." Neil had written the chords that were to go with it, although it was in a different key than the version he eventually recorded. Neil changed his mind regarding the third and fourth lines of the verse that starts, "And who's comin' home on old ninety-five?" The familiar lines are "though having it, sharing it ain't quite the same, it ain't no gold nugget, you can't lay a claim." Stricken out with thick pencil marks are the original lyrics:

And who's gone away to the place she once stayed?
While they're sellin' cat food to cover a raid
One more small thing I hasten to add
Nowadays Clancy ain't singin' too bad.

Neil and Clancy were reunited at Kelvin High's 75th Reunion Banquet, held at the Winnipeg Convention Centre in June 1987. Someone pointed Neil out, and Clancy decided it was an opportune time to introduce himself. Confined to a wheelchair for many years after being diagnosed with multiple sclerosis in 1977, Clancy wheeled himself up to Neil and initiated a conversation. Neil recognized him immediately; they spoke briefly and there were no startling revelations.

DESPITE HIS INCREASING INVOLVEMENT IN the music scene, Neil did appear to make an effort to improve his flagging marks. In an October 1961 letter[51] to Scott, Rassy reports that Neil is "well and happy and is quite vocally enamoured of life here — he's president of the Community Club and seems to have a deal of more or less important class stuff to do at school for his room." Rassy also sent along Neil's term-test results:

English Literature 69
English Composition 69
Social Studies/Geography 69
Maths 68
Science 76
Industrial Arts/Drafting 75

She noted that Neil did not take the French test, but "[he] is coming along very well with it, however." This could be chalked up to differences in curricula between the Manitoba and Ontario school boards.[52] French was not taught as early or as intensively in Ontario as it was in Manitoba, which has a large francophone population. Neil had to play catch-up and was given extra help and tutoring.

Neil's marks were important to Scott, and he continued to stress the value of a solid education to his son. Rassy was more sensitive to Neil's interest in music and acknowledged the depth of his dedication and talent. "Rassy was the biggest supporter of my musical endeavors," Neil remarks, "and believed in me from the very beginning, offering her encouragement always."[53] Scott's and Rassy's different outlooks would create considerable friction during Neil's school years. "Well, as my Dad wasn't living with me at the time," Neil recalls, "he didn't have the perspective on it that my mother had. If he had, he'd have seen how 'into the music' I was, but at the same time he'd have been pushing me to stay on at school, just like my mother was. And I definitely think he'd have certainly been stronger at persuading me to stay on. The classic thing that happens in family break-ups . . . the perspective gets changed. The father will always have a negative reaction to what the mother does particularly if she's being 'soft' on the child. Without the true understanding of what's going on, he'll just say that 'it's wrong.' It's a reaction created out of frustration over not being able to really voice an opinion. So . . . to say that my father was less into my music than my mother would be unfair. Although my mother was more supportive."[54]

In the October letter, Rassy tells Scott, "I have bought [Neil] a better guitar for his upcoming birthday. He craves an amplifier still and is saving for one — perhaps, if you are wondering about a gift for his sixteenth birthday, a cheque would really be what he wants. He needs some more money for the amp — it's a Fender Champ if you want to send him one."

It was an important gift — his first electric guitar. Rassy bought him a pre-owned 1956 "tobacco sunburst" Gibson Les Paul Junior with one pickup and two control knobs — one for volume and one for tone.[55] Neil must have had his eye on this particular guitar in advance of his 16th birthday and would have given his mother some broad hints regarding the model he wanted and where to get it.

Neil finally had an electric guitar, but he still needed an amp. No doubt disappointingly, Scott had sent Neil another sweater for his birthday instead of the amplifier. That meant Neil had to borrow an amp from friends or resort to cruder methods of amplification, such as plugging his guitar into his record player/radio unit at home. (Radios and some record players in the 1950s and early '60s had a tube-driven amplifier section built in. The output from a guitar could be patched into the amp if a compatible jack could be found or rigged — some soldering work was usually necessary. This was useful only for practice; a domestic radio unit's four- or six-inch speaker and single watt or less of power would have been worse than useless onstage.)

For many young musicians putting together their first band, amplification was almost an afterthought. The first priority was the instrument itself: the right guitar for your style of music and your way of playing. Next, you needed to find other competent players to complete the group and assemble a repertoire. At least at first, a band might need only a small amp for the practice room. A more powerful amplifier is required once the band begins to play small halls, schools and church basements, and an even larger one becomes necessary if the band progresses to more substantial venues.

Relatively few brands of guitar amplifiers dominated the market in the early '60s. There were high-priced Fender and Gibson amps for those who could afford them, while more reasonably priced, but of lesser quality, were the Ampeg and Harmony line. Expensive imported amps from the U.K., such as VOX and later Marshall, were also available, while for cash-strapped players there was a selection of amplifier kits from EICO and Heathkit. Homemade amps were also an option. It was common practice to exchange amplifiers with other bands to test them out. Borrowing an amplifier was sometimes possible, and rental was a common last resort.

KEN KOBLUN, WHO WAS ATTENDING Grade 10 at Churchill High School on the eastern edge of Fort Rouge, began to grow closer to Neil in November 1961. It was at this point that Ken "worked up enough nerve" to call Neil and ask if he would "play something for him on the guitar. . . . I didn't know anything about music then," Ken recalls. "It was before I even had my first guitar." Neil was pleased to hear from Ken and a date was set up to meet at Neil's place. This was Ken's very first visit to the apartment at 250 Hugo Street. He recalls, "I think even when I first met him, Neil wanted to be a songwriter or singer or something like that. I asked him to show me some things on the guitar because I was interested in playing guitar and he obliged by taking his electric guitar and amplifier[56] [most likely a loaner from a friend] and strumming some things in his mother's apartment. And I said, 'Neat song, what is it?' He said, 'It's something I wrote.' That was the first exposure I had to that idea."[57] Neil then played a chord progression Ken found interesting. Ken asked Neil if he could show him some more; Neil told him he would have to get his own guitar if he was going to do that.

Inspired by the visit, Ken asked his biological father, Arthur Koblun, for an acoustic guitar for Christmas. He received an archtop Harmony Monterey — just like Neil's first guitar, but without a pickup — shortly before Christmas. His foster brother Richard received a flat-top Harmony Sovereign from his father on Christmas Day. It was agreed that Ken and his foster brother would share the two guitars. Ken paid another visit to Neil's place shortly thereafter, and Neil showed him how to finger some basic chords.

NEIL FORMED HIS SECOND BAND, the Stardusters, during the fall of 1961. All the members hailed from Kelvin except pianist Linda Fowler, who attended Churchill High, the same school as Ken Koblun. Linda had heard through a friend that Neil was looking for a piano player for his band, and she offered her talents.

Linda had played in the Esquires for a brief period, but only after Neil and Jim Atkin left the band. Don Marshall rated her highly: "She was a very good, trained piano player." The bespectacled 14-year-old had been classically trained — in both technical skills and theory — since age six, and had shown a talent for playing by ear. She had played her first church service by age 11. Both of her parents were musical: her mother also played the piano and her father played the fiddle. Linda was a popular and willing player. While classical music was her passion, and would eventually become her career, she played popular music in bands "for the sheer joy of playing."

Neil made regular visits to her parents' home at 866 Fleet Street at Stafford in Fort Rouge. When he first received his Gibson Les Paul Junior, he brought it over to show Linda and her parents. Neil sat in the family's kitchen eating peanut-butter sandwiches and twanging the same note: *Ping! Ping!* It drove Linda and her parents crazy. He would fixate on one note and play it obsessively, then switch to a second note and repeat the process. *Ping! Ping!* It got so bad that her parents had to cover their ears. "Neil still plays this way," Linda jokes. Musicologist William Echard, describing Neil's later work, makes a similar observation: "Young frequently uses repeated chords or repeated notes to explore textural variation and to build intensity."[58] A classic example is the guitar solo in "Down by the River," in which Neil somehow coaxes a melody out of the rich tonalities of a single sustained note. His efforts in Linda's kitchen were no doubt less sophisticated.

Other musicians who were in the band from the beginning included Jim Atkin on percussion and vibes, and someone named Ken (*not* Koblun) on drums (later replaced by another drummer). Linda confirmed that Jim was a highly skilled player and served as timekeeper in the band. The band held its practices in the living room at Linda's home, where the piano was located — a small upright black spinet. Linda recalls that on at least one occasion Neil patched his guitar through the family's old stand-up RCA radio. Linda's parents obligingly retreated to the kitchen when the band monopolized the living room.

During their earliest gigs, the Stardusters plugged into the in-house PA systems at the schools, churches and halls where they performed. These systems were often less than ideal, but the band had to work with what it found. On other occasions — when no other source of amplification was available — Neil would try to borrow an amp from a friend. Linda had to be flexible enough to play whatever piano was available at the venue. Many times these pianos were not in the best condition — out of tune, or with dead or sticky keys — and she was often forced to improvise.

Richard Koreen, a Grade 12 student at Kelvin who lived with his family at 170 Elm Street, joined the Stardusters as their bass player in the late fall. This gentle, soft-spoken and intellectual student had met Neil earlier in the school term, in

one of the corner rooms of the labyrinthine basement. Neil and Richard naturally gravitated to each other. They both liked to escape the student crowds during the lunch period and sought out a quieter place to perch and talk.

"My conversations with Neil in the basement of Kelvin delved into life and the future through the eyes of teens," Richard recalls. "I remember our one conversation about 'Tintern Abbey' — the poem [by William Wordsworth]," which Richard introduced to the less-well-read Neil. They discussed the poem as "an example of a euphoric state linked to a setting." Richard feels it was "part of a discussion about setting up a perfect goal or life path. [Neil] had goals but they lacked the focus created through being clear. The poem presented an example of complete perfection." Richard was pleasantly surprised years later when Neil referred to "Tintern Abbey" during an interview.

"Another item that came up later were two books he pulled out of the waste paper," Richard says. "[They were] Hilroy notebooks used by a student suffering from severe arthritis." The student was well-known in the school and was often seen poring over his notebooks. "Every page was filled with letters

---

CLOCKWISE FROM TOP: *Richard Koreen and Linda Fowler heading out to attend Richard's graduation at Kelvin High School, June 1962.* [© 1962 Richard Koreen]; *Linda Fowler and Richard Koreen at the Koreen family home, December 24, 1962. Linda, Neil's first piano player, is holding a 3/4 size guitar.* [© 1962 Richard Koreen]; *Linda Fowler at the Koreen family home, December 24, 1962.* [© 1962 Richard Koreen]; *Richard Koreen, Pikwitonei, northern Manitoba, February 1963.* [© 1963 Richard Koreen]; *Richard Koreen, Neil's first bass player, playing his brother's classical guitar in his bedroom at home, December 24, 1962.* [© 1962 Richard Koreen]

of the alphabet written over and over. It seemed to improve a bit in each session." Richard guessed the arthritic student was perhaps "loosening up his fingers for the day." There was no perceptible change in the writing other than "a slight easing of the wiggling in each session." Neil "saw the pain" and understood about the "easing." Richard recalls that Neil said something akin to "If I could only do this, I'd be able to do anything." Years later Richard came across a published interview in which Neil mentioned the two notebooks as examples of "an individual overcoming obstacles." The books had obviously made a deep impression.

As serious as Neil was about the band, he hadn't entirely abandoned his interest in chicken farming. Richard was intrigued when Neil mentioned the subject. "Neil had the whole thing worked out. . . . He wanted to raise chickens that laid those brown eggs.[59] He even knew some market prices."

But Neil also shared his thoughts on more music-related concerns — such as how a band might be televised to good effect. "He wanted to have each member of the band on a separate platform (mini-stage)," recalls Richard, "and have the cameras flying past them on the floor. We discussed this and I had many doubts. Sure enough, years later there it was — a Buffalo Springfield televised piece (not a full concert) with that set-up. It wasn't as magical as Neil had imagined, and the bass guitarist looked a bit tense, but it happened and I recognized the fruit of our talking in the Kelvin basement."

Neil spoke enthusiastically about the Stardusters, the band he had formed a month or two earlier, and asked if Richard might be interested in joining. Richard didn't own an instrument at the time and asked Neil what he could play.

The answer came promptly: Neil had already pegged Richard as a bass player.

Bass players were a rare commodity in most bands in the early 1960s, even though an entry-level bass was no more expensive than an entry-level guitar. It was cooler and more prestigious to play guitar; rhythm and lead guitarists were more prominent onstage, and a guitar was a more versatile instrument — always in demand at campfire singalongs, for instance. And, not least, it was considered a truism that girls were attracted to guitar players.

But Richard agreed that playing the bass sounded like a good idea. Ever the enterprising salesman, Neil suggested a particular used bass that was for sale. "[Neil] knew the guitar and claimed it was a good one," Richard recalls. The asking price was $50 — the same amount that a pawnshop would have paid for the bass. Richard came up with the cash and Neil returned with the bass.

Unknown to Richard, the bass Neil procured for him was Jim Kale's old Danelectro — a brown 1960 double shorthorn model, originally purchased by Jim for $130 from a Sears-Roebuck mail-order outlet in North Dakota. Jim's first guitar had been a Silvertone electric, six-string, single cutaway in black with white trim that he sometimes played as a bass by tuning down the lower four strings. By the fall of 1960 he had graduated to the Danelectro bass, which he played in the Silvertones before progressing to a Fender Precision in the fall of 1961. It was at this point that Jim decided to sell the Danelectro.

Jim often loaned his equipment to other musicians when he didn't have a gig scheduled, and he may have allowed Neil to borrow his Danelectro for a few days at the end of June 1961. (Neil had become acquainted with Jim when he had played with the Esquires on a few occasions.) In a photo taken on the day of his Grade 9 graduation from Earl Grey, Neil holds a Danelectro bass that may well have been Jim's.

Richard knew nothing about playing the bass, although he did have a modicum of musical experience, including fooling around with a guitar. He had played piano for a few years and was able to read music. "Most homes during that era still had a piano," he says, "and it was almost understood that you'd take piano as a kid." He enjoyed listening to jazz and spent a few nights per week, until about 3:30 a.m., hanging out at the Stage Door, a club on Fort Street, to watch acclaimed Winnipeg jazz guitarist Lenny Breau perform. (Oddly, Richard never took Neil on one of his "jazz nights.") Neil taught Richard the basics on the bass to get him started. Bass players don't play chords, so he had to learn how to adapt a bass line to a song's chord changes. "Neil gave me my first lessons," Richard remarks. "He was years ahead of me in musicianship." Richard felt Neil's high level of musical knowledge was characteristic of his remarkable willpower. "He was a driven person and always was. Everything he did he saw relative to delivering a goal he was working on at the time." Neil needed a bass player in the band, and he did what he had to do to recruit one.

Richard noticed that Neil had an amp during his first practice with the Stardusters. (Most likely an Ampeg:[60] Richard recalls Neil talking about this brand of amplifier in a later conversation.) Richard didn't have an amp of his own, but said he could get one: his parents had a "co-axial" unit that was part of the family's overall sound system. Richard was allowed to borrow the amp for band practices and gigs. "At the second practice I arrived with my amp and everyone thought I had brought the Queen's jewels," he recalls. The amplifier[61] "was about seven inches high, 15 wide and 10 deep. It was a radio-tube amp with four or five input channels using Philips jacks on the back. The amp had a metallic grey, slotted-for-ventilation metal cover that wrapped up the sides and over the top. Each input channel had a volume knob on the front. It was not a stereo amp, so had only the one output channel. There were four speaker jacks on the back. It could handle large-format speakers. The unit was transported by taking the two open-back speaker boxes (one 12-inch speaker in each), putting the two open backs together, placing the amp in the bottom space and snapping the two halves together. There was a sturdy handle on top." This single unit allowed the band to use more mikes and permitted a more balanced sound. Prior to Richard's arrival, the piano, drums and vibes had not been miked. This changed once Richard brought his "treasure."

The Stardusters already had a polished repertoire, so Richard had to learn quickly or risk falling behind. "The difficult part for me," he says, "was remembering all the songs," mainly popular instrumentals of the day. During one of their basement discussions at school, Neil raised the possibility of performing original material instead of just instrumental covers. This was well before he had penned his first song or sung a vocal. Richard recalls, "Although many of the pieces we did had words, we just played the instrumental part." According to Richard, two songs stood out as regular selections on the band's set list — "Can't Help Falling in Love with You" and "Ku-U-I-Po," both from the Elvis Presley movie *Blue Hawaii*. They practised at Linda Fowler's home several times a week. Although he can't remember exactly which were performed onstage, Richard does remember Neil mentioning additional numbers, usually with the words "Okay, let's play . . ." These included "Runaway" by Del Shannon, "Let's Twist Again" by Chubby Checker, "Harbor Lights" by the Platters, "Torquay" by the Fireballs, "(The) Green Door" by Bob Davie and Marvin Moore, "Road-Runner" by the Wailers and "Sleepwalk" by Santo & Johnny. Linda remembers one additional number that was a regular on their set list — "Tall Cool One" by the Wailers, with a distinctive strong piano lead.

Linda had a firm idea about her role in the Stardusters: "A piano player was the anchor in a band, and usually the only band member who had any formal training and the ability to read music, call out chords and figure them out by ear." Neil valued Linda's abilities, and he understood how reading music worked, but according to Richard, "[Neil] wasn't practiced in using what skill he had in this area. This became evident when he personally transcribed a few of his guitar compositions to be played on the piano. It was impossible to reach the notes with a human hand on the keyboard. On the guitar there was no problem."

Richard adds, "Neil usually played rhythm guitar and Linda usually played the melody and accompaniment on the piano. . . . Neil was very capable on the guitar and was able to play runs and take the lead as required."

Linda was impressed with Neil's business sense. "He was the one who would go out and get us gigs," she recalls. "He displayed confidence and bravado right from the start as well as a burning desire and drive to succeed." Linda felt he possessed "unshakeable confidence," which she felt she was lacking. She was nervous about playing in front of large crowds, while Neil revelled in the spontaneity and atmosphere of live performances.

Neil was definitely perceived by the other members as the band's leader. It was Neil who conducted, gave the count, set the play list, approved the gigs, got the gigs and was at the mike onstage. Richard remarks, "He was the only one of us who was looking at the horizon, so to speak. I remember him talking once about each of us having a mike so we could sing. This was greeted with stunned silence and dropped."

There were two "extras" attached to the group — a designated manager and a tech person — both also habitués of the social scene in Kelvin's basement. The manager was supposed to get the band gigs and was to be paid on a commission basis. Richard recalls that the manager "talked a good game" but never produced any results. The tech person was more useful: he could interconnect the band's equipment, and do it effectively in a short time. "Back then if you were in a group you brought your own amp, cables, extension cords, everything," Richard recalls. "And at the site you scrambled to get it all plugged in and working. After a few events we had this tech guy help us — just a friend, but he got part of the gate." It took about 20 minutes to set up the band's equipment.

The Stardusters usually played high school dances, coffeehouses or teen dances in church basements. They occasionally rented a small hall on Osborne Street, put up posters and charged admission at the door. "The hall was really a hole-in-the-wall place with its entrance on Osborne," Richard says. "It was perhaps 24 feet wide and 35 feet deep, had a bit of a cloakroom near the entrance and a washroom."

The band changed its name several times, depending on the occasion. "We were the Teen Tones at one event," Richard recalls, "and then something else the next. We had little vision of this being any kind of a career — we were having a ball." They played as the Teen Tones at two of their Osborne Street gigs and also at River Heights Junior

High. The gigs at the hall were put on without a sponsor. Whatever the band earned at the door was its take, and they usually managed to fill the place. Richard estimates the date of these gigs as late November or early December 1961, possibly even January 1962. They became the Twilighters for a gig at St. Ignatius.

Jim Atkin faced some medical challenges while in the band. Richard recalls, "Jim suffered from a kind of youth arthritis for which he had surgery in late 1961 or early 1962. He was always in pain, but had a stoic outlook." He adds, "The surgery was not small. He had the muscle in his thigh split and wrapped around both sides of his thigh bone so he could use that muscle to move his leg. He used a cane and was obviously in pain a lot of the time."

Meanwhile, Neil faced a sobering family event at this time. His grandfather, Percy Andrew Young, passed away on January 30, 1962, after suffering a stroke. Scott flew to Winnipeg for the funeral. During this visit Neil told his father he was keeping busy playing rhythm guitar in a band with some friends, but Scott still didn't grasp the degree of his son's commitment or what might follow from it.

The 1961-62 Kelvin yearbook reports that during February "[a] dance was held after the [basketball] game, in River Heights gym, and entertainment was provided by the Stardusters, a Kelvin group that was really fabulous! A Mexican Hat Dance and a few Twists broke the ice at the beginning of the dance, and it was pretty hot from then on!"

Neil's musical knowledge was growing exponentially, but he still had to deal with the constant distraction of school, homework and exams. Vice-Principal F. A. Hodgkinson reported on Neil's academic progress in a February 1962 letter[62] sent to Rassy (and then relayed to Scott):

Neil Young wrote a set of examinations in December at Kelvin High School. Although there is room for improvement, Neil is making a good attempt at handling his year. He is still handicapped to some extent by his transition from the Ontario to the Manitoba school system. With the aid of a tutor, Neil is trying to do two years' French in one year, and hopes to be able to handle the school examination in June.

Neil's December mid-term exam marks were unimpressive:

| SUBJECT: | MARK: |
| --- | --- |
| English Literature | 45 |
| English Composition | 62 |
| Geography | 44 |
| Algebra & Geometry | 55 |
| General Science | 69 |
| Industrial Arts | 65 |
| Physical Education | D |

When a pen and paper were handy, Neil sometimes distracted himself from schoolwork by drawing a character he referred to as a "Crot-Bonk," a comical line drawing that took about a minute to complete. He usually wrote *"I am a miserable Crot-Bonk"* under the drawing. There were slight variations in the drawing intended to indicate emotions, but usually it was the same dull face. Neil's Crot-Bonk drawings were often taped to walls or tucked into the notebooks of unsuspecting friends as a sign that Neil had been there. Sometimes his drawings were delivered to his friends via messenger. "You'd be sitting there," Richard recalls, "and someone would give you a Crot-Bonk and you'd look around to find [Neil]."

Come spring, there were troublesome signs that the Stardusters were beginning to unravel. Richard recalls that "things were sort of falling apart — we were teenagers." An incident in April reflected Neil's discontent. Richard and Linda, who were developing a romantic interest, went to a downtown coffeehouse called the Java Hut. A piano was available for patrons to play if they wished, and Linda gamely banged out a few tunes. While they were there, Richard got a phone call from Neil: Richard had no idea how Neil had found them, but "[he] was incensed that Linda was playing in such a public place." Richard felt it was Neil's opinion that "nice (good) women don't go to places like that and play the piano (making a public display of themselves)." It was the first time Richard had been exposed to this aspect of Neil's character — "a very straightlaced, very partitioned bit of him, I imagine." In a conversation with Richard later that day (or the next), Neil mentioned a few other perceived social infractions he thought Linda had committed. Fortunately none of this reached Linda, though she was familiar with Neil's temper: she had seen him get upset with the band more than once. She admittedly had a "different focus" than Neil did. He was "serious about the band," while she was "playing for fun." Richard felt Neil didn't make these distinctions; it never occurred to him that anyone in the band was or should be more committed than anyone else. They were all in it together, equally.

Linda and Richard "got serious" during the late spring. Richard recalls, "[Linda] and I spent every waking moment clinging to each other — true love and all that. . . . On any day I could probably have told you what she had for breakfast and dinner, who was at home, etc. And she likely could have done the same for me." Linda confirms that Richard was her "first serious boyfriend." At the time, Linda's home life was tumultuous; her father was an alcoholic and her mother an enabler, creating a stressful and sometimes violent environment for Linda and her four younger siblings. Richard provided a welcome and calming influence on her life. She was also starting to experience troubling health issues: she suffered from occasional spells during which she would pass out for about two minutes. These episodes became more frequent and of longer duration, and Richard insisted she see her doctor. She was admitted to the hospital and kept under observation for a month, but no definitive diagnosis was made. (It was felt that her condition was stress-related, possibly due to her problems at home, and she was prescribed appropriate medication.) Richard and Linda "technically" remained a couple until the 1963 Easter break, but it was basically "a summer romance," Richard says. In September he accepted a teaching position in the Cree community of Pikwitonei, situated at mile 214 along the Hudson Bay Railway line in northern Manitoba. He and Linda corresponded and then dated during his return for Christmas break, but their relationship dissolved shortly after he returned for the Easter holiday. Linda was devastated that he had "deserted her," and he came back to an unforgiving "wall of ice."

Frustrated, Neil had already left the band by the end of April. Attempts were made to replace him, but that was more easily said than done. A guitarist recruited from St. Boniface proved no match for Neil – he lacked the creative vision, leadership and sheer drive that Neil possessed in spades. A few practice sessions were held, but the band never played another gig and fell apart by mid-May.

A NUMBER OF DANCES WERE held at Kelvin during the second half of the academic year. The Avalanche Danche on Friday, January 19, was sponsored by *Et Cetera*, the student newspaper. The yearbook reported:

> "It's coming!" "What's it?" "Avalanche!" "Well run!" "No Danche!" was the well-remembered ad for this decidedly different dance. Abominable snowmen played hosts to a large crowd of Kelvinites who twisted, bunny-hopped and did other things under the streamers, tinsel and snowballs. The Del Rios[63] entertained with such numbers as "When the Saints Go Marching In," "The Twist" and "Night Train." For a grand climax, an avalanche of balloons descended on students and twisting teachers alike.

The yearbook-sponsored Reign Dance was held in March and included the crowning of Kelvin's king and queen. The Co-Ed Dance in May was a "girl-ask-boy" affair with proceeds going to the Kelvin Charity Drive. Entertainment was provided by the Sherwood Three, who played folk songs. According to the yearbook, "tables were set up in the auditorium, where 7-Up with lime sherbet was served. The decorations were extra-special, and added an extra touch to a terrific evening."

With a booming youth population, enthusiasm for teen dances spread rapidly throughout the city in tandem with an explosion in the number of rock-and-roll bands. St. Ignatius church on Stafford Street sponsored regular Friday- and Saturday-night Catholic Youth Organization dances. Barry Brazier recalls, "Everyone went to the CYO dance. Classic

*Happy Days* stuff. Boys on one side, girls on the other, lights were low but certainly not too low, and when a slow one came on there was a stampede to get to the girls on the other side of the dance floor." Other popular CYO dance spots were St. Mary's, St. Paul the Apostle and Our Lady of Victory.

CJAY-TV tried to keep up with the times by airing *Teen Dance Party* on Saturday afternoons in the fall of 1961. The show, taped at the Polo Park studio and sponsored by Pepsi-Cola, featured teens dancing to the latest records or local bands. It was hosted by popular CKY disc jockey Peter Jackson (a.k.a. PJ the DJ). The Chord U Roys played the first show, were well-received and became the show's house band for the next two years. PJ the DJ was replaced by Bob Burns in 1963. Regular dancers on the show included Jacolyne and Marilyne Nentwig, identical twins who attended Kelvin High, both of whom Neil dated at different times. They were members of the so-called "Pepsi Pack," a group of three boys and three girls selected to learn the latest dance crazes and demonstrate them on the show and at schools throughout the city. Their status as *Teen Dance Party* regulars lent the twins a certain high-school celebrity cachet. Neil visited the set once during the time he dated Jackie in late 1962/early 1963 but stayed offstage; he was too self-conscious to expose his rudimentary dancing skills to the camera.

FROM MAY TO AUGUST, NEIL performed on an ad-hoc basis with a number of different bands and musicians. It was during this period that he played rhythm guitar for Carmine La Rosa and the Thunderstorms[64] at a few community club gigs. Carmine played guitar and handled vocals; the other regular members of the band were Bill Craining (guitar), Ron Macri (sax) and Garry Rogers (drums). According to some accounts, Neil played bass and was fired from the band, but that's not how it happened, according to Carmine La Rosa: "During the time that Neil played with me he definitely played the guitar and not the bass." He adds, "I do not know how the rumour started that I fired him from the band. It seems to me that the media thrives on sensationalism. Every time Neil comes to Winnipeg the media badgers me to say that I fired him. I hope this will now lay [that story] to rest." Neil quit the band after about a month.

Mike Sambork,[65] a fellow student from Kelvin High, played a few "one-off gigs" with Neil. Neil and Mike practised with friends in a basement and on occasion managed to get a functioning band together. He recalls playing a session at Lord Roberts Community Club. Neil "wanted to play things his own way."

NEIL'S MARKS DURING EASTER EXAMS in April were again disappointing. The downward spiral had begun in earnest. In a letter[66] to Scott in early May, Neil first mentions some good news and then some not-so-good news:

> Dear Dad,
>
> I just got home from Tuxedo golf course. We were playing the practice round for the Kelvin Tournament. The temp was 40 degrees, the wind was 40 mph and it was raining, however. I was low man with 82 (43 – 39). The tournament is on Friday, at least, the qualifying round. My marks were bad.
> SC 50
> Geog 50

Maths 39
Lit 50
Comp 47
Fr 24
I will be much higher than this in June. However, I have already started studying for the exams.

Scott sent his prompt and pointed response:[67]

I was happy to hear about your good score in the practice round for the Kelvin tournament, but that didn't diminish the shock of those marks to any great extent. Your mother said in her letter that some of your exam papers were better than the marks showed, because of the 1-2-3 system, but since the marks generally seemed worse than the Christmas ones, which were bad enough, it's difficult to understand where the improvement was.

I think that somebody has to do some new and serious thinking about where you are going in life. . . . You could do yourself a lot of good if you made a substantial improvement in your final exams, but with the record you have that will take hard, unremitting work — not sitting around assuring people, including yourself, that everything is going to be all right.

Neil's brother Bob visited Winnipeg during May 1962, prior to participating in a major amateur golf tournament back east. Bob was a skilled golfer and hoped one day to make a living as a tournament player. (Alas, it would remain an ambition unfulfilled.) Scott asked Bob, who was more serious about his studies and had already graduated from Pickering High School, to speak to Neil about his poor grades. In a May 1962 letter[68] to his father, Bob wrote:

> I've been talking to him [Neil] about his schoolwork, etc. He is trying and I'm sure he'll make it. He wants to come in the summer for about 3 weeks. You'll hear more about that in a week or two.

NEIL WAS ALREADY PLANNING TO make Ken Koblun his next bass player, for a new band called the Classics. He took the same blunt approach he had used with Richard Koreen: "Why don't you play the bass?" Ken readily agreed — the idea appealed to him.

In *Waging Heavy Peace*, Neil reports that Ken ordered his first (or second) bass through Cam's Appliances on Osborne Street, but according to Ken, "I bought my first bass second-hand, not new. A new one would have been too expensive for me at the time. I may have gone with Neil once to Cam's on Osborne Street to check something out or inquire, but that was all."

Neil knew Richard wanted to sell his Danelectro, the one that had earlier belonged to Jim Kale. Ken confirms, "I was just learning to play and he [Neil] asked me to get a bass guitar from this guy [Richard Koreen] who had one for sale. It was a Danelectro bass that used to belong to Jim Kale."[69]

Richard agrees: "Yes, I sold the magic bass [Jim Kale's] to Ken." Wanting to recoup his investment, Richard pegged the price at $50. After a little haggling — Ken wanted a lower price because he'd have to invest $15 in new strings — Richard agreed to part with the bass, cables and case for $35. He was trying to be nice about it but remembers being "a bit pissed" that he didn't get his full investment back.

Now Ken had his electric bass, but he still needed an amplifier. Arthur Koblun and Harvey Clayton joined forces to build one from parts. Ken remarks, "I diversified and divided the labour between my foster father and my biological father." Harvey assembled the vacuum-tube electronics and installed the tiny amp in a large "top box" with holes on the sides for ventilation and holes in the back for access to connectors. He also procured a 10-inch jukebox speaker. "I was grateful he did it," Ken says. "It showed that he was interested in what I was doing." Arthur built the cabinet and painted it black. Ultimately, however, the amplifier proved inadequate for Ken's needs — it simply wasn't powerful enough.

Ken practised playing his Danelectro for a month before he landed his first official gig, on an outdoor stage on the grounds of the Red River Exhibition. The date was July 1, 1962 — then called Dominion Day — and it was Canada's 95th birthday celebration. The show was filmed by local station CJAY-TV. Ken accompanied a pianist and an accordion player. He can't remember which song they played, but he does remember that it was in the key of E flat. He didn't know what he was doing, and his performance didn't add up to much: he just played some random notes and was "underwhelmed" by the whole experience.[70] By the mid-1960s the Red River Exhibition recognized the drawing power of bands and began staging a Teen Fair, with local groups showcased on six outdoor stages in the large parking lot on the grounds.

NEIL SAW ONE OF HIS idols in a memorable performance at the Winnipeg Civic Auditorium[71] in the early 1960s: "I saw Roy Orbison at the top of his fucking game in '61 or '62. Winnipeg. Roy and the Candymen. They kicked ass."[72, 73]

The auditorium was located at 200 Vaughan Street near St. Mary Avenue and Memorial Boulevard, a block from Portage Avenue. Grant Park student Glenn Church recalls that it was "a weird auditorium — like a glorified basketball-gym atmosphere." The building was constructed of Manitoba limestone, the same material used for the interior of the Parliament Buildings in Ottawa. The auditorium space was on the main floor, which also housed a municipal museum and an office. A second level provided additional seating for the auditorium.

Neil had been an Orbison fan since he first heard "Only the Lonely," a hit when Neil was in Toronto visiting Robinson's Records with Comrie Smith. Neil has singled out Orbison's "Evergreen" as "one of the most beautiful sentiments ever recorded"[74] and has cited "Blue Bayou" as another Orbison song he particularly liked. "I loved Roy Orbison from the beginning. . . . Great singing, great arrangements, great records. . . . They were revolutionary records. Hit after hit after hit . . . totally off the wall."[75] Just as Neil recognized that Bob Dylan had a unique voice, he recognized and admired the same quality in Orbison. "[He's] got a weird voice. Beautiful — but weird. Opera-velvet kind of a sound."[76]

Roy Orbison's influence would be lasting. Neil cites Orbison in the lyrics to "Twisted Road," included on *Psychedelic Pill* (2012): *Singin' in the place where I first saw Roy / Playin' in that place gave me so much joy.* Given that Neil never played at the Winnipeg Civic Auditorium,[77] he may be referring more broadly to the City of Winnipeg.

Decades later Neil revealed to Nick Kent that he had seen Orbison many times during 1962. "I saw him in Winnipeg, saw him all over the place that year," Neil recalled. "Got to talk to him once outside a gig. He was coming out of his motor-home with his backing band the Candymen. That had a profound effect on my life. I always loved Roy. I looked up to the way he was, admired the way he handled himself. That aloofness he had influenced me profoundly. It was the way he carried himself . . . with this benign dignity."[78]

Neil admitted to deejay Tony Pig in a 1969 KSAN radio interview that the melody for "Flyin' on the Ground Is Wrong" was partly inspired by "Blue Bayou." "There's a little piece of Roy on every album I've done," Neil said. He has admitted that "Don't Cry," which appears on *Eldorado* — a 1989 EP released only in Australia and Japan — is heavily indebted to Orbison. Neil describes it as "Roy Orbison meets heavy metal."[79]

Also important for Neil was an appearance by the post–Buddy Holly Crickets at a roller rink in the old dance pavilion at Winnipeg Beach, a resort 95 kilometres north of the city. "I remember watching them set up their own stuff," he says. "They had a Cadillac and a U-Haul."[80] It was around the same time that Neil caught Dick Clark's Cavalcade of Stars — eight artists and a band, with Fabian as master of ceremonies — at the Winnipeg Civic Auditorium: "Those were my glory days."[81]

SCOTT GREW INCREASINGLY CONCERNED ABOUT Neil's lack of progress at school, where things had gone from bad to worse. He wrote a letter to Kelvin High principal R. J. Cochrane to see if anything could be done to pull Neil out of his academic nose-dive. He received a pointed response from Vice-Principal Hodgkinson in late June 1962:[82]

Dear Mr. Young:

I am answering your letter to Mr. Cochrane as I have had more to do with Neil.

Neil has had a very poor year at Kelvin. We have tried to help him but have not succeeded. I have talked to Neil and his mother, and so has Mr. Hunter from the Child Guidance Clinic.

Neil is very emotionally disturbed, I feel. Unless there is a complete change in his outlook, I am afraid that Kelvin cannot help him. He has played truant and flouted Kelvin rules on several occasions. We came very close to asking Neil to withdraw but realizing that he is very mixed-up in this thinking, we decided to give him a second chance.

As you probably know, Neil has the ability to do well in high school. But until his thinking is straightened out, there is not a chance of academic success. At Neil's age, it is imperative that he be helped immediately if his capabilities are to be realized.

If your son will be spending some time with you this summer, you may be able to do something about his difficulties. Perhaps you would be wise to get professional help, but you

---

FROM TOP: *Richard Koreen's rendering of a Crot-Bonk, similar to the type of simple comical line drawings that Neil was known to make.* [© 2012 Richard Koreen]; *1123 Grosvenor Avenue, Crescentwood. Neil and Rassy lived in the upper duplex.* [© 2009 Sharry Wilson]

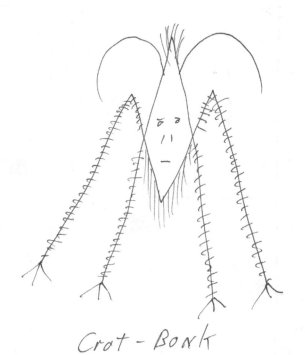

Crot - Bonk

will be able to judge this matter better after you have spent some time with him.

Sincerely,
F. A. Hodgkinson,
Vice-Principal.

Scott responded in a letter[83] in early July:

Dear Mr. Hodgkinson:

Thank you very much for your letter of June 21, which will be helpful to me in trying to help my son when he visits here for a few weeks this month.

His brother, who lives with me, and is twenty, also will do what he can to help.

I have been very concerned about this matter for more than a year but previously did not wish to get in touch with you directly lest my action caused further confusion and upset to Neil.

Any time there are problems in the future in which I can help, in any way by coming out there, I will be glad to do so.

Yours sincerely,
Scott Young

Neil flew to Toronto in mid-August to visit Scott and Astrid shortly before the birth of Neil's half-sister, also named Astrid. He stayed for about a week at their spacious home at 280 Inglewood Drive in Moore Park, the same neighbourhood where Neil had lived while attending Grade 4 at Whitney School. (By this time Bob was no longer living with Scott and Astrid — he had apparently been disrespectful toward Astrid, and it was thought best that he relocate.) Scott spent "every spare minute" with Neil, working hard to rekindle their faltering relationship. They spoke about school — Scott had taken Vice-Principal Hodgkinson's words to heart — and also about Neil's passion for music. They bonded over a game of golf, driving to the course in Astrid's TR-3 sports car.

Neil returned to Winnipeg for the rest of the summer. He and his mother had recently moved to classier digs at 1123 Grosvenor Avenue in Crescentwood, closer to Kelvin High and a step up from their Fort Rouge apartment. They lived on the upper floor of the lovely old home and enjoyed access to a spacious third-floor attic room.[84]

But Neil failed his year at Kelvin, and as summer drew to a close he was faced with the prospect of repeating Grade 10. Musically, the coming year would be an exciting and fertile time for him. But his school career had hit bottom.

★ 9 ★
# KELVIN HIGH SCHOOL (YEAR TWO):
## The Classics, The Squires

THE FALL OF 1962 WAS a busy time for Neil. As well as juggling the incessant demands and irritations of school, he was carefully assembling his third band, the Classics.

The lineup seemed solid. Neil himself would play rhythm guitar. Ken Koblun had already been groomed to fill the slot as bass player — when Neil formally asked Ken if he'd like to join, he had jumped at the chance — and Linda Fowler agreed to lend her talents on piano once again. Neil was looking for a drummer, and Linda suggested Buddy Taylor, who lived seven houses down the street from Linda's family. She often heard him practising when she walked past his house, and she could tell he was a skilled drummer. Neil agreed, and asked Buddy to join the band. Rounding out the band were Jack Gowenlock on lead guitar and John Copsey[85] on vocals. (Neil and Jack occasionally switched positions, Neil playing lead and Jack playing rhythm.) Jack and John had met at River Heights Junior High and were already friends.

Jack, now enrolled at Kelvin, became musically acquainted with Neil in the early fall. He recalls that on one occasion — prior to the formation of the Classics — he, Neil and Jim Atkin played together in a park. John Copsey's bio in the River Heights Junior High yearbook describes him as "a guitar player," although he specialized in his vocal talents while attending Kelvin.

Practice sessions were usually held at Linda Fowler's home, where the band had access to a piano. Linda helped Ken find the appropriate notes on his bass, since his playing was still rudimentary. "He was not a blazing talent," Linda recalls. "He didn't have a natural flair for bass playing." His skills must have improved quickly, however, given that Neil thought highly of Ken's bass playing once the Squires — Neil's next band — became a cohesive unit. "We worked together well, supported each other," Neil remarks. "Ken was a good friend. He was always ready to go. And he was into it. There was a good bass player — when Ken was into it, he was pretty fuckin' cool."[86]

Ken's large hands — complementing his nearly six-foot-six frame — were ideally suited to span the longer scale on the bass guitar's fretboard. But his acoustic guitar skills couldn't simply be transferred to the larger instrument. Neil suggested Ken take in a show by Allan and the Silvertones. "They were the best musicians in town. . . . They played everywhere and got all the big gigs," Neil declares. "They were simply the best."[87] Ken had played the Danelectro three or four times at gigs with the Classics when he heard a deejay announce on CKY that Allan and the Silvertones would be appearing at the Riverview Community Club one evening during the fall. He went on his own to the show and was so impressed with what he heard that he went up to the stage afterwards to have a word with Jim Kale. He said, "I like your work. I like how you play. Can you show me a few things?" Jim agreed, and the two arranged to meet.

Ken went to Jim's home at 53 Clonard Avenue in St. Vital. Jim asked him what he knew how to play and then said, "Here. Play my guitar." (It was Jim's Fender Precision bass that he had ordered through Cam's Appliances the previous fall. Ken recalls that Jim's bass was highly distinguishable because it had an indentation where Allan Kowbel's Jazzmaster guitar had accidentally been dropped on it. There was a mark in the indentation that resembled a circle with an X in it, like the head of a Phillips screw.) Ken proceeded to play "Blues in G," a simple chord progression. Jim pronounced, "You can now play the bass." Jim put a copy of *The Shadows* (the band's first album, available only as a U.K. import) on the record player. Ken was immediately taken with the band's melodic instrumentals, and when he came back for a second visit he brought along a tape recorder to capture the sounds for himself. He listened to the tape obsessively, trying to reproduce those sounds. The album included a version of "Apache," which Ken and Neil knew from a cover, performed by Danish jazz guitarist Jørgen Ingmann in 1961, that had reached No. 1 on Canada's CHUM Chart. The number would become a regular entry on the Classics' set list.

The Shadows were an English instrumental group comprising Hank Marvin on lead guitar, Bruce Welsh on rhythm guitar, Brian Bennett on the drums and Jet Harris on bass.[88] Originally a backing band for U.K. pop sensation Cliff Richard, they called themselves the Drifters in 1958 but changed the name to the Shadows after they secured a recording contract with EMI the following year. The Jerry Lordan tune "Apache," released in July 1960, was their first hit single. The song enjoyed huge success in the U.K. but flopped in the American market, where surf-music instrumentals by bands such as the Ventures and the Fireballs were more popular. The Shadows, known for a clean and distinctive melodic sound complemented by echo and vibrato effects, were pioneers of the four-member rock-group format — lead guitar, rhythm guitar, bass and drums.

Ken was able to obtain a U.K. import of *The Shadows* through Roger Herring, a friend of his foster brother, and he remembers "playing it to death." Because his father worked at the British Consulate in Winnipeg and had connections in the U.K., Roger became an important source of British record imports. Through Roger, Ken managed to score a handful of important titles, including *Out of the Shadows*, the Shadows' second album (not yet released in Canada), and *Please Please Me*, the Beatles' first U.K. import. He shared these records with Neil as soon as he got them, well before they were available to the broader Canadian audience.

Allan and the Silvertones were also enthusiastic fans of the Shadows and adopted many of their songs early on. Wayne Russell, a friend of Allan's, shared import albums from England, which meant the group was always playing the latest hits from the U.K. long before anyone else. Shane Fenton & the Fentones, Johnny Kidd & the Pirates and Mike Berry & the Outlaws were other bands whose tunes they covered.

Neil and Ken went to see Allan and the Silvertones as often as their schedule permitted. Neil had profound respect for the band: "Randy's playing was an inspiration for a lot of my sound. . . . The Silvertones did not have a weak link. Their singer Allan Kobel [sic] was really great. Bob Ashley on piano was unreal. He could really rock and play anything from Floyd Cramer to Professor Longhair. Jimmy Kale, the bass player, was totally unreal, and he helped us a lot. . . . He was a good friend."[89] Neil and Ken liked to stake out a place close to the stage where they could scrutinize the guitarists' fingering and figure out which chords were being played. While Neil focused on Randy's playing, Ken kept a close eye on Jim Kale. "I mostly learned all that stuff from watching Randy Bachman, though," Neil remarks. "He knew more about music than I did, so he'd learn it, and I'd learn it by watchin' him."[90] Randy recalls, "I remember both Neil and Ken coming to many gigs. . . . I remember Neil asking me about the songs and where I got them and how I learned them. I was playing 'Apache,' 'Kon-Tiki,' 'Man of Mystery' and 'Mustang,' and our lead singer Chad Allan was singing Cliff Richard songs like 'Living Doll,' 'Move It,' 'Dynamite,' 'Pointed Toe Shoes,' 'We Say Yeah' and 'Summer Holiday.' We were totally different than any other local band because of this British repertoire we played."[91]

Randy Bachman had picked up some of his chops at an early age, during the late 1950s, when he was fortunate enough to meet future jazz legend Lenny Breau, then working with his parents Hal "Lone Pine" Breau and Betty Coady. They were appearing as part of the CKY Caravan event being held in the parking lot of Gelhorn Motors on North Main Street in West Kildonan, near where Randy lived. Randy bicycled to the concert from home one Saturday. He was enjoying the show when Lone Pine and Betty left for a break and turned the stage over to "Lone Pine Jr." Randy took immediate notice

FROM TOP: *John Hart Copsey, vocalist in the Classics.* [Courtesy of John Michael Copsey, nephew of John Hart Copsey]; *Playlist for the Classics, 1962.* [Courtesy of Jack Gowenlock]

23. Let's Twist Again.
24. Harbor Lites.
25. Torquay
26. Jammy
27. Handy Man
28. Green Door.
29. Where Have They Gone.
30. Bo Diddly
31. Road Runner
32. The Breeze & I
33. Teardrop
34. Sleepwalk
35. Ivory Marbles
36. Fright Water
37. Chu my sne.
38. Fried Egg.
39. Wonder Land by Night
40. Granada.
41. Apache'
42.

1. Don't Make Me Cry
2. " Ever Leave Me
3. Wise Men
4. Su-pu-ill-pi
5. Diana
6. Dream Lover
7. Tall Cool One
8. Lest We Forget
9. Panic Button
10. Vaquero
11. Summertime
12. Greensleeves.
13. Twilight Time
14. Midnight Has Been
15. Doin the Best I Can
16. Bunny Hop
17. Sarah Lockman.
18. Green Velvet
19. Runaway
20. Alley Cat
21. Kansas City.
22. Baby Blue

of the beautiful guitar a young Lenny was playing. Randy recalls, "He had a big orange Gretsch with a big black letter G burned into the body like a brand on a cow. It was called a Gretsch 6120 Chet Atkins G Brand Model."[92] (A photo taken at the Rainbow Dance Gardens in 1958 shows Lenny holding the1956 model with its distinctive letter G branding and an unusual custom-installed Bigsby tremolo bar in an S shape. The Chet Atkins line of guitars was introduced in 1955, with the first few model lines clearly oriented to the country-and-western market.) Randy approached Lenny and asked him what style of music he was playing. Lenny told him it was Chet Atkins, so Randy went to the record store and bought a copy of "The Third Man Theme." He took it home, listened to it repeatedly and taught himself first the bass line and then the melody. Equipped with this new knowledge, he approached Lenny a few weeks later at another CKY Caravan at a car lot in the North End. Lenny recognized Randy, who asked if he could come to Lenny's home sometime and have him show him a few things on the guitar. Randy was thrilled when Lenny agreed. For the next few years the informal teaching arrangement continued. First Randy learned how to play Chet Atkins–style guitar, and later, rock and roll, in a first-rate if informal musical education.

Although he originally owned an acoustic guitar, Randy began seriously practising on his first electric instrument — a black, single-cut, one-horned Silvertone model U2 1303 made by Danelectro and ordered through the Sears catalogue for $35. In 1961 Randy bought an orange Gretsch 6120 Chet Atkins guitar similar to Lenny's for $400 from Eddy Laham at the Winnipeg Piano Co. Randy's first Gretsch — visible in photos taken with Chad Allan and the Reflections — was a 1959 model, distinguished by the small "neoclassic" inlays that replaced the old-model "hump-block" fretboard markers. Randy's Gretsch also featured the company's own "humbucking" Filtertron pickups in place of the older models' DeArmond single-coil pickups. All Chet Atkins models featured his signature printed on the pickguard.

Using the Gretsch, Randy mastered the echo effect (in addition to the guitar's vibrato arm) that was crucial to recreating Hank Marvin's distinctive sound. His mentor Lenny Breau had been one of the first musicians in Winnipeg to employ an echo effect, using an EchoSonic amp. Designed by Ray Butts in the 1950s, the EchoSonic was the first commercial amp with a built-in tape echo instead of the more common spring reverb, and it had been used to great effect by Chet Atkins and Scotty Moore (Elvis's guitarist). The next advance was the Echoplex, an external tape-delay effect designed by Mike Battle in 1959.

Hank Marvin of the Shadows used an Echoplex, but the devices were hard to come by in Winnipeg, and Randy contrived a way to make a home-brewed equivalent. Bob Ashley's mother, a French schoolteacher, had an old German Körting tape recorder, and Bob mentioned that you could get an echo effect if you swapped the Record and Play heads. Randy convinced Bob to let him use the tape recorder. "I had special patch cords made," Randy recalls, "and plugged my Gretsch guitar into his tape recorder and from that into Jim Kale's Fender Concert amp. I got the most incredible echo sound from that little homemade system. That became *my* sound."[93]

"Randy was definitely the biggest influence on me in the city," Neil says. "He was the best. Back in those days he was years ahead of anybody else in the city. He had a homemade [E]choplex from a tape loop on an old tape recorder. He did the Shadows' style better than anybody else."[94] Neil zeroed in on the guitar Randy was playing and decided that he needed to get one, too: "He was playing a big orange Gretsch guitar and I got one just like his [in September 1963]. I still play an orange Gretsch like that one today. My heroes were guys like Bachman and Kale. I always thought Randy's guitar playing was great."[95]

In the meantime Neil continued to play his Gibson Les Paul Junior, with an eye to eventually acquiring the orange Gretsch. "I tried to make a reverb out of a garden hose," he recalls. "It didn't work too well. You stick a mike in the end of the hose and wrap the hose along the way — about fifty feet of it. You have a small speaker on the other end and you put, like, a funnel on — the sound goes into the garden hose, through a funnel, out the other end into the microphone, back into the fuckin' amp. . . . I could never get it to work."[96]

THE CLASSICS CONTINUED TO REHEARSE and began to play their first gigs. Band member Jack Gowenlock, who played a 1960 Silvertone, recalls practising with Neil in the attic at 1123 Grosvenor Avenue. (Jack met Rassy on several occasions and thought she was well-suited to her nickname: she was "irascible" — "Quite a woman!") Neil used a small Ampeg amp, likely the same one he had used in the Stardusters, and Jack had a small Fender amp.

Jack has kept a playlist from his time in the Classics. Instrumental songs with guitar and piano leads predominate. "Apache" is one notable inclusion, as is the Santo & Johnny hit "Sleepwalk," also covered by the Shadows on their first album. "Teardrop," another popular instrumental by Santo & Johnny, is also represented. "Panic Button," "Vaquero" and "Torquay" by the Fireballs are prominent, while "Ivory

Marbles" and "Alley Cat" are two of the piano-led songs. And although it doesn't appear on the playlist, Jack remembers the band performing a rocked-up version of Beethoven's "Moonlight Sonata." A few other novelty songs lightened the mix, including "The Bunny Hop" and "Sarah Jockman" (a play on "Frère Jacques"). "Don't Ever Leave Me" and "Diana" by Paul Anka are included, as is "Dream Lover" by Bobby Darin; John Copsey provided the vocals for these. Some of the songs Neil originally played with the Jades and the Stardusters are on the list, such as "Fried Eggs," "Ku-U-I-Po," "Can't Help Falling in Love with You," "Tall Cool One," "Road-Runner," "Runaway," "(The) Green Door," "Let's Twist Again" and "Harbor Lights." Interesting additions on the Classics' playlist include "It Might Have Been" and the iconic folk tune "Greensleeves," two favourites that would often appear on Neil's future set lists. Another folk-sourced inclusion is "Where Have All the Flowers Gone?" The Kingston Trio's cover had been a huge success in 1961; Peter, Paul & Mary's 1962 version was even more successful.

The Classics played their first gig on November 17 at Churchill High, the school Ken and Linda attended. Another Churchill student, Clive Morrison, helped the Classics land a better gig on December 21. Clive commuted to Kelvin to attend an electrical shop class, which was where he had met Neil — Clive was a smoker, and Neil occasionally bummed cigarettes from him. They soon discovered a common interest in music. Clive happened to be a member of the teen council at Riverview Community Club. Sensing an opportunity, Neil asked Clive if the Classics could be booked there. At the time Riverview mainly used deejays to spin records for teen dances, but Clive was able to arrange a booking for the Classics. They were allotted one hour to perform between the traditional record-spinning sessions. The Classics were one of the first live bands to perform at the venue, for which they were paid the grand sum of $25.

During this time, Neil became much tighter with Ken Koblun: "He [Ken] was one of the nerdiest and I was one of the geekiest. We hit it off." Ken recalls, "I'd go over to Neil's house often and we'd sit in his room and talk about music."[97] Something else Neil and Ken enjoyed doing together was smoking: "Real men inhale," Neil insisted.[98] (Neil was eventually able to give up the habit, but Ken was not as successful.) Every once in a while, when Rassy was out of the house, Neil would filch a few Black Cat Plain cigarettes — her favourite brand — and he and Ken would sample them. Ken would even, at least occasionally, light Neil's cigarettes for him.

Ken was a list-maker by nature, and he began to compile a record of all the live shows he played, beginning with the Classics' first official gig at Churchill High. Ken originally titled this the "List of Shows,"[99, 100] while Neil later referred to it as "the Gospel According to Ken."[101, 102] (See Appendix A.)

Ken explains why he started keeping the list: "I thought I would not be in music all the rest of my life. At least that's what I thought later on. At the time I thought I wanted memorabilia of the things I had done in music. I wanted a list of things I had done, so that I would know I had done them." Looking at the six-page list from the perspective of the present, it's impressive how many gigs he played over the years — 141 with the Classics and the Squires. "Some of those early gigs were scary," Ken remarks. "When you don't know what you're doing, it can be really frightening."[103]

Ken's record of the live shows is meticulous, but he admits it's not flawless: "I kept the list as accurate as possible under the circumstances. Sometimes I had to insert information later on when I had the time, and my recollection of the dates might have been imperfect. It's quite possible that I missed listing a few gigs as well."

In a supreme display of historical detail-mindedness, Ken noted which members of the Classics appeared at each gig by writing their initials beside the venue. The Classics were booked at Kelvin High School on November 24 for their second live show. Buddy Taylor wasn't able to make their third show at the Wentworth High Club on December 8, so a Kelvin High student named Jack Harper took his place. Neil and Jack shared a homeroom class and had recently become friends. Jack was a successful athlete who devoted much of his spare time to sports, but it was music that connected him to Neil. From the moment Jack told Neil he played drums, he and Neil became lifelong friends. Jack would play an important role in helping Neil form the Squires, his next band — by December Neil was already making plans in this direction.

Jack had attended Grade 9 at J. B. Mitchell Junior High on the western edge of River Heights the previous year, and he lived with his family on Carpathia Road. Jack had become friendly with Allan Bates, another J. B. Mitchell student, who lived at 566 Beaverbrook Street and would also become a founding member of the Squires.

Allan played a German-made Framus 5/130 Hollywood guitar. The instrument, Allan recalls, "had a single pickup which was mechanically moveable. It could be moved toward the neck for a more mellow sound or back toward the bridge for a harder sound." Allan had begun playing the guitar when he was nine, his first lessons given to him by "Dusty" Despins, the janitor at the elementary school he attended — Dusty gigged at various lounges in the evenings. Allan began taking formal instruction but quit after about four sessions. He learned more from friends of his older brother, some of whom played guitar and were willing to show him how to finger various chords.

At one point Allan and Jack appeared on a local TV show called *Junior Highlights*, playing an arrangement of Duane Eddy's "Forty Miles of Bad Road" for guitar and drums. They were also part of a four-piece band that played the Grade 9 graduation dance at J. B. Mitchell in June 1962. A photo from the event shows Allan with his Framus guitar, and two giant flags — a Union Jack and the Canadian Red Ensign — adorning the wall behind the band. He and a second guitarist, Jim Hatch, plugged in their instruments to a record player provided by the school; Beverly Mazur played the piano and Jack played the drums.

Unlike Neil, Allan excelled in academics and sports as well as music. He moved on to Grade 10 at Grant Park High School, while Jack attended Kelvin. Glenn Church was in Allan's Grade 10 class at Grant Park. "Allan sat at the desk right in front of me in homeroom in Grade 10, so we talked," Glenn remarks. "He was very friendly and very popular with the guys and girls. Very bright too." The 1962-63 yearbook notes that Allan was a member of a singing group (Bernie and the Vampires) that supplied entertainment at the Freshie Dance on September 12. They sang "The Football Mash,"[104] "Let's Dance" and "Cotton Fields." Allan was captain of the basketball team and would serve as president of the school during 1964-65, his final year at Kelvin. While still in high school he appeared on the CBC as a studio musician and later played with jazz greats Lenny Breau and Reg Kelln: "I played bass for Lenny Breau in the late '60s and early '70s, about five times at places like the Coach Manor Lounge and Jazz A Go-Go."

Neil himself was notably absent for a Classics gig on December 8 at the Morse Place Community Club. He came back for their gig at the Riverview Community Club on December 21 but was AWOL again for the Classics' last performance, a CYO dance at St. Ignatius on December 29. By this time the band was concluding its business, fulfilling previous commitments.

Neil was busy assembling what would become his next band, the Squires. Jack Harper, who agreed to take on drumming duties, recommended his good friend Allan Bates to play rhythm guitar, and Neil agreed. Bassist Ken Koblun moved directly from the Classics to the Squires. The group rehearsed over the Christmas break in Jack's basement. A photo taken at the time shows a crude homemade amp that Allan and Neil shared — it features two globe-shaped vacuum tubes mounted on a square wooden cabinet. Neil holds his Gibson Les Paul Junior, while the back of Allan's Framus guitar is visible. Ken, in the background, sits next to the homemade bass amp his foster father and biological father had built for him.

The band practised hard, trying to master enough songs to fill a full evening's performance. They concentrated on popular rock instrumentals by the Ventures, the Fireballs and the Shadows. "I was mainly into instrumental groups," Neil says, "so I paid a lot of attention to them."[105] He admired Lonnie Mack and wanted to play like him, but he wasn't skilled enough for that just yet. "As time went by I got better. I learned how to play like Hank Marvin a little bit. But I *still* couldn't figure out what Lonnie Mack was doing. What a great player he was. 'Memphis,' 'Wham!' That was great stuff."[106] Neil adds, "I always liked primitive rock and roll." He cites Link Wray as another early influence: "He was the

245

beginning of grunge way before anyone else."[107]

December proved especially busy for Neil. The Christmas examination schedule had been posted at Kelvin High School on November 29, amid the ongoing nuisance of construction work aimed at modernizing the school. The Kelvin yearbook reports, "Ominous signs in many classrooms greeted students with a warning, 'DO NOT OVERLOAD.'" The upheaval was especially evident on the second floor. Students disregarded *Keep Out!* notices and took shortcuts through the construction site, flirting with danger and risking injury.

Rassy wrote Scott a letter[108] in early December to tell him he could expect a large dental bill soon. She had had some necessary but extensive work done on her teeth, and so had Neil. Rassy wrote:

> Neil's front tooth, which you may recall was broken off some years ago, abscessed and had to be removed. He now has a temporary plate, for a year or so and there is a possibility his second incisor may have been affected by the infection.

Neil's left front tooth was the one most affected. At Earl Grey Junior High he was known for his discoloured tooth, described as having a bluish tinge. Neil discovered he could crack up his friends by yanking the temporary replacement tooth from its socket and grinning broadly.

Neil added a note on the end of the letter:

> Dear Dad,
>
> . . . I had a few tough breaks on exams but did well enough to stand eighth. The first [tough

break] was losing my British Hist notes which cost 20 out of 25 term marks bringing me a 43. The second was leaving out a section in the maths worth 15 marks for a 55. I failed French — 34 and will have to work still harder to pass it in June. Others were Science 77, Geography 57 (class average 54) and I have last year's credits in Comp & Lit [English]. From a realistic point of view I must consider summer school for French, in the event that I don't pass it at June, so I will not apply for any summer jobs this early. If I see that my report is good in June I will get some kind of job here.

Neil's exam marks may have been less than inspiring, but he still received a much-welcomed Christmas gift. Neil had been expressing his keen desire for an amplifier for over two years now. In the meantime he had begun using a "small Ampeg" during his time with the Stardusters/Twilighters/ Teen Tones and then during his time with the Classics. "First I was using another guy's amp and then I got my own,"[109] he says. Neil was familiar with his friend's Ampeg and almost certainly asked his mother for a similar unit.

A photo[110] of the Christmas celebration at Toots and Neil Hoogstraten's home shows family members gathered in the living room. A large, gaily wrapped package (obviously containing an amplifier) sits in the middle of the floor. The photo is date-stamped "JAN 63," and a caption written by Rassy on the back of the photo reads: "Xmas at Toots' & the famous amplifier over which so much anguish was spent."

Anguish aside, it was surely a more pleasing gift than the usual sweater. Ken Koblun remembers an Ampeg "combo" amp with its distinctive blue Tolex skin and a chrome control panel on top. It was equipped with a 12-inch speaker and could generate 30 watts of power. Neil confirms, "My first amp that I had was an Ampeg Echo Twin."[111] The Ampeg ET-1 was first produced in November 1961, so it was most likely a year old when Neil received it, and it would last a couple of years more: Neil references the demise of this amp in a letter written to his father in May 1964.[112] It was a prestigious instrument for the leader of a young band to own. Ken Smyth, who would soon replace Jack on drums, remembers visiting Neil shortly after he received the amp from Rassy. "She bought him a good amp," Ken says. "We all went over to his place and we walked in and there was this big amp and we thought 'oh boy!' She was behind Neil, no doubt about that. He was her pride and joy."[113]

Reverb and tremolo effects, necessary for emulating the distinctive sound of the Shadows, were built into the amp. By this time Neil had also become interested in distortion as a musical effect. The 1958 hit instrumental "Rumble" by Link Wray & His Ray Men, one of Neil's favourites, featured a distortion-laden "dirty guitar sound." He had first heard the song in Toronto with Comrie Smith, and it was one he still admired after moving to Winnipeg. "That was just hairy," Neil recalls. "It was great. I wanted to play like that. I learned how to do that and then I became fascinated with why it sounded like that. It was the beginning of Fuzztone and effects."[114] Gibson had introduced the Fuzz-Tone pedal under their Maestro brand in 1962, although musicians had been experimenting with the effect since the late 1950s.

Neil's love affair with distortion and feedback became a hallmark of his collaborations with Crazy Horse over the years. Their performances since 1986 are notorious for "lengthy instrumentals in which distortion and extended playing techniques would considerably elaborate upon the aspects of 'rock as pure sound,'"[115] writes musicologist William Echard. Author and Neil Young aficionado Robert Clark Young coined the colourfully appropriate term "grunge-jazz-feedback"[116] to describe this style of playing. Neil remarks, "I love distortion. I thrive on distortion."[117, 118]

ONE OF WINNIPEG'S IMPORTANT SEASONAL social events happened shortly before the end of the year. It was the Humpty Dumpty Ball, held on December 28 at the River Heights Community Club, and Neil attended with Jacolyne Nentwig as his date. (Neil's friend Rick Dubord attended with Jackie's twin sister, Marilyne. The four of them are joined by two other couples in a photograph taken at the event, a larger-than-life-size figure of Humpty Dumpty looming ominously in the background.) The Humpty Dumpty Club was a charitable organization that raised funds for sick children in hospitals. Membership in the club was exclusive, the annual ball was rather snobbish, and you needed an invitation to get inside. The Nentwig sisters from the Fort Rouge area were not considered social equals by the Humpty Dumpty crowd, but had somehow managed to score an invitation for themselves and their dates. The girls wore fancy dresses, white gloves and corsages; the boys dressed in dark suits with carnations in their lapels. There is no record of how they were received at the dance, but Neil would continue dating Jackie casually over the next few months.

The Squires continued to practise and played some informal local gigs, including a teen dance in a church basement. The rehearsals conflicted with Jack Harper's hockey and school athletics schedule, and Jack chose to leave the band, another hockey casualty.

Allan Bates suggested as a replacement Ken Smyth, who played drums in music class at Grant Park. Ken's father had bought him his first set from a pawnshop when Ken was 13 and attending River Heights Junior High. In the school yearbook, the caption next to Ken's name describes him thus: "Nice looking boy with a cute little curl in the middle of his forehead is Room 13's Ken. His mind wanders from girls to girls and back to girls. He is very easy to get along with and is always full of fun." Ken learned to drum on the pawnshop kit, but it proved to be substandard. His next set — the one he played during his entire career with the Squires — was a 1950s John Grey Autocrat Super kit from the U.K. His parents were impressed by his devotion to the Squires and allowed regular weekly practice sessions — usually on Saturday afternoons — to be held in their basement at 735 Waterloo Avenue. Ken remarks, "We always practised at my parents' house as I was the drummer." The family's 12-foot-long tournament snooker table was an added attraction. Friends of the band and curious neighbours often dropped by just to hang out, listen and lend support.

Neil's friend Clive Morrison, who had helped book a gig for the Classics, arranged for the Squires to play their first official gig at the Riverview Community Club on February 1,

---

CLOCKWISE FROM TOP: *Humpty Dumpty Ball, River Heights Community Club, December 28, 1962. Group photo with Neil standing at extreme right with his date Jacolyne Nentwig et al.* [Courtesy of Wayne Smith with assistance from the late Richard Dubord]; *Ken Smyth, drummer in the Squires.* [Courtesy of Ken and Sharon Smyth]; *Portage Avenue, circa 1960s.* [Courtesy of Stan Milosevic]; *Allan Bates, rhythm guitarist in the Squires.* [Courtesy of Allan Bates]

1963. They were paid the impressive sum of $5 for the appearance. Two weeks later they played Grant Park High and earned twice the amount. Sometimes the band played for free, accepting gigs for the sheer pleasure of performing before a live audience. "We used to just play on the weekends and practise a little bit during the week in basements or garages," Neil recalls, "and we played high school dances and community club dances and stuff like that in our dark glasses and our suits we had. Sometimes the band would share 10 bucks or something among us — that was pretty good, just the fact that we were getting paid something to do it was great, kind of reassuring at the beginning."[119]

One of the Squires' earliest gigs was a basement party in South River Heights. The invitation-only private party took place at the home of Linda Gibbons, a classmate of Glenn Church and Allan Bates from Grant Park High. Linda's father was a U.S. consular official, and the family resided in Winnipeg for only one year. Several fellow students attended, including a healthy representation from Glenn's homeroom class. Glenn fondly remembers the party, though not the set list. He felt lucky to have received an invitation: "I was in the right homeroom at school."

Soon the Squires were securing weekend bookings at various high schools, community clubs and church basements. Richard Koreen, Neil's old bass player from the Stardusters/Twilighters/Teen Tones, was present at one of the Squires' earliest gigs at St. Ignatius church. The Squires played a "coffeehouse" in the basement, and Richard remembers them covering "Kansas City." Ken Koblun ventured a bass solo on the Danelectro he had purchased from Richard and seemed pleased with the result.

Allan Bates recalls that "Harbor Lights" was an important

song during this period — "I think it was Rassy's favourite." Allan also remembers singing "You Belong to Me" in a comical Donald Duck voice.

The Squires developed an extensive repertoire of material by the Shadows, including "Apache," "FBI," "Kon-Tiki," "The Savage," "Shindig," "Spring Is Nearly Here," "The Rise and Fall of Flingel Bunt," "Blue Star" and "Wonderful Land." (Neil and Randy Bachman would later collaborate on a version of "Spring Is Nearly Here"[120] for inclusion on *Twang! A Tribute to Hank Marvin and the Shadows*, released in 1996.) Hits from the Ventures and Fireballs were also part of their constantly expanding repertoire.

"We could all play our instruments, right from the beginning," Allan Bates remarks. "Ken Koblun was on bass and it was rare to find a bass player who could play, never mind own his own instrument. And Ken Smyth was really good. Every night he'd do a long drum solo, where we'd put our guitars down and all the kids would gather around."[121] Although the Squires concentrated on instrumentals, vocalist John Copsey occasionally sat in for a few songs. Jim Atkin joined the band as percussionist in mid-May and would remain with the Squires for three months.

Allan's older brother Ray built him an EICO hi-fi component amp from a kit. The EICO 2536 receiver, able to pump out 36 watts into an 8 ohm speaker, meant that Allan now had an amp that more or less matched Neil's in power. Allan has strong memories of his EICO amp: "Mainly he [Neil] had the Ampeg and I used the EICO, which was a hi-fi kit my brother soldered together. I had a huge homemade speaker cabinet."

Ken would sometimes borrow an EICO HF-12 integrated amp from Jim Kale. The 12-watt mono amp was actually owned by Allan Kowbel of Chad Allan and the Reflections, but it was the amp Jim most often used. (Allan also owned a 35-watt EICO HF-35 that Ken would eventually purchase from him in April 1965.) The HF-12 was designed as a hi-fi component, and Allan Kowbel constructed a 10-inch speaker box to connect to it. Jim Kale stored the amp at his place and was willing to loan it to Ken when he wasn't using it.

Jim was well-known for his willingness to help young bands in need of decent equipment. Both Ken and Neil appreciated his help. Ken remarks, "Jim Kale took me and Neil under his wing." Don Marshall, drummer of the Esquires, says of Jim's excellent reputation, "Jim would help all the musicians anytime, whether backing them up or loaning his equipment. He was generous to other up-and-coming musicians, bad or good."

In addition to the EICO amp he periodically lent to Ken Koblun, Jim sometimes allowed the Squires to use his Fender Concert amp. Jim's Concert amp was well-known in the Winnipeg music community. "He had the best amplifier in town at the time," Don Marshall recalls. Jim had purchased the Concert amp and a black Fender Precision bass in the fall of 1961 at Cam's Appliances. The Fender P-bass had a tortoise pickguard and a mounted bridge cover, which most bass players removed. No inventory was kept at the store, but instruments could be special-ordered from a desk at the back. Jimmy Gillies had given Jim a good deal — $960 for both the amp and the bass. Unfortunately, his order got mixed up — unusual for Cam's, which had a sterling reputation.

Jimmy and his two brothers, Bud and Gar, owned and operated Cam's, which would continue to cater to the evolving Winnipeg music scene. In the mid-1960s Thomas Garnet "Gar" Gillies began custom-building more powerful amps for rock-and-roll bands, and by 1966 these had evolved into the Garnet line of amplifiers, which became the most popular brand in the city. The Garnets were sold out of a new location dedicated solely to music, on Ellice Avenue near Ferry Road. The Gillies brothers were considered amplifier gurus, pioneers in the field who were willing to extend credit to cash-strapped young musicians in need.

Nevertheless, Jim Kale still had a problem. He had ordered a Fender Bassman, but received a Concert amp instead. Unsure how to go about making an exchange, Jim decided to keep the Concert amp even though it wasn't meant to amplify a bass guitar but was designed to handle the less demanding midrange of a conventional guitar; low frequencies could drive it into noisy, buzzing distortion. Jim decided to press on, but played with "great frustration," and the amp produced a sound he compared to "an elephant passing gas." The amp was covered in brown Tolex, had two channels and four inputs, and drove two pairs of 10-inch speakers with 40 watts of power. "It was the biggest amp in Winnipeg at the time," Jim recalls. Neil remarks, "Kale let me use his Fender Concert amp. I thought I was in seventh heaven. He'd lend us stuff all the time. He was in a band that was doing a lot better than mine, yet it didn't bother him to help us."[122]

Jim was a welcome visitor at 1123 Grosvenor. He met Rassy on several occasions and was impressed by her strength of character. "Neil is very much like Rassy. She had the biggest balls in the world." Jim adds, "Neil is very driven. He acts like he has 'something to prove.'" Both Jim and Neil took their involvement with music seriously — it wasn't just a hobby to them. Jim recognized that he and Neil were alike in this respect.

Neil began to show an interest in learning to play the piano. He tried out his skill on an old, out-of-tune piano stored in the basement of the duplex at 1123 Grosvenor, much to the consternation of the tenants on the main floor. Classmate Sue Cox believes she gave Neil his first piano lesson (though he would have been exposed to plenty of piano players within his extended family). Sue and Neil had both attended a school pep rally in January 1963 aimed at selling tickets to *The Fortune Teller*, a Victor Herbert operetta that would be presented at the Playhouse in February. The yearbook reports, "Mr. Belyea, Mr. Hoole and Mrs. Cuddy were involved in hysterical practices for the operetta as opening night was fast approaching. A pep rally was held at which students were encouraged to 'SELL! Sell! Sell!'" Sue remembers sitting down to the piano with Neil at a friend's house after the rally and showing him the basics. "He had this wonderful ear and he played in that fashion," she says, "so the thought of knowing the notes was totally unnecessary to him."[123]

One of Neil's major piano influences was Floyd Cramer, who had had a huge hit with "Last Date," an instrumental released in 1960. Cramer was famous for his "bent note" or "slip note" style, which influenced a generation of musicians. Chad Allan and the Reflections were part of that generation, releasing a piano instrumental called "Back and Forth," the B-side of "A Tribute to Buddy Holly," released on the Canadian American label in 1962. Although Neil's piano playing was in its infancy, he persevered and began to regularly feature piano selections at his concerts by 1970.

NEIL WOULD SPEND A LOT of time that year in his bedroom writing songs — guitar instrumentals with strong, catchy melodies. He knew instinctively that it was important for musicians to write their own material — to create their own distinctive sound — and had said as much a year ago, in

Kelvin's basement with Richard Koreen. Now the Squires began incorporating some of Neil's original instrumentals into their repertoire of old pop tunes, waltzes and covers of the Shadows, Ventures and Fireballs. Two of these songs — "The Sultan" and "Aurora" — would eventually give the band their first big break.

The other Squires were conscious of Neil's prolific output. "Right from the beginning," Ken Smyth remarked, "Neil had his own stuff. Half of our stuff, easy, was his own. It just kept comin', one after another . . . it seemed to be endless. 'Come to practice, I got a new tune.' And it always seemed to be catchy."[124] Allan Bates also noticed Neil's songwriting talent: "Neil was writing really nice melodies with nice harmonic changes in 'em. Something your ordinary run-of-the-mill guitar player wasn't doin'."[125] Randy Bachman remarks, "He was already writing his own songs. Other than us [Chad Allan and the Reflections] most bands in the city weren't doing that yet."[126]

This lineup of the Squires, after the departure of Jack Harper, proved to be the most stable, lasting almost two and a half years. Ken Koblun says it was also the strongest lineup:[127] "I think it was good because we kind of grew together for a while. We became better as a group."[128] Ken adds, "[Neil] was pretty serious about the band. We'd rehearse really well so we knew the songs, and of course, Neil would be writing his own stuff. The Squires' music went in the form of a progression, from instrumentals to vocals and then original songs."[129]

The members of the band were becoming very close, doing things together. Allan remembers excursions with Neil to the Winnipeg Piano Co. Pianos, organs and sheet music occupied the main floor of the shop, but the real attraction was the guitar section in the basement, where brand-new electric guitars by Fender, Gretsch and Gibson lined the walls and amplifiers were displayed on the floor. Guitarists avidly studied the equipment and were allowed to try out different makes and models. Business cards and want ads for musicians were pinned on the wall in the basement, and a lot of casual networking happened there. "Neil loved playing hooky from school," Allan recalls. "He thought it was a total waste of time, so we'd go to Winnipeg Piano, where they had these great guitars in the showroom. We'd get the guy to take the guitars out of the cases and you could even smell them. We'd spend an afternoon doing that."[130] Another destination was Lowe's Music on Kennedy Street.

Both music stores were located near the main intersection in downtown Winnipeg. Randy Bachman famously mentions the intersection — *Portage and Main, fifty below* — in the song "Prairie Town," and acoustic and electric versions of the song bookend *Any Road*, an album released in 1993. (Neil appears on both tracks.) Winnipeg's Main Street follows the course of the Red River, while Portage Avenue follows the flow of the Assiniboine. The two rivers meet at "the Forks," just behind the intersection of Portage and Main. A gigantic Coca-Cola sign looming over the intersection relentlessly flashed the time and current temperature.

Every weekend, teenagers were drawn to Portage and Main by a kind of relentless adolescent instinct. They typically congregated along a six-block strip of Portage Avenue between T. Eaton & Co. and the Hudson's Bay Company, rival chain department stores. The S. S. Kresge and Co. store, with its distinctive large red lettering facing the street at 368 Portage, offered a soda fountain with generous seating in plush vinyl-covered booths. The store also had a popular record counter. Woolworth's, on the southeast corner of Donald and

Portage, had its own lunch counter but no booths. Hot beef and turkey open-face sandwiches slathered with gravy were the specialty of the house. Other attractions near Portage and Main included clothing stores, record shops — and, of course, the movies. The Capitol Theatre was handy on the northeast corner of Portage and Donald, while the Rialto Theatre was located a bit farther west at 362 Portage Avenue. The Metropolitan Theatre — popularly known as the Met — stood at 281 Donald Street near Portage. Other movie houses were located along Main Street, not far away.

The Paddlewheel, a restaurant on the sixth floor of the Bay, was often the final destination for teens after an afternoon spent patrolling the strip, checking out records, clothing and musical equipment. The restaurant's decor included a replica paddlewheel spinning in a trough of water that also served as a wishing well. Affectionately called the P-Wheel or the Wheel, the restaurant was a place where band members and their fans mingled in a casual, fun and exciting atmosphere. According to Kelvin student Natalie Pollock, "On Saturday afternoons it was *the* place to pick up boys. You met everyone there." Randy Bachman recalls, "Besides meeting your fans, that's where all the bands would catch up with each other and find out what we were all doing, where the good and bad gigs were, what new songs were being played, or who was in or out of a lineup. Because you were gigging all the time, you rarely got the chance to hang out together and compare notes."[131]

The Squires continued to have a hectic schedule. Fran Gebhard, then a student at St. Mary's Academy, attended their performance at a CYO dance at St. Ignatius in May. Fran's friend Natalie Pollock recalls, "She [Fran] looked like Mary in the group Peter, Paul and Mary . . . blond hair with long straight bangs were so in style."[132] This was Fran's first experience of the Squires, and she was immediately captivated by Neil. She told Natalie, bluntly, "I'm in love with this guy and plan to go out with him." She began to follow the Squires' gigs just so she could see and be near Neil, who was "the livin' end." At this point they still had not yet met face to face or talked. She simply admired Neil from afar and, in classic teenage fashion, wrote about him at length in her diary. She liked his "quiet presence" and considered him a "master guitar player"; he had "terrific charisma," but "didn't flaunt it like Burton Cummings." An observant Catholic, Fran went to mass for four months and prayed that Neil would notice her and ask her out.

June was a whirlwind month at Kelvin. School awards were presented early in the month, followed by the election of the school president. Neil received no academic awards (unsurprisingly), but he did participate in activities in support of one of the candidates for school president — Pete "the Magic Dragon" Barber. Neil and friends Tim Henry, Charles "Chic" Bell and Don Thompson composed a parody sung to the melody of "Puff the Magic Dragon," retitled "Pete the Magic Dragon" for the occasion. Tim held up signs with the lyrics so students could sing along. Posters Tim had made incorporating *Mad* magazine icon Alfred E. Neuman festooned the hallways at school, urging students to cast their vote for Pete. The campaign was only partly successful — Pete didn't garner enough votes to be president, but was given the second-place slot of vice-president.

The middle of June brought final exams and high anxiety for most Kelvin students. This time Neil managed passing grades, except in typing, which he was required to repeat the following September. He was still a year behind in French, and would be enrolled in Grade 10 French in September as well. Otherwise it was full speed ahead for Grade 11.

School was finally out for the summer, and Neil intended to focus his energies on music. He knew he wasn't alone. Winnipeg's rock-and-roll scene had already spawned more than a hundred ambitious young bands, all competing for an audience. Popular local groups included the Shondels, the Deverons, the Crescendos, the Eternals, the Viscounts, the Roadrunners, the Del Rios, the Continentals and the Phantoms, to name just a few.

Teenagers typically latched on to a favourite band and followed it from gig to gig. Fan clubs were formed and members recruited to swell their ranks. Diana Halter,[133] daughter of Nola Macdonald (one of Rassy's co-panellists on *Twenty Questions*), started the one and only fan club dedicated to the Squires. One day when Diana was backstage visiting her mother and waiting for shooting to begin, Rassy approached her and exclaimed, "OH! You HAVE to come to my house on the weekend and hear my son and his friends play the guitars! Gawd! They drive me CRAZY!" Diana accepted the invitation and decided to start the fan club after watching a couple of rehearsals at 1123 Grosvenor. "I began the fan club standing on the back of the sofa in Rassy's living room," she recalls, "after taking a lot of photos of the Squires with Rassy's baby Brownie camera. We prepared sheets of paper with basic fan information: birthdate, favourite colour, pet peeve, etc. My friend Susan Gee and I hand-drafted each sheet, and gave them out to friends." Diana was a member of the teen council at the River Heights Community Club, where she helped to recruit bands for performances. She recalls that the Squires' shows were always sold out.

Another popular gathering spot for teens was the Salisbury

House restaurant,[134] which had several locations throughout the city and is considered, even today, a Winnipeg institution. Two popular locations in the 1960s were the original site on Fort Street with its distinctive "little red roof" (opened in 1931) and another on Pembina Highway at Stafford. The Squires often stopped by "Pembina Sals" after a gig. Neil liked listening to popular hits on the old Rock-Ola jukebox.[135] One play cost a nickel, and among Neil's favourites was the song "Four Strong Winds," written by Ian Tyson. The single by Ian and Sylvia, featured on their second album by the same name, was released on the Vanguard label during the early fall of 1963. "Four Strong Winds" became a Canadian classic, the song most readily identified with Ian and Sylvia. Neil first heard it at Pembina Sals: "There was this place where we used to go where you could put a nickel in the jukebox and 'Four Strong Winds' was on it. . . . I used to play it all the time. That's where I heard it for the first time and I loved the song. I listened to it over and over. It just caught my attention."[136] He adds, "I've always loved it. It was the most beautiful record I heard in my life and I could not get enough of it."[137] Neil later wrote, "'Four Strong Winds' by Ian & Sylvia speaks to me always. It occupies part of my heart. There is a feeling in it. I love the prairies, Canada, my life as a Canadian."[138] He would eventually include the song on the *Comes a Time* album in 1978, and he continues to perform it regularly.

Winnipeg bands traditionally frequented their favourite Sals location after they finished jamming, practicing or playing a gig. The Pembina Sals opened in 1954, but was demolished to make way for a new edition of the restaurant, which opened on April 2, 2012. A memorabilia collection at the new Pembina Sals includes among its artifacts a

Winnipeg Jets electric guitar, signed by Neil and hockey legend Bobby Hull.

The Red Top Drive-In Restaurant at 219 St. Mary's Road in St. Vital was another popular meeting place for teens, especially on weekends. It opened in 1960 and was an almost instant success. Bands congregated there during their off-hours, but the weekend evenings were when it was really hopping. According to former Earl Grey student Barry Brazier, "It was just like *Happy Days!*" — a perfect place to hang out with friends, enjoy a burger and root beer, and meet your favourite band members. CKRC deejays including Boyd Kozak, Jim Paulson and Bob Washington blasted the latest rock-and-roll hits from a trailer in the parking lot under the restaurant's distinctive circular red sign, announcing bands and their members as they pulled in for car service. Future Squire Jeff Wuckert remarks, "It was quite a thrill to hear your band name and some bandmates mentioned." Barry fondly remembers the Red Top's friendly car-hop service, with pretty young girls delivering orders to the cars. "The guys really loved that. . . . Cars would drive round and round in the parking lot, rarely taking the time to pull in and order something, just preferring to cruise in circles until it was time to leave and cruise another hangout."

Neil seldom had enough money to buy a meal at the Red Top. According to Jeff Wuckert, it was Neil's routine as the driver of Rassy's car to collect a few dollars from passengers for gas expenses. Neil would then use the cash to dine on cheaper fare at Paul's Hamburgers on Pembina Highway, where the burgers were only 19 cents (as opposed to the Red Top's higher-priced — but far more palatable — 25-cent burgers). Jeff Wuckert explains that his long-time girlfriend and then-wife Judy Wallis hated Paul's because "the drive-through window was infested with flies and she didn't trust the food." Nevertheless, Neil would buy four Paul's hamburgers and then go to the Red Top to be "announced," meet other members from bands and allow the other passengers in the car to get something more appetizing.

Some local bands had already issued recordings, and local radio stations CKY and CKRC supported the development of the youth music scene by promoting favoured bands on the air. Individual deejays identified bands they felt worthy of support, played their records on air and perhaps even served as an announcer at their gigs. The deejays also announced upcoming teen dances for community clubs, church basements and high schools throughout the city. In turn, the deejays became celebrities in their own right. Peter Jackson — PJ the DJ — was extremely popular, as were Dino Corrie, Mark Parr, Daryl B, Dean Scott, Chuck Dann, Jimmy Darin and Gary Todd from CKY. Popular counterparts at CKRC included Doc Steen, Boyd Kozak, Bob Bradburn, Frank Todd, Don Slade, Jim Paulson, Ron Legge and Bob Washington. Both stations recorded live bands — there were few other formal recording venues available to emerging bands.

The Squires became more popular and were beginning to draw significant crowds by mid-1963. This attracted the attention of deejay Bob Bradburn, who was always on the lookout for new talent. Bradburn began plugging their engagements on his CKRC radio show and hosting their gigs at community clubs.

On July 12, Bradburn arranged an audition for the Squires with the station's recording engineer Harry Taylor. Taylor recorded many of the city's earliest rock sessions and was a huge supporter of the local music scene. The small two-track recording studio was on the second floor of the radio station's offices at 300 Carlton Street, in the old Winnipeg

Free Press building. According to Ken's "List of Shows," both of Allan Kowbel's EICO amps were loaned to the Squires for this audition.

The band ran through 15 to 20 of the best selections from their repertoire. Neil recalls, "The first day we played all of our songs so we could hear how they sounded when recorded. It was very exciting, and I was really jacked up."[139] They were invited back for another session a week later so Taylor could once again hear two promising instrumental songs Neil had written — "The Sultan" and "Image in Blue." It was at this session that they worked on possible arrangements. "At the time," Neil recalls, "it was decided that 'Image in Blue' needed a name change so that Bob Bradburn could say the title at the end of the record in echo."[140] The band picked "Aurora" as the title without any input or complaints from Neil, who was happy just to be given the opportunity to record. Taylor was impressed, and a July 23 recording date was booked. Neil recalls that the CKRC recording studio "had a pair of mono tape recorders, some EQ, some echo, and a control board. The mixing was done live."[141]

Both songs are notable for their evocative melodies and an obvious stylistic debt to the Shadows and surf-guitar bands such as the Ventures. Prerecorded gong accents added by Taylor to "The Sultan," and Bradburn's portentious whisper at the end of "Aurora," gave both songs an exotic ambience.

Bob Bradburn pitched the songs to local record labels. Surprisingly, V Records — a label that specialized in ethnic music, most notably Ukrainian polkas — agreed to release it. Owner Alex Groshak, who started V Records in 1962, hoped the Squires' single might help the label capture a share of the burgeoning youth market.

Groshak ran V Records out of the basement of his

family home at 15 Fleury Place in the Windsor Park area of St. Boniface. The most successful act on the label was the duo of Mickey and Bunny, who played Ukrainian polka music and traditional tunes.

Mickey and Bunny Sklepowich[142] released several successful albums on V Records, including *This Land Is Your Land*[143], *Ukrainian Country Music*, *Country Roads* and *Faces from the Past*. Mickey had constructed his own recording studio, Studio Star by Bunny, in the basement of *his* home — a three-bedroom bungalow at 11 Gilia Drive in Garden City, West Kildonan. The duo felt they could cut costs by recording their own albums, and they made the studio available to other bands for a reasonable rate. Mickey himself was the recording engineer. It was a "sound-on-sound" or "low-tracking" studio, using a basic one-track reel-to-reel tape machine. The studio had a cement floor, and the walls were treated with acoustic material to absorb sound and dampen echoes. The only other options for bands seeking to record were the tiny but better equipped two-track studios at CKY and CKRC, also available for a modest fee, or, more expensively, Arbuthnot Recording Studios on Tache Avenue in St. Boniface or Inland Broadcasting on Notre Dame Avenue. (Mickey and Bunny also made use of their living room, where they photographed the front cover for two of their Christmas albums — *Mickey and Bunny Sing English Xmas Carols in Ukrainian* and *Mickey and Bunny Sing Traditional Ukrainian Carols*. The cover for an album by the D-Drifters 5, *D-Drifters 5 Sing and Play at a Ukrainian Concert*, was also photographed there.)[144]

Mickey and Bunny's basement evolved into a popular hangout for musicians, especially the other acts on V Records. (The Squires would later record here.) Dave Roman (Romanyshyn) of the D-Drifters 5 was one of those who frequented the studio. His band, known as the originators of Canadian-Ukrainian rock and roll, also recorded on the V label and were Mickey and Bunny's backing band for four years in the mid-to-late-1960s. They also released their own albums, including *The D-Drifters 5 Sing and Play Beatles Songs — and Other English Hits — in Ukrainian.* Their cover of "Farmer John" appears on this recording. The song — written by Don and Dewey — was a band staple of the day, and the Squires included it in their repertoire when they played the Fourth Dimension coffeehouse in Fort William. "Farmer John" was also the first song during which Neil really abandoned himself to his guitar: "The first time I really got off playin' a guitar, I just went nuts. We were playing 'Farmer John' — something happened. I went completely berserk. I just got lost in it. And then when I came off the stage, people were looking at me different."[145] He adds, "I was just startin' to find myself."[146] The song remained a sentimental favourite, and he would record a version with Crazy Horse for the 1990 album *Ragged Glory.*

THE SQUIRES' 45 RPM SINGLE, "The Sultan" b/w "Aurora," was listed in V Records' catalogue as V-109. About 300 copies were pressed in Montreal and distributed locally in November,[147] with promotional copies going to radio stations. The majority of the copies were sold through local record shops. (Surprisingly, Ken Koblun never received a free copy; he had to go to a store to buy one.) The 45, with its distinctive yellow label, has since become a much sought-after collectible. Decades later, Jack Harper gifted Neil with a copy signed by all of the other Squires who played at the recording session.

Bob Bradburn played the single during his mid-morning

time slot at CKRC, and Neil heard it while he was driving with Ken Koblun in Rassy's car. "I felt so good," he recalls. "I am sure I was walking on air for weeks."[148] After an initial burst of interest, the single failed to catch fire, but reaction was positive enough to garner increased attention for the Squires. It was quite a coup for a young band whose members were still attending high school to have a single played on local radio. It was suddenly much easier to land gigs.

In an attempt to secure copyright on the songs, Neil had a friend transcribe the chords and lyrics on staff paper, which he then tucked into an envelope and mailed to himself, along with an affirmation that "I, Neil Young, wrote this song." (The idea was that the sealed letters, sent via registered mail with a date-stamped cancellation, would prove he was the author.) When Rassy passed away in 1990, Neil found among her possessions the two still-sealed envelopes.[149]

Neil mentions the Squires' single in an important if typographically imperfect letter[150] to his father in late December. He says (verbatim):

Dear Dad,

I am trying to type this letter on the typewriter that Mother gave me for Christmas. You can tell that I am not used to it yet. I'm sorry that I didn't answer your birthday present. I just found the letter that I forgot to mail to you the other

---

FROM TOP: *Distinctive circular red sign advertising the Red Top Drive-In Restaurant, St. Vital.* [© 2009 Sharry Wilson]; *"The Sultan" b/w "Aurora" was the Squires' only single.* [© 2001 Stephen Cross]

day. some of these sentences have grave errors in them but if I started over again I would be at it all night. Thanks for the sweater and the money, L an making very good use of both of them. Our record will be released on January 8, and rather than me sending a copy to you, I would like you to buy one there. This would not be too easy. You might have to have it ordered specially. The Sultan/Aurora are the titles of the songs/ I wrote both of them. the promotion copies are doing very well on the radio stations here. It is on the "V" lable. Thanks again and love to everybody.

Love,
Neil

Neil's mention of a release date of January 8, 1964, is puzzling, since there is evidence that the single was released locally much sooner. Perhaps a second press run was planned but never materialized.

A nugget of additional information about the Squires' single can be gleaned from a short (and also typographically imperfect) piece by an "uncredited author" that appeared in the October 16, 1963, issue of *Et Cetera*, the Kelvin student newspaper:

TWANG!

In our midst, we have a future recording star. Neil Young and the Squires, sponsored by CKRC, have made a recording on the Vee label. On one side is "The Sultan" and on the other,

"Aurora." Neil plays lead guitar, while Al Bates is on lead??? Ken Smyth on drums and Ken Koblen on Bass. The record now being pressed in Montreal is expected to be released in the near future. The squires now have a contract with CKRC for weekly Friday Night High School Dances this year. This is an up and coming instrumental group with a bright future.

After a hiatus of over four decades, Neil resurrected "The Sultan" during his 2007 Chrome Dreams Continental Tour. First playing it as the final number of a three-song encore at the Chicago Theatre on November 13, 2007, Neil included it as an encore number throughout the tour and during his 2008 tour of Europe.

A PAIR OF GIGS AT the Crescentwood Community Club bookended the Squires' recording time at CKRC, followed by gigs at Glenwood and West End Memorial during the end of July and the first two weeks of August 1963. Jim Atkin was still in the band but would soon be departing. We know Jim left the band because song entries under the listings for *Vibes (Fast)* and *Vibes (Slow)* — as well as "Bongo Rock" under *Drums* and songs listed under *Vocals (Jim Atkin)* — have been crossed out in one of Ken Koblun's encyclopedic song lists. (See Appendix B.) What's striking about this particular list is that it includes a number of Neil's earliest instrumental compositions. Under the entry for *Guitar (Fast)* are "Image in Blue (Aurora)" and "The Sultan." (Ken added "Aurora" in parentheses after the song was retitled at their recording session.) At least four other original compositions — "Banana Mashed," "Red Eye," "Comanche" and "The Ghost" — are also included. ("Comanche" is crossed out with the notation by Ken that it "needs work.") "White Flower," "Green Velvet" and "The Shepherd" — all original instrumentals written by Neil — are listed under *Guitar (Slow)*. Ken confirms that Neil had written a number of different instrumentals at the time, in addition to the two songs recorded for their single. Many of the same numbers on the song list — such as "Apache," "Panic Button," "Ku-U-I-Po," "Summertime," "Runaway," "Walk Don't Run," "Fried Eggs," "It Might Have Been," "Alley Cat," "Harbor Lites," "Torquay," "Teardrop" and "Greensleeves" — were played earlier by the Classics, and earlier still by the Stardusters/Twilighters/Teen Tones.

Another summer was drawing to an end. The Squires played a Labour Day gig on Monday, September 2, from the back of a Coke truck in the parking lot at Topp's Discount Fair at 700 St. James Street, across the street from Polo Park, the city's largest shopping mall. A Topp's ad in the August 31 edition of the *Winnipeg Free Press* advertises the gig as an "Open Air Dance Party" taking place from 7 to 10 p.m. As an added incentive, Topp's offered "free Coke for everyone," records (20 of Elvis Presley's latest LP, *It Happened at the World's Fair*) and other prizes. The weather was brisk, even for early September in Winnipeg. CKRC was broadcasting live from the event, and Bob Bradburn introduced the band. Ken Koblun recalls that Jim Kale loaned him his Fender Precison bass: "It was really cold that day and a member of the audience handed me a pair of well-worn brown leather gloves to wear." Ken managed to play even with gloves on, since the Fender's frets were more widely spaced than those on his Danelectro. He played wearing gloves until the audience member asked for them back. The band earned $40 for the performance.

The new school term began the next day. But for Neil, school and music had become warring nations competing for his time and attention. He was ready to declare his loyalty, and he knew which side he was on. His third year at Kelvin would be his last.

## ⋆ 10 ⋆
## KELVIN HIGH SCHOOL (YEAR THREE):
### The Squires (Continued)

FOR NEIL, SCHOOL HAD BECOME a frustrating distraction. If music was everything that mattered, school was everything that got in the way. It was a place that demanded his presence and his attention but offered nothing that spoke to the deepest part of him.

Kelvin's student government had introduced a new house system in an effort to encourage school spirit, and the student body was divided into four houses: Kerr, Roblin, Saunderson and Gilbert. Neil was assigned to Saunderson House in Class XI-33, along with his friend (and former Squire) Jack Harper.

Uniforms were still obligatory. Red and grey were the official school colours. Grade 10 Kelvin student Lynne "Hammy" Hamilton, who would soon begin dating Allan Bates, recalls the dress code: "We had to wear a drab grey skirt, a white shirt, white bloomers/shorts with elastic bands around the top of the legs and a cherry-red-coloured scarf around the neck." Boys could be expelled for wearing hair that fell below their collar. Many students, both male and female, supplemented their uniforms with a complementary sweater of their own choosing.

Kelvin placed heavy emphasis on sports, a world in which Neil felt perennially misplaced and self-conscious. The school's shiny new gym did nothing to improve his performance. Classmate Roger Currie recalls, "His [Neil's] somewhat frail health was largely unknown to our phys. ed. teacher, Mike Kachmar.[151] Mike was also the football coach, and in gym class he could have been mistaken for a military drill sergeant as he whipped us through sit-ups and pushups. I recall more than one occasion when Neil was just about in tears and Kachmar spared him no quarter."[152] Coach Kachmar seemed to delight in berating Neil for his lack of suitable gym attire and his general ineptitude. Interviewed by Jimmy McDonough many years later, Neil's phys. ed. teacher said, "[Neil] was a tall, gawky-looking character — I always worried that if there was a strong wind we'd have to put lead in his running shoes just to keep him down. Throwing a football at Neil? Well, you hope it didn't hit him in the head. Kind of an awkward individual."[153]

"I think I just was different," Neil later remarked. "I wasn't athletic and I just wanted to play in my band. And I wanted to go and play on the weekends and write songs. And I used to draw pictures of stages and the way the equipment would be set up to get a certain sound and what would be the best. I spent a lot of time researching that in school when I should have been doing other things."[154] Roger Currie confirms, "Truth is, Neil didn't have many close friends at Kelvin, unless they were into music. Academic studies certainly took a back seat to his guitar."[155]

NEIL WAS WRITING NEW SONGS at a furious pace. On September 15, he recorded one such song, the instrumental "White Flower." ("At present Neil Young and the Squires are booking local dances and preparing themselves for their new release 'White Flower,'" the *Winnipeg Free Press* reported a year later.) Neil recalls, "It was an instrumental that was supposed to be the follow-up to 'The Sultan.' It was pretty cool."[156] The tape has been lost,[157] but luckily Ken Koblun recorded the chord progressions on one of the song lists he kept from his time with the Squires. (See Appendix C.) As Ken notes, "They're common chord patterns of the time. . . . A number of different melodies could work." Neither Ken Koblun nor Allan Bates nor Ken Smyth remember the melody — apparently it was a slow-tempo number. "It was a pretty thing,"[158] Neil recalls.

Writer, musicologist and Neil Young historian Ralf Böllhoff has studied the chord progressions in greater detail and reports, "It can be seen that the intro is a typical '50s rock-and-roll chord progression: C, Am, F, G7. The verse is a bit unusual. There's no repeated structure (each line is different), and the Em and Dm chords are odd for a song written in C major. The bridge contains two bars in each line with half bar chord changes (four chords in two bars). The chord progressions contained in the bridge — C, Bb, Bb, C7, and then C, Bb, Bb, G7, are strange. The use of the G7 (dominant 7th inside the

CLOCKWISE FROM TOP: *Ken Koblun holding his 1962 Höfner 182 bass.* [Courtesy of Ken Koblun, © 1965 Don Baxter]; *Ken Koblun's transcription of chord progressions for "White Flower," dated April 13, 2012.* [© 2012 Ken Koblun]; *Dinner party held in the basement of Lynne Hamilton's house at 414 Brock Street in Winnipeg, December 1963. Left to right: Neil, Betty Wood, Sharon Krentz, Ken Koblun.* [© 1963 Lynne Hamilton]

WHITE FLOWER
CHORDS by Neil Young

Transcription
by Ken Koblun 9.13.12

C major key) makes more sense than the C7 in the previous line. However, the chord structure works somehow. It's a song composed by a teenager, not a Beethoven masterpiece."[159]

Allan Bates was impressed with Neil's songwriting. He sometimes went to 1123 Grosvenor to practise guitar with Neil: "I'd . . . sit in his living room and he'd say, 'Here's a new one I've just written.' And even then this guy had that creativity. He used to blow me away. I'd say, 'Man, is that ever a great song.' These songs he was writing in Grade 10 and 11 were really something, songs like 'Mustang,' 'The Sultan' and 'I Wonder.' Most bands would only be doing covers back then, but we'd be playing Neil's original stuff too."[160]

NEIL'S GIBSON LES PAUL JUNIOR guitar began to show some shortcomings as time went on. One day in the early fall of 1963, the Squires were rehearsing in Ken Smyth's basement as usual. ("[Neil] was a real rehearsal guy," Allan remarks. "There was no messing around.")[161] According to Allan, Neil was getting electrical shocks from the guitar.[162] He grew increasingly frustrated and tossed the instrument down on the floor. Allan recalled, "He just really wanted this band to work so bad." The story may have become exaggerated over time, however: Allan reflects, "I know that Neil doesn't remember it. Neil told Jack [Harper], 'Smyth's parents were so nice to let us practise in the basement — why would I do that?'" Allan adds, "Well, when you get the final-straw shock, you don't immediately think how nice Ken's parents were. You get mad and chuck. Maybe it was a lesser chuck — but it stood out for me for many years. That's my story and I'm sticking to it." Ken Smyth has no memory of the incident; Allan thinks Ken may have been upstairs when it happened.

Neil himself reports a more significant problem: the Gibson

Les Paul Junior "was hard to keep in tune. I didn't know that the intonation could be adjusted, so it went on like that until I got my next guitar."[163] The Les Paul Junior — Gibson's low-end electric guitar at the time — had a cheap and primitive bridge. The strings were wrapped around the bridge, and the intonation had to be fixed by adjusting the entire bridge using two small screws on the back. A common problem of the Les Paul Junior was that it could break where the intonation screws hit the bridge. Neil was either unaware that the intonation could be adjusted by means of the two screws, or he found the process of adjusting them frustratingly difficult.

Other guitars were more attractive. Neil had long had his eye on an orange Gretsch 6120 Chet Atkins model, similar to the one Randy Bachman played.[164] That fascination would eventually lead him to Jon Glowa, former guitarist for the Silvertones, who owned one of the only other orange Gretsch guitars in the city.

According to Esquires drummer Don Marshall, "Jon Glowa was *the* ultimate rhythm guitar player. He knew more chords than any other guitar player I have ever met then or since." Jon had left the Silvertones in September 1961 to devote more time to his studies. Larry Wah — who played guitar for the Silvertones immediately after Jon Glowa's departure and just prior to Randy Bachman's arrival — says, "I think Jon's mom was covering some of his bills on the Gretsch at the time. . . . [Jon] had expressed an interest in folk and bluegrass guitar and I felt he was pursuing that." Jon occasionally played in the Brothers Grymm with Ken Johnson (vocalist from the Esquires) and Laurie Nowicki (who would later fill in at least once as rhythm guitarist in the Squires). Ken Johnson remarks, "We sang folk songs like the Everly Brothers."

Jon's musical focus had changed since his time in the Silvertones. He needed a different sort of guitar now, which meant he was looking for someone to assume the remaining loan payments on the Gretsch and reimburse him for what he felt was the instrument's current worth. He found a willing customer in Neil, who set about raising the cash necessary to seal the deal: "I came to a new realization about a lotta things when I turned eighteen,[165] and I sold my golf clubs and bought another guitar which was good enough for me to play in front of more people."[166] The funds he raised from the sale of his golf clubs reimbursed Jon for what he had decided was the guitar's value, and Neil took over the remaining loan payments demanded by the contract. A letter[167] from Neil to Scott in early May 1964 suggests that he succeeded in paying off the loan: "I just paid for my guitar. It is beautiful. There are only 3 or 4 like it in the whole city." Neil added, "I paid $275 for my guitar between October and April 15, so you can see how well we do."

The most identifiable feature of Neil's Gretsch was the assembled Bigsby vibrato — a V-Cut B6 — first introduced for the company's 1960 models. The 1961 model also had this feature, but was distinguished by the height of the guitar shell. The 1960 model was streamlined compared to its 1959 counterpart — 2.5 inches versus 2.75 inches. The height of the 1961 model was streamlined further still to 2.25 inches. Neil's was the 1960 model. There were additional distinguishing characteristics: a horseshoe design inlaid on the top plate, the lack of a cowboy-style G branded on the ceiling, the metal "bar-bridge" that gave the guitar its "twangy" effect, a "zero fret" immediately behind the saddle, and the Filtertron "humbucking" pickups with ridged plastic pickup frames.[168]

Neil sold the Gretsch a few years later, during the late fall of 1965, when he was trying to make it as a folksinger in Toronto's Yorkville music scene. "I sold my Gretsch and got an acoustic twelve-string,"[169] he recalls. "The Gretsch had a white case that had been signed by everyone I had met to that time . . . and I am sorry I sold it. I was out of money and didn't know what else to do. . . . I sold it at a music store on Yonge Street, and of all the things that are out there of mine, that is the one I wish I still had. That was my first Gretsch, just like Randy Bachman's, but it was gone. . . ."[170, 171]

NEIL DEBUTED HIS 1960 ORANGE Gretsch 6120 Chet Atkins guitar when the Squires played a CYO dance in the basement of St. Mary's church on September 20, 1963. The Gretsch would be Neil's axe for the rest of his time with the Squires, and it was a significant improvement over the Gibson Les Paul Junior.

Fran Gebhard, who had been attending the Squires' gigs regularly since she first saw them at St. Ignatius in May, showed up at the CYO dance at St. Mary's. She was still "head over heels in love with Neil," and the CYO dance was being held in the basement of the church affiliated with her school. During the break, Neil asked her to dance with him while some records were being played. She swooningly agreed. They would connect again a few weeks later, at a Squires gig at River Heights Community Club.

Kelvin student Lynne Hamilton frequently accompanied her boyfriend Allan Bates to gigs. Often this meant travelling with Neil in Rassy's small, light-blue Standard Ensign. (The Squires' official second car was Ken Smyth's father's big Chrysler.) It took extraordinary effort and finesse to squeeze all of the band's musical gear into the compact car. "We always spent a lot of time loading and unloading [Rassy's] small Ensign, an English car made by Standard Motors," Neil recalls. "It wasn't big enough for our band's gear, but we made it fit."[172] Loading the gear was no easy task, especially in the depths of winter, and Lynne was often called on for help: "It sure was hard to date seriously in 50 below weather!" Allan recalls, "I don't think the heater worked very well and we certainly noticed that in the Winnipeg winters."[173] Neil adds, "[W]e used to have to go out and warm up the cars before we could put the guitars in them because [the instruments] would crack in the cold."[174]

Allan remembers travelling in the car one night with Neil to a gig at River Heights Community Club: "It was the winter and we ended up right up against a big tree on the boulevard. No damage was done. Neil just backed up and carried on." Rassy's car was also commandeered for out-of-town gigs. On these occasions the car would be even more tightly packed. "We had my mother's little Ensign packed so full," Neil says, "that I could never see out the back when I was driving to the gigs. It's a wonder we weren't pulled over. We never were."[175]

Although Neil was playing his orange Gretsch now, he still held on to his first electric guitar. "The Les Paul did not disappear," Allan recalls. "We had it onstage sitting on a guitar stand. We used to joke that we could always use it as a weapon if needed. In particular, it was onstage at the Cellar."

The Cellar was a notorious subterranean club in a seedy laneway off Fort Street near Portage. It had begun its existence as a jazz club, but changed course in late 1962 when the Duguay brothers took over and started booking rock bands. The club's trademark was its bright red door, on which the words *The CELLAR* were printed in large white letters.[176] The venue was always dark and smoke-filled, its atmosphere infused with a sense of potential (and often real) danger. A small platform served as the stage, and the walls were painted black and decorated with menacing paraphernalia, including a chain-link ceiling with exposed plumbing. Bikers frequented the club and fist fights were not uncommon. On occasion, gunshots were heard and knives were brandished. Beer bottles served as missiles, often whizzing past band members. "Neil didn't give a damn where he played," Allan Bates remarks. "If we had a gig, we were playin', and that was that."[177]

The Squires appeared at the Cellar several times before it closed in late 1964. The Crescendos played the Cellar regularly, as did Chad Allan and the Reflections, and the Deverons. Burton Cummings famously played there one night when he was only 14 or 15. The band that was scheduled hadn't shown up, and he was called at the last minute as a potential replacement. Cummings jumped at the chance and had a remarkably successful evening, sitting at the Cellar's upright piano and banging out a two-hour repertory that included virtually every song he knew how to play.

In early October the Squires played a gig at River Heights Community Club. Even though Neil had asked Fran Gebhard to dance a few weeks earlier, he had still not asked her personally to attend one of his gigs. She decided to show up at the River Heights performance with a few girlfriends, wearing a tight-fitting blue sheath dress in an attempt to attract Neil's attention. It seemed to work: after the gig they walked out to the parking lot for a long conversation. Fran was a good listener, and Neil was in the mood to talk. He opened up to her about his hopes for his music career. "Neil's goal was to make a living at music, not being a star," Fran recalls. "He had a very strong work ethic and school wasn't important." Neil told her he wanted to quit school and go to the States to work — he was trying to figure out how to accomplish that goal. She told him school was "a waste of time" and he had "bigger things on the horizon." He was "destined for great things."

Fran felt she had made a real connection with Neil. Ken Koblun, meanwhile, had fallen hard for Fran's best friend Phyllis Freedman, who had accompanied Fran to some of the Squires' gigs. (Phyllis was Natalie Pollock's cousin, so Fran was friendly with her as well.) Neil and Fran tried to set up a meeting between Ken and Phyllis at one of the Salisbury House locations after the Squires' next River Heights gig at the beginning of November, and Neil and Fran made it to the restaurant, as did a hopeful Ken, but Phyllis never showed up. Apparently her father disapproved of the arrangement. Neil and Fran's matchmaking career was short-lived.

The relationship between Neil and Fran began to fizzle during the later part of autumn. Fran thinks she may have "misunderstood Neil's intentions." He was casually dating other girls at the same time he was dating Fran, which upset her. She went back to him after a few of these heartbreaks, but was continually unhappy that he wouldn't commit to being with her exclusively. She admits to being "crazy mad for Neil," but he was never crazy mad for her, at least not to the same degree.

According to Natalie Pollock, "Neil was with girls all the time. They were always following him around." On one occasion Neil confided to Natalie, who considered him a "friend boy" rather than a boyfriend, "I wish these girls would stop bothering me." She was convinced Neil didn't really care about girls. "He was not sexual. He only cared about his music and his guitar."

THE FALL SEASON MEANT IT was time for Kelvin High to host its Freshie Dance in the school's new cafeteria, "transformed into a ballroom for the year's first social fling," according to the yearbook.

Along with the dance came what the yearbook called a "practical Freshie Day." The school advocated a "clean up, paint up slogan." Kelvinites were armed with "brooms and shoe polish, while soapy water, chalk dust, and shaving cream was lavished upon the once stately interior," in the cryptic words of the yearbook account. Under the old hazing tradition, freshmen were required to perform menial chores such as carrying books for older students, but Freshie Day hazing had been banned for the first time this year.

Katharine Bruce, a freshman who lived on Yale Street (separated by a back laneway from Neil's home on Grosvenor), encountered Neil while walking to school that day. Neil was aware that Katharine was a freshman and suggested they resurrect the hazing tradition in the spirit of fun. Katharine readily agreed: "I had to meet him between every class all day and make sure he had the right books for each class. It was great fun for both of us, one of my happiest memories of high school." She liked Neil, and she double-dated one of Neil's friends just so she could be around him: "He was a charmer — funny, funny, funny. He was always making everyone laugh."

Kelvin High's theatrical production for 1964 was soon announced: a revival of the operetta *Ruddigore*. Music department head Mr. Belyea was charged with finding potential performers. Near the beginning of the school year he surprised students by asking them to sing "O Canada" (or some other well-known selection) — students who refused had to sit in the hallway as punishment. Lynne Hamilton managed to secure a spot in the chorus, and she formed the habit of studying her libretto while walking home from Kelvin, singing away at the top of her lungs.

Much preparation had to be done, since the musical was scheduled for February. Students were encouraged to sell tickets; a Ticket Selling Party would be held for the three classes reporting top ticket sales.

The year's first issue of *Et Cetera*, titled "Welcome, Kelvinites," was distributed on October 16, 1963. The "Twang!" article in that issue, announcing the imminent release of the Squires' single, lent Neil a special cachet among other students. Roger Currie recalls, "It certainly got played to death in the Kelvin cafeteria, and on the local airwaves at CKRC."[178]

The Squires began to spread their wings. They booked their first out-of-town gig for November 1: a high school dance in Portage la Prairie, the same town, 75 kilometres west of Winnipeg, where Neil had seen the Fendermen perform in 1961. The Squires came back to Winnipeg the same night, then played a high-profile gig at the River Heights Community Club on November 2. Their next out-of-town gig was another high school booking, this time in Dauphin on December 13. Dauphin was farther than they had ever travelled for a performance — more than 300 kilometres northwest of Winnipeg — and they were paid $125, their biggest fee to date. The band members rode to Dauphin on a passenger bus, along with all of their equipment. Ken Smyth remembers that night because of an incident with his bass drum: "Al was carrying my bass drum and he tripped over my dad's toe rubber [shoe protector] at the top of the step. We were coming home from a gig in Dauphin, Manitoba. Al and I came home while Neil and Ken stayed overnight in

Dauphin." To everyone's relief, the bass drum survived the trauma. So did Allan Bates.

A far more tragic and devastating trauma occurred on November 22, 1963. Roger Currie, who sat three seats away from Neil in Dr. Golubchuk's chemistry class, had just finished handing out test papers when the school's PA system announced that U.S. President John F. Kennedy had been assassinated in Dallas, Texas. "I looked up and gazed around the room," he recalls. "Some of the girls were crying. Neil and I looked at each other with expressions that spoke volumes without any words. Why on earth were we trying to do this stupid test? I'm sure we both failed that day, but what did it really matter?"[179]

The Football Dance scheduled for that evening was cancelled, and students were sent home early. The Squires had booked a gig for the night of November 22 at St. Peter's Mission. According to Ken Koblun's "List of Shows," the Squires did perform that night (he didn't list gigs that had been cancelled), but it could only have been a haunted, difficult performance.

Kelvin's 1963-64 yearbook would be dedicated to John Fitzgerald Kennedy, "who gave his life in the pursuit of world peace."

KEN KOBLUN DEBUTED HIS NEW pride and joy — a 1962 Höfner 182 bass — at the St. Mary's CYO dance on December 6. "I got it from Lowe's [music store] on Kennedy Street for $150," Ken recalls. "I traded in my Danelectro and got a $35 credit. I also got a loan co-signed by my foster father [Harvey Clayton] to cover the rest." This is the bass — with its readily identifiable red alligator vinyl finish — that Ken would play for the rest of his time with the Squires.

287

Heather Tozeland, another Kelvin student, remembers an evening during the winter of 1963 when she and her boyfriend Erwin Ploner — Neil's old friend from Earl Grey — were hanging out with Neil and a female friend. Bored and looking for entertainment, they decided to play an impromptu game of "automotive hide 'n' seek." Heather recalls, "Neil and I decided to hide [in a car] in my parents' garage and see if the second car [driven by Erwin with Neil's female friend as a passenger] would find us." Much to their dismay, it was Heather's father and brother who discovered them. "My dad was none too pleased. I can imagine what he was thinking. Me, in a dark garage, with this beatnik . . . in my mum's car. I was toast! But it was totally innocent fun."

Close to Christmastime, a group gathered for a buffet-style dinner in Lynne Hamilton's basement at 414 Brock Street, prior to attending the annual Stardust Prom. Lynne was there with Allan Bates. Neil's date was Betty Wood, daughter of Chris and Howard Wood Jr., Rassy's long-time friends. (Neil occasionally spent lunchtime at the Woods' large and welcoming home on Harrow Street, conveniently located across the street from the side entrance to Kelvin.) After his failed matchup with Phyllis Freedman, Ken Koblun now had a steady girlfriend in Sharon Krentz, whom he would continue to date off and on until he left Winnipeg for good with the Squires in the spring of 1965. Sharon was Ken's date at the dinner, and two other couples were also present. The dinner menu was classic postwar suburban fare, Lynne says: "Neil's favourite — macaroni and cheese, lime-green Jell-O salad and buns." More specifically, Lynne recalls that the macaroni and cheese was "just good old KD [Kraft Dinner][180] with the orange/yellow packaged cheese mixed in. I liked it and so did everyone else, including Neil and the rest of the gang." Lynne believes it was her mother who prepared the "lime-green Jell-O mixed with fruit cocktail — the kind you used to get in a can. It added some pizzazz to the meal." A bun was thrown in for good measure.

Two musical instruments appear in a photograph taken by a Hamilton family member: the family's Chickering Square grand piano,[181] and a guitar leaning against a wall. Neil had been known to play the piano when he came over, and this was a basement where the Squires sometimes practised. The guitar was an old Stella, used by Lynne's siblings Gail and Bill when they were first learning to play. In the photograph Neil and Ken wear dark-coloured suits with white carnations in the lapels; the girls are dressed in colourful party frocks with corsages.

Although Neil took some time out for socializing, music continued to be the dominant force in his life. The Squires' single, "The Sultan" b/w "Aurora," had been played regularly by Bob Bradburn on CKRC since its release a few months earlier, but the record never took off — already, the tide was turning from instrumentals to songs with vocals.

Beatlemania was in full swing, and Winnipeg was becoming a mini-Liverpool, with an intense music scene that was fully conscious of its British counterparts. "Canada was pretty musically aware," Neil remarks. "You got a lot of off-the-wall records that didn't even make it into the States. For instance, the early Beatles records. We were into them way before the Sullivan Show."[182] He adds, "The Beatles were number one in Canada before the States. All the real early ones, 'From Me to You'/'She Loves You,' was number one, and it never made number one in the States. So we got all the English stuff immediately."[183] *Please Please Me*, the Beatles' U.K. import on Parlophone, was released on March 22, 1963, and Ken Koblun was able to obtain a copy of this early. *With the Beatles* was released by Parlophone U.K. on November 22, 1963; the Canadian version, *Beatlemania! With the Beatles*, was released by Capitol Canada on December 2, 1963, well before the band's first U.S. release, *Introducing . . . the Beatles* on the Vee-Jay label on January 10, 1964. *Meet the Beatles!* was released by Capitol (U.S.) 10 days later.

Chad Allan and the Reflections were the first to perform Beatles songs in Winnipeg, and Neil and Ken were impressed by what they heard. Ken shared his copy of *Please, Please Me* with Neil, who was blown away by it. After leaving Ken's place, Neil ran into Allan Bates at the Crescentwood Community Club and eagerly shared his enthusiasm: "Man, you've gotta hear these guys from England! They've got this long hair and it goes down over their forehead. Damn, they're good."[184]

The surging popularity of the Beatles and other British Invasion bands prompted Neil to consider singing for the first time. Instrumental-only bands had fallen out of favour, and the Squires needed a lead singer if they wanted to continue landing gigs. Neil, initially timid about his vocal abilities, resolved to do what was necessary despite his nervousness. Ken Koblun felt there was another reason why Neil took the plunge: "I think it was the economics of the situation that actually drove him to sing, because if we added a singer, that would cut down the share of each person in the band."[185]

"I remember singing Beatles tunes," Neil said in a 1975 interview with Cameron Crowe. "The first song I ever sang in front of people was 'It Won't Be Long' and then 'Money (That's What I Want).' That was in the Calvin [sic] High School cafeteria. My big moment."[186]

There are also reports that after an instrumental performance at the St. Ignatius CYO dance on January 3,

1964, the Squires donned wigs and came back onstage to perform "She Loves You" as an encore. The audience's response was apparently tepid. According to one account, an audience member shouted out "Stick to instrumentals!" at the end of the number. Neil and the Squires persevered, of course, and would improve over time. Says Neil, "People told me I couldn't sing but I just kept at it!"[187]

Other accounts vary. Ken Smyth recalls, "Neil announced at a practice that they were going to do a couple of vocals. It was around the time of the British Invasion." Allan Bates remembers the Squires donning Beatles wigs and singing "She Loves You" on just one occasion — earlier than January 3, 1964, and not at their St. Ignatius gig. Allan believes it occurred at one of their two shows at River Heights Community Club during fall 1963. The corresponding dates would be October 5 and November 2, according to Ken Koblun's list of gigs. Ken Smyth remarks, "I recall some wigs, but don't think we all wore them — I know I didn't — I think it was just Neil and Al."

Capitol Canada released "She Loves You" as a single during the early fall of 1963, so the timing seems correct. *Beatlemania! With the Beatles,* the Beatles' first LP, was released by Capitol Canada in Canada in early December 1963.

"The Beatles were exciting because they were a group," Neil has said. "They made bands popular. That's how they affected me."[188] In 2012, at a ceremony during which former Beatle Paul McCartney was given a long-overdue star on the Hollywood Walk of Fame, Neil described McCartney's influence on him:

> Let me tell you a little bit about our friend Paul here just as a musician. When I was in high school

and the Beatles came out, I loved the Beatles and I tried to learn how to play like them, and no one could figure out what Paul was doing on the bass. Not only was he playing differently because he plays left-handed, he played notes that no one had put together before — in a way that made us stand in awe of this great musician.

I'm so proud to be doing this. As a musician, as a songwriter, Paul's craft and his art are truly at the top of his game, the way Charlie Chaplin was an actor. He has an ability to put melodies and feelings and chords together, but it's the soul that he puts into everything he does that makes me feel so good and so happy to be here.[189, 190]

The Beatles didn't perform in Winnipeg during their first North American tour, but in the summer of 1964 their plane stopped for refuelling at Winnipeg International Airport. A few hundred Beatle-crazed teenagers crammed the airport's observation deck, hoping for a glimpse of their musical heroes. Bruce Decker, rhythm guitarist in the Deverons, broke past the security line and began to run up the stairway of the plane. He was quickly apprehended, but his stunt — dubbed "Decker's Dash" — made the local newspapers the next day.

Neil, like many others of his generation, was immediately influenced by the Beatles' style of dress and mod haircuts. He let his hair grow down over his forehead and below the collar, and began to wear black turtlenecks and pointy shoes.

A selection of Beatles songs quickly became *de rigueur* at the Squires' performances. In addition to "She Loves You," "Money" and "It Won't Be Long," the band's repertoire expanded to include "I Saw Her Standing There," "Do You

Want to Know a Secret?", "A Hard Day's Night," "Kansas City," "Twist and Shout," "Ringo's Theme (This Boy)," "I Call Your Name," "I'll Cry Instead," "What'd I Say," "Slow Down" and "I Got a Woman."[191] (See Appendix D.) Other bands took up Rickenbacker guitars, the Beatles' instruments of choice, but Neil continued to play his prized orange Gretsch exclusively.

The Squires also included other hits from the British Invasion in their repertoire, such as "Can't You See That's She's Mine?", "Glad All Over," "House of the Rising Sun," "How Do You Do It?", "Needles and Pins" and "Sugar and Spice."[192] (See Appendix E.) The Shondels, the Deverons and the Crescendos, already well-established, also jumped on the Merseybeat bandwagon. New bands multiplied exponentially, all in response to the exciting new sounds coming out of the U.K.

The Squires were also beginning to include more of Neil's originals in their performances. According to Ken Koblun's 1964 song lists, these included Neil's earliest songs with vocals — "I Wonder," "Be My Girl" and "High School Playboy." (See Appendix F.) Some fast and slow instrumentals were still part of the Squires' repertoire, including "Mustang" (recorded by the Squires at the CKRC studio on April 2, 1964), "The Sultan" and "White Flower." They also began to perform "Made in England," a Hank Marvin–style instrumental written by Randy Bachman and included as the A-side of a single released on Reo Records in 1963, recorded under the one-time name Bob Ashley & the Reflections. It appears that the Squires covered a Randy Bachman song three or four years earlier than the Guess Who covered one of Neil's songs — "Flying on the Ground Is Wrong," recorded at Mills Music in London in 1967.

Winnipeg's folk-music scene also had a loyal following, though folk enthusiasts tended to disdain rock-and-rollers. Jazz enthusiasts were also a breed apart.

The Fourth Dimension coffeehouse, at 2000 Pembina Highway near the University of Manitoba campus in Fort Garry, was a hotspot for university students, hip intellectuals, would-be beatniks and folk/poetry enthusiasts. Neil's interest in folk had begun to develop shortly after his move to Winnipeg. His first folk influences were the Kingston Trio and Peter, Paul and Mary, followed by — far more significantly — Bob Dylan.

Neil was first introduced to Dylan's music by a group of older private-school students he became friends with. Someone in this group knew of a job opening on the railroad, and Neil was intrigued by the possibility of work that would take him to the U.S. "[W]hen I first heard Bob, back in '63," he recalls, "I was just getting used to being independent, looking for a reason to stay in Winnipeg and finding a reason to leave. . . . I went down to the railroad station and could not get a job. I thought workin' on the railroad would be a good way to get out of town and go to the USA. Then I found I needed a work visa."[193] His friends were sitting around listening with rapt attention to a record, hanging on to every word sung by a musician who accompanied himself on harmonica and acoustic guitar. "There was something about that, the way it sounded. I thought it was folk music, but not like the

---

FROM TOP: *Bob Dylan, backed by Levon and the Hawks, performs at Massey Hall, November 15, 1965.* [York University Libraries, Clara Thomas Archives & Special Collections, Toronto Telegram Fonds, F0433, ASC01210. Photographer: Madison Sale]; *Massey Hall.* [© 2012 Sharry Wilson]

folk music of the Kingston Trio."[194] Neil adds, "They had *Freewheelin'* or his first album. . . . I was diggin' it."[195]

For Neil, Dylan's distinctive voice was both unpretentious and inspirational: "I listened to Bob Dylan and I'd think, 'He's got a great voice,' and then he'd say, 'I'm not a singer like Caruso. I have my songs and I sing my songs.' That made sense to me. So I figured I'd just sing and see what happened."[196]

IT'S IMPOSSIBLE TO OVERSTATE THE continuing influence of Dylan on Neil's music, style, repertoire and approach to composition. Asked by Josh Tyrangiel in a September 2005 *Time* interview which musician he most admired, Neil's response is unhesitating:

> Bob Dylan, I'll never be Bob Dylan. He's the master. If I'd like to be anyone, it's him. And he's a great writer, true to his music and done what he feels is the right thing to do for years and years and years. He's great. He's the one I look to. I'm always interested in what he's doing now, or did last, or did a long time ago that I didn't find out about. The guy has written some of the greatest poetry and put it to music in a way that it touched me, and other people have done that, but not so consistently or as intensely. Like me, he waits around and keeps going, and he knows that he doesn't have the muse all the time, but he knows that it'll come back and it'll visit him and he'll have his moment.[197]

There would be many "Dylan moments" in Neil's later life. He has described, for instance, hearing "Like a Rolling

Stone" for the first time during the summer of 1965: "I can still remember that afternoon in Toronto. It changed my life. The poetry, attitude, and ambience of that piece are part of my makeup. I absorbed it."[198] Neil recalls, "[H]e came over the speakers of my radio singing 'How does it feel?' over and over. The lyrics pounded their way into my psyche, this new poetry rolling off his tongue. He spoke for a lot of us without knowing it. I felt connected to him in a moment."[199]

Neil referenced his Dylan memories in the lyrics to "Twisted Road" from *Psychedelic Pill* (2012): *First time I heard "Like a Rolling Stone" / I felt that magic and took it home / Gave it a twist and made it mine, / But nothing was as good as the very first time / Poetry rollin' off his tongue / Like Hank Williams chewin' bubble gum / Askin' me, "How does it feel?"*

"Like a Rolling Stone" was released by Columbia Records on July 20, 1965, and Dylan performed it at the Newport Folk Festival five days later, as part of his controversial "electric" set. The song reached the No. 2 position on the U.S. charts and achieved Top 10 status on the Canadian charts. Neil would have seen Dylan perform the song at one of Dylan's two shows at Massey Hall in November 1965.

And the influence was not entirely one-way: Dylan has periodically expressed his awareness of Neil's work. When Dylan first heard "Heart of Gold" on the radio, it spooked him:

> The only time it really bothered me that someone sounded like me was when I was living in Phoenix, Arizona, in about '72 and the big song at the time was "Heart of Gold." I used to hate it when it came on the radio. I always liked Neil

Young, but it bothered me every time I listened to "Heart of Gold." I think it was up at number one for a long time, and I'd say, "Shit, that's me. If it sounds like me, it should as well be me."[200]

It may have been Neil's use of the harmonica that made "Heart of Gold" sound so Dylanesque. "Eventually I was able to pick up the harmonica without thinking I was copying Bob, just influenced by him,"[201] Neil says. Neil "had to avoid listening to [Dylan] for a long time in the late sixties and seventies because I thought I would assimilate so much that I would suddenly be copying him. It was a conscious thing, to avoid being too influenced. I am like a sponge in that when I like something, I become so influenced by it that I almost start to *be* it."[202]

When Dylan was in Winnipeg in 2008 for a November 2 show, he paid a visit to Neil's old home at 1123 Grosvenor. The current owners invited him and his manager in for a brief tour. Dylan took in everything with an interested eye and asked some thoughtful questions. Standing in Neil's old bedroom, Dylan remarked, "OK, so this was his view, and this was where he listened to his music."[203] John Kiernan, owner of the house, wondered if Dylan might have been thinking about his own childhood, listening to music and gazing out of his bedroom window in Hibbing, Minnesota. "It suddenly dawned on me, when you're looking at Bob Dylan standing in a hallway, that he had a very parallel experience 200 miles to the south, sitting in his room, listening to his music, looking out his window."[204]

THE 4-D WAS AT THE EPICENTRE of the folk-music ferment in Winnipeg, and Neil was along for the ride. The nascent folk-rock movement he encountered at the club would become a key ingredient in the mixture of styles that defined his career as a musician.

There were three 4-D coffeehouses, one in Winnipeg, one in Regina and one in the town of Fort William. Charlie Clements managed the Winnipeg club.[205] Situated on the northeast corner of Pembina Highway and University Crescent, the 4-D operated seven days a week, and customers paid 25 cents per hour for admission (and to keep a seat). Once inside, customers could choose a place at one of a number of small tables. Checkered tablecloths and burning candles enhanced the bohemian atmosphere, and specialty coffees and teas filled out the menu.

Gene Cuica owned the Winnipeg and Regina locations, while Gordie "Dinty" Crompton was the owner of the 4-D in Fort William. One of Charlie Clements's many duties as manager was booking acts for the 4-D circuit.[206] Sunday-night open-mike hootenannies at the Winnipeg location were wildly popular events, and Neil often attended.

The Squires made a big impact when they landed a gig on January 25, 1964, becoming the first rock-and-roll band to play at the folk-music venue. The band played for free that night, and would again on other occasions, and the audience was always welcoming. The band was supplied with food in lieu of payment, which Neil happily accepted. At a February 1964 gig, the Squires tested out some Beatles covers, with Neil doing vocal duty. "When we did 'It Won't Be Long' at the 4-D, we actually got a hand," Allan Bates recalls.[207] Neil was encouraged by the audience's positive reaction.

Fran Gebhard, still harbouring a major crush on Neil, worked at the 4-D as a waitress on Friday and Saturday nights. The situation was awkward for her, and would become even more so when Neil began bringing his first steady girlfriend to the club in the fall of 1964. But that was still in the future.

Richard Koreen's younger brother Terry Koreen[208] also worked as a waiter at the 4-D. Terry and Charlie Clements were good friends, and Terry, a skilled guitarist, was able to play with some of the musicians who were booked there. Richard became increasingly familiar with the 4-D. His first impression as a teenager was that it was "rundown and marginal. You entered from the dirt parking lot, the one full of potholes, and passed through a dark tunnel-like entranceway. You were now beside a cash register behind a counter and were given a time slip. . . . I remember being charged by the hour for being there. . . . There was a railing funnelling you past the counter with the sitting area now on your right. The tables were small and the area crowded. There were tablecloths on some and others were bare. The chairs were rickety and not all matched, as they came from different sources. The stage was beyond the sitting area and could be viewed by standing behind the rail. To your left was the espresso machine — a monster about eight feet high with at least two copper towers. As steam flew and waiters delivered, your little chit of a bill got added to and added to. The washrooms were an event, being a mixture of ancient, impossible-to-really-clean fixtures with even dimmer lights. The acts were excellent — mostly blues. I recall Sonny Terry and Brownie McGhee."

Fran Gebhard remembers a few other big-name acts who performed at the 4-D, including Tim Hardin and José Feliciano. Neil has mentioned seeing Sonny Terry and Brownie McGhee, Tim Rose and the Thorns, the Allen-Ward Trio, the Dirty Shames and Don McLean, among many others. He was impressed by the travelling musicians he met at the 4-D: "I saw myself as a part of it all, the music scene, the writers and performers. I wanted to do just what they did, too — get in a truck after they finished their set and leave."[209]

Local acts booked at the 4-D, in addition to the Squires, included the Down to Earthenware Jug Band,[210] Three Blind Mice, the Brambles and classical guitarist David Stone. According to Bernie Barsky,[211] a member of the Brambles, "Neil was just one of the guys who used to come to the 4-D. It was a haven for everybody. Nothing like it existed anywhere. Wherever we played, if we didn't want to go home after a gig we'd go to the 4-D. That's just what you did."[212]

ANOTHER MUSICIAN NEIL WOULD MEET at the 4-D was Joni Mitchell. Annis Kozub of Three Blind Mice was there when it happened. "I remember being at the 4-D during the day when Joni Mitchell was there with her husband Chuck. They were doing a sound check and Neil and I both sat together and listened to them. I think that's when he met Joni for the first time."[213] Neil visited Rassy in Winnipeg in December 1965. Joni retains a strong memory of this time. "We were there over Christmas," she recalls. "I remember putting up this Christmas tree in our hotel room. Neil came out to the club and we liked him immediately."[214] This is when Neil first sang "Sugar Mountain" for Joni.

They discovered that they had much in common. Both had been stricken with polio as children in the early 1950s, and both came from families that moved around a lot. (Joni's father was an officer in the Canadian Air Force.) Both had spent their teenage years in the Canadian prairie provinces, and both had played the ukulele when they were first discovering their aptitude for music in the late 1950s.

Joni famously wrote "The Circle Game" as a response to

Neil's "Sugar Mountain." Neil says, "It was a real feeling of recognition that Joni wrote her song to answer mine. I didn't even hear it until she had already been singing it for a year."[215]

They would reconnect often over the years. Neil wrote a song for Joni — "Sweet Joni,"[216] which was captured in an audience recording at its debut at the Civic Auditorium in Bakersfield, California, on March 11, 1973. (It remains unreleased.)

Neil, members of the Band and Joni Mitchell performed "Helpless" during the Band's farewell performance — "The Last Waltz" — at the Winterland Ballroom in San Francisco on November 25, 1976. Joni and Neil, side by side, shared a mike for "I Shall Be Released," the finale. They were next to each other again in February 1985 for the recording of "Tears Are Not Enough," a fundraising effort to aid Ethiopian famine relief by a collection of Canadian artists dubbed the Northern Lights.

JOE BARNSLEY AND JOHN TESKEY — Kelvin High students who were friendly with Neil — shared an interest in folk music. Joe was a member of the Down to Earthenware Jug Band, composed entirely of fellow students from Kelvin. The band mainly played gigs at the Fourth Dimension and at high schools and community clubs. Fellow member John Robertson recalls that Neil occasionally helped the group with song arrangements, though he never actually performed with them.[217]

Joe played guitar and banjo with a fingerpicking style, and Neil was intrigued enough to ask for some advice on the technique. Joe met Neil at 1123 Grosvenor and brought along a copy of the folk-movement magazine *Sing Out!* featuring a technical article on fingerpicking. He spent 20 minutes showing Neil the basics, which Neil quickly mastered.

Joe brought Neil over to good friend John Teskey's house, where John gave Neil a demonstration of the potential of the harmonica in rock-and-roll songs. "I played the harmonica for him," Teskey recalls, "and I swear some light went on for him. It was something he hadn't thought of before. You could see it in his eyes."[218] Teskey later adds, however, "It would be a wildly presumptuous overstatement to seriously suggest that I personally contributed anything whatsoever to Neil Young's musical development."

Nevertheless, by the spring of 1964 Neil "was listening to blues stuff like Jimmy Reed and getting into the harmonica."[219] There is evidence that he began playing harmonica with the Squires as early as September 1964, inspired by John Lennon's harmonica work on the classic Beatles song "I Should Have Known Better."[220] Neil admits to learning much of what he knows about the harmonica from Sonny Terry: "I learned more about playing harmonica from Sonny Terry than Jimmy Reed, 'cause I could watch Sonny night after night. . . . I saw them in Winnipeg."[221] Glenn MacRae of the Crescendos remembers Neil teaching him to play harmonica in the fall of 1964 during breaks at the Twilight Zone on St. Mary's Road in St. Vital.[222] Neil's first recorded harmonica-playing is his enthusiastic break on "Hello Lonely Woman,"[223] recorded in October 1965 with former schoolmate Comrie Smith in the attic of his family home at 46 Golfdale Road in north Toronto. "The sound of a harmonica hits you directly," Neil says. "There's no language barrier."[224]

Folk music infiltrated Kelvin High in a big way. On January 24, the Squires performed a free gig at Kelvin's "Hootenanny and Dance," sponsored by the school newspaper. (They played at the dance itself, not the hootenanny prior to the dance, although Neil was known to sit in occasionally with a few of the school-based groups.) The co-editors of the newspaper were the folk-music lovers Joe Barnsley and John Teskey. "Not to be left behind in the era of folk-song popularity," the yearbook reported, "Kelvin held its first hootenanny. The evening surpassed all expectations, drawing the largest crowd in Kelvin history. Entertainment was provided, featuring Miss 'Dominique' Redmond, The Jesters, The Stubby Six (and One), Wendy and Joe, Val Stewart, and the Kelvin Combo, with Mr. Glass on guitar. And then there were the Ladybugs."

After the dance, Neil offered a ride to fellow Kelvin student Maureen Goldberg. Maureen was not among those who, like Fran Gebhard, considered Neil fatally attractive: in her judgment, Neil was "very skinny, older than everyone and a 'loser.'" Not very promising dating material. "Besides," Maureen adds, "he wasn't Jewish." Janice Booth, a good friend of Lynne Hamilton, agrees with Maureen's assessment: "He wasn't especially good-looking, was skinny, not social and no scholar." "Mr. Disappointment," at least to some.

Marilyne Nentwig, on the other hand, saw Neil as a diamond in the rough. Jackie Nentwig's twin sister began dating Neil regularly. Marilyne readily accepted Neil's commitment to the Squires, and when he complained to her about not having enough places for the band to rehearse — other than Ken Smyth's basement — she asked her mother if they could use the basement at their family home at 1111 Fleet Avenue in Crescentwood. Her mother initially agreed but was unprepared for the racket the band made. The neighbours were equally displeased, and the arrangement lasted just a week. Nevertheless, Neil felt comfortable in the Nentwig home. He and Marilyne spent many pleasant hours in the family room. "We really had a good time together," Marilyne recalls, "but we never got into any trouble. We weren't bad kids. I always felt comfortable with Neil. I never had to fend him off. He was a gentleman and never made inappropriate advances. He was really cuddly even though he was so skinny. He was very kind, sensitive and romantic."[225]

A typical date would be going to one of the Squires' gigs with Neil (and, of course, helping to carry the equipment). Marilyne loved to dance — she still occasionally appeared as a dancer on *Teen Dance Party* — but at these gigs she was usually left sitting on the sidelines while Neil performed. Neil made it up to her one night in mid-March at a community club, when he unveiled a new song he had written for her: it was called "Be My Girl."[226] He had managed to keep it secret until the performance, and Marilyne was thrilled.

Neil often lent a hand at music-based school functions and sat in with a number of the bands. Jack Gowenlock, who had performed with Neil in the Classics, played guitar with the Stubby Six, and Neil might "pop in and out of the group as a guitar player." The band took its name from the recent introduction of "stubby" (short) bottles in the Canadian beer market. (Beer was available in six-packs, and there were originally six members in the band.) The group favoured another iconic Canadian item, the lumberjack shirt, and Jack recalls, "One of [band member] Bryan Robertson's friends worked at Molson's [brewery] and got some four-foot-tall plastic 'stubby' bottles that we would put at each end of the stage. The label was [Molson's] Canadian, so we figured, 'What's more Canadian than a lumberjack?'" Other members of the band included Brian Hunt, Fred Kemp (playing a four-string guitar), Grant Boden and Vern Paul (bongos). The "and one" in the Stubby Six (and One) was George Padovan, who "had a part-time job that prevented him from being at all the gigs." Jack recalls, "Sometimes John Copsey [once the Classics vocalist] would fill in for him when he wasn't available. Sometimes Copsey wasn't there." The group was very fluid. "We were a folkie group. . . . It was never more than a hobby for fun," Jack remarks. "We used to do hootenannies wherever we found them, usually in church basements, coffeehouses and teen drop-in centres. We would walk around singing three- and four-part harmony just for laughs. Talk about your shopping-mall mobs."

Neil also joined the Ladybugs for at least one performance. The band was led by fellow Kelvin student Shirley Tilghman, who would go on to become Princeton University's first female president. In a 2001 *Princeton Alumni Weekly* profile, Shirley recounted Neil's "mortification after she convinced him to sing backup in her short-lived girl band, the Ladybugs."[227]

According to Roger Currie, "[Neil] gave a number of memorable impromptu performances in the gym and the cafeteria, and I remember them as being very funny. One song in particular called 'A Letter to Freddie' stands out. Freddie was Fred Hodgkinson, the vice-principal of Kelvin, who gave Neil more than a few detentions for his various antics."[228]

During school lunch hour, students often congregated at Stan's, a drugstore near the corner of Grosvenor and Stafford. Lynne Hamilton recalls that her typical lunchtime routine entailed buying a cup of chicken noodle soup from the dispenser in the cafeteria, to go along with a sandwich brought from home. She hastily gobbled this down so she could spend the "sacred lunch-hour time" at Stan's, at rehearsals for the school play or just hanging out with the boys and other friends. During one lunch hour at Stan's, Lynne noticed that Neil was finishing off a composition for an upcoming English class. The story was about "a turtle without a shell and a bird without wings and their meeting and travels, struggles and journey together." Neil confided that he planned to submit it as a marked assignment in two different classes.

A SELECT GROUP OF STUDENTS who were known to skip classes occasionally would convene — hoping not to get caught — at what was called Peanut Park, just down the way from the mansion-like Blick family home on Harvard Avenue in River Heights. Brian and Barry Blick were twins; both attended Kelvin, and Neil was friendly with both, although he socialized mostly with Brian. Their father was John Oliver "Jack" Blick, founder of CJOB radio station. The many well-known musicians who visited the Blick home were a topic of deep interest to the students at Kelvin.

In their free time, Brian and Barry enjoyed working on their pet project: restoring a dark blue, two-door 1940 Packard they kept in their laneway. (Girls were known to sneak down the laneway to see if the brothers were at work on their drool-worthy car.) Neil, already a certified car enthusiast, was fascinated. A mutual love of automobiles and music made for a fast social bond.

Although they spent a lot of time restoring the Packard, Brian and Barry were often spotted driving their father's huge white 1959 Cadillac convertible. The car had an internal speaker system that was used for parades by the radio station. "The 'speaker system' was a loud hailer which had a siren with a few different types of siren sounds," Brian recalls. "It also had a button on the unit that, when pressed, would slow the siren. Then when it was released the siren would speed up, making it sound like an old ambulance. The unit was illegal to have in a car, so we didn't use it that often. Mostly to get girls' attention."

Neil was impressed by John Oliver Blick's Cadillac convertible: "It was red [it was actually white] with a red leather interior. The car made a big impression on me, so I used to sit in the YMCA in Fort William figuring out how long I would have to work gigs like the Flamingo Club until I had enough money to buy a car like that. I checked all the ads in the paper for similar cars and compared prices."[229, 230]

FEBRUARY'S BIG SCHOOL EVENT WAS a Ticket Selling Party for *Ruddigore*, the Gilbert and Sullivan musical the school was presenting later that month, to reward those with the highest ticket sales. The yearbook reports, "These loyal workers and super-salesmen were fested on cookies and donuts, as well as being entertained by the cream of Kelvin's talented crop." Neil and friends Chic Bell and Don Thompson performed at the Ticket Selling Party, and a photo of them in action was published in the yearbook. The enigmatic caption reads, "Oh Chick, you beautiful thing, don't you ever die!!" Chic thinks this was written by Tim Henry as a joke. Tim was supposed to join Neil and Chic, playing parodies of popular Beatles songs of the day. According to Chic, he, Neil and Tim — Chic's best friend since kindergarten — assembled at 1123 Grosvenor one day to rehearse. But at the last minute Tim was replaced by Don Thompson for their performance in the school auditorium.

On February 7, the Squires performed for the first time at Patterson's Ranch House. Having played there with the

---

*Ticket Selling Party for* Ruddigore, *February 1964.*
*Left to right: Charles "Chic" Bell, Neil, Don Thompson.*
[© 1964 Ron Coke. Courtesy of Stephen Cross]

# Ticket Selling
# Party

"Oh Chick, you beautiful thing, don't you
ever die!!"

Esquires, Neil was acquainted with the venue's country-and-western roots. In a 2011 interview with John Jurgensen, Neil recalls his introduction to country music: "I just know that playing this kind of music is something that's always been a part of my life. Even when I first started playing, there was a place called Patterson's Ranch House on the outskirts of Winnipeg, Manitoba, if you can imagine that. I worked there with my band. It was way out in the sticks. Growing up in Winnipeg, travelling around Canada, the ruralness of my surroundings from little Omemee in north Ontario where I really started getting into music. It's always been the backdrop. That's why I am the way I am."[231]

The Squires played Patterson's Ranch House next on February 29, and again on March 26 and 28. It was during this cluster of closely spaced gigs that Lucille Emond, a teenage celebrity, briefly sang with the Squires. Emond had scored a hit single on the charts when she was just 12, after making three consecutive winning appearances on CJAY TV's talent show *Amateur Hour*. It was CKRC deejay Bob Bradburn who arranged for Lucille to record some commercials at the station and to make an appearance with the Squires. Ken Koblun says she sang one song with them at Patterson's. Lucille laughingly recalls, "[Bradburn] wanted Neil to have me in the band, but it just didn't work out. They didn't want a girl in their band. But I did do a couple of gigs with them [when] I was only about 12. Here was this little girl being backed by Neil Young. It just wasn't meant to be."[232]

The Squires enjoyed the services of an unofficial manager, Grant Park student Lorne Saifer.[233] "Lorne was a friend of mine," Ken Smyth remarks, "and he did do a limited amount of so-called managing — nothing official." Ken had attended River Heights Junior High with Lorne; they were in the same

Grade 9 class and lived close to one another. The biographical information in the River Heights yearbook attests to the fact that Lorne was outgoing and liked to talk — good qualities for a band manager: "Not too quiet, he always gets his point across to the teacher. Ambition is to be a lawyer and the way he argues he should be a good one."

Lorne met Neil through his friendship with Ken Smyth. One Sunday afternoon Lorne heard music coming from a nearby house. This was where the Smyth family lived. Heading over to investigate, he discovered Neil enthusiastically playing guitar. Introductions were made, and Lorne and Neil became friends. Lorne soon began to handle some of their bookings; during evening phone conversations he and Neil thrashed out where and when it was best to seek gigs.

Lorne claims to have supplied Neil with a microphone he "borrowed" from the Shaarey Zedek Synagogue for his vocal performance in Kelvin's cafeteria in early 1964. Neil needed a mike, and Lorne knew the synagogue had one set up for a banquet later that evening. The mike was eventually returned undamaged and no one was the wiser.

Randy Bachman was also a friend of Lorne Saifer, and it was Lorne who introduced Randy to Neil at a show at the River Heights Community Club. "Neil was a skinny, dark-haired kid who stood to the right of the stage, my side, and watched me all night," Randy recalls. "I'd heard of him because in Winnipeg you tended to know of other guitar players who were good."[234] Randy recognized a kindred spirit when Neil, a determined look in his eyes, began to quiz Randy about the chords in some Shadows instrumentals. "Neil Young has had a parallel kind of life to mine,"[235] Randy has said. Over the years Randy maintained a steady friendship with Neil and has seen him evolve as an artist: "Neil's best qualities are:

hard work, honesty, generosity, determination, setting goals to complete each dream and then working step by step to get it done. This was evident when we first met and every time I've seen him since over the years."[236]

IN FEBRUARY, KEN KOBLUN BOUGHT a new amp through his uncle, a high school music teacher. It seemed like a good deal: a black Tolex Bassman amp with a pair of 12-inch speakers for $400. As the name suggests, the Bassman was designed as a bass amp, but guitarists liked it for its rich tonality and power. Ken debuted the Bassman at the Squires' gig at the Glenwood Community Club on February 1, 1964, exactly one year after the Squires' debut at the Riverview. The amp served admirably for several shows, until one of its speaker units blew out during a gig in Transcona. Ken had to scurry to find a replacement speaker. The bargain bass amp wasn't quite the bargain it had seemed.

April was a busy period for Neil, both at school and with the Squires. On April 2, 1964, the Squires were back at the CKRC studio to record some new songs (including vocal numbers this time) with Bob Bradburn and Harry Taylor. Bradburn recalled his sessions with the Squires: "Neil was a great kid and he'd work for hours on something. He and the Squires put the music first. . . . As far as producing went, I'd suggest to Neil that he maybe put in a certain riff here or there. Or that a drum roll would work well in a certain part of a song. Neil was always open to suggestions. But you've got to remember that given the technology of the day, there wasn't a whole lot you could do in terms of effects."[237]

Although about 20 songs were recorded, only a few survive. Two recordings from this session were found, decades later, on master tapes in Bradburn's basement. One of the songs was "I Wonder," the first recording of Neil singing, and the other was an untitled instrumental, "Mustang."[238] When Randy Bachman was offered an opportunity to hear them, he was amazed; he broadcast the songs for the first time on November 12, 2005, on his CBC Radio One show *Vinyl Tap*, as part of a 60th birthday tribute to Neil.

(For decades prior to Bradburn's discovery, Neil had only a lesser-quality dub of "I Wonder."[239] The tape was in such poor shape that it could be played back only once, to create a digital computer file; the audio was then enhanced to improve the sound and fill in any obvious gaps. The lesser-quality dubs of "I Wonder" and "Mustang" were taped at 7.5 inches per second, while the master tapes were recorded at 15 ips. Higher tape speeds yield higher quality sound.)

Neil later adapted parts of "I Wonder" in his 1965 song "The Ballad of Peggy Grover," and resurrected the song again when it became a major part of "Don't Cry No Tears" on the 1975 album *Zuma*. The April 2, 1964, recordings of "Mustang" and "I Wonder" remained unreleased until they were included on *The Neil Young Archives (Volume 1)*.[240]

A further instrumental, "Cleopatra," has unfortunately been lost. One of Neil's first songs with lyrics, called "No," may have also been recorded at this session. "Ain't It the Truth," another from these sessions, was resurrected by Neil for live performances in his 1987-88 tour with the Bluenotes. Ken Smyth recalls that the 1964 recordings were demos for a proposed recording contract with London Records of Canada that never materialized.[241]

After the session Taylor gave Neil a blunt opinion about his talent: "You're a good guitar player, kid — but you'll never make it as a singer."[242] Bradburn concurred: "I've admitted if before, I just didn't think Neil would make it as a singer;

I thought he'd find success as a writer and guitar player, but this was all before FM rock radio came along."[243]

BY APRIL 1964, THE SQUIRES were doing remarkably well. A radio poll had ranked them third among the roughly 150 teenage bands in Winnipeg at the time. Ken Koblun believes the first- and second-place bands were Chad Allan and the Reflections and the "Club 63" Galaxies, respectively. Neil wrote to Scott about their ranking in a letter[244] from early May:

> We are rated no. 3 of the 150 odd teenage bands in the city. This is a rating from engagements and popularity unofficially taken by DJ's at CKRC and CKY. We will not stop at no. 3. I know we will be no. 1 by next summer.

Neil was confident about the songs and the band's ability to play them. "The Squires . . . got really good. We had the most original material of all the bands. I was writing a lot, because I was always thinking about music," Neil recalls. "First it was instrumentals, and then songs with words that I had to start singing. That set us apart. I knew that and I took advantage of it."[245]

THAT APRIL THERE WAS A minor scandal at Kelvin. A substantial number of students, allowed out of class to attend the regional/provincial track meet, skipped the sporting event and went elsewhere. Principal Cochrane had expected that all students would attend track meets to support their respective schools. From then on, he declared, all track meets including the Field Day in June would be considered regular school days — attendance was mandatory. Angry students, in a move that reflected the increasing restiveness of young people in the increasingly radical 1960s, decided to stage a strike. A group of them, including Neil and Lynne Hamilton, gathered in student council vice-president Peter Barber's backyard to practise chanting and singing strike songs. Students taking part in the strike gathered in front of the school on the scheduled day, where they conspicuously ignored the bell announcing the start of the school day, and all subsequent bells.

"I think it only lasted for a couple of hours," Lynne recalls, "but those stragglers 'on the line' who stayed out eventually went in and became members of 'the sunshine club' and had to come to school for the next couple of weeks [for detentions] beginning at 7 a.m. Not fun, and I think there were only about 20 people who suffered this punishment." She adds, "I don't remember ever getting a free day off for sporting events after that." Neil's first foray into political activism had achieved, essentially, nothing. But like the rest of his generation, he was moving toward a deeper political engagement with the world.

Neil and classmate Stuart Adams performed at the climax of Charity Week in the "Cavalcade of Stars," singing covers of three Beatles songs. The April 17 event, which replaced the traditional Co-Ed Dance usually held at that time of year, attracted an audience of 350 to 400. According to the April 28 edition of *Et Cetera*, several notable Kelvin acts performed, "including such groups as the renowned Stubby Six; Wendy Wiens; the hilarious Hydraulic Banana Peel Jugband Stompers including such outstanding (ha) Kelvin personalities as John Robertson, Joe Barnsley, Dave Nesbitt and of course Grant Boden armed with his water pistol; Pascoe's Petalpickers, a take-off on the New Christy Minstrels; and last but not least, the lost Beatle, Mr. Glass, accompanied by Stuart Adams also on guitar and Bill Edmundson [sic] on the drums. In addition to the fine playing of this trio, the audience also vigorously enjoyed three Beatle songs which were sung by Stuart Adams and Neil Young." Adams' performance — complete with an English accent — was singled out as something special, and Bill Edmondson was described as "the unforgettable drummer, Kelvin's answer to Ringo Starr."[246]

Near the end of April, Easter exam marks were released. Neil's school career had reached a crisis point. Vice-Principal F. A. Hodgkinson, sent a letter[247] to Scott detailing the results of Neil's Christmas and Easter terms. The marks were dismaying:

| SUBJECT: | CHRISTMAS: | EASTER: |
|---|---|---|
| Literature | 55 | 53 |
| Composition | 67 | 58 |
| History | 34 | 39 |
| Mathematics | 68 | 50 |
| Biology | 32 | 43 |
| (X) French | 61 | 46 |
| (X) Typing | 22 | 47 |

"As you can see," Hodgkinson continued, "Neil will have to dig in and work if he is to make the grade. I shall see him and try to spur him on."

The X's in his report indicated that Neil had taken those subjects at a Grade 10 level, not Grade 11. English literature and composition were still relatively strong subjects for him. His mathematics results also touched on the minimally respectable. All else was disastrous.

About a week later, Neil wrote an important letter[248] to Scott that touched off a flurry of letters between the two of them and Rassy. Neil mentions his schoolwork vaguely and in passing ("I'm doing better in school and am finally beginning to settle down . . ."), but adds that "a very serious thing happened two weeks ago. . . . We were playing at a school dance[249] and about ten pm my amplifier blew up." With obvious reluctance, he goes on to ask his father for a loan. "This is very important to me as you no doubt know. I have decided to divide my life work into teaching Jr. High English and Comp.[250] and composing and playing music. . . . I don't like to ask you for money but I have tried every other way, so I'm sort of asking for a $600 advance on my education."

On the same day, and without having had a chance to see Neil's letter, Scott wrote to Rassy commenting on Neil's poor grades: "I know you must be as upset by the way he is going at school, as I am. I wonder what can be done. . . . In Bob's case — and he was quite a bit better at school than Neil has been — once he got out and started to make his own living, he was all right. Have you considered this for Neil?"[251]

As soon as he received Neil's message about the amplifier, Scott responded with another letter.[252] He was clearly unhappy. "I would have been a lot more impressed with your request," he wrote, "if you [would] have included your marks in your letter and commented on them directly. . . . I cannot help thinking that however well you are doing in music, it is partly or all at the expense of school work and it is time that you made up your mind which is more important." Neil needed to face facts, Scott suggested: "If I had read that letter you wrote to me without knowing the facts, I would have thought everything was going great. . . . You have to be able to distinguish between what you HOPE is going to happen, and *what is really true.*"

The amplifier was apparently out of the question. "Now, you ask for $600 to buy an amplifier for your band," Scott continued, "and ask this on the basis of an advance against your college education. If you had an average of even around 70 and a good school record, I would send it to you as a loan in the next mail. As it is, I am offended that you should try to float a loan with me, with part of the pitch being NOT to come clean about your school marks." He did hold out a sliver of hope as an incentive, however: "There is one way I will back you toward that amplifier. . . . When I receive your report card . . . showing your term-end marks and you pass in *everything*, I would co-sign a note at the bank for you to get the money for the amplifier, on the basis that any missed payments would be subtracted from the monthly allowance sent to your mother. . . . In other words, you produce for me and I will produce for you."

Before Neil could receive this, Rassy wrote a response[253] to Scott's letter from four days earlier. She acknowledged Neil's difficulties at school but felt they could be surmounted: "I went immediately to Kelvin where I had a long discussion with Mr. Hodgkinson regarding Neil's plans for the future, which are as he outlined them in his letter to you. . . . Mr. H. feels that Neil is definitely college calibre, and that provided he applies his native ability, he should have no difficulty. It was my impression that the last thing the school feels is that Neil should become a drop-out." Rassy added, "I also discussed the problem regarding Neil's amplifier and told Mr. Hodgkinson that Neil had asked you for the funds to cover a new one. It is our mutual feeling that it would be most unfortunate should Neil have to curtail his musical career at this point — might even make all the difference in the world to his future. So I do hope that you can find your way clear to send him the money for this as soon as possible."

Shortly after Rassy had written this, Neil received Scott's "you produce for me and I will produce for you" missive. Peter Barber was with Neil that day: "We were walkin' home after school and he had the letter with him. Neil was disappointed, hurt — you might even say angry. It was a painful thing."[254]

Rassy read the letter and was incensed. Neil didn't respond to Scott's negative letter, but Rassy did. "I am highly amused," she wrote, "at your gracious offers — co-signing loans indeed. What kind of a father are you anyhow? . . . He did not ask for $600 to buy an amp for his band, he asked for it to buy a new amp for himself. He is the lead guitarist in the band and is essential to the functioning of it. In other words, they cannot function without him. . . . I take great pleasure in informing you that I will see that Neil gets his amplifier and that I have not the slightest doubt in the world that he will repay me as he can as he earns the money."[255]

The family quarrel escalated when Scott wrote to Vice-Principal Hodgkinson on May 16:[256] "I am sorry to have embroiled you unwittingly in the recent Battle of Neil's Marks. . . . Am I unreasonable in getting a little restive, when he's been five years trying to get through three grades of high school?[257] I've never expected or demanded too much of Neil, but in all realism I haven't been able to reconcile the idea of four failures out of seven subjects (his Easter record) with a college future (which my former wife, bless her irascible hide, tells me you think highly of, as a possibility for Neil)."

Vice-Principal Hodgkinson's reply[258] of May 21 took a diplomatic tone: "I, too am sorry to be 'embroiled unwittingly in the recent Battle of Neil's Marks.' . . . All standard tests show that Neil has high intelligence and mentally is of University calibre. But we both know that success in University depends

By BOB
HOLLYWOOD
do they do it?"
sion viewer asks
tinguished acto
commercial pitch
They do it fo
else could an act
for one day's wor
will pay that
names.
Take the exam
G. Robinson. He'

STILL BREAK
ATTENDANCE
FOLK SIN
RON, LAURI
in the BALINESE

Piggra's

CITY CENTRE
MOTOR HOTEL
CARLTON at ELLICE
* Banquet Facilities

F
Jean He

N
AL

Music b
Supper
No Cove
except
WE
From ou
CHINE
Served N

CLUB
RUT
Star of
Dancing
OU
SM
6 to
11 p

wants
score-
first
, de-
pair
Bob
A's.
, 5-0.
Laurie
i did

e
y a
ocal
test
One
vis.
ball
rles
t on
der.

G RETURNS

on academic background and study habits as much if not more than on mere intelligence. Neil's background is weak and by the looks of his marks his study habits leave much to be desired. . . . Am I making myself clear? What I'm trying to say is that Neil's past record doesn't indicate that he is heading toward a University career. But, if he has a goal and a deep desire to reach that goal, he has the native intelligence to achieve [it]." Mr. Hodgkinson sums up: "There has been, as I have said, a tremendous improvement in [Neil] as a person. I like the lad now, but I would gladly have got rid of him during his early days at Kelvin."

Many years later, Neil told *Shakey* author Jimmy McDonough, "I don't remember that much of it. I wanted an amp. I asked my dad if he'd lend us some money to buy an amp. He said my grades weren't good enough. If I got good grades, I could get an amp. My mom freaked out — that was just one of their arguments, y'know. I probably woulda done what my dad said. Hard to say."[259]

The flurry of letters subsided, but Neil's school career, such as it was, went on. Kelvin Awards Day was held on June 5 in the new gym; students with high enough marks were exempted from final exams, but Neil wasn't among them.

The Squires had booked four gigs during June. Neil was still without an amplifier, and he had to make do with rentals and loaners. An odd booking for the Squires was the Special Rock & Roll Intermission at Winnipeg's Notre

---

CLOCKWISE FROM TOP: *George Wolak holding the brand new guitar, a Gibson SG Special, he received for Christmas, 1962.* [Courtesy of George Wolak]; *Ads for the Squires.* [*Winnipeg Free Press*, April 3/4, June 15, and April 8/9, 1964]

Dame Auditorium on June 9 — the main event was "All Star Wrestling," featuring an eight-man tag match. The Squires were paid nothing for this performance. A gig at the Maple Leaf Community Club on June 12 was more rewarding: it paid $40.

Another significant (although unpaid) gig occurred on June 15 at the Town 'n' Country, a supper/nightclub at 317 Kennedy Street near the University of Winnipeg. The Town 'n' Country was really a double venue. The Towers, the larger upstairs room with seating for 300, attracted an older and more upscale clientele. (A 19-year-old Barbra Streisand had played a two-week engagement at the Towers in July 1961, her first out-of-country booking.) By the mid-1960s the room featured up-and-coming local acts, in an atmosphere more formal than at the Gold Coach Lounge on the mezzanine level. The lounge was where university students gathered to hear rock bands, a relatively new phenomenon in Winnipeg in the early 1960s. An advertisement in the June 15, 1964, edition of the *Winnipeg Free Press* shows the Squires booked on the same bill as "Chad Allen [sic] and the Reflections, Lenny Breau, Judy Scott, Phil Sanchez and Miss Mickey [sic] Allen." It was highlighted as "A Gala Two Hour Show," part of "The Parade of Stars" for *The Mark Parr Show* taking place in the Towers from 11 p.m. to 1 a.m.

Allan Bates knew in advance that he would be unavailable for the gig at the Town 'n' Country, so Neil had to find a temporary replacement. George Wolak, a drafting student at Tec-Voc High School, heard through a mutual friend that Neil was looking for someone. George had played guitar in a Winnipeg band called the Belmorals since its formation in 1961. The Belmorals, which mainly played community clubs, high schools and church basements, folded in mid-1964. Neil and George connected, and Neil agreed to use George for the Town 'n' Country gig. George, who played a Gibson SG Special he had received for Christmas 1962,[260] recalls that he practised with Neil three times in the living/dining room at 1123 Grosvenor and once in the attic at his own home at 697 Aberdeen Avenue in the North End. The performance at the Town 'n' Country was a success.

Neil headed back to Kelvin for the last week of school before the doors officially closed on June 30. The summer that followed would alter the course of his adult life.

## ★ 11 ★
## GET GONE

*Well, I worked so hard*
*I flunked out of school*
*And everybody said*
*I was a teenage fool*
*Meanwhile I wrote me*
*a new set of rules*
*'Bout how to get gone*
*and how to be cool.*

— Neil Young, "Get Gone"

THE SUMMER OF 1964 STARTED on a high note with a July 5 appearance at the ProTeen, a teen dance hall on Pritchard Avenue off Arlington Street in the North End. Two gigs at the Cellar followed.

An advertisement in the *Winnipeg Free Press* from July 27 shows that the Squires played the Town 'n' Country again that night (though Ken Koblun's "List of Shows" fails to note the appearance). Acts on the same bill included Chad Allan, Vicki Knight, the Steiner Brothers, Jose Poneira and Jose Bolero. Once again the Squires were part of "The Parade of Stars" for *The Mark Parr Show*, "A Gala Two Hour Show" in the Towers from 11 p.m. to 1 a.m. (Ken mistakenly dated this show as August 6; he admits he often listed gigs days after the Squires played them.)[261]

Over the summer, Neil's resolve to leave school and make music a full-time career hardened. Ken Smyth recalls Neil talking about wanting "to go on the road," adding, "Neil made a commitment to music. . . . He knew what he was going to do. His vocation was going to be music. Going to school at the time was not seen as necessary." That put Neil at odds with Allan and Ken, who were serious about finishing high school. (Allan would be entering Grade 12, and Ken would be in Grade 11 at Grant Park High.) Ken Koblun, on the other hand, had just finished Grade 11 at Churchill High and was ready to follow Neil anywhere. A rift had developed in the band, and the conflict would soon come to a head.

In early August, Neil and Ken Smyth decided to make a day trip in Rassy's car to Falcon Lake, a resort town 145 kilometres east of Winnipeg in Whiteshell Provincial Park. "I think Neil had something in mind," Ken recalls. "There was a hotel and bar up there." Everything was going well until the car stalled on the highway, halfway to their destination. "I think the motor blew," Ken says. "A fellow came along and towed us all the way back to Winnipeg, right to his [Neil's] home. . . . We went back to Winnipeg, and Neil went back up to Falcon Lake later on."[262]

Jack Harper and Jim Atkin joined Neil for a camping trip to Falcon Lake once Rassy's car had been repaired. It was a turning point for Neil: it was here that he met Pam Smith, his first serious girlfriend. Pam and her twin sister, Pat, attended high school in the East Kildonan area of northeast Winnipeg, but worked summers at Falcon Lake.

Jack Harper documented some of the happy moments from this trip in a group of three photos dated August 1964.[263] One photo shows Neil and Pam Smith sitting, with his arm affectionately wrapped around her, against a sunny background of water and boats. Another shows Neil posed on his knees at the flap of his half-collapsed tent; the third shows Neil and Jim Atkin in shorts and T-shirts, arms slung over each other's shoulders in a display of camaraderie on the beach along the water's edge.

Lynne Hamilton, whose family owned a cottage on the south shore of Falcon Lake, recalls that Pam and Pat "were very pretty, smiling all the time." Pam worked in a drugstore, Pat in a restaurant and Lynne at the local grocery store. The Hamilton family frequently hosted barbecues at their cottage, and Neil (ever grateful for a free meal) said that Lynne's mother made the best burgers around.

Roasting marshmallows at night over a campfire on the beach was a favourite activity, and Neil could usually be counted on to strum his guitar and sing one or two songs. On weekends, everyone looked forward to the hootenannies held at various cottages in the area. Lynne remembers Neil coming to her family's cottage along with Jim Atkin — who was now dating Pat — and a few others, trying to teach everyone "Four Strong Winds," the song he had first heard on the jukebox at Pembina Sals. He loved the song's simple melody and poignant message, and he insisted that the group sing it over and over until he was satisfied with how it sounded. In the 2006 documentary *Heart of Gold*, Neil introduces "Four Strong Winds" with a memory of his time at Falcon Lake. He recalls being at a restaurant there: "I think I spent all my money playing that song over and over again." The restaurant was most likely the Falcon's Nest, still renowned for its burgers and fries and massive ice-cream cones.

Neil and Pam often went for walks along the beach. Opening up to her, Neil confided that he was self-conscious about his skinny physique and didn't like to wear swim trunks, so he wouldn't go swimming. He was also sensitive about the fact that he didn't play sports like other boys. An empathetic Pam remarks, "It was something Neil wasn't capable of doing — he almost felt apologetic about it. Neil was insecure as a person — I think that's why playing music was so good for him. He had all the confidence in the world in that role, whereas in the person role he had so many misgivings. . . . He wanted to be a regular guy, he wanted to fit in. He didn't feel that he did, and even if you told him he did, he wouldn't believe it. Neil knew he was different."[264]

Pam was drawn by Neil's imagination and respected his commitment to music: "He struck me as a very sincere person. Outwardly, he'd present an attitude of being very lighthearted, laugh at a lot of things — he seemed like a leader with the group of friends he was with. But I think underneath it he had a much more serious side. I felt his mind was always working. He was a loner."[265] The connection Neil forged with Pam continued after they returned to Winnipeg. Before long, Neil asked Pam to go steady, presenting her with his Kelvin High School ring to seal the deal. "Pam was my steady girlfriend," he recalls, "my first real love."[266]

Images from Neil's time at Falcon Lake with Pam would surface in two songs. "I'll Love You Forever" was about "a beautiful, soulful girl I met a Falcon Lake who was my first love . . ."[267] The song was set by the ocean, a place Neil had never seen — "We used the sound effects of waves. I thought it was really cool."[268] "I'll Love You Forever" remained unreleased until it appeared on *The Neil Young Archives (Volume 1)* in June 2009. The song was recorded by Ray Dee in Fort William at radio station CJLX on November 23, 1964. A second song, "Falcon Lake" — originally written and recorded during the first half of 1968 at two separate recording studios — remained unfinished and unreleased until it was remixed by Tim Mulligan at Plywood Digital in February 1998 and subsequently included as the track "Falcon Lake (Ash on the Floor)" on the *Buffalo Springfield Box Set*. The main melody would appear in another song, "Here We Are in the Years," from Neil's first solo album, *Neil Young*. Hints of other early Neil song melodies, such as "One More Sign" and "There Goes My Babe," can also be heard in "Falcon Lake (Ash on the Floor)."

Jack Harper believes Neil had a personal revelation at Falcon Lake that August: "Neil saw this band, the Crescendos, come down to the lakefront and plug in to the concession stand — just plug in to an outlet with a couple of amps and start playing. I think that sort of tweaked Neil's mind — 'Hmmm . . . *touring*.'"[269] Neil may also have noticed the VW bus the Crescendos used as their band vehicle; the Squires would need that kind of transportation if they were serious about touring. Neil spoke to the management at the hotel soon after seeing the Crescendos perform and convinced them to book the Squires, payment to consist of room and board. He excitedly called Ken Smyth and told him, "Get all your equipment . . . all expenses paid . . . bring everything up here. We're going to start playing this weekend and we are going to play up here for a week."[270]

But complications soon dampened Neil's excitement. Both Allan and Ken Smyth had plans that weekend. Nor would it have been easy for them to take time off from their summer jobs. Ken Smyth recalls, "In the summertime it was very hard to get any work as a band. People were off of school and they'd go to the lake. . . . In fairness to Neil, maybe we could have tried harder to get time off, but it's hard to get time off from a summer job you're only working for two months."[271]

Ken spoke to Allan, who reported to Neil that he didn't think they could make it up there to play. "So Neil said, 'Fine,' and I could tell he was irritated, and he hung up." Ken continues, "The next time he saw me in Winnipeg he said, 'Okay, we're going to finish our engagements, then we're breaking up.'"[272] Neil no longer wanted Smyth, Bates or Koblun in the band.

The verdict seemed abrupt and harsh to Ken Smyth and Allan. Ken Koblun had been noticeably absent through most of the "difficulties," but he was even more distressed over being fired than either Allan or Ken Smyth. He made tentative steps to join a new band, but his heart just wasn't in it. He remembers auditioning for a band at Rick Pollock's place in the North End, but he couldn't generate much enthusiasm. What he really wanted was to be a Squire and play with Neil.

Everyone ultimately remained friends, but Ken Smyth recalls, "There was an unpleasant moment when the band had to split up equipment that belonged to so-and-so, and then there was a little struggle regarding who 'the Squires' were after that."[273] Ken Smyth and Allan wanted the name for a new band they were planning to put together, but Neil wanted to retain it himself. Eventually it went to Neil, with no animosity involved.

In retrospect, Ken Smyth admits that Neil's frustration was understandable. "I mean, he's committed," he explains. "In fact, at this point, I think Neil had actually quit school. So he knew where he wanted to go — and if something like that came up, and all of a sudden your band's not going to show up to play — so I can understand that."[274]

Neil reflected on his actions years later: "I dislike firing people. Since my first high school garage band, I have had to make those decisions and have those conversations. . . . It hurts to be honest, but the muse has no conscience. If you do it for the music, you do it for the music, and everything else is secondary."[275]

Ken Smyth and Allan Bates, along with guitarist Doug Campbell — who would ultimately play with a later incarnation of the Squires — formed a new band called the Dimensions. Ken recalls, "The Dimensions kind of fell apart after Doug Campbell left. It was a blow to the band."

KEN KOBLUN WOULD RETURN TO the Squires after a couple of weeks, but in the meantime Neil sought out the services of another bass player. George Wolak was recruited to replace Allan Bates, and Neil asked George if he could recommend a bassist. George suggested Bob Wall, a North End friend with a homemade electric bass. It was during this time that George played a gig with Neil at the 4-D ("that beatnik place") — it may have been one of the open-mike hootenanny nights, since, as George recalls, it was just himself backing Neil.

One evening George went with Neil to the Red Top, where Boyd Kozak was the on-site CKRC deejay. Neil asked Boyd for the lyrics to "House of the Rising Sun," a traditional folk song that had been a recent hit for Eric Burdon and the Animals. "Neil was trying to learn all the verses," George recalls.

Meanwhile, Neil needed a new drummer to replace Ken Smyth. One candidate was his friend Bill Edmondson, who had attended Kelvin during the 1963-64 academic year and who owned a drum kit. Bill had come to Winnipeg from Montreal with his older brother Peter and their mother, Marg, after his parents divorced. They moved into the home of their widowed grandmother, Myrtle Blodgett, in the upper duplex at 1076 Grosvenor Avenue, and their troubled mother soon moved out, leaving Bill and Peter to live with "Myrt," as

Neil and Bill referred to her. Peter saw Rassy as a "socialite" who was too often away from home, and the family tried to make Neil feel especially welcome for that reason. Neil often brought over his guitar and played for them. Their grandmother thought he was "brilliant"; Peter thought Neil was "very intelligent and with it. He knew exactly what was happening in his music and the world in general." He adds, "Neil had a vision."

Toward the end of August, Neil called Ken Koblun to say, simply, "C'mon back," and Ken happily complied. Ken Smyth confirms, "His loyalty was always with Neil."

The next person to join the band was Jeffrey Dack Wuckert, who played piano and tenor sax. He was known simply as Dack — pronounced with a kind of twang to it — by his high school buddies at St. James Collegiate Institute in west Winnipeg. Jeff first learned to play the family's upright piano when he was ten. Both of his parents had musical backgrounds and encouraged him. During the summer of 1964, he played in a band called the Concepts, and on one memorable occasion he backed Bobby Curtola at Melrose Park Community Club. There were relatively few piano players in rock bands in Winnipeg at the time, so Neil was aware of him. Jeff recalls how he first met Neil: "One weekend we were playing Friday and Saturday night at St. Vital Community Club. We played there alternating sets with Carmine La Rosa and the Thunderstorms. . . . All of a sudden, as we were finishing a set, in walks two guys. One in a wrecked sweatshirt and the other guy looked like he was six foot four. It was none other than Neil and Ken. Judy [Jeff's girlfriend and future wife, Judy Wallis] was of course with me and I got her to come over and meet them, as they wanted me to join the group. Neil had just fired two band members and was looking for replacements. I jumped at the chance." Although he appreciated the opportunity of joining the Squires, Jeff had "no love of the music the Squires played. I'm a dyed in the wool R&B guy."

He and Neil may not have been as far apart in that respect as Jeff believed. Neil had become increasingly immersed in rhythm and blues, at least since April 1964, when he recorded "Ain't It the Truth" at the CKRC studios. This is when Neil first began listening to Jimmy Reed and learning to play the harmonica. Two R&B-influenced songs on the Squires' future set list at the Flamingo Club in Fort William were "Hi-Heel Sneakers" and "Baby What You Want Me to Do?" (The former was written by Robert Higgenbotham, recorded by Tommy Tucker and released in January 1964. The latter was written and recorded by Jimmy Reed, released in November 1959.)[276]

Neil premiered the new lineup of the Squires on August 23 at the 4-D in Winnipeg. Also premiering was Neil's new amp — a blond Tolex Tremolux piggyback. Rassy had come through with her promise to Neil. The Tremolux was the smallest of Fender's piggyback amps, with 35 watts of power and a two-by-ten-inch speaker cabinet. It offered a tremolo effect but no reverb. "I remember my first Fender amp," Neil recalls. "I got it as a gift from my mom. She always supported my music. It was a piggyback model. The amp was on top of the speaker cabinet. Two ten-inch speakers delivered the

---

CLOCKWISE FROM TOP: *Jeff Wuckert and Judy Wallis at a YMCA house party in the basement of the Elliot family home in Winnipeg, December 1962.* [Courtesy of Jeffrey Dack Wuckert]; *Ads and press for the Squires.* [*Winnipeg Free Press*, July 27, and October 3, 1964]

JAN 63

## Presenting The Squires

Left to right: Neil Young, Bill Edmonson, Jeffrey Dack and Ken Small.

The original Squires began in December 1962 strictly as an instrumental group; a year later they released their first disc, "Aurora." The group as it now appears includes Neil Young and Ken Small of the original Squires, with Jeffery Dack and Bill Edmondson, two new members of the group.

Neil Young, originally from Toronto came to Winnipeg in 1966. For two years he played in various groups and in 1962 organized the Squires. Shortly after he wrote "Aurora." Aside from being lead guitarist, he writes songs for the group.

Ken Small, bass guitarist, stands a dainty 6'5½". Ken is at present a grade 12 student in Churchill High School. His interest in music began in 1961 and he has been playing ever since.

Jeffery Dack, pianist, is at present a grade 12 student at St. James Collegiate. Jeff's interest in music began at an early age; in addition to piano, he plays saxophone, vibes and the organ. Jeff has backed Bobby Curtola, at stop-overs in Winnipeg.

Bill Edmondson, originally from Montreal, came to Winnipeg in 1963. In Montreal he backed singer Pierre Lalonde, and also found time to play in various other groups. Living across the street from Neil, the boys became good friends, and Bill became the drummer of the group.

At present Neil Young and the Squires are booking local dances, and preparing themselves for their new release "White Flower."

whopping sound of the smallest piggyback amp Fender ever made. But to me it was HUGE."[277]

It was around this time that Neil suggested a name for the band. Bill Edmondson recalls Neil telling him and Ken Koblun, "I'm gonna be in this business the rest of my life, guaranteed. Do you mind if I put my name in front of the band — Neil Young and the Squires?"[278] His proposal met with little objection and was quickly adopted. On August 30, Neil Young and the Squires played their second gig at the 4-D.

ALTHOUGH KEN KOBLUN HAD RETURNED to the fold, George Wolak claims to have played one final gig with Neil and the Squires at Winnipeg Beach, a resort on the southwestern shore of Lake Winnipeg, about 56 kilometres north of the city, over the Labour Day weekend.[279] George remembers that they performed at the Midnight Dance (that took place from midnight to 3 a.m.) in the old dance pavilion, which had been converted into a roller rink.

According to George, he, Neil, Bill Edmondson and Bob Wall played this gig. The Labour Day weekend performance isn't listed in Ken Koblun's "List of Shows," perhaps because summer school and a temporary job kept Ken from playing. (The list is exclusively a record of shows that Ken played; any appearances by Neil with George Wolak and/or Bob Wall would not have been included.)

Neil asked George if he would be interested in going to Toronto with the Squires, but George politely declined. He wanted to return to Tec-Voc to finish his Grade 12. Obviously Neil was already thinking about taking the band on the road, and he needed a rhythm guitarist to replace Allan Bates.

IT WAS DURING THE EARLY fall that Neil became the proud owner of the 1948 Buick Roadmaster hearse he called "Mort" — more formally, "Mortimer Hearseburg."[280]

Mort had been custom-built as a hearse by the oddly named Flxible Company in Loudonville, Ohio — the name *Flxible* was inscribed on the side of the front fender. The company, originally known as the Flxible Sidecar Company, began production in 1913 with motorcycle sidecars that featured a flexible mounting. The company name changed to the Flxible Company in 1919, and in 1924 — faced with a falling demand for sidecars — it moved on to produce a line of hearses, ambulances and buses.[281]

"Mort was real important. My first car. It was part of my identity," Neil says. "It was like this weird thing — The Band and The Car. I remember getting the hearse. A hundred and fifty bucks. Kinda gave the group something that made them different."[282] Neil recalls, "We always used a hearse to carry our equipment because it was like a giant station wagon. It was fantastic! It was like they built it for us."[283]

Mort was a gift from Rassy: "Rassy paid the bill. . . . I couldn't believe my good fortune. I was high as a kite!"[284] But Ken Koblun remembers that both he and Neil contributed to the purchase of Mort, albeit in a smaller capacity than Rassy. Ken had been setting aside a portion of both his and Neil's engagement earnings for the express purpose of buying a band vehicle. "[Rassy] may have paid the lion's share, but both Neil and I helped out," he says.

Cosmetically, Mort sported a blue velvet trim interior in the back compartment. "In the back there were really nice curtains and a headliner of plush velvet with pull-down shades," Neil recalls, "and there was a sliding divider window between the front and the back. There were rollers on the floor for moving the caskets easily in and out of the back through a gigantic rear door. . . . Perfect for rolling amps and PAs in and out, sleeping and storing equipment."[285]

Physically, "the wheelbase was 156 inches" and the hearse was "at least eight inches taller in the hood than a normal Roadmaster."[286] Technically, the hearse had a straight-eight engine and three-speed manual transmission, two side doors and a tailgate, so it wasn't a true rear-loading hearse. (It was known as a three-loader — three doors in the back.) It may be that Neil's 1948 Buick hearse was one of the last equipped with a three-speed manual transmission.[287]

Neil unintentionally inflicted some additional wear and tear on the vehicle. "Mort was a good runner," he recalls, "and to save gas I used to go into neutral on downgrades, not knowing this practice was putting unnecessary strain on the drive train which I would pay for later."[288] Ken Koblun was asked in a 2006 *Broken Arrow* interview if he thought Neil was "totally nuts" when he bought his first hearse. "I thought it was reasonable and logical," he replied, "except that I was afraid that if it broke down there would be some big bills to play and we'd never get parts!"[289] Ken's worries proved well-founded: Mort's entire transmission would drop as one heavy steaming mass onto a highway near Blind River, Ontario, at the end of June 1965. The manual transmission could not be replaced, and Neil would be forced to abandon the vehicle.

Neil later wrote a song for Mort, the affectionate "Long May You Run."[290] It became a trademark song and remains a Canadian favourite — Neil performed it at the closing ceremonies of the Winter Olympics in Vancouver in 2010.

Ken Koblun is aware of only one other band in Winnipeg during the 1960s that used a hearse: "[T]here was one other group with an organ player who had a [Hammond]

B3 and his group would travel around in a hearse. I don't know who got the idea first."[291] It became commonplace during the 1960s-70s for bands to use a hearse to transport band members and equipment — especially the California-based surf bands, who discovered that a hearse was also a convenient way to carry surf boards.

Brian Blick recalls a story involving Neil and Mort:

> One day, I was sitting at home on Harvard Avenue in Winnipeg when I received a call from Neil. He was very excited that he had just bought a 1948 Buick hearse and he was just doing a few things to clean it up. I told him I would be right over to give him a hand. So I jumped into our 1940 Packard two-door business coupe and went over to Grosvenor. I pulled into the back land and there was the Buick, and Neil vacuuming out the back.
>
> He was beaming. [The vehicle] was in pretty good shape and the straight-eight engine was sound. The hood lifted up from the side after undoing a couple of ornamental "spears" on the side of the hood. He took an unusual delight in showing me how all the rollers and coffin slides worked. We cleaned up that car for most of the afternoon.[292]
>
> One day Neil came over to our house on Harvard Avenue, parking right in front. There was no one home except my grandmother, who was upstairs. Neil and I were just hanging out listening to some music in the bar as we called it. About 30 minutes later my mother arrived home

Sept 22/64

Dear Scott –

Neil has decided
to follow your advice
and become a drop-
out. He hopes to return
to school next year.

I hope this arrives
in time to aid you in
figuring your next
payment.

Rosso

by taxi. She ran into the house and, with panic in her voice, shouted, "Is Grandma okay?"

"Yeah, what's the big problem?" I asked calmly.

"Well, why is there a hearse outside?" she asked.

"Oh . . . that's mine," Neil said, as I burst out laughing.

"Thank God!" she said. "I thought Grandma died."

NEIL WAS STILL SEEING PAM steadily after her return from Falcon Lake in the early fall of 1964. He often arrived at her home driving Mort, though "Pam Smith's dad was not so sure about it [Mort] when I pulled up in front of their house in the residential area where they lived." Much like Brian Blick's mother, "the neighbors all thought that someone had died."[293]

One of their favourite places to go was the 4-D. Pam Smith recalls, "Neil used to eat there a lot. When the band played there, we could have anything there we wanted to eat."[294] Fran Gebhard, who worked at the club as a part-time waitress, was still carrying a torch for Neil and recalls that Pam was "a real problem" for her. She felt "uncomfortable" in their presence and would try to make herself "disappear,"

---

FROM TOP: *Publicity photo of the Squires taken at the CKRC studios in September 1964. Clockwise from left: Neil (holding his 6120 Gretsch electric guitar), Bill Edmondson, Ken Koblun, Jeff Wuckert.* [Courtesy of Ken Koblun]; *Letter dated September 22, 1964, from Rassy to Scott informing him that Neil has dropped out of Kelvin High School.* [Trent University Archives, Scott Young fonds (90-003 Box 26)] so she wouldn't have to be around them. She knew Neil was serious about Pam and saw her as "a threat." It took a long time for Fran to get over Neil, and Pam wasn't helping the situation. But the Squires continued to perform at the 4-D and Neil continued to participate in the open-mike nights. Neil and Pam dated throughout the fall and winter of 1964, breaking up sometime before their first anniversary. "We went together for about a year," Neil recalls, "maybe less, as I remember it, a long time for someone that age."[295] Neil still thought of Pam occasionally after he left Winnipeg and wrote her "long, rambling letters," which she did not answer. He retains warm feelings for her to this day.

THAT AUTUMN, NEIL BEGAN SPENDING more time with Squires pianist Jeff Wuckert and Jeff's girlfriend, Judy Wallis. On the way to a gig at the River Heights Community Club in mid-September the three of them stopped by Neil's place. Neil decided to make a pot of coffee in Rassy's Pyrex double-decker coffeepot. "Neil put the glass coffeepot on the stove on high because we were in a hurry," Jeff recalls. "I guess we left without making the coffee." River Heights Community Club was located close to Neil's place, so they returned between sets. "We come in," Jeff says, "and the whole place is dark, except for this funny red glow coming from the kitchen. And there it is . . . the glass pot on the stove with no water in it just sitting there glowing from the red burner under it." Neil turned down the burner while everyone stood back. "A minute later, the stove clicks down as the element starts to cool. As it clicked, the pot exploded and shattered into pieces of little tiny glass particles in a heap on top of the burner. I think we then turned the element off and wondered what we were going to tell Rassy." No one was looking forward to that encounter, especially Neil. Rassy's reaction is unrecorded.

Meanwhile, Bill Edmondson had moved out of his grand-mother's home on Grosvenor to live with his girlfriend, Sharon McRae, after being hired as the drummer in the Squires. They shared the third floor of a grand old brick house at 874 Dorchester Avenue, on the corner of Dorchester and Wentworth. Sharon had a hand in making the pink cummerbunds the Squires wore as part of their stage outfits: "They all wore black pants, pink cummerbunds and white tops. I tore up my grad dress to make those silly things for a weekend show at some school." The laundry room was located in the basement of their apartment, so Sharon had to "tread many stairs to wash those pink cummerbunds before ironing them for the next show."

Sharon worked at CKRC and repeatedly encouraged Harry Taylor and deejay Doc Steen to take a promotional photo of the Squires. A photo session was finally booked in late September. Jeff's mother made vest pullover tops for the band, and Jeff made the ascot ties on his mother's sewing machine. Jeff recalls that Neil — typically not fond of fancy dress clothes — didn't much care for the vest outfits. Jeff himself dressed meticulously and often kidded Neil about his less formal attire: "I was always bugging Neil about what he wore." The publicity photo of Neil Young and the Squires appeared in the October 3 issue of the *Winnipeg Free Press*. Jeff recalls that stage names were a big thing back then — he was listed as Jeffrey Dack, while Ken Koblun chose the ironic surname Small.

The band sometimes rehearsed in the living room at Sharon and Bill's apartment. The landlady who owned the house lived on the second floor, but since she was deaf she allowed them to practise unimpeded. Neil parked Mort in the back, so instruments could be quickly loaded for gigs. He was a frequent visitor at Sharon and Bill's place, and Sharon noticed that he "would [seem to] drift off all the time, and sure enough he would be writing something down on his arm, a napkin or whatever he could get his hands on." Sharon adds, "Neil was a good poet," although she didn't care for his voice. "I never liked Neil's singing, and told him so, lots of times, when I got mad." When things were more amicable, Neil liked to share his notes with her — ideas for a song, for lyrics or for something to do with their gigs. "Neil was actually quite shy, but had a very dry and sharp sense of humour." His shyness vanished whenever he picked up an instrument; then he became outgoing and self-assured.

NEIL'S SCHOOL CAREER WAS APPROACHING its ultimate crisis. He had thought long and hard that summer about how to resolve the conflict between school and music. When Aunt Snooky — Rassy's sister who lived with her family in Texas — visited Winnipeg, Neil told her about his plan to leave school. "Neil," she said, "you're nearly finished — why don't you wait and get your high school degree?" He replied, "I can't, Aunt Snooky — my music, it *has* to come out."[296]

Near the end of the spring term, Neil had spoken to Vice-Principal Hodgkinson about his musical ambitions. When the vice-principal asked, "Neil, waddya wanna do with your life?" Neil replied in all sincerity, "Well, I'd like to play music in a bar." Hodgkinson tried to convince him this was folly: "That's a flash-in-the-pan kind of thing, y'know. In the music business, people come and go real fast. Look — you hear about somebody one year, and the next year they're gone."[297] But the vice-principal's remarks only steeled Neil's resolve: "Well, that made a big impression. That wasn't gonna be *me.*" He realized the odds were against him, but he also knew he had to follow his dream. Principal Cochrane, in a similar confrontation, seemed to side with Neil: "Go and give it a try,"[298] he said — once Neil was forced to confront the unpleasant reality of making of a living, he would recognize the importance of a high school diploma and return to Kelvin.

Rassy delivered the news to Scott in a tersely worded letter[299] dated September 22, 1964:

> Neil has decided to follow your advice and become a drop-out. He hopes to return to school next year. I hope this arrives in time to aid you in figuring our next payment.

Her comment about Neil hoping to return to school was likely wishful thinking. She must have known Neil was determined to make a success of his music career and that nothing would stop him. And, ultimately, she supported him in his quest.

Scott received official confirmation in a letter[300] from Vice-Principal Hodgkinson a week later:

> Neil has not returned to Kelvin High School this year. I have no idea if he is attending school elsewhere or not.
>     Sorry.
>
> Yours truly,
> F. A. Hodgkinson

Scott immediately responded with a surprisingly temperate letter[301] to Neil:

There is no importance in being a school dropout as long as you now can set a course and follow it successfully. Your Uncle Bob did that and many others. . . . Some day when you are older you will understand that in the troubles in our family, nobody has been either black or white.

One visitor we had this summer was Barbara Digou, the stepdaughter of my cousin Alice. She said she had met you and had heard you play at dances and that you were terrific, both at playing and singing.

This was perhaps Scott's way of acknowledging what Rassy already knew: that music had become absolutely central to his son's life. Neil's course had been set, and there would be no steering him away from it.

---

## ✶ PART THREE ✶
# LEAVING SUGAR MOUNTAIN

---

*Oh, to live on Sugar Mountain*
*With the barkers and the coloured balloons.*
*You can't be twenty on Sugar Mountain*
*Though you're thinking that*
*You're leaving there too soon.*
*You're leaving there too soon.*

— Neil Young, "Sugar Mountain"

---

## ✲ 12 ✲
## OH CANADA

*Oh Canada*
*We played all night*
*I really hate to leave you now*
*But to stay just wouldn't be right.*[1]

— Neil Young, "Don't Be Denied"

ALTHOUGH NEIL'S CHILDHOOD EFFECTIVELY ENDED once he quit high school at the age of 18, he still needed periodic financial support from his mother during the following year. He lived with Rassy at 1123 Grosvenor until mid-October, at which time he and the Squires left on their first sojourn to Fort William, 705 kilometres east of Winnipeg at the head of Lake Superior. It was in Fort William that Neil began to develop what generations of listeners would come to recognize as his own musical style, transitioning from rock-and-roll/R&B to a characteristic folk-rock sound.

The Squires, then composed of Neil, Ken Koblun and Bill Edmondson, played a six-day series of shows at the Flamingo Club before returning to Winnipeg for some gigs during the latter part of October. They left for Fort William a second time in early November, playing a long string of gigs at the Flamingo once again and then the Fort William 4-D coffeehouse for the first time. Members of Donny B and the Bonnvilles,[2] the top band in the Fort William–Port Arthur area

347

at the time, caught the Squires performing at the Flamingo and became fast friends. Local guitarist Terry Erickson, who often backed other musicians during coffeehouse gigs, also became friendly with Neil. Neil famously wrote "Sugar Mountain" on his 19th birthday while staying at the Victoria Hotel in Fort William. The lyrics suggest he was aware that his carefree childhood years were behind him.

During this period, Neil came to the attention of Ray Dee, the deejay at local station CJLX, who would record another version of "I Wonder" plus "I'll Love You Forever"[3] (Neil's ode to Pam Smith and Falcon Lake) and "Together Alone"[4] in the radio station's recording studio on November 23. Neil later remarked, "My favourite 'I Wonder' is the Ray Dee production. . . . It features Bill Edmondson on drums."[5]

Neil and the Squires returned to Winnipeg in mid-December to play a lengthy engagement at the Twilight Zone, the popular teen club that had recently opened in St. Vital. The club had become a hangout for musicians, including Neil, who wanted to catch other bands performing. Randy Bachman name-checks Neil and the Twilight Zone in "Prairie Town": *On the other side of Winnipeg / Neil and the Squires played the Zone / But then he went to play / for a while in Thunder Bay / He never looked back and he's never coming home.*

Neil remained in Winnipeg for three months, playing gigs with different aggregations of the Squires. He fired Bill Edmondson — who had proved unreliable and had some personal issues to deal with — shortly after they'd returned to Winnipeg, and lured away guitarist Doug Campbell from the Dimensions (Allan Bates and Ken Smyth's band), with Terry Crosby replacing Edmondson on drums. Terry remained with the band briefly and was then replaced by Al Johnson, who was also with the band for only a short time. Neil has admitted to favouring the next lineup of the Squires: Ken Koblun on bass, Doug Campbell on rhythm guitar and Randy Peterson on drums.

In the spring of 1965, V Records expressed interest in two of Neil's songs — "I Wonder"[6] and "(I'm a Man and) I Can't Cry" — and the band recorded a demo on March 15, 1965, in Mickey and Bunny's basement studio at 11 Gilia Drive. Neil, Ken Koblun, Doug Campbell (guitar) and Randy Peterson (drums) played at the session. V Records never released the songs, which were eventually included in *The Neil Young Archives (Volume 1)*.[7]

It was a turbulent time for the band. There seemed to be a revolving door through which different Squires passed for varying lengths of time and with various degrees of success. "We kept morphing and changing," Neil remarks. "People would join and then we'd go do gigs out of town. They'd quit because they didn't want to leave town and weren't ready to take a chance. Some of the guys I wanted to take I couldn't because their parents would say, 'You're going to screw up your life.' Suddenly the timing would derail. Some good musicians who just couldn't step out and take a chance got left behind."[8]

The Squires departed for Churchill in early April 1965. By this time Bob Clark had become their drummer. (Fifteen-year-old Randy Peterson had to stay in Winnipeg to finish high school.) Doug Campbell also decided to remain in Winnipeg and not pursue his career. The Squires were a trio once again. They played a string of gigs at the Hudson Hotel, including one night at the Navy Club, and returned to Winnipeg briefly in mid-April, setting out for Fort William one last time a few days later.

An iconic photo shows the Squires dressed for a gig, posing in front of Mort in Fort William shortly after their arrival. Publicity photos of the band were taken backstage at the Flamingo Club by Don Baxter, who tended bar at the Blue Swan Inn.

Neil gave Ray Dee a copy of the basement recording the Squires had made in Winnipeg on March 15, hoping he could bring it to the attention of record companies. Ray had tried to do the same thing with the Squires' earlier recording of "I'll Love You Forever," but to no avail.

It was during their last sojourn to "Fort Bill" that Neil met Stephen Stills, then a member of a band called the Company, who performed at the 4-D on April 18. Neil recognized Stephen's abilities as a vocalist and introduced himself after the Company's set. They found they had much in common, and vowed to reconnect and play together sometime in the future.

In addition to gigs at the 4-D, Ray Dee secured some one-nighters for the Squires. One of these gigs was on May 21 at Westgate High School in Fort William, where an unknown audience member took some photos of their performance.

Terry Erickson began to regularly sit in with the band at the 4-D during May, and by the end of the month there was talk of him joining as rhythm guitarist. He was with the band when they played three gigs at Smitty's Pancake House at the

---

FROM TOP: *Victoria Hotel & Grill, Fort William, circa 1949.* [Courtesy of Dave Cano]; *Ad for the Squires' appearance at the Twilight Zone in St. Vital.* [*Winnipeg Free Press*, December 18, 1964]; *Posed in front of Mort in Fort William, April 1965. Left to right: Ken Koblun, Neil, Bob Clark.* [Courtesy of Ken Koblun]

Edward Island (skip Art    fireplaces, radiators and

**~INGS~**

50  12—Weathervane

00  6—News, Viewpoint

**TWILITE ZONE**
539 St. Mary's Rd., St. Vital
Something New and Different
FRI. - SAT. - SUN. NITE
**THE SQUIRES**
SUN. AFTERNOON 3 to 7 P.M.
HOOTENANY
Full Course Meals

GL 3-7948

**Pinetr~**

YOUR

end of May, appearing as the High Flying Birds. The name
derived from the popular Billy Edd Wheeler folk song "High
Flying Bird," a song the Company performed in Fort William
with Stephen Stills on vocals. Neil included his arrangement
of the song on their set list, and it proved extremely popular.
The High Flying Birds performed two gigs at the 4-D in mid-
June; Don Baxter once again took a series of publicity photos
of the band, this time posed with their instruments on an
empty boxcar behind the club.

Without much forethought, Neil consented to drive Terry
Erickson to a gig he had lined up with another band in
Sudbury, 650 kilometres away. (Squires drummer Bob Clark,
as well as Tom Horricks and Donny Brown of the Bonnvilles,
went along for the adventure. Ken Koblun remained in
Fort William, unaware of Neil's plans.) Much of the route
followed the rugged coastline of Lake Superior through a
sparsely populated area of the Canadian Shield. It was near
Sault Ste. Marie that the hearse's engine began to knock
and bang, and just outside Ironbridge, Ontario, the entire
transmission dropped out of the chassis onto the highway.
The hearse was hauled to Bill's Garage in Blind River, but
finding a replacement transmission proved more difficult
than Neil had anticipated.

He left Mort in the garage before making his way to
Toronto on the back of Terry's Honda motorbike, which
Neil had been transporting in the back of the hearse. Neil
figured they could stay with his father until they got their
footing. He contacted Bob Clark and Ken Koblun and
persuaded them to join him in Toronto for the reformation
of the Squires, now composed of Neil, Terry, Ken and Bob,
and they were rechristened 4 To Go. Prospects were slim,
and Bob soon departed for Winnipeg, followed shortly

afterward by Terry, who had lined up some gigs in England.

In the meantime Neil tried to play on his own whenever and wherever he could. This meant mainly playing for free. Agent and promoter Martin Onrot witnessed one of Neil's informal solo performances, was suitably impressed and signed him as a client. He urged Neil to get a band together and was confident that he would be able secure some bookings. Guitarist Jim Ackroyd, a former member of the Galaxies in Winnipeg who had relocated to Toronto a year earlier, was recruited for the band next. Neil found Geordie McDonald's name on the back of another musician's card pinned up on the bulletin board at the Long & McQuade music store on Bloor Street West, and McDonald agreed to drum for the band.

Neil had earlier determined that nothing further could be done to resuscitate the badly ailing Mort. A postcard to Rassy from Parry Sound, Ontario, in mid-July 1965 mentioned Mort's demise: "Please cancel the insurance as Mort is dead. The transmission fits but the rear-end is ruined."[9]

With Mort formally retired, Neil bought a 1947 Buick convertible that he formally christened "Tinker Bell." It cost $75, but Neil was so cash-strapped that the purchase left him without money for either a licence or registration for the car. He abandoned the Buick a few months later when he couldn't keep up with the ongoing expenses.

It was during this time that Neil composed "Casting Me Away From You"[10] and "There Goes My Babe," which he recorded with Comrie Smith (along with another recent song, "Hello Lonely Woman"),[11] in his parents' attic at 46 Gulfdale Road[12] in October. Neil was living in Geordie's old apartment at 88 Isabella Street, which he immortalized in the song "Ambulance Blues" — *Oh Isabella, proud Isabella /*

*They tore you down / And plowed you under* — and worked briefly as a stock boy at Coles bookstore at Yonge Street and Charles Street.[13] The band followed a rigid rehearsal schedule and tried in earnest to make a go of things, but Martin Onrot was unable to secure any gigs for them. The writing was on the wall and the group disbanded, disheartened. It had been the last gasp of the band formerly known as the Squires.

Neil visited Rassy in Winnipeg for two weeks that fall. His mind was on his music (as usual), and he talked about going back east and perhaps making a trip to New York City. Shortly after his return, Neil and Ken Koblun decided on a whim to go to New York to visit Jean Gurney, the female singer from the Company. Neil was also anxious to reconnect with Stephen Stills, who had given him his address six months earlier in Fort William. Richie Furay, Stephen's roommate, answered the door when they knocked and told Neil that Stephen had left for L.A. a few months before. Neil played some of his songs for Richie, who was especially impressed by the new tune "Nowadays Clancy Can't Even Sing." Neil and Ken stayed in New York City a few more days and then headed back to Toronto, where their prospects were still dim.

In a decision he later regretted, Neil traded his beloved Gretsch for a Gibson 12-string acoustic guitar and tried to make it as a solo folksinger in Yorkville. Neil was listening to Bert Jansch's and Phil Ochs's earliest recordings — they would both prove to be major influences on Neil's own work. In a 1969 KSAN interview with deejay Tony Pig, Neil remarked, "Melodically, speaking, Phil Ochs was a big influence on me. I really think Phil Ochs is a genius. He's written fantastic, incredible songs — he's on the same level as Dylan in my eyes." While introducing a cover of Ochs's "Changes" at Farm Aid in July 2013, Neil glowingly spoke of Ochs as "one of the greatest songwriters that ever lived." Neil was also in awe of Bert Jansch's musical prowess. He listened to Jansch's first album repeatedly during the time he lived in Yorkville and called it "some of the greatest guitar playing I ever heard."[14] Neil has admitted that he borrowed liberally from Jansch's "Needle of Death" while composing "Ambulance Blues," which he and Bert played together at the 2006 Bridge School Benefit Concert. Jansch later opened for Neil during his 2010 Twisted Road Tour. Two years after Jansch's death in October 2011, Neil covered "Needle of Death," and a film of his performance was shown at "A Celebration of Bert Jansch," a tribute to the folksinger held in London at the Royal Festival Hall in December 2013.

Absorbing these new influences and others, Neil was able to secure a few solo gigs at the Bohemian Embassy and the New Gate of Cleve, and he played at least one informal solo gig at the Riverboat in late 1965.[15] He also played casually at some of the Riverboat's Monday-night hootenannies as a member of the Public Futilities, a folk group.

Neil became increasingly depressed and frustrated over his inability to secure steady bookings and began to compose deep and introspective "serious songs," such as "Runaround Babe," "The Ballad of Peggy Grover,"[16] "The Rent Is Always Due,"[17] "I Ain't Got the Blues"[18] and "Extra, Extra." He recorded these songs — as well as "Nowadays Clancy Can't Even Sing"[19] and "Sugar Mountain" — at a demo session in Studio B at Elektra Records in New York City in the late fall,[20] but nothing came of the session.

Some luck came his way in January 1966 when he was recruited as a member of the Mynah Birds, a popular, much-booked band led by Ricky James Matthews (later and more famously known as Rick James). Bass player Bruce Palmer

was the one who notified Neil about the vacancy after their guitarist suddenly departed. But at a recording session in Motown,[21] Ricky was busted. He was a draft dodger and was AWOL from the U.S. Navy, a serious offence. He turned himself in and did some prison time before finding fame in the late 1970s as a funk artist. Ricky's arrest effectively ended the recording sessions with Motown, and the group's contract was cancelled.

Neil and Bruce Palmer hatched a plan to make their way to L.A. They decided to sell some of the band's equipment (which they did not own) to raise a grubstake to finance the trip, including the purchase of a vehicle. Toward the end of March, after their short and wild careers with the Mynah Birds, Neil and Bruce (and four other passengers)[22] left for L.A. in a 1953 Pontiac hearse, which Neil christened Mort II.

His next band would be Buffalo Springfield.

DURING AN INTERVIEW AT THE June 1987 Shakin' All Over event in Winnipeg, Neil was asked whether he regretted losing the innocence of the early years.

"Sometimes," he replied. "Everyone regrets innocence

---

FROM TOP: *Behind the Fourth Dimension, Fort William, June 1965. Clockwise from lower left: Neil, Terry Erickson, Bob Clark, Ken Koblun.* [Courtesy of Ken Koblun, © 1965 Don Baxter]; *Fourth Dimension, Fort William, May 8, 1965. Left to right: Neil, Bob Clark, Ken Koblun.* [Private Collection of Owen Clark and Brighit Morrigan]; *Backstage at the Flamingo Club, Fort William, April 1965. Left to right: Neil, Bob Clark, Ken Koblun (holding Terry Erickson's Fender White Jazz bass).* [Courtesy of Ken Koblun, © 1965 Don Baxter] FOLLOWING PAGE: *Westgate High School, Fort William, May 21, 1965. Left to right: Ken Koblun, Bob Clark, Neil.* [Courtesy of Ken Koblun]

lost. No way to get it back. It's better to go forward. In the next world we'll get it back."[23] As for the original members of the Squires, "They never wanted to make it like I did. We had a great time together while we were together."[24]

Randy Bachman recognized in Neil the same drive and determination that he possessed. Neil had "a 'look' in his dark eyes," says Randy. "A focused determination of getting to a place far from where he was. I've been told I had the same look. When one knows at an early age that their gift, talent and direction is musical, one tends to focus on that and let nothing interfere or impede the forward motion toward the end of that rainbow." He adds, "I saw Neil play many times in several different bands. In those days many band members revolved or went in and out of bands. Some guys didn't have the dream and discipline, some chose sports or girlfriends over being in a band, but the ones who were constant figures in the bands were the ones that made it. No obstacle was too big to overcome."[25]

Bob Young feels his parents made a significant contribution to Neil's career: "I think my brother's success and what he's done as a singer-songwriter, is largely attributable to the support he got from my parents. And some of that support was critical."[26]

It's true that, despite family conflicts, Neil retains pleasant memories of his childhood and his parents. Although Scott's fortunes as a writer waxed and waned, the family enjoyed a high standard of living. Neil and Bob suffered no significant material deprivation, and the family enjoyed such perks as winter holidays in Florida. "I remember really good things about both my parents," Neil said in a 1979 interview with Cameron Crowe. Scott and Rassy's separation and the resulting divorce had complex repercussions, but whatever anxiety Neil experienced in the wake of their conflict could be transmuted and redeemed, in a kind of psychological alchemy, through the medium of music.

Winnipeg was fertile ground for Neil's musical ambition, and he enjoyed the consistent and enthusiastic support of his mother. Rassy was proud of his accomplishments, as Scott would be once Neil's career began to progress. In Winnipeg, Neil was allowed a degree of freedom other teenagers envied, and he forged ahead with his dream with considerable independence, though at the expense of his conventional education. "Neil is like a lighthouse beam," Neil's long-time photographer and archivist Joel Bernstein remarks. "He has an incredibly intense focus in a very narrow area to the exclusion of all else."[27]

THE YOUNG FAMILY'S MANY MOVES may have inadvertently fostered Neil's ability to cope with and adapt to change. In a 1992 interview Neil recalls, "That's the way I was brought up — to keep changing. . . . I went to 12 different schools before I finished Grade 11 or whenever I dropped out, and my family moved around a lot. All the time, there was always different things happening. So in my life, I can roll with that."[28] Neil referenced his numerous childhood moves in the song "Born in Ontario": *I left home at a tender young age / 'Cause Mum and Daddy never seemed to stay / In any one place for very long / So we just kept moving, moving on.*

All that time on the road may also have deepened his fascination with vehicles: "I have a thing for transportation. Cars, boats, trains. Travelling. I like moving."[29]

The continual change — moving, meeting different people and struggling to find a place among them — bears an obvious relationship to Neil's life as a working musician and songwriter. A capacity to adapt to and even embrace sudden change has served Neil well throughout his career, although it has meant that many people have been left by the wayside. His dedication to the Muse is unwavering, but bandmates and musical styles have come and gone. "I only care about the music," Neil states with uncompromising conviction. "It's sad. Sometimes people are damaged by it. But if people understand me, they can understand what that is."[30]

In addition to his passion for music, Neil continues to enjoy many of the hobbies and interests he first developed as a child. An entire barn at Broken Arrow Ranch is devoted to model railroading, and he restores and drives vintage automobiles, especially those from the period of this childhood. Jonathan Demme remarks that the "whole world of cars and music, that's a big chunk of Neil's DNA. He's all about cars and driving and music in motion."[31] Chicken farming, too, has never lost its appeal for Neil; his son Ben proudly carries on the family tradition with his organic egg business. "Neil has always been into toys," Neil's sister Astrid confirms, "and the things he loves most are the things he loved as a boy: trains, cars, chickens."[32]

Adulthood is almost a postscript to childhood in the lyrics of the song "Born in Ontario": *That's where I learned most of what I know, / 'Cos you don't learn much / When you start to get old.*

NEIL IS A WRITER'S SON, and writing has always been a presence in his life. As a boy he was surrounded by his parents' friends and acquaintances, many of whom were writers or editors. His brother Bob remarks, "Pierre Berton, Farley Mowat, June Callwood [and] Robertson Davies — they were just a natural part of the social environment that [Neil and] I grew up in."[33] English was always Neil's best subject at school, up to the time he quit high school. Most of his other subjects were disasters, so his success at English stands in stark contrast. He even toyed with the idea of becoming a junior high school English teacher.

Neil also considered becoming a writer himself. In a 1968 interview for *Teen Set*, Judith Sims wrote, "Neil understandably wanted to be a writer before he ever thought of making music."[34] The ambition would be realized with the 2012 publication of his memoir, *Waging Heavy Peace*. "I felt like writing books fit me like a glove," he said in a news release about the book. "I started and I just kept going." And in an interview with Patti Smith at a June 2012 BookExpo, Neil said, "I do think of my father all the time when I'm writing, because it feels so natural." In *Waging Heavy Peace*, Neil writes, "I am beginning to see that the rest of my life could conceivably be spent as an author, churning out books one after another...."[35]

About his time in Toronto in the mid-'60s, Neil says, "I was a complete failure. . . . I like [Toronto] and grew up here, but we tried and tried, but we couldn't get work here. I got some really terrible reviews. But I knew I was good. I was just in the wrong place."[36] The "right place" turned out to be L.A., but Neil returned to Canada at the end of January 1969 for three shows at Le Hibou in Ottawa and three more in Toronto in early February at the Riverboat. His performances were reasonably well-received, but it would be his two gigs (an early and late show) on January 19, 1971, at Toronto's Massey Hall that would bring far greater accolades and attention.

"When I walked out onstage [in 1971]," Neil recalls, "the place really got loud. It was a feeling like no other. [Toronto] was where I had worked at Coles Bookstore, played at the Riverboat Hootenanies, lived on Isabella Street in my little flat writing songs, gone to school, experienced my mom and dad's breakup, bought records by Roy Orbison, delivered newspapers. It was a big moment in my life to be sure."[37]

Terry Gross asked Neil about his 1971 Massey Hall performance(s) in an October 2012 interview. "The concert," says Neil, "was a great time because I was coming home. . . . I wasn't a big success when I was there the last time before this visit. So going back there and playing at Massey Hall and having a couple of sold-out shows in one day . . . it was a real rush. . . . It was like all the Canadian kids that were there, they felt like, 'If this can happen to this guy, this can happen to me and it can happen to anybody.' So there was a lot of that. It was sort of a celebration. It's a Canadian spirit thing."[38]

Musician and producer Daniel Lanois is well-acquainted with the "Canadian spirit thing." When he and Neil worked on *Le Noise*, Lanois remarked, "There's nothing like getting to know somebody as a friend to find out what it's all about. We're both Canadian, and I know we've travelled the world plenty, but it's always comforting to be with someone from your own backyard. There's an awful lot that gets spoken without words."[39]

Neil has occasionally spoken ambivalently about being Canadian. In a 2012 BBC radio interview with John Wilson,

---

CLOCKWISE FROM TOP: *An informal solo gig at the Riverboat, late 1965.* [© 1965 Manfred Buchheit]; *Handbill for the Riverboat listing upcoming shows from January to March, 1969, including Neil Young.* [Courtesy of Nicholas Jennings]; *Riverboat at night. Photographer unknown, January 1965.* [Courtesy of Nicholas Jennings]

Neil remarks, "I'm a Canadian, but mostly I'm a citizen of the planet and a student of history." But his sister Astrid confirms, "Neil's still Canadian. He still holds his Canadian passport, so that's a hugely telling thing. He's very proud of being Canadian."[40] In an interview with Josh Tyrangiel for *Time* in 2005, Neil elaborates: "I guess I could be a dual citizen, but if I ever had to give up my Canadian citizenship to become American I wouldn't do it because I wouldn't want to hurt Canada."[41]

NEIL EXPLORED HIS OWN EARLY history during a road trip taken with director Jonathan Demme for *Neil Young Journeys*. They visited a few of the places Neil had lived in as a child growing up in Ontario, including Omemee and Brock Road. Both were rural idylls for Neil — settings in which he has always been most comfortable. Demme remarks, "[It] was kind of amazing to get to that town in North Ontario and see, what do you know, it is gorgeous. It is dreamlike. And, amazingly, it's still here."[42]

That wasn't the case with Brock Road. In Neil's words, "[We] discovered some missing things like my school, which was an old school that was built in the 1800s, an old stone school, two-room school that I went to when I was living up there and that was gone. The road has been moved and it went right through where the school was and there was this tree that used to be in front of the school. It was beautiful! And we used to play baseball right in front of it and it was gone!"[43]

Also gone was the Young family's former home on Brock Road. All that remained was the lawn. Earthmovers were plowing up the golf course across the street, transforming it into a housing development. Demme was impressed by "[the] symbolism of actually seeing the earthmovers right at work even as he's driving away. It's almost like, 'You better get out of there, Neil, before they gobble you up like that old house.' "[44]

"Oh, man," Neil says in the film, "it's all gone. But it's in my head. That's why you don't have to worry when you lose friends. Because they're still in your head, still in our heart."

HIS EARLY YEARS IN ONTARIO and Manitoba abound in Neil's music. "I love Canada. As I get older, more and more I start singing about Canada,"[45] he says. In a conversation with Jonathan Demme before the filming of *Neil Young: Heart of Gold*, Neil talked about "my home in Canada, my dad, my mom, my upbringing, my dad's hometown on the prairies, my dad's passing, my cousins singing under the directions of my uncle Bob, who was a great musician and my dad's brother; we talked a lot about those things."[46]

Many songs on *Prairie Wind* invoke the Young family's roots in the prairies and Neil's childhood memories — the album is dedicated "For Daddy." *Back when I was young the birds blocked out the sun / Before the great migration south / We only shot a few / They last the winter through / Mother cooked them good and served them up*, Neil sings in "No Wonder." The song "Far from Home" is especially eloquent:

> *When I was a growing boy*
> *Rockin' on my daddy's knee*
> *Daddy took an old guitar and sang*
> *"Bury me on the lone prairie"*
>
> *My uncle Bob sat at the piano*
> *My girl cousins sang harmony*
> *Those were the good old family times*
> *That left a big mark on me*

*Bury me out on the prairie*
*Where the buffalo used to roam*
*Where the Canada geese once filled the sky*
*And then I won't be far from home*

*Bury me out on the prairie*
*Where the buffalo used to roam*
*You won't have to shed a tear for me*
*'Cause then I won't be far from home*

*Walkin' down the Trans-Canada Highway*
*I was talkin' to a firefly*
*Tryin' to make my way to Nashville, Tennessee*
*When another car passed me by*

*Someday I'm gonna get some money*
*And buy myself a big old car*
*Make my way down the promised land*
*Then I'm gonna really go far*

*The Red River still flows through my hometown*, Neil writes in "It's a Dream," recalling his early years in Winnipeg. He claims two hometowns in Canada — Toronto (the city of his birth) and Winnipeg (where his musical ambition first flourished). He invokes his father in "Prairie Wind," the title track from the album: *Tryin' to remember what my Daddy said / Before too much time took away his head / He said we're goin' back and I'll show you what I'm talkin' about / Goin' back to Cypress River, back to the old farmhouse.*

Neil elaborates on his childhood remembrances: "Old memories are wonderful things and should be held on to as long as possible, shared with others, and embellished if need be. Whenever I go back to Canada, my heart is flooded with them, memories that is."[47]

On *Americana* (2012), Neil and Crazy Horse recreated some of the songs he first learned in grade school and then played on his plastic ukulele in Toronto in the late 1950s. He had performed many of these same songs with the Squires — first in Winnipeg and then in Fort William: "Oh Susannah," "Clementine," "She'll Be Comin' 'Round the Mountain" (retitled "Jesus' Chariot" on *Americana*) and "High Flyin' Bird." The arrangements resemble those Neil used with the Squires in Fort William. "Fort William," Neil recalls, "was the beginning of this kind of folk rock that we played. . . . We got into a thing in Fort William where we did classic folk songs with a rock 'n' roll beat and changed the melody." Neil adds, "We did 'Oh Susannah'[48] based on an arrangement by a group called The Thorns. Tim Rose was in The Thorns. We saw them at the 4-D."[49]

Neil's references to Ontario in "Helpless" from *Déjà Vu* (1970) are well-known: *There is a town in north Ontario / With dream comfort memory to spare / And in my mind I still need a place to go / All my changes were there.* The title track from *Time Fades Away* (1973) proclaims, *Back in Canada I spent my days / Riding subways through a haze / I was handcuffed, I was born and raised.* In "Journey Through the Past," also from *Time Fades Away*, Neil is *goin' back to Canada / On a journey thru the past / And I won't be back 'til February comes,* while "Don't Be Denied" contains references to Manitoba with a nod to Ontario:

*When I was a young boy,*
*My mama said to me*
*Your daddy's leavin' home today,*

*I think he's gone to stay.*
*We packed up all our bags*
*And drove out to Winnipeg.*

*When we got to Winnipeg*
*I checked in to school.*
*I wore white bucks on my feet,*
*When I learned the golden rule.*
*The punches came fast and hard*
*Lying on my back in the schoolyard.*

*Well pretty soon I met a friend,*
*He played guitar.*
*We used to sit on the steps at school*
*And dream of being stars.*
*We started a band,*
*We played all night.*

*Oh Canada*
*We played all night*
*I really hate to leave you now*
*But to stay just wouldn't be right.*
*Down in Hollywood*
*We played so good. . . .*

"Ambulance Blues" (from *On the Beach*, 1974) details Neil's time in Yorkville trying to make it as a folksinger. The highly biographical song includes repeated references to mid-'60s Toronto:

*Back in the old folky days*
*The air was magic when we played.*

*The Riverboat was rockin' in the rain*
*Midnight was the time for the raid.*

*Oh, Isabella, proud Isabella,*
*They tore you down and plowed you under.*
*You're only real with your makeup on*
*How could I see you and stay too long? . . .*

*Well, I'm up in T.O. keepin' jive alive,*[50]
*And out on the corner it's half past five.*
*But the subways are empty*
*And so are the cafés.*

*Except for the farmers' market*
*And I still can hear him say,*
*"You're all just pissin' in the wind*
*You don't know it but you are."*

In 2010 Neil recorded *Le Noise* with Daniel Lanois. Two of the songs — the highly autobiographical "The Hitchhiker"[51] and "Love and War" — mention Toronto. From the latter: *There've been songs about love / I sang songs about war / Since the backstreets of Toronto.* And in "The Hitchhiker," Neil sings of his experimentation with drugs:

*You didn't see me in Toronto*
*When I first tried out some hash*
*Smoked through a pen and I'd do it again*
*But I didn't have the cash*
*I didn't have the cash.*

*Then I tried amphetamines*
*And my head was in a glass*
*Taped underneath the speedometer wires*
*Of my '48 Buick's dash.*[52]
*But I knew that wouldn't last.*

More recently Neil referenced Ontario, and Toronto in particular, in a few songs from *Psychedelic Pill* (2012). "Twisted Road" mentions both Manitoba and Ontario, while "Born in Ontario" is obviously more Ontario-centric. "When where you are from keeps returning to you," he writes in the lyrics booklet that accompanies the album, "it may be time to go back."

FOR NEIL, IT HAS OFTEN been "time to go back" to Canada.

He reaffirmed his feelings about Ontario (and Manitoba — and Canada in general) in his memoir *Waging Heavy Peace*: "Someday I want us to live on a lake up there in North Ontario for a while. . . . This is not the time for us to go there, though. Maybe it will never come, and that's all right, but I want to do it someday, and that is important to me. It is part of my Canadian self. I feel it stronger these days than in days past."[53]

Whether Manitoba or Ontario, the lyrics to "One of These Days" from *Harvest Moon* (1992) come strongly to mind: *One of these days / I'm going to sit down and write a long letter / To all the good friends I've known / And I'm going to try / To thank them all for the good times together / Though so apart we've grown.* Neil adds, *My friends are scattered / Like leaves from an old maple / Some are weak, some are strong.*

AT THE 2011 JUNO AWARDS ceremony in Toronto, Neil was presented with the Allan Waters Humanitarian Award — as well as a few individual JUNOs for his work, including Artist of the Year. A radiant Amber Jean Young proudly escorted her father along the red carpet at the ceremony held at the Air Canada Centre, where venerable journalist Robert Fulford described Neil as "a fellow Canadian whose songs (rooted firmly in Canada) have become a part of our culture. The fact that he lives in the United States doesn't alter that."[54]

It isn't unusual for Canadians to find success elsewhere in the world. An estimated 3 million Canadians currently live and work abroad. But most of us remain mindful of our country of origin — we carry it with us as a fundamental part of our character and identity. Neil is no exception. His career took him to the United States, and he has lived and worked there for most of his adult life. But the memories he brought with him from Canada — the bucolic summer days in small-town Ontario and the pitiless winters of the Canadian prairie; the privations and possibilities of the post-war years; the complex cruelties and kindnesses of home and schoolyard — are the building blocks from which he has constructed his life's work.

Perhaps Neil himself sums it up best — and with a characteristic economy of words: "I feel pretty Canadian."[55]

⭐

# APPENDIXES

*Appendix A: Ken Koblun's "List of Shows"*
see Buffalo Springfield Box Set for more accurate dates of gigs
in January and February 1967 when Ken Koblun played with them

*Appendix B: Early Squires Songlist, circa 1963*
includes fast and slow guitar instrumentals

*Appendix C: Squires Songlist, circa 1964*
includes chords for "White Flower"

*Appendix D: Squires Songlist, circa 1964*
includes Beatles covers

*Appendix E: Squires Songlist, circa 1964*
includes British Invasion covers

*Appendix F: Squires Songlist, circa 1964*
includes original songs penned by Neil with vocals

*Appendix G: Young and Ragland Family Trees*
circa March 1966

# List of Shows

| | Place | | Date 1962 | Gross | Adv | Out | Amt. |
|---|---|---|---|---|---|---|---|
| Classics | Chonodil H.S. | JC, JG, NY, LF, BT, KK | Nov.17 | 5 | — | — | unit & 10' |
| | Kelvin High | JC, JG, NY LF, BT, KK | N.24 | 5 | — | — | |
| | Westworth H.C | JC, NY, LF, JH, B, KK | D.1 | 8 | — | — | |
| | Morse Place C.C. | LF, JC, BT, JG, KK | D.8 | 25 | 5 | — | |
| 5 | Riverview C.C | NY, BB JG, JC LF, KK | D.21 | 25 | 4 | — | |
| Dec 26 Squires Rons. Aronsides | St. Agnutous C.Y.O. | BT, JG, JC, LF, KK | D.29 | 30 | 6 | — | |
| | | | 1963 | | | | |
| | Riverview C.C | | F.1 | 5 | — | — | Minus 12 |
| | Grant Park H.S | | F.15 | 10 | 2.10 | — | |
| | Crensentwood C.C. | | M.2 | 35 | — | 2.50 | |
| 10 | Sir John Franklin C.C. | | M.8 | 20 | — | 5 | cellophane |
| | Grant Park H.S | | M.22 | 20 | 2 | 3 | |
| | Glenloe C.C. | | M.29 | 0 | — | — | |
| | Westworth H.C | | A.19 | 20 | 5 | — | Kalos 12 + 12 |
| | Nelson Mac. High | | A.26 | Battle of Sounds | | | |
| 15 | Sir John Franklin | | A.26 | 20 | 5 | — | |
| | Sir Andrews H.C | | A.27 | 25 | 625 | — | |
| | Youth Council | | M.10 | 20 | 4 | — | |
| | Sir John Franklin | | M.17 | 20 | — | 5 | |
| June 4th thing | St. Peters H.C. | | M.18 | 20 | — | 4 | |
| 20 | St Agnatous C.Y.O. | | M.25 | 0 | — | — | Kalos current |
| | Earl Grey C.C. | | J.7 | 37.50 | 7.20 | — | |
| | Lipset Hall C.Y.O. | | J.27 | 60 | 11 | — | |
| | Cresentwood C.C. | | J.2 | 35 | 7 | — | |
| | CKRC | | J.12 | Audition | | | Tobels 25 + 12 |
| 25 | CKRC | | J.19 | Practise | | | |
| | CKRC | | J.23 | Recording | | | |
| | Cresentwood C.C. | | J.30 | 36 | 7 | — | 5 |
| | Glenwood C.C. | | A.7 | 0 | — | — | |
| S.A-out | West. End. Memorial C.C. | | A.15 | 30 | 4 | — | 10 |
| 30 | Torps | | S.2 | 40 | 15 | — | Kalos Band 1½ |
| | St. Mary's C.Y.O (Gretsh) | | S.20 | 52 | 9 | — | 10 |
| | the Cellar | | S.27/28 | 68/40 | 10.50 | — | 20 |
| | River Heights C.C. (Drums) | | O.5 | 0 | — | — | |
| | Grant Park H.S. (Gibson) | | O.18 | 25 | 5 | — | |
| 35 | West End Memorial CC. | | O.19 | 30 | 650 | — | |
| | Our Lady of Victory mull tolas | | O.26 | 35 | 3.25 | — | 40 |
| | Portage la Prairie comes | | N.1 | 60 | 12.50 | — | 10 |
| 38 | River Heights CC | | N.2 | 30 | 7.50 | — | My amp. |

| | | | 1963 | | | | | |
|---|---|---|---|---|---|---|---|---|
| groups 70,160 +A's 75 each | St. Peter's Mission | | N. 22 | 45 | 11.25 | - | | miss 154 12 · 16 week |
| 40 | St. Agnatius P.Y.O. | | N. 29 | 50 | 10 | - | | |
| | St. Marie C.Y.O | (HORNER) | D. 6. | 415 | 2.25 | - | | mins 126 19 10 gallon |
| v | Dauphin | | D. 13 | 125 | 287.5 | = | | |
| v | Charleswood Coll. | | D. 20 | 60 | 12.00 | - | | |
| v | St. Agnatius C.Y.O | 1964 | J. 3 | 50 | 10 | - | | |
| 45 | Kelvin H' | | J. 24 | 0 | - | - | | |
| | 4th Dimention | | J.25 | 0 | - | - | | |
| v | Miles MacDonell Coll. | | J. 31 | 60 | 11.30 | - | | Jazz men |
| v | Glenwood C.C | | F.1 | 57 | 11.25 | - | | |
| v | 4-D | | F. 5 | 0 | - | - | | |
| 50 | Paterson's Roadhouse | | F. 7 | 25 | 7.50 | 1 | | |
| | 4-D | | F.8 | 2 | - | - | | |
| v | St. Pauls of the Apostil | | F. 9 | 50 | 100 | - | | |
| v | Our Lady of Victory. | | F. 14 | 50 | 10 | - | | |
| v | Portage la Prairie | | F. 21 | 60 | 10 | - | | |
| 55 | Meleans United Church | | F. 22 | 16 | 4 | - | | |
| | 4-D | | F. 29 | - | - | - | | |
| | Paterson's Roadhouse | | M. 7 | 25 | 5 | | | |
| | Glenwood. C.C | | M.14 | 24.25 | 7.50 | - | | |
| | Paterson's | | M.26 | 0 | - | - | | |
| v 60 | Patersons. | | M.28 | 50 | 9 | 1 | | |
| | Inland Broadcasting | | A. 2 | 70 | 1 | | | |
| | C.K.R.C | | A. 2 | Recording | | | | |
| | Crescentwood | | A 3. | 40 | 10 | - | | |
| v | Norberry C.C. | | A.4 | 60 | 12.50 | - | | |
| v 65 | St. Paul's of the Apostil | | A. 5. | 50 | 10 | - | | |
| Practice CKRC #7 → | Paterson's (Neil is paid 75) | | A.11 | 55 | 5 | | | |
| | Winiakwa C.C (Amped) twin | | M. 8 | 75 | 6.50 | | | |
| | Grendell CC | | M.15 | A.35 | 3.87 | | | |
| | Nortes Dome. Aud. | | J. 9 | 0 | - | - | | |
| 70 | Maple Leaf C.C. | | J.12 | 40 | 6.25 | | | |
| | Towers - Tap | | J. 15 | - | - | - | | |
| | Weston. C.C | | J. 19 | 0 | - | - | | |
| | Preteen | | J. 5 | 20 | 5 | - | | |
| No Neil | Cellar | | J. 24 | 30 | ? 10 | | | |
| Neil Powers | Cellar | | J 31 | 36 | 9 | | | |
| | Towers T+C | | A. 6 | 0 | - | - | | Bass amp. |

1964

| | | | | | |
|---|---|---|---|---|---|
| 3points | 4 - D | (Tomulux) | A.23 | 0 | - |
| 8.00 Iff | 4 - D | | A.30 | - | - |
| | River Heights. C.C | | S.11 | 60 | 15 |
| 85 | River Heights C.C | | S.18 | 60 | 15 |
| | St. Pauls of the Apostil | | S.19 | 50 | 10 |
| | Holy Cross Gym | | S.25-35 | 8.25 |
| | Glenwood C.C. | | O.3 | 35 | - |
| | Glenwood C.C. | | O.9 | 70 | 12 |
| Jet out 90 | Murdock MacKay | | O.10 | 70 | 11 |
| | Flamingo Club (F+B:11) | | O.12-17 | 325 | 41 |
| | West Kildonan Coll. | | O.23 | 70 | 6 |
| | River Heights C.C. (UNION) | | O.31 | 70 | 10 |
| | Flamingo club | | N.2-7 | 350 | 105 |
| 95 | Flamingo Club (Bassman) | | N.9-14 | 350 | 105 | 5 |
| | 4-D - F+B:11 | | food. |
| | 4-D | | N.20 | 15 | 5 |
| | 4-D | | N.21 | 15 | - |
| 100 | CJLY | | N.23 | recording |
| | Collisium - F+B:11 | | D.12 | 75 | 25 |
| | Twilight Zone | X | D.15-20 | 150 | 33 |
| Ken's | Selkirk - Memorial Hall | X | D.23 | 90 | 15 |
| Terry+Doug | Neepawa - Drill Hall | | D.31 | 200 | 33 |
| 105 | Brandon Roller Rink | | 1965 J.2 | 100 | 25 |
| | St. Pauls of the Apostil | X | J.3 | 60 | 15 |
| | Weston Memorial C.C | X | J.8 | 40 | 10 |
| Ken Rug+Terry | Churchill High School | | J.15 | 60 | 15 |
| - Bill+Doug | River Heights C.C | X | J.23 | 85 | 11 |
| 110 | MacGregor Man | | J.29 | 115 | 14 |
| | Glenwood C.C. | X | J.30 | 35 | 15 |
| | United College | X | F.5 | 60 | 24 | X5 |
| | Oxenlawn Colleg. | X | F.12 | 85 | 15 |
| | Gerour, Man. | X | F.13 | 100 | 25 |
| Al-Doug 15 | Holy Cross C.40. | X | F.14 | 60 | 9 |
| Terry+Doug | Nelson Mackentire H.S. | X | F.19 | 90 | 20 |
| 115 | Selkirk Memorial Hall. | X | F.26 | 90 | Tea |
| | River Heights | X | F.27 | 85 | |
| | Selkirk Lutheran Hall | X | M.5 | 85 | |
| 120 | 4-D | | M.7 | 30 | 10 |

378

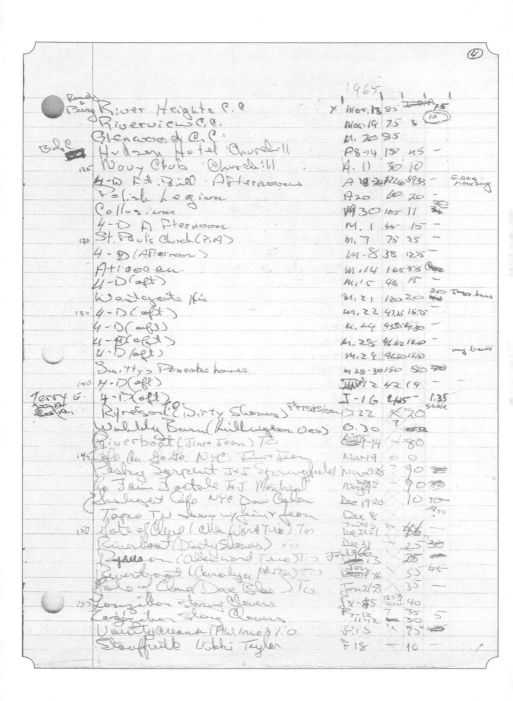

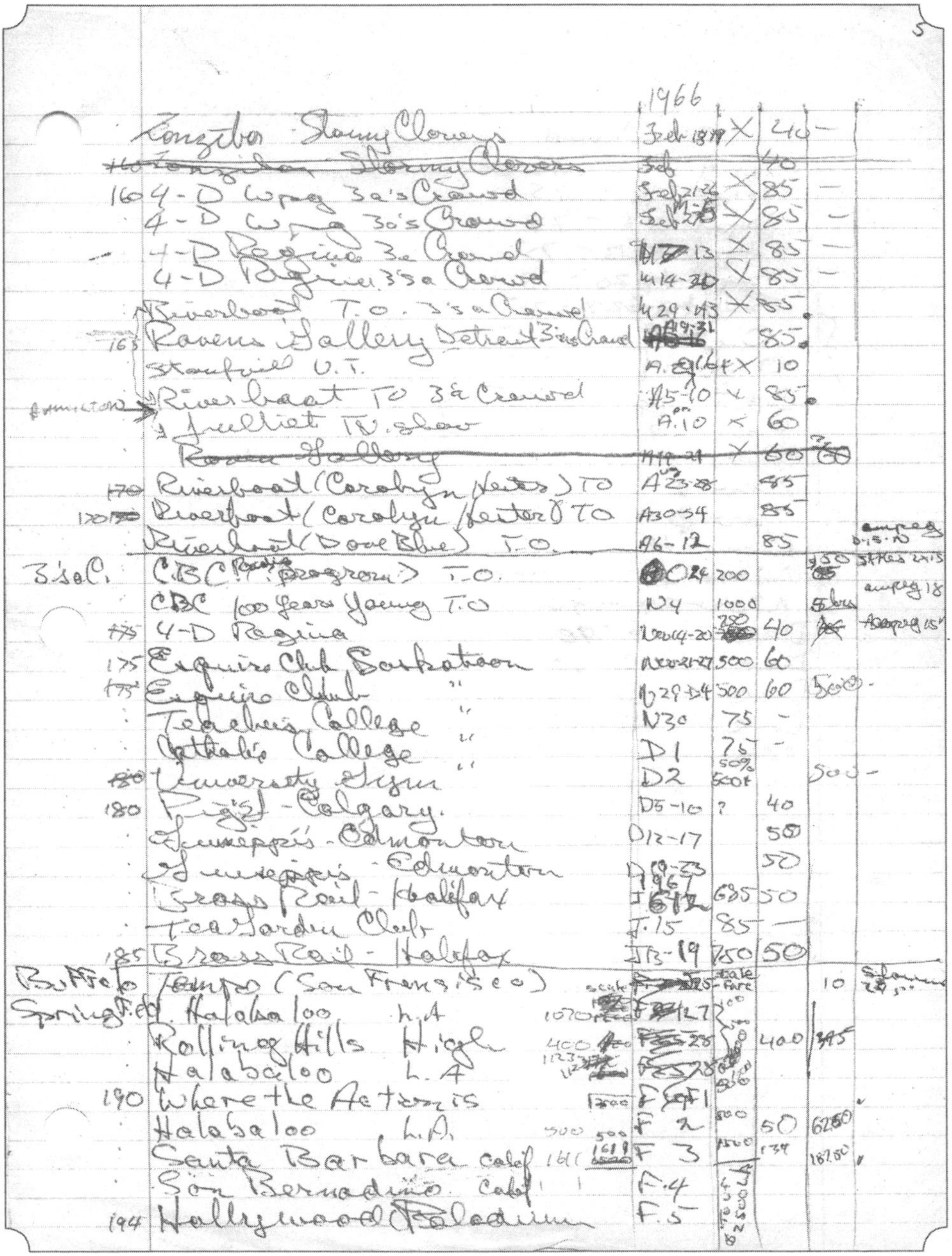

| | | 1967 | | | |
|---|---|---|---|---|---|
| 195 | Cinnamon Cinders, Long Beach | F 6 | | | |
| | Albuquerque . N.M. | F 8 9 | | | |
| | Santa Fe N.M. | F 8 9 | | | |
| | Lubbock Tex | F 8 10 | | | |
| Clark — | Youth Pavilion Montreal EXPO | M 14-9 | 700 | 150 | Kent |
| 200 | New Penelope Montreal Monster Rama | J 11-16 | — | 100 | Hosmer |
| | Venus de Milo Montreal Clyne | J 25-27 | 310 | 7200 | |
| | Le Hibou Ottawa Clyne | July 10-15 | 600 | 1120 | |
| | Buffalo - Luria Park Clyne | F J 26 | 160 | 3700 | |
| | Toronto City Hall Clyne | Aug 3 | | | |
| 205 | Marifred - Clyne | Aug 10 | 200 | 50 | 300 |
| 350 Crowd | Expo Ontario Pavalian Aug 17 | Aug 20-25 | 1250 | — | 75 |
| | Expo Ont. Pav. | A 27-31 | 1250 | — | 75 |
| | Expo Ont. Pav. | S 3-88 | 1250 | — | 75 |
| | CBC Take 30 | S 12-13 | 600 | — | 75 |
| 210 | Canadian Film Awards | S. 23 | 350 | 25 | Sauder |
| | C.B.C - Folkworld | S. 29 | 450 | | |
| | EXPO - Canadian Pav. | O 2-9 | 1250 | 45 | Standel |
| | UCLA Student Union | O 20 | 250 | | |
| | Beware King - Dunhill L.A | O.Q 108 | 12-09 | | Standel |
| 215 | Neil McNeil H.S. Tor | N. 11 | 950 | | |
| | Jonny's T.O | N 12-17 | 1250 | | |
| | Jonny's T.O | N 19-24 | 1250 | | |
| | Jonny's T.O | N. 27 | 350 | | |
| | Ohio State U. Columbus | D 2 | 750 | | |
| 220 | Riverboat T.O | Dec 19-24 | 600 | | |
| | Riverboat T.O | D 26 | 825 | | |
| | Hamilton - Business Lunch 350 C | A 18/66 | | | |
| 225 | | | | | |
| 230 | | | | | |
| 232 | | | | | |

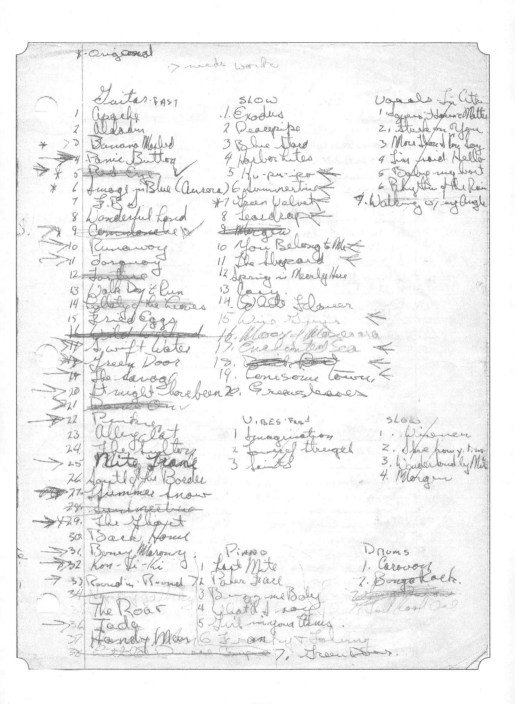

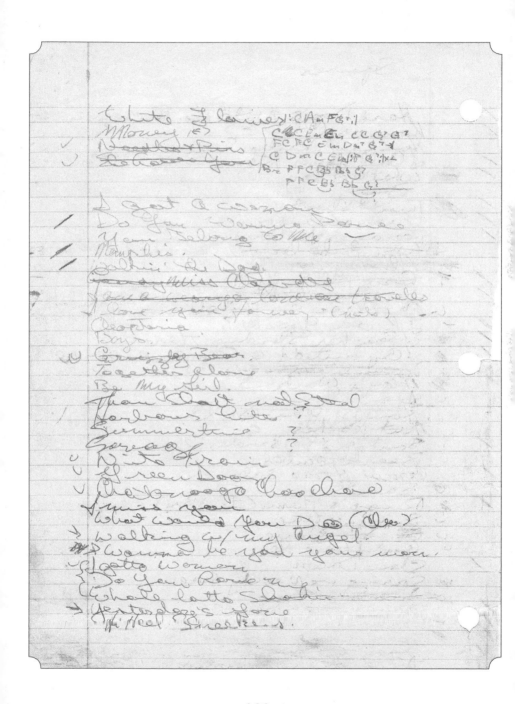

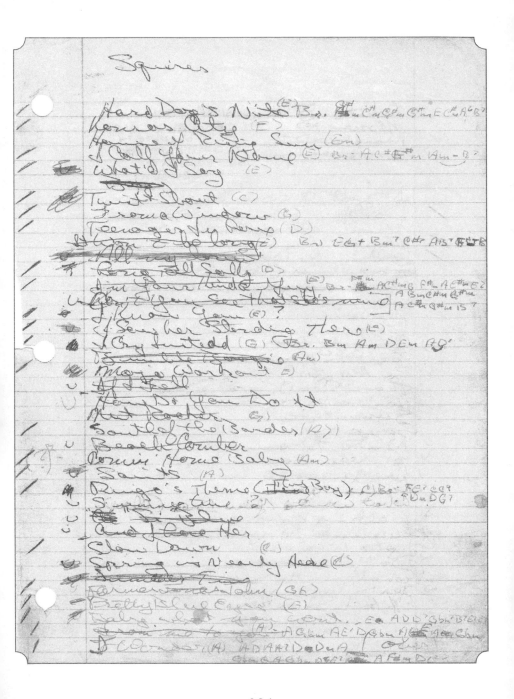

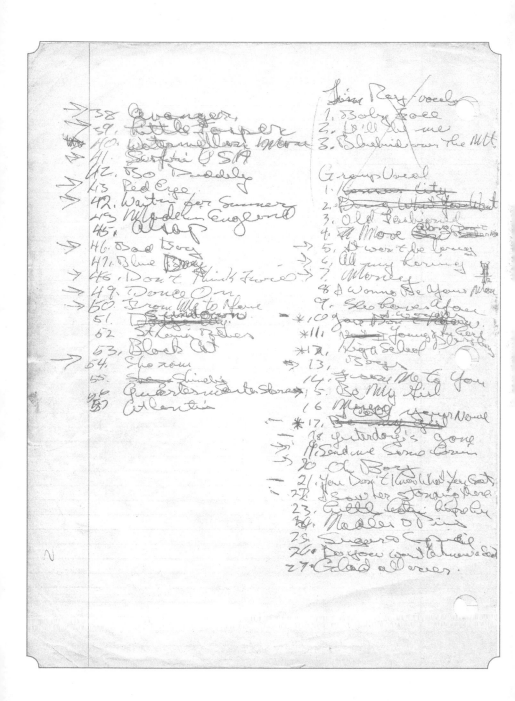

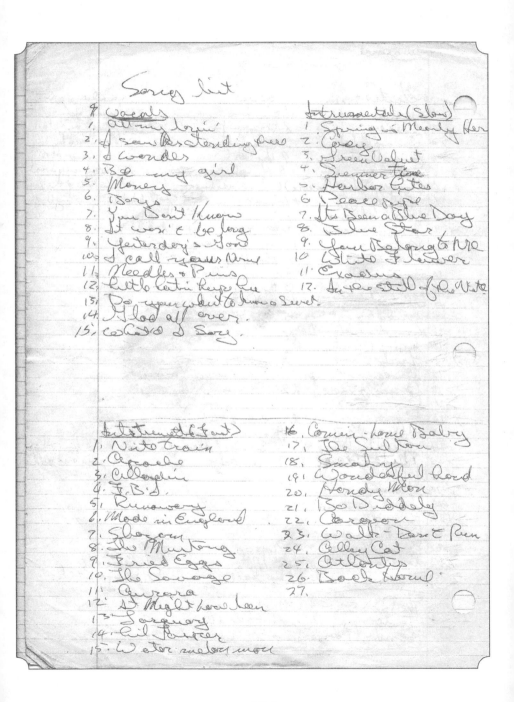

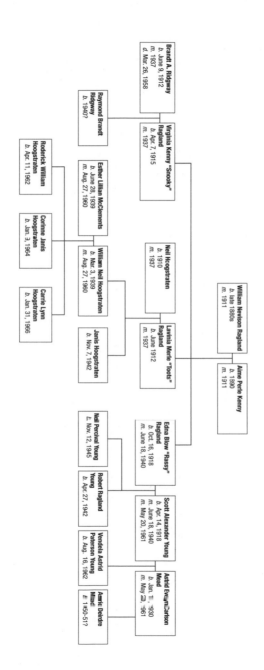

## Ragland Family Tree
### (circa March 1966)

**Brandt A. Ridgway**
*b.* June 9, 1912
*m.* 1937
*d.* Mar. 26, 1958

**Raymond Brandt Ridgway**
*b.* 1940?

**Virginia Kenny "Snooky" Ragland**
*b.* Apr. 7, 1915
*m.* 1937

**Roderick William Hoogstraten**
*b.* Apr. 11, 1962

**Esther Lillian McClements**
*b.* June 28, 1939
*m.* Aug. 27, 1960

**Corinne Janis Hoogstraten**
*b.* Jan. 3, 1964

**Neil Hoogstraten**
*b.* 1910
*m.* 1937

**William Neil Hoogstraten**
*b.* Mar. 3, 1939
*m.* Aug. 27, 1960

**Carrie Lynn Hoogstraten**
*b.* Jan. 31, 1966

**William Nevison Ragland**
*b.* late 1880s
*m.* 1911

**Lavinia Merle "Toots" Ragland**
*b.* June 1912
*m.* 1937

**Janis Hoogstraten**
*b.* Nov. 7, 1942

**Aime Perle Kenny**
*b.* 1890
*m.* 1911

**Neil Percival Young**
*b.* Nov. 12, 1945

**Edna Blow "Rassy" Ragland**
*b.* Oct. 16, 1918
*m.* June 18, 1940

**Robert Ragland Young**
*b.* Apr. 27, 1942

**Scott Alexander Young**
*b.* Apr. 14, 1918
*m.* June 18, 1940
*m.* May 20, 1961

**Vendela Astrid Paterson Young**
*b.* Aug. 16, 1962

**Astrid Evelyn Carlson Mead**
*b.* Jan. 1, 1930
*m.* May 2, 1961

**Aenie Deirdre Mead**
*b.* 1450-51?

## Young Family Tree
### (circa March 1966)

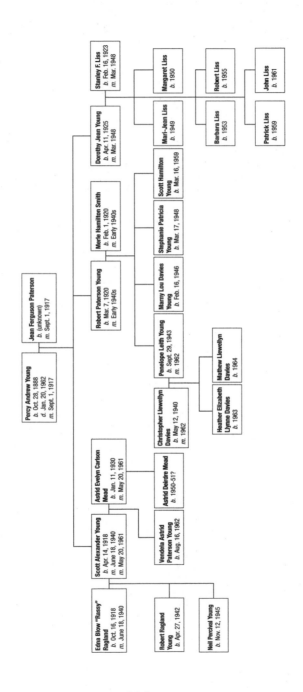

# ✷ END NOTES ✷

## PART ONE

### 1: In the Beginning . . .

1    Ian Munro worked for the Canadian Press news agency for more than 50 years, starting as a copy boy and retiring as head of technical operations on his 65th birthday. He died from heart problems at 98 in Sunnybrook Hospital in Toronto on September 10, 2011. Ian was Neil's godfather. Scott Munro — Ian and Lola's son — was named in honour of Scott Young, who was also his godfather.

2    Scott Young, *Neil and Me* (McClelland & Stewart Ltd., 1984), 23-24.

3    Born in the late 1880s to an old southern family living on a plantation near Petersburg, Virginia, Bill Ragland quit the Virginia Military Institute when he was 17. His father died, leaving the family in debt. In 1905 Bill secured employment in New York City with Barrett Roofing. After three years he was sent to Winnipeg to head the company's operations in western Canada. He loved prairie life and eventually married Aime Perle Kenny, a dark-haired American beauty of Spanish/French/Italian/Irish descent who worked for the Grand Trunk Railway near Sault Ste. Marie. In the late 1970s Neil bought a 1913-vintage Baltic trading schooner and named it *W. N. Ragland* in honour of his grandfather.

4    As a young boy Scott idolized his uncle, who had travelled in and written about the Canadian north. Jack also enjoyed writing fiction; some of his short stories were published in the *Saturday Evening Post*.

5    The Young family's former home at 335 Brooke Avenue no longer exists. The large dwelling that replaced the modest post-war bungalow is now 315 Brooke Avenue.

6    The building was torn down in 2001 to make room for the new Clinical Services Building, which opened in 2005. The original portico from the Thomas J. Bell Wing has been preserved in the Ne Gasperio Conservatory in the new building.

7    Burcher, "The Largest Single Hospital, Medical, Educational Unit on the Continent."

8    Connor, *Doing Good*, 212.

9    McDonough, *Shakey*, 37. Fan legend has it that he was born "Neil
     Percival Kenneth Robert Ragland Young," but Neil's full name
     is recorded in Scott Young's Last Will and Testament, held in the
     Scott Young fonds. Neil's half-sister Astrid confirms that Neil
     Percival Young is his full name in *Being Young*, 16.

10   Scott Young, *A Writer's Life*, 145.

11   Percy married Jean Ferguson Paterson on September 1, 1917. His
     drugstore in Glenboro went out of business in 1926; the family
     moved to Winnipeg but failed to achieve financial equilibrium.
     Percy and Jean separated in 1930. Scott was 12 at the time, Bob
     was 10 and Dorothy was four. They tried to get back together in
     Flin Flon in 1936, but didn't succeed. Jean stayed in Flin Flon and
     made a life for herself and Dorothy.

12   Pierre Berton would later interview Neil on *The Pierre Berton
     Show* (1962–1973). Unfortunately, Screen Gems erased many
     shows to re-use the tape, and Neil's interview was one of the
     casualties. Scott Young recalls that Neil was interviewed around
     the time he was first becoming famous.

13   Gzowski, "Pierre Berton, fresh from a 47th book tour, still calls
     me Pete."

14   McDonough, *Shakey*, 38.

15   Scott Young, *Neil and Me*, 25.

16   Scott Young, "Polio Recalled: Sickness a Time to Think." Held in
     the Trent University Archives, Scott Young fonds (95-001/4/1).

17   Beryl enjoyed success as an actor and married actor John Hart in
     1957 after meeting him on the set of television's *Hawkeye and the
     Last of the Mohicans*. Hart starred as Hawkeye and Beryl had a bit
     part in one episode.

18   Scott's older brother — Robert Paterson Young — married Merle
     Hamilton Smith, one of Scott's earlier girlfriends. They had three
     daughters and a son.

19   Astrid Young, *Being Young*, 15.

20   McDonough, *Shakey*, 39.

21   Scott Young, "Family Journey Problems."

**2: Omemee and Beyond**

22  Fax dated February 9, 1992, held in the Trent University Archives, Scott Young fonds (95-001/2/5).

23  McDonough, *Shakey*, 36.

24  Video excerpt of Patti Smith's interview with Neil Young at BookExpo in New York City, June 6, 2012. us.penguingroup .com/nf/Book/BookDisplay/0,,9780399159466,00.html.

25  Skippy was the first of many dogs to whom Neil would form a warm attachment. His dog Winnipeg posed with him for the front cover of *Everybody Knows This Is Nowhere*, photographed by Frank Bez in Topanga Canyon, September 1968. Henry Diltz took a photo of Neil and his dog Harte at Broken Arrow Ranch in northern California in 1971, and one of Neil posed with his dog Art — wearing huge sunglasses — in front of a beach house in Malibu. Neil wrote "Love Art Blues" while Art was with him. He later wrote "Old King" in memory of his hound dog Elvis. Carl, a Labradoodle, was Neil's constant companion for 14 years until he died in 2010. Carl is featured prominently in *Fork in the Road*'s video "Johnny Magic," riding in the back seat of Lincvolt. Pegi's dog Nina now accompanies Neil on many road trips.

26  McDonough, *Shakey*, 39-40.

27  Ibid., 42.

28  Ibid., 40.

29  Neil Young, *Waging Heavy Peace*, 27.

30  Ibid., 298.

31  McDonough, *Shakey*, 43.

32  Neil Young, *Waging Heavy Peace*, 270.

33  John Hart — husband of Neil's earlier saviour, Beryl Braithwaite — published a cookbook in 2000 titled *Cowboys in the Kitchen*, featuring one of Beryl's best recipes for imperial chicken, as well as Scott's spaghetti recipe.

34  "Scott Young's Spaghetti Recipe" is held in the Trent University Archives, Scott Young fonds (06-002/2/15).

35  Neil Young, *Waging Heavy Peace*, 271-272.

36  Scott Young, "Polio Recalled: Sickness a Time to Think."

37  Rutty, "Helpless: The 1951 Ontario Polio Outbreak; the Neil Young Case."

38 Neil Young, *Waging Heavy Peace*, 28.

39 Ibid., 29.

40 Ibid., 28.

41 Ibid.

42 Scott Young, *Neil and Me*, 36.

43 Neil Young, *Waging Heavy Peace*, 28.

44 Ibid., 29.

45 Scott Young, *Neil and Me*, 36.

46 Kent, "I Build Something Up, I Tear It Right Down: Neil Young at 50."

47 McDonough, *Shakey*, 605.

48 Fussman, "What I've Learned: Neil Young."

49 McDonough, *Shakey*, 46-47.

50 Scott Young, "Polio Recalled: Sickness a Time to Think."

51 Sean O'Connor, "Rock star gets honorary degree."

52 Henry Mason's family lived at 45 King Street East in Omemee. This building currently houses the Youngtown Museum, which Neil visited with his brother Bob and close friend Dave "Snow Bear" Toms in October 2011. Neil told proprietor Trevor Hosier that his "best friend" Henry Mason used to live in the same house and it might be nice to have a photo of him somewhere in the museum. Henry was located — still living nearby and working as a farmer — and he supplied a childhood photo of himself for the museum.

53 Neil Young, *Waging Heavy Peace*, 297.

54 Fussman, "What I've Learned: Neil Young."

55 Neil Young, *Waging Heavy Peace*, 29.

56 Scott Young, "Dr. Young Says Penny Ante Psychology Backfires." Held in the Trent University Archives, Scott Young fonds (06-002/1/5).

57 Ibid.

58 Rassy returned to Florida in the 1960s to live in a modest bungalow Neil purchased for her in New Smyrna Beach. She returned to Winnipeg each summer to stay with close friends Howard and Chris Wood, at their Winnipeg home or their cottage on Clementine Bay in Whiteshell Provincial Park. She made the return journey by car every summer until 1986, and remained in

New Smyrna Beach until cancer claimed her life at 72 on October 15, 1990.

59    It's not clear which of the cottages the Youngs lived in. The 1950 New Smyrna Beach Directory has the three cottages listed as occupying the lots at 315, 317 and 319 South Atlantic Avenue. They were all listed as "vacant" (used for rentals only).

60    The Allen family spent many winters in the Coronado Beach area, ultimately purchasing a home on the northwest corner of Ninth Avenue and South Atlantic Avenue when their eldest daughter, Jane, began high school. She attended New Smyrna Beach High School, as did her younger sister Mary.

61    "Born in Ontario" is included on *Psychedelic Pill*, Neil and Crazy Horse's October 2012 release.

62    The Ward Motel, owned by Al Ward, at 423 Flagler Avenue at South Atlantic, took up an entire block on the southwest corner and is now called the Seahorse Inn. Ward later expanded his motel properties to other locations nearby, including one at 301 Buenos Aires Street, where the Turtle Run Inn now stands. Some additional motel rooms were later opened across the street from the original Flagler Avenue motel. The Wards lived in a spacious home with a wraparound porch on the southeast corner of Columbus and South Atlantic Avenue. Their property extended to Buenos Aires, where their two-bay garage was located.

63    Sea Fox, a retail women's clothing store at 501 Flagler Avenue, now stands on the former premises of Pop Thornal's gas station. Many of the local children referred to it incorrectly as Pop Thornton's.

64    Scott Young, "$100 a month — 'You-All Should Be in Florida Too.'" Held in the Archives of Ontario at York University, Scott Young fonds (F1134-3-3-1, MU 3665, B240661).

65    Uhelszki, "Neil Young and Daniel Lanois: Love and War."

66    McDonough, *Shakey*, 47.

67    Ibid.

68    Neil has fond memories of his old friend. At his performance with Crazy Horse at Molson Park in Barrie, Ontario, on August 31, 1996, Neil asked, "Is Garfield 'Goof' Whitney in the house?" There was a loud affirmative response from a section of the

audience. Neil then announced, "Garfield 'Goof' Whitney. This note's for you," and launched into a rousing version of "F*!#in' Up."

69    McDonough, *Shakey*, 42.

70    *Neil Young Journeys* (2011) was the third film Demme shot with Neil's co-operation. The first two were *Neil Young: Heart of Gold* (2006) and *The Neil Young Trunk Show* (2009).

71    During the Q&A session after the world premiere screening of *Neil Young Journeys* at the Princess of Wales Theatre on September 12, 2011, during the Toronto International Film Festival, a friend of Goof's presented Neil with a manila envelope from his old friend and said Goof was unable to attend the screening. Neil accepted the mysterious envelope and said, "Well, say hi to him and his brother, too." He jokingly added, "This is that guy who gave me money to walk up to that lady and tell her she had a fat ass. God knows what he wants me to do now."

72    Neil Young, *Waging Heavy Peace*, 484.

73    Foster child Eric Basciano would join the family at a later date.

74    Astrid Young, *Being Young*, 17.

75    Letter dated August 3, 1952, held in the Trent University Archives, Scott Young fonds (90-003/26/2).

76    The image of the Indian has always been strongly associated with Neil. In another early photo taken in 1955, nine-year-old Neil is holding a bow and arrow while brother Bob holds a rifle. During Neil's time with Buffalo Springfield he wore a fringed leather jacket with decorative beads around his neck; his bandmates called him "the Indian in the group." Neil would later write songs with explicit references to Native peoples, including "Pocahontas," "Cortez the Killer" and "Broken Arrow." ("Broken Arrow" is also the name he gave his ranch in California.) He usually performs with a classic wooden cigar-store Indian onstage, and his band Crazy Horse took its name from the famous Sioux warrior. In July 1989, he gave a benefit performance at the Paha Sapa Music Festival on the Pine Ridge Indian Reservation in South Dakota. The cover of *Americana* (2012), originally designed by Tom Wilkes in 1975 for an album that was never released, consists of a 1905 photograph of Geronimo and three other Native Americans in a

vintage automobile with modern images of the members of Crazy Horse superimposed. In January 2014, Neil played four benefit concerts in Canada ("Honour the Treaties") in support of the Athabasca Chipewyan First Nations legal defence fund to aid the band's legal challenges against oil companies and the government in regard to the perceived injustices they felt had been committed against their traditional lands and rights.

77    Birchbark arrowhead place setting held in the Trent University Archives, Scott Young fonds (90-003/26/2).

78    Scott Young, "Long may you run. Neil and me: a father's memories of his famous son." Held in the Trent University Archives, Scott Young fonds (06-002/1/6).

79    Principal Curtis also taught grades 7 and 8 at Omemee Public School.

80    Letter dated February 10, 1953, held in the Trent University Archives, Scott Young fonds (90-003/26/2).

81    McDonough, *Shakey*, 47.

82    Ibid., 47-48.

83    This cottage has been replaced by a three-storey condo at 1901 Hill Street. It stands on a double lot, suggesting that the Youngs used to reside in the cottage that inhabited the lot at 1903 Hill Street. The old Finney home is now at 1905 Hill Street and the Shepard home is at 1907. The 1950 New Smyrna Beach Directory lists the houses on Hill Street without specific numbers. The entry states the homes were "irregularly placed along Hill Street." The addresses on South Atlantic Avenue beyond Third Avenue had no house numbers.

84    Kay Shepard still lives at 1907 Hill Street and has rebuilt the house to look as it did when her parents first purchased the property, complete with its wonderful wraparound porch. Kay's great-grandfather, Berlin Hart Wright, built the cottage in the late 19th century and named it Heart's Content. A sign reading *Heart's Content* was located on the ocean side of the cottage.

85    Bob Young visited his mother in New Smyrna Beach on occasion and returned to live there in the 1990s. He was part-owner of a jewellery shop on Flagler Avenue and enjoyed playing golf in his spare time.

86    Neil Young, *Waging Heavy Peace*, 396.

87 The note from Principal Curtis at Omemee Public School and dated February 10, 1953, regarding Neil's poor behaviour in Miss Doris Jones's class, serves as evidence that the Youngs were at home in Omemee during this time.

88 Photo held in the Trent University Archives, Scott Young fonds (90-003/26/1).

89 Neil Young, *Waging Heavy Peace*, 5.

90 Ibid.

91 Neil later acquired a 1953 Buick Skylark, the first one ever made. He considers it "the big Kahuna" of his vintage car collection.

92 Zimmer, "Blue Notes for a Restless Loner."

93 A reference to Neil's little-known earlier time with his family in Winnipeg can be found in the April 1968 issue of *Teen Set* in the article "Neil Young Profile," by Judith Sims. Sims interviewed Neil and wrote, "He 'lived all over the place' for years, twice in Winnipeg, where he did most of his growing up." (He actually spent more time growing up in Ontario, but his formative teenage years were spent in Manitoba.)

94 Social Column, *Winnipeg Free Press*, November 11, 1954, 17. "Mr. and Mrs. Scott Young and their children have left for Toronto, Ont. after spending the summer months in Winnipeg."

95 Confirmed by Neil via Will Mitchell in an e-mail dated July 22, 2010: "Definitely Hillcrest Ave. I remember that very well. Might be number 95, that rings a bell."

96 According to Bill Hoogstraten, Virginia Ridgway had been Lyndon Baines Johnson's campaign manager. Virginia Ragland Ridgway would later write *After Tomorrow* (1998), a book about "life, love and laughter in the retirement world."

97 McDonough, *Shakey*, 26.

98 Ibid., 28.


**3: An Uneasy Time in Toronto**

99 133 Rose Park Drive was "House of the Week" in the *Real Estate News* section of the *Toronto Star* on July 31, 2009. Its past association with the Young family was mentioned prominently. The property was sold shortly after it was featured in the article.

100 There is a brief mention of Mary Ellen Blanche [sic] as Neil's "first female friend" in Johnny Rogan's *Neil Young, Zero to Sixty*, 19.

101 There were other instances when Neil threw Coke bottles. Geordie McDonald, a member of Neil's early Yorkville-era band 4 To Go, recalls that Neil sometimes got upset during their rehearsals: "[Neil] was very intense and highly focused. When things went wrong he would throw a Coke bottle across the room." (Einarson, *Don't Be Denied*, 145.)

102 Mary Ellen would again have brief contact with Neil more than 50 years later. During the Q&A after the screening of *Neil Young Journeys* by Jonathan Demme at the Toronto International Film Festival in September 2011, she was selected as one of the audience members to speak with Neil and Demme. As soon as she introduced herself, Neil's eyes lit up and he exclaimed, "My first girlfriend!" Neil relayed the amusing story about winning the sparkly little prize at the fair and giving it to Mary Ellen. He later found out it was actually a dog collar. "I still haven't lost my touch," Neil joked. He mentioned Mary Ellen and the "dog collar" story again at the Slamdance Film Festival in Park City, Utah, where *Neil Young Journeys* was screened in January 2012.

103 Rassy's sister Vinia Hoogstraten wrote about the flood in a *Chatelaine* article, "Heartbreak of Coming Home," which won a memorial award from the Women's Canadian Press Club. She worked tirelessly in the canteen at the Norwood dike to support the hundreds of volunteers assisting with sandbagging efforts.

104 McDonough, *Shakey*, 49.

105 Neil Hoogstraten was a commercial artist who also painted finely detailed, realist landscapes and buildings of rural Manitoba. His paintings are well-regarded and he was a past president of the venerable Winnipeg Sketch Club, having joined in 1928. He remained a member until two years before his death at 93 on December 8, 2003.

106 Scott rented a top-floor garret space (Room 309) at 47 Dundonald Street near Church Street. He was determined to finish the novel; he had been working on it for four years and finished it after four more months of steady work. It was published in Canada and the U.K. in September 1956.

107   Scott Young, *Neil and Me*, 39.

**4: Brock Road: A Rural Idyll**

108   Scott Young, *Neil and Me*, 242.
109   Scott Young, "The Foundling Budgie."
110   Ibid.
111   Ibid.
112   Denberg, "Music just takes you wherever you want to go:
        A conversation with Neil Young."
113   Neil Young, *Waging Heavy Peace*, 300.
114   *Ibid.*
115   McDonough, *Shakey*, 52.
116   The "little shack" or "tool shed" becomes a "hobo's shack" in
        Nick Kent's interview with Neil ("I Build Something Up, I Tear It
        Right Down: Neil Young at 50"). Neil remarks on "The Wayward
        Wind." Neil told Kent, "I used to walk by a railroad track on
        my way to school every day. There was even a real 'hobo's shack'
        there. The song and the image have always stayed with me. When
        I hear it, I always think of being five or six walking past that
        old shack and the railroad tracks gleaming in the sun and on
        my way to school every day with my little transistor radio up to
        my ear." (He must have misremembered his age because he was
        between nine and 11 while attending the old Brock Road School.)
        Gogi Grant's cover of "The Wayward Wind," written by Stanley
        Lebowsky and Herbert Newman, was one of the biggest hits of
        1956. Neil references Frankie Laine's 1968 cover of the song in the
        Kent interview.
117   Neil's interest in model railroading, and Lionel trains in particular,
        was rekindled in the 1970s with the birth of his son Ben.
        Neil remarks, "I was just getting back into trains at the time,
        reintroducing myself to a pastime I had enjoyed as a child. Sharing
        the building of the layout together was one of our happiest times."
        (*Waging Heavy Peace*, 2.) Neil began collecting Lionel O gauge
        trains, both pre- and post-war, amassing an impressive collection.
        In 1995 he became a shareholder in the Lionel train company,
        and invested in the development of a wireless control device that

could be used by physically challenged individuals such as Ben, a quadriplegic born with cerebral palsy: "I devised a switch system run by a big red button that he could work with his hand. It took a lot of effort, but it was very rewarding for him to see the cause and effect in action. Ben was empowered by this." (*Waging Heavy Peace*, 3.) Neil played an important role in developing the Lionel TrainMaster Command Control (which allows multiple trains to run at the same time), as well as Lionel RailSounds (which provides realistic railroad audio effects) and the Lionel Legacy Control System. Although he lost money on his investment in Lionel, Neil remains a board member. A massive Lionel model train layout, including living plants and a mist irrigation system, is housed in one of the barns on his ranch in California; the terrain is accented with miniature novelties including collectible tin cars, lead figures, vintage structures and tiny animals. The layout has grown into 3,000 square feet of track and trains over the years. Two full-sized old rail cars sit behind the model-train barn and appear to frame it.

118     Bunte, "Railroading Together."

119     From Neil's spoken introduction to "Mellow My Mind," performed during the Chrome Dreams Continental Tour at the Chicago Theater on November 12, 2007.

120     Neil Young, *Waging Heavy Peace*, 497.

121     Pickering District High School was located in the old Village of Pickering, which is not the same as the City of Pickering. The old Village of Pickering is now part of the City of Ajax, while the hamlet of Brock Road is now part of the City of Pickering. Bob Young graduated from Pickering High School — the word *District* was dropped in the ensuing years — with his Secondary School Graduation Diploma in the summer of 1961.

122     Scott Young, "Presents Not Easy to Choose."

123     Neil Young, *Waging Heavy Peace*, 300.

124     Scott Young, "Company Report: Neil's Chicken Business." Held in the Trent University Archives, Scott Young fonds (06-002/1/5).

125     In an oral composition presented to his Grade 8 class in Toronto a few years later, Neil gives the number as nine. Scott reported the number as 10 in his *Globe and Mail* column.

126 Scott Young, "Company Report: Veritable Business Cyclone."
Held in the Trent University Archives, Scott Young fonds
(06-002/1/5).

127 In Neil's outline for the Grade 8 oral composition, he notes that he
found nine dead chickens, which he sold for 75 cents each to make
a total of $6.75 — not $7.50 as Scott reported in his May 2, 1957,
*Globe and Mail* column.

128 McDonough, *Shakey*, 51.

129 In his May 3, 1957, *Globe and Mail* column, Scott reported that
Neil ordered 25 chicks. However, in the outline to Neil's Grade 8
oral composition he notes that he ordered 26 more chicks. Scott's
figure seems more accurate since Neil started out with Petunia,
obtained two more chicks from Don Scott and Howard Bath, and
then lost two to an owl attack. If he ordered 25 more chicks, this
would make his total 26, which is the correct number.

130 Neil Young, *Waging Heavy Peace*, 301.

131 Scott Young reports that the first egg was laid on December 3.
However, Neil notes in his Grade 8 oral presentation that one of
his hens laid the first egg on December 27, 1956.

132 Scott Young, "Company Report: Veritable Business Cyclone."

133 From Neil Young's Grade 8 oral presentation. Held in the Trent
University Archives, Scott Young fonds (90-003/26/2).

134 Neil likely took the name *Hoiman* from a popular Paramount
Pictures cartoon of the time called *Herman and Katnip* ("Save
us, Cousin Hoiman! Save us!"), a clone of MGM's *Tom & Jerry*.
Herman was a mouse and Katnip was a cat.

135 Neil evidently liked the name *Hoiman* because he used it again in
an undated script (likely from his time on Brock Road) for a play
he wrote called *The Rise and Fall of Jake Bell*. Bell is "a hard-
working cleaner man" who works for Hoiman, his "very snippy
boss who needs everything [to be] 'just right.'" The script is held in
the Trent University Archives, Scott Young fonds (90-003/26/2).

136 From Neil Young's Grade 8 oral presentation about his chicken
farming business.

137 Multiple pages of financial records for Neil Eggs are held in the
Trent University Archives, Scott Young fonds (90-003/26/2).

138 The original sign is held in the Trent University Archives,

Scott Young fonds (90-003/26/2).

139  The original note is held in the Trent University Archives,
     Scott Young fonds (90-003/26/2).

140  The correct spelling of the surname is *Vernoy*, according to an
     ex-Brock Road resident.

141  Neil never abandoned his interest in chickens, even as an adult.
     In 1999 he helped organize a chicken-farming operation on three
     acres of his sprawling ranch in La Honda with his middle child
     Ben. The eggs are produced from free-range chickens, and in 2002
     the company, Coastside Farms, was certified organic. Currently
     Ben raises 250 red sex-links, similar to Rhode Island Reds. The
     hens are all named Georgette and the roosters George. Neil's
     chicken mania was on full display when he was interviewed by
     Conan O'Brien on *Late Night* on March 19, 2004. He related
     different types of chickens to the political situation in the U.S.

142  From Neil Young's Grade 8 oral presentation about his chicken
     farming business.

143  McDonough, *Shakey*, 51.

144  Marlene shared something else in common with Neil. She was
     stricken with poliomyelitis in 1953. Like Neil, she was considered
     a "lucky polio." She suffered some lasting muscle weakness on one
     side, but was not paralyzed.

145  Neil Young, *Waging Heavy Peace*, 299.

146  Ibid.

147  Information received from Neil via Will Mitchell in an e-mail dated
     July 19, 2010.

148  Neil Young, *Waging Heavy Peace*, 302.

149  Ibid., 299-300.

150  The bridge was replaced by a steel culvert when the area was
     filled in.

151  Neil Young, *Waging Heavy Peace*, 300.

152  Ibid., 301.

153  Scott Young, *A Writer's Life*, 156.

154  McDonough, *Shakey*, 51-52.

155  Crowe, "Neil Young: Still Expecting to Fly."

156  McDonough, *Shakey*, 51-52.

157  Ibid., 53.

158   CHUM was launched as a dawn-to-dusk radio station on October 28, 1945. Allan Waters took over the station in December 1954 and instituted the Top 50 format on May 27, 1957. Beginning in 2006, the Allan Waters Humanitarian Award — recognizing "a Canadian artist whose humanitarian contributions have positively enhanced the social fabric of Canada" — has been presented at the annual Juno awards. The award went to Neil Young in 2011.

159   The last CHUM Chart was released the week of June 14, 1986, when Madonna's "Live to Tell" was the final No. 1 song.

160   Kent, "I Build Something Up, I Tear It Right Down: Neil Young at 50."

161   Arthur Godfrey was an American radio and television broadcaster and entertainer who hosted two popular weekly TV series during the 1950s — *Arthur Godfrey's Talent Scouts* and *Arthur Godfrey and his Friends*. Godfrey sang and played a ukulele and lent his name and support to plastics manufacturer Mario Maccaferri's line of inexpensive plastic ukuleles called the Islander. Competitor Emenee was also able to use Godfrey's image to promote its line of Flamingo ukuleles that came with an Arthur Godfrey songbook. It has been suggested by Ralf Böllhoff (in *"Das Rätsel um Neil Youngs erste Plastik-Ukulele"*) that Neil appears to have had a mixed set consisting of a Meccaferri Islander and an Arthur Godfrey songbook by Emenee. These mixed sets were also popular at the time. www.rusted-moon.com/2011/04/das-ratsel-um-neil-youngs-erste-plastik.html.

162   Bienstock, "Rider on the Storm."

163   Denberg, "Music just takes you wherever you want to go: A conversation with Neil Young."

164   The Knopfs' two eldest daughters, Monika and Rosemary, were in the senior class with Neil at Brock Road School during the 1955-56 academic year.

165   The scorecards are held in the Trent University Archives, Scott Young fonds (90-003/26/2).

166   Neil's golf handicap is reported at www.golfdigest.com/golf-tours-news/2007-12/musicianrankings_gd2007.

167   Scott Young, *Neil and Me*, 40.

168   Eldon "Sunny" Wingay practised his guitar playing for the next

two years with friend Rick Capreol, whose sister Suzy was in Neil's Grade 4 class at Whitney School. Rick also had a Stella acoustic guitar with an electric pickup in addition to an Ampeg amplifier. Eldon and Rick formed a band with Eldon's older brother Eddie, who was in Neil's Grade 4 class at Whitney School, and friend Peter Plant. They first played for money at an evening dance on the tennis courts at the 1960 Mayfair in Rosedale Park. Rick and Eldon went on to become professional musicians with their own groups and played venues throughout Ontario in the 1970s. From the late 1960s to the late 1970s, Eldon was lead guitarist in the group Brutus and then left to join Tribe, while Rick won accolades locally as guitarist with Little John & the Friars. During the early days of the Mynah Birds — before Neil and bassist Bruce Palmer were members — the only place the band was able to practise was in the basement of Rick's parents' house on Heath Street East. Two other former members of Little John & the Friars — Goldy McJohn (keyboards) and Richie Grand (drums) — went on to become members of the Mynah Birds, with McJohn continuing his musical career more famously with Steppenwolf.

169   The June 27, 1958, edition of the *Pickering News* reports: "Mr. and Mrs. Young and family, of Brock Road, have gone to live at Willowdale. We wish them the best in their new home."

170   Scott Young, "Cutups All, Grass Type, That Is."

171   Scott Young, *Neil and Me*, 42. The original copy of Neil's oral composition is held in the Trent University Archives, Scott Young fonds (90-003/26/2).

**5: Sad Movies**

172   The house the Young family lived in was demolished in 2012. A new dwelling with the same number was built in its place.

173   Scott Young, *Neil and Me*, 45. Neil says the plastic ukulele was purchased in Pickering a few months before they moved to Toronto. Scott recalls that the ukulele was a Christmas gift at 49 Old Orchard Grove. This would have been during December 1958, at least seven months after the Youngs had moved there. Neil's recollection makes more sense.

174   The 1956 Sears-Roebuck catalogue advertises a ukulele classified as "BETTER" for $9.95. This is likely the sort of ukulele Neil played as his first upgrade after the plastic model.

175   McDonough, *Shakey*, 59.

176   In his interview with Nick Kent, Neil remembers the number and order of his earliest instruments a bit differently. "My first was this little plastic Arthur Godfrey ukulele, then I seem to remember a baritone 'uke,' then I had a banjo. So I had these different sounding instruments which I played the same way."

177   The address of the school was later changed to 245 Fairlawn Avenue.

178   John Wanless, born August 28, 1862, was an inveterate supporter of the public school system. To encourage students to work harder he presented an annual award called the Optimus Cup (also known as the Wanless Cup). Wanless died on July 15, 1941.

179   Crowe, "Neil Young: The Last American Hero."

180   Neil Young, *Waging Heavy Peace*, 299.

181   Bunny maintained a close friendship with Neil at John Wanless Public School and then at Lawrence Park Collegiate. They are still in contact. Bunny's name appears prominently in a letter written by Neil to his mother (dated August 1965), displayed on pp. 32-33 of the Archives Book, part of *The Neil Young Archives (Volume 1)*. Neil stayed at Bunny's mother's place with Bunny when he was first getting settled in Toronto during the summer of 1965. In the letter Neil reassures his mother that he is doing well and has some prospects lined up. He mentions he's "writing some good stuff" and that many people seem interested. He also notifies her about the condition of his broken-down hearse, which is "still up north." Bunny adds his own personal message to Neil's mother at the end of the letter, reassuring her that Neil is being well taken care of and that his mother is "enjoying his stay here and doesn't mind in the slightest."

182   McDonough, *Shakey*, 61.

183   Crowe, "Neil Young: The Last American Hero."

184   Ken Koblun says Neil told him this story when they were classmates in Grade 9 at Earl Grey Junior High School in Winnipeg. According to Ken, the notorious dictionary episode

did not occur at Earl Grey, as others have claimed. (He recalls
Neil speaking about the incident as if it were an earlier event
that happened in Toronto.) The version of the story Neil told to
Cameron Crowe finished with, "Few years later, I just felt it. All
of a sudden I wanted a guitar and that was it," which suggests
the dictionary episode occurred at John Wanless. (Neil purchased
his first guitar shortly after arriving in Winnipeg in August 1960,
two years after he began Grade 8 at John Wanless.) Neil himself
suggested the school in question might have been John Wanless
when he was interviewed by Jimmy McDonough (*Shakey*, 61).

185   McDonough, *Shakey*, 61.

186   From Neil Young's Grade 8 oral presentation about his chicken
farming business.

187   Scott Young, *Neil and Me*, 41.

188   Scott changed the year to July 1956 in a slightly revised version
of Neil's composition that appears in *Neil and Me*. He also
corrected Neil's spelling and punctuation. He incorrectly identifies
the composition as being presented while Neil was in Grade 7,
but there is hard-copy evidence that Neil was in Miss MacKay's
Grade 8 class at the time.

189   From Neil Young's Grade 8 oral presentation about his chicken
farming business.

190   Cameron Crowe misidentified Neil as a *Toronto Sun* paper boy
and Scott as a sportswriter for the same newspaper in an interview
with Neil ("The Last American Hero"). The *Sun* did not exist at
that date. The paper he delivered was the *Globe and Mail*.

191   The receipt from Art's Cycle & Sports at 1945 Avenue Road, dated
Nov. 6, 1958, is held in the Trent University Archives, Scott Young
fonds (90-003/26/2).

192   Scott Young, *Neil and Me*, 44.

193   Wheeler, "Lanois' Neil Young project proceeds with caution."

194   The Glendale Theatre holds the record for the longest Cinerama
screening of Stanley Kubrick's *2001: A Space Odyssey*. The film
played for two years, four months and five days during the late
1960s, according to Arthur C. Clark's book *The Lost Worlds of
2001* (Signet, 1972). It was popular among young, hip moviegoers
to drop LSD prior to a screening and trip out on the bizarre images

on the screen. A Nissan car dealership has since replaced the Glendale Theatre at 1661 Avenue Road.

195  Shea's Bowl was located at 1654 Avenue Road.

196  Hall's Pure Milk Dairy Store was located at 3353 Yonge Street, between Snowdon Avenue and Golfdale Road.

197  Composition held in the Trent University Archives, Scott Young fonds (90-003/26/2).

198  John Flower, president of the John Wanless Alumni Association, has a copy of the Class of 1959 Graduation Program. Flower arranged for a framed photo of an adult Neil, along with his Grade 8 class photo and a short biography, to be displayed in the school.

199  Astrid Jr. remarked that Astrid Sr. (her mother) and Rassy "both drank a lot, and they both had the same drink — rye whiskey and water" (McDonough, *Shakey*, 99).

200  McDonough, *Shakey*, 85.

201  The "love letters" written by Scott and Astrid are held in the Trent University Archives, Scott Young fonds (90-003/1/23-26).

**6: It Might Have Been**

202  "It Might Have Been" (Harriet Kane/Ronnie Green). Lyrics to this song borrowed heavily from John Greenleaf Whittier's 1856 poem "Maud Muller."

203  Scott makes no reference to Lawrence Park Collegiate in *Neil and Me*.

204  Scott Young, *Neil and Me*, 45.

205  Ciccone's, established in 1951 by Frank and Mary Ciccone, was located at 601 King Street West (between Spadina Avenue and Bathurst Street). The restaurant closed in 2000.

206  Telegram dated October 17, 1959, from Scott to Astrid, held in the Trent University Archives, Scott Young fonds (90-003/1/26).

207  McDonough, *Shakey*, 69.

208  Goddard, "Neil Young's childhood friend walks down memory lane."

209  McDonough, *Shakey*, 60.

210  Comrie Smith, "Notes on Neil Young" (dated November 11,

1970), provided by Sheila (Smith) Edgar, Comrie's sister.

211 Ibid.

212 The McConnell family lived at 74 Snowdon Avenue, one block east of Yonge Street near Bocastle. They resided in the lower duplex and his aunt and uncle lived in the upper duplex. Bob was born in 1944 and was a year ahead of Neil at Lawrence Park Collegiate.

213 Comrie Smith, "Notes on Neil Young."

214 Letter from Comrie Smith to Scott Young dated October 16, 1990, held in the Trent University Archives, Scott Young fonds (90-001/2/5).

215 Goddard, "Neil Young's childhood friend walks down memory lane."

216 "The Loner," *UNCUT,* March 2009, 32-45. Complete transcript of Comrie Smith's interview by John Einarson — "Part 5: High School Friend Comrie Smith Interview" — published online at www.uncut.co.uk/neil-young/part-5-high-school-friend-comrie-smith-interview.

217 McDonough, *Shakey,* 60.

218 Halpern's was located at 3376 Yonge Street, just south of Melrose Avenue.

219 Undated letter sent to Scott Young from Comrie Smith titled "Neil Young," held in the Trent University Archives, Scott Young fonds (90-003/27).

220 Letter dated November 1959 held in the Trent University Archives, Scott Young fonds (90-003/26/2).

221 The "white bucks" reference in "Don't Be Denied" is usually attributed to Neil's arrival in Winnipeg in August 1960. However, this is not the case. Neil first started wearing white bucks at Lawrence Park Collegiate in Toronto prior to moving to Winnipeg. By the time he arrived in Winnipeg his bucks were becoming worn out and he saved them for special occasions only.

222 McDonough, *Shakey,* 62.

223 Comrie Smith, "Notes on Neil Young."

224 Ibid.

225 McDonough, *Shakey,* 62.

226 Letter from Comrie Smith to Scott Young dated October 16, 1990.

227 McDonough, *Shakey,* 130.

228 Comrie Smith, "Notes on Neil Young."

229 McDonough, *Shakey*, 60.

230 Ibid.

231 Undated letter from Comrie Smith to Scott Young, held in the Trent University Archives, Scott Young fonds (95-001/2/5).

232 Robinson's Radio Service was located at 3331 Yonge Street, just south of Snowdon Avenue.

233 McDonough, *Shakey*, 64.

234 Ibid., 65.

235 Comrie Smith, "Notes on Neil Young."

236 Confirmation received from Neil via Will Mitchell in an e-mail dated July 19, 2010. Neil wrote, "Comrie Smith is the friend on the school steps." Neil must have relayed this information to Jimmy McDonough when he was writing *Shakey* because on p. 130 McDonough wrote, "One day in the fall of 1965, Neil had Comrie drive him by all of their old Toronto haunts. There were glimmers that Young was feeling the pull of his dreams, feeling the urge to move on. He insisted they stop at their old school, Lawrence Park. 'I have to do this, Comrie,' he said, and then sat on the steps with his guitar and played song after song." The reference to the school steps in "Don't Be Denied" is often attributed to Earl Grey Junior High in Winnipeg, but it's a reference to the steps at Lawrence Park Collegiate. In the song, Neil combines his remembrances from his year at Lawrence Park in Toronto, his memories of Winnipeg and his early days with Buffalo Springfield in L.A.

237 Bob McConnell recalls that Comrie's first guitar was a flat-top acoustic Harmony Sovereign Jumbo. He thinks Comrie may have received this guitar for Christmas 1961. He did not yet have this guitar when Neil was attending Lawrence Park Collegiate.

238 "The Loner," *UNCUT*, March 2009, 32-45. Complete transcript of Comrie Smith's interview by John Einarson — "Part 5: High School Friend Comrie Smith Interview" — published online at www.uncut.co.uk/neil-young/part-5-high-school-friend-comrie-smith-interview.

239 Harold comes from a large, musical family. The Greers lived at 46 Teddington Park Avenue. Harold's youngest brother, Ken, is a

long-time member of Red Rider, Tom Cochrane's band. He plays
pedal steel guitar as well as guitar and keyboards. Ken and his
girlfriend were in the car with Comrie and friend David Bradley
when they drove to Hamilton to attend Neil's show with Crazy
Horse at Copps Coliseum on October 31, 1996. Neil had pre-
arranged with Comrie to bring the tape of the songs they had
recorded in the attic of his parents' home at 46 Golfdale Road in
fall 1965. Three of the songs on this tape are featured on Disc 0 of
*The Neil Young Archives (Volume 1)* — "Hello Lonely Woman,"
"Casting Me Away from You" and "There Goes My Babe."

240   Harold was a member of the school orchestra and a student in the
strings music class. His teacher and orchestra leader was Natalie
Kuzmich (nee Belz). Harold was in Dr. Dickinson's homeroom
art class (form 9H) during the 1959-60 academic year. This was
considered an "experimental" gifted class and students took
both music and art, learned at an accelerated pace and graduated
in four years instead of five. The students from the gifted class
stayed together for all of their classes during this time. Owen
Charlesworth, who attended John Wanless Public School with Neil
and was in Harold's homeroom class, recalls that Dr. Dickinson
was a "wonderful teacher," who "invited the homeroom class to a
picnic at his farm at the end of the school year."

241   St. Leonard's Anglican Church is located at 25 Wanless Avenue.

242   St. Timothy's Anglican Church is located at 100 Old Orchard
Grove.

243   Perhaps remembering the name of this band, Neil later used the
title "The Sultan" as the A-side of his one and only single with the
Squires on the V Records label.

244   Carl Scharfe was in class 10A — Mr. Humphries' homeroom class
— during the 1959-60 academic year at Lawrence Park Collegiate.

245   Undated letter sent to Scott Young by Comrie Smith titled "Neil
Young," held in the Trent University Archives, Scott Young fonds
(90-003/27).

246   Ronnie Hawkins, originally from Arkansas, found success in
Toronto in the taverns along Yonge Street playing with various
incarnations of the Hawks, his backing band. Some of the more
notable Hawks included musicians who would go on to form the

Band. Hawkins' first hit single was a cover of "Hey, Bo Diddley," released in 1958.

247 Kent, "I Build Something Up, I Tear It Right Down: Neil Young at 50."

248 From an audience recording of Neil Young and the International Harvesters performing at the Canadian National Exhibition Grandstand in Toronto, September 1, 1984.

249 Franklin Men's Wear was located at 3278 Yonge Street, north of Brookdale Avenue and south of Fairlawn Avenue. The proprietor was Joe Franklin. The store is incorrectly identified as Halpern's in *Shakey* by Jimmy McDonough.

250 Scott Young, *Neil and Me*, 46.

251 It was during this time that Bob finished his last year at Pickering High School. The school most likely held good memories for him since he attended it at a time when the family was happier and he was busy with school, his friends and his sporting activities. Scott's downtown apartment was a considerable distance from the school, which may have been another reason — apart from its small size — why Bob found living with his father unsuitable. Bob's Secondary School Graduation Diploma from Pickering High School (held in the Scott Young Fonds) is dated and signed July 4, 1961. After graduating, Bob worked in the pro shop at the Pickering Golf Course for a few seasons. He also played in many golf tournaments, but his hopes for a professional golf career never came to fruition.

**PART TWO**

### 7: Earl Grey Junior High School

1    Scott Young, *Neil and Me*, 28.

2    Neil's daughter Amber Jean is named after Jean Young.

3    Jean Ferguson Paterson Young also wrote the Social News column for the *Flin Flon Daily Reminder* from the 1950s to the 1980s.

4    Neil Young, *Waging Heavy Peace*, 256.

5    McKay, "Neil Young — London Hammersmith Apollo, March 16, 2008."

6    Neil Young, *Waging Heavy Peace*, 256.

7    Bienstock, "Rider on the Storm."

8    Neil revealed during a live "Legends on Twitter" event on October
     24, 2012, that he no longer has his first guitar. Tom Dunning
     asked, "What was your 1st guitar and do you have it still?" Neil
     responded, "it was a harmony. don't have it still." twitter.com/
     neilyoung/with_replies.

9    The 1959 Harmony Monterey Catalog shows the price as $46 U.S.

10   McDonough, *Shakey*, 79.

11   In an e-mail message from Neil, forwarded by Will Mitchell
     on July 19, 2010, Neil confirms, "I think I got the Monterey in
     Winnipeg, not Toronto."

12   KSAN radio interview, Neil Young to Tony Pig, November 12, 1969.

13   McDonough, *Shakey*, 81.

14   Neil would retain his fondness for sweaters up to and including his
     time with the Buffalo Springfield. Many photos from that period
     show him posed in a striking yellow, green and black geometric
     print sweater — obviously one of his favourites. He also owned a
     similarly patterned sweater in red.

15   A play on the Sealy Posturepedic mattresses that were first sold
     to the public in 1950. They were advertised heavily on TV and in
     print at the time.

16   Comments received from Neil Young via e-mail forwarded by
     Will Mitchell on July 19, 2010.

17   Bienstock, "Rider on the Storm."

18   Erwin left Kelvin High School after Grade 11 and attended United
     College (now the University of Winnipeg). He lost track of Neil for
     some time but did go to Woodstock and saw him perform there
     with Crosby, Stills and Nash.

19   The use of the strap was banned in Manitoba in the early 1980s.
     All schools in the province had a strap available for use in the
     office until that time. Only the principal and vice-principal were
     authorized to use the strap, and it was only used sparingly during
     the later years.

20   Undated letter held in the Trent University Archives, Scott Young
     fonds (90-003/26/2).

21   Neil Young, *Waging Heavy Peace*, 58.

22   Allan Kowbel legally changed his name to Chad Allan in the early
     1970s.

23 Letter dated November 2, 1960, held in the Trent University Archives, Scott Young fonds (90-003/26/2).

24 Letter dated November 13, 1960, held in the Trent University Archives, Scott Young fonds (90-003/26/2).

25 Einarson, *Don't Be Denied*, 47.

26 *Ibid.*, 48.

27 Letter from Rassy sent to Scott dated November 13, 1960.

28 "The Loner," *UNCUT,* March 2009, 32-45. Complete transcript of Ken Koblun's interview by Rob Hughes — "Part 2: The Gospel According to Ken Koblun" — published online at www.uncut. co.uk/neil-young/part-two-the-gospel-according-to-ken-koblun-interview.

29 McDonough, *Shakey*, 82-83.

30 The building that housed Patterson's Ranch House was purchased by a church in 1975. The Holy Ghost Ukrainian Centre now stands on the property.

31 It can be determined from the headstock of Neil's guitar, and by the shadow the guitar casts against the wall, that Neil is not playing his Harmony Monterey with DeArmond pickup, but a Gibson Les Paul Junior. It is unclear if this is the same guitar he played prior to the 1960 orange Gretsch 6120 "Chet Atkins" model he purchased from Jon Glowa. There is solid evidence that Rassy purchased the Gibson Les Paul Junior for Neil's 16th birthday. In a letter to Scott dated October 28, 1961, Rassy wrote, "I have just bought him a better guitar for his upcoming birthday." Perhaps she gave Neil a very early birthday present, but told Scott she was giving Neil the guitar for his birthday. If this was not the case, Neil may have been playing a borrowed Gibson Les Paul Junior in the Esquires that he later received as a birthday gift from his mother.

32 B'nai Brith, "an independent voice of the Jewish community, representing its interests nationwide to the government, NGOs and the wider Canadian public," regularly held dances for members of Winnipeg's Jewish community and in other large Jewish population centres across the country.

33 McDonough, *Shakey*, 83.

34 Ibid.

35 Ibid., 84.

36    Ibid.

37    The April 10, 1961, issue of *Billboard* reports that the Fendermen were then touring Canada.

38    Scott and Astrid were wed on May 20, 1961.

39    Scott Young, *Neil and Me*, 42.

40    Neil appears to be holding a Danelectro guitar. Due to the poor photo quality and because some of the characteristic parts of the guitar are covered by either Neil or Susan Kelso, the exact model cannot be determined. The "Coke-bottle" style headplate, the small white pickguard and the short-horn body seem to suggest it's either a four- or six-string bass made by Danelectro. Its origins can only be speculated upon. Jim Kale has confirmed that his second guitar was a brown-coloured four-string 1960 Double Shorthorn Danelectro purchased from a mail order Sears-Roebuck location in North Dakota during the fall of 1960. It's possible Jim loaned the guitar to Neil near the end of June 1961. Even though Neil has never been associated with playing a bass, he was likely curious about it since bass guitars were relatively uncommon then. He was also giving some thought to forming his second group, the Stardusters. (He had quit playing with the Esquires in May, but it wasn't Neil who had formed that band.) Neil realized he would need a bass player in the band and had the opportunity to check out a Danelectro. Both Richard Koreen and Ken Koblun would later own this same bass and both played with Neil, but at different times. Neither can confirm if this is the same bass guitar Neil is playing in the photo. However, it seems likely this might be the case. Ken recalls that the pickguard did not cover the pickup and the guitar Neil is holding seems to have a similar pickguard.

**8: Kelvin High School (Year One)**

41    Not to be confused with Ross F. "Clancy" Smith, a Grade 10 student at Kelvin. Neil used Clancy as a source of inspiration for "Nowadays Clancy Can't Even Sing."

42    The F in Clancy's full name stands for *Fingard*, the anglicized spelling of his mother's maiden name. The nickname Clancy was selected for Ross while he was still *in utero*. Family members were

trying to think of a suitable name and his mother joked that they should give him an Irish name like Kelly or Clancy. (The Smiths were a non-traditional Jewish family.) Clancy's then five-year-old brother said he liked Clancy best, so the name stuck. The Smith family's original surname in the old country (Germany) was Mackler, but it was changed to the more anonymous Smith after his grandfather moved to Winnipeg during the early part of the 20th century.

43 "Who Was Clancy?," KSAN radio excerpt, Neil Young to Tony Pig, November 12, 1969, *The Neil Young Archives (Volume 1)*.

44 "Valerie, Valera" is found in the lyrics of a popular song called "The Happy Wanderer" by Friedrich-Wilhelm Möller. It was written shortly after World War II and became an international hit after a children's choir sang it on a BBC radio broadcast in 1953.

45 "Who Was Clancy?," KSAN radio excerpt.

46 Neil Young interview with Jeffrey C. Alexander, *Los Angeles Times Calendar*, September 1967.

47 Tim Henry was a friend of Neil's at Kelvin. Tim's mother was Ann Henry, noted journalist, playwright and *Winnipeg Tribune* columnist. She married Max Smith, Clancy's father, in the mid-1960s. Tim remembers a party held in the basement home on Oxford Street where Neil played with the Squires. This is likely the same party where Clancy remembers meeting Neil.

48 The two versions include the demo recording from Elektra Records (December 1965) and the live recording from Canterbury House in Ann Arbor, Michigan (November 10, 1968). The previously unreleased Elektra demo appears on *The Neil Young Archives (Volume 1)*, as does the version of "Clancy" from July 1966 that appears on *Buffalo Springfield*. Neil says he didn't want to use the 1968 recording of "Clancy" from the acoustic set at Canterbury House because it's too good: "I was too on it." (See McDonough, *Shakey*, 125.)

49 Sandie, "The Original Lyric Manuscript: 'Nowadays Clancy Can't Even Sing.'"

50 Neil remembered that Ken had the lyrics to "Clancy" and called him in 1990 to see if he still had them. Ken did, and Neil came to see them. He later dispatched his long-time archivist Joel Bernstein

to fetch the lyric sheets along with other material Neil wanted
to use for the *Buffalo Springfield Box Set* and *The Neil Young
Archives (Volume 1)*. The material was returned to Ken
nine years later.

51 Letter dated October 28, 1961, held in the Scott Young fonds
(90-003/26/2).

52 Differences in the curricula between Manitoba and Ontario schools
are discussed in letters exchanged between Rassy and Scott during
1960-64. These letters are held in the Trent University Archives,
Scott Young fonds.

53 Neil Young, *Waging Heavy Peace*, 47.

54 Kent, "I Build Something Up, I Tear It Right Down: Neil Young
at 50."

55 Neil's long-time guitar tech Larry Cragg confirmed the year and
model in issue 23 of *The Fretboard Journal* (Fall 2011). Photos
from the article were posted online by Jason Verlinde as an
addendum — "Photo Outtakes: Guitar Tech Larry Cragg."
www.fretboardjournal.com/photos/photo-outtakes-guitar-tech-
larry-cragg. Neil had spotted Larry's 1956 Gibson Les Paul Junior
and remarked that it was exactly the same as his first electric
guitar. Larry said, "I sold Neil a Les Paul Jr. in 1978. It has no
finish on it." Neil played both Larry's 1956 Gibson Les Paul Junior
and the unfinished Les Paul during his 2009 Continental Tour.
(Information received from Larry Cragg via e-mail dated January
13, 2012.)

56 In an audio clip from an interview included on a bonus track of
the Bonus DVD edition of *Neil Young: Heart of Gold* by Jonathan
Demme, Neil is asked about his earliest amplifiers. He remarks,
"First I was using another guy's amp and then I got my own." The
amp Ken saw Neil playing with at his home in November 1961
must have been a friend's, as Neil did not receive his own first amp
— an Ampeg Echo Twin — until Christmas 1962.

57 Mike Currie, "An Interview with Ken Koblun."

58 Echard, *Neil Young and the Poetics of Energy*.

59 Ben Young's free-range chickens at Coastside Farms lay organic
brown eggs.

60 Both Richard Koreen (while a member of the Stardusters/

Twilighters/Teen Tones) and Ken Koblun (while a member in the Classics) remember Neil having a "small Ampeg." This must have been the amp Neil borrowed from a friend that he refers to on an audio clip from an interview included on a bonus track of the Bonus DVD edition of *Neil Young: Heart of Gold* by Jonathan Demme.

61    The amplifier was possibly a British-made Selmer Truevoice PA system.

62    Letter dated February 6, 1962, held in the Trent University Archives, Scott Young fonds (90-003/26/2).

63    Kelvin student Mike Sambork, who also attended Earl Grey Junior High earlier, was a member of the Del Rios at this time. He played some one-off gigs with Neil after he left the band later in the year. Ed Klym, who had played at some early practices with the Esquires but never performed with them onstage, rehearsed and played a few gigs with the Del Rios. His younger brother Brian recalls that their father, a tailor, made red shirts for the band with the band's name embroidered on the front pocket. Mike recalls, "Ed had a good guitar and amp but wasn't a great live player. He was more of a 'basement guitarist.'"

64    Squires drummer Ken Smyth played with Carmine La Rosa from 1989 to 1995 when the band was called Carmine La Rosa and Guests. They were the house band in the Pompeii Lounge upstairs at Vesuvio's Restaurant. Guitarist Mike Sambork, formerly of the Del Rios, was also a member of the band and had played with Carmine La Rosa for many years. He was the one who initially asked Ken to sit in with the band one night when he was in the audience. This turned into a regular gig for Ken.

65    Mike Sambork played in the Del Rios in the early 1960s and then with the Dimensions in the mid-1960s. (Allan Bates and Doug Campbell were also in this band; Doug went on to play with the Squires briefly in 1965.) Mike then played for a long period in various incarnations of Carmine La Rosa's bands. He played with Carmine La Rosa and the Thunderstorms at the Shakin' All Over Sixties Winnipeg Bands Reunion concert held at the Winnipeg Convention Centre on June 28, 1987. The band played the 6 p.m. slot before Neil came onstage and performed with some other

well-known 1960s Winnipeg musicians such as Randy Bachman, Burton Cummmings and Chad Allan.

66    Undated letter held in the Trent University Archives, Scott Young fonds (90-003/26/2).

67    Letter dated May 16, 1962, held in the Trent University Archives, Scott Young fonds (90-003/26/2).

68    Letter dated May 23, 1962, held in the Trent University Archives, Scott Young fonds (90-003/26/2).

69    "The Loner," UNCUT, March 2009, 32-45. Complete transcript of Ken Koblun's interview by Rob Hughes — "Part 2: The Gospel According to Ken Koblun" — published online at www.uncut. co.uk/neil-young/part-two-the-gospel-according-to-ken-koblun-interview.

70    Ken neglected to include his very first live performance in his meticulously kept "List of Shows." He felt it wasn't worthy of inclusion.

71    Neil has referred to the venue as the Winnipeg Municipal [sic] Auditorium. wbi.lib.umanitoba.ca/WinnipegBuildings/showBuilding.jsp?id=239.

72    McDonough, Shakey, 94.

73    The exact date Neil first saw Roy Orbison is not known. No details regarding gigs at the Winnipeg Civic Auditorium from 1960-62 have emerged, but there is solid evidence he played a gig at the auditorium on October 18, 1963. An ad for the show ran in the October 16, 1963, Winnipeg Free Press. Orbison's hit record at the time is noted: "Blue Bayou." There were two opening acts scheduled — Skeeter Davis and Bob Luman. Nevertheless, it is unlikely Neil attended this show. The Squires were playing the Freshie Dance at Grant Park High that same evening. Ken Koblun confirms that they played at the high school the entire evening and it would have been difficult to make it to the Orbison show on time. Ken does remember seeing Orbison perform around this time and thinks Neil may have been with him. He remembers Roy singing "Blue Bayou" and possibly "Pretty Woman." If it was "Pretty Woman," the date of the concert — also held at the auditorium — must have been September 22, 1964 (an ad appeared in the Winnipeg Free Press on September 5, 1964.) The Squires did not

have a gig scheduled that night and they were playing in Winnipeg, just prior to departing on their first foray to Fort William. So it's possible both Neil and Ken attended this show.

74    Neil Young, *Waging Heavy Peace*, 10.

75    McDonough, *Shakey*, 65.

76    Ibid., 98.

77    Venues in Winnipeg Neil has played since 1971 (as posted on the "Sugar Mountain: Neil Young Set Lists" site): www.sugarmtn.org/getshows.php?city=Winnipeg.

78    Kent, "Neil Young: This Young Will Run and Run."

79    McDonough, *Shakey*, 628.

80    Ibid., 94.

81    Neil Young, *Waging Heavy Peace*, 378.

82    Letter dated June 21, 1962, held in the Trent University Archives, Scott Young fonds (90-003/26/2).

83    Letter dated July 3, 1962, held in the Trent University Archives, Scott Young fonds (90-003/26/2).

84    Neil's grandfather, Bill Ragland, would later live with them after Perle was placed in a nursing home. He stayed in the attic room. Rassy, always the apple of her father's eye, was a good companion for him in his later years.

**9: Kelvin High School (Year Two)**

85    John's older brother William was instrumental in forming some Winnipeg rock-and-roll bands in the late 1950s and early '60s, including "Wild Bill" Copsey and the Rhythm Rockers (a.k.a. the Rhythm Rebels) and the Playboys.

86    McDonough, *Shakey*, 81.

87    Neil Young, *Waging Heavy Peace*, 58.

88    Tony Meehan was the original drummer in the Shadows but left in 1960 and was replaced by drummer Brian Bennett. Jet Harris left the band in 1962 and was replaced by bass player Brian Locking, and later, John Rostill.

89    Neil Young, *Waging Heavy Peace*, 58-59.

90    McDonough, *Shakey*, 80.

91    "The Loner," *UNCUT*, March 2009, 32-45. Complete transcript

of Randy Bachman's interview by Rob Hughes — "Part 4: Randy Bachman" — published online at www.uncut.co.uk/neil-young/part-4-randy-bachman-interview.

92    Bachman, *Vinyl Tap Stories*, 83.

93    Ibid., 121.

94    Einarson, *Don't Be Denied*, 65.

95    Ibid.

96    McDonough, *Shakey*, 80.

97    The Loner," *UNCUT*, March 2009, 32-45. Complete transcript of Ken Koblun's interview by Rob Hughes — "Part Two: The Gospel According to Ken Koblun" — published online at www.uncut.co.uk/neil-young/part-two-the-gospel-according-to-ken-koblun-interview.

98    McDonough, *Shakey*, 80.

99    "The List of Shows" covers Ken's musical career from November 1962 to December 1967. The shows date from the start of the Classics, through the entire Squires' period, to his membership in Three's A Crowd and then the earliest days of the Buffalo Springfield and beyond.

100    Neil references Ken's "List of Shows" in his memoir: "Ken, my classmate and an original Squire from the beginning, had been keeping a diary since our first gigs" (*Waging Heavy Peace*, 51).

101    McDonough, *Shakey*, 80.

102    Neil mentioned how much he values Ken's "List of Shows" during a Twitter Q&A on December 2, 2012, sponsored by Blue Rider Press to promote *Waging Heavy Peace*. "There is a diary kept by my friend (of the Squires era) which was a great help to me for both books." (In his memoir Neil mentions that he wrote another book, to be regarded as part two of *Waging Heavy Peace*.)

103    The Loner," *UNCUT*, March 2009, 32-45. Complete transcript of Ken Koblun's interview by Rob Hughes — "Part Two: The Gospel According to Ken Koblun" — published online at www.uncut.co.uk/neil-young/part-two-the-gospel-according-to-ken-koblun-interview.

104    A parody of "The Monster Mash" was first released by Bobby (Boris) Pickett and the Cryptkicker Five in 1962. The song was a huge hit, recycled every year around Halloween. Glenn Church

remarks, "I remember the one time I heard Bernie Barsky and the group play their song ['The Football Mash'] at Grant Park High. I was a brand-new freshie — the time was about late September 1962 and there was an election for high school president, vice president, etc. There were several speeches and then Bernie's 'application' was having his group [which included Allan Bates] sing a 'Mash' song. Of course I cannot remember the words but the song was funny and the crowd ate it up, much to the dismay of the other candidates. I remember some people in the halls later saying they were opposed to his doing that — no speech, just a song. Anyway, Bernie came in second and was vice-president of the student council that year."

105   *Neil Young: Don't Be Denied*, documentary directed by Ben Whalley and initially shown on *American Masters*, BBC Four, October 31–November 2, 2008.

106   Bienstock, "Rider on the Storm."

107   *Neil Young: Don't Be Denied*, documentary directed by Ben Whalley.

108   Undated letter held in the Trent University Archives, Scott Young fonds (90-003/26/2).

109   From an audio clip of an interview included on a bonus track in the bonus DVD edition of *Neil Young: Heart of Gold* by Jonathan Demme.

110   Archives Book, *The Neil Young Archives (Volume 1)*, 17.

111   Neil Young, *Waging Heavy Peace*, 58.

112   Letter dated May 5, 1964, held in the Trent University Archives, Scott Young fonds (90-003/26/2).

113   Einarson, *Don't Be Denied*, 66.

114   Gross, "In Memoir, Neil Young Wages 'Heavy Peace.'"

115   Echard, *Neil Young and the Poetics of Energy*, 43.

116   Robert Clark Young made his original post coining the term "grunge-jazz-feedback" to the Yahoo! Groups Rust list on April 11, 2003. Bob Young — not to be confused with Neil's older brother — made his post in response to an earlier comment made by Scott Sandie ("Surfer Joe"). launch.groups.yahoo.com/group/rust/message/46190.

117   Gross, "In Memoir, Neil Young Wages 'Heavy Peace.'"

118  Neil's fascination with distortion has continued throughout his career. The ultimate example is the album *Arc-Weld*, released as a limited-edition three-disc set in 1991. The *Arc* portion, later released as a single disc, consists in its entirety of a sound collage of guitar noise and distortion. William Echard, in *Neil Young and the Poetics of Energy*, devotes an entire chapter — "The Liquid Rage: Noise and Improvisation" — to this aspect of Neil's music.

119  Simmons, "Crazy Horse: Ralph, Billy, Poncho . . . and Neil."

120  Randy Bachman dedicated the November 12, 2005, instalment of *Vinyl Tap* — his regular radio show for CBC Radio One — to Neil's 60th birthday. Included among the songs played was their collaboration on "Spring Is Nearly Here." Randy reminisced about how the song was recorded. All the other musicians who contributed to the tribute album had picked the Shadows' more popular numbers, and there was one slot left for Neil and Randy. Neil suggested "Spring Is Nearly Here," and Randy agreed. They recorded the song from memory because a copy of the song couldn't be located in time.

121  "The Loner," *UNCUT*, March 2009, 32-45. Full transcript of Allan Bates's interview by Rob Hughes — "Neil Young: The Squires' Years by Allan Bates" — published online at www.uncut.co.uk/neil-young/neil-young-the-squires-years-by-allan-bates-interview.

122  Einarson, *Don't Be Denied*, 63.

123  Ibid., 53.

124  McDonough, *Shakey*, 87.

125  Ibid.

126  Bachman, *Vinyl Tap Stories*, 44.

127  Neil's opinion regarding the best Squires lineup differs from Ken's. Neil states, "The best group was with Doug Campbell and Randy Peterson [circa early 1965]. That group was fine!" (Einarson, *Don't Be Denied*, 107).

128  Mike Currie, "An Interview with Ken Koblun," 45.

129  "The Loner," *UNCUT*, March, 2009, 32-45. Full transcript of Ken Koblun's interview by Rob Hughes — "Part Two: The Gospel According to Ken Koblun" — published online at www.uncut .co.uk/neil-young/part-two-the-gospel-according-to-ken-koblun-interview.

130    "The Loner," *UNCUT*, March 2009, 32-45. Full transcript of
        Allan Bates's interview by Rob Hughes — "Neil Young: The
        Squires' Years by Allan Bates" — published online at www.uncut
        .co.uk/neil-young/neil-young-the-squires-years-by-allan-bates-
        interview.
131    Bachman, *Vinyl Tap Stories*, 8.
132    From comments written by Natalie Pollock that accompany a
        youtube video posted at www.youtube.com/watch?v=teBlRsBlhBY.
        The video shows a tattered poster advertising a gig at the University
        of Manitoba Student Union (UMSU) by Neil Young and the Squires
        and the Crescendos on Friday, May 14, 1965. This gig remains
        a mystery because it is not mentioned in Ken Koblun's "List of
        Shows" — another gig is listed on this date at Atikokan High
        School. A few documents included in the DVD and Blu-ray editions
        of *The Neil Young Archives (Volume 1)* shed some light on the
        subject. A letter addressed to CJLX deejay Ray Dee in Fort Willliam
        from Atikokan High School principal Shirley Kostesky dated April
        26, 1965, reads: "Dear Ray — I have spoken to our Head Boy Bob
        Muir who is in charge of the Spring Prom. I talked to him about
        your costs of $145 for the band and $20 for travel expenses from
        Lakehead. Bob apparently likes what he has heard. But there is
        something that could change the whole perspective. That is the date
        of the dance. I told you that the date was May 21st but it isn't. The
        Spring Prom is to be held on May 14th. The dance is from 8 to 12,
        with a 1/2 hour intermission. Please answer asap if Neil Young and
        the Squires are able to play on May 14th for our Spring Prom."
        Ray Dee responded in a letter dated May 4, 1965: "In reply to your
        letter of April 24, 1965, 'Neil Young & the Squires' will attend
        your 'Spring Prom' on May 14, 1965." The gig at the UMSU was
        likely booked first with posters being printed and circulated. (The
        Squires originally thought they had this date available.) Then they
        received the letter from Principal Kostesky about the date mix-up.
        The Spring Prom paid more, so another band must have replaced
        the Squires at the UMSU dance on May 14 with the Crescendos.
133    Diana would later participate with Doug Mackenzie in the
        folk-singing duo Doug and Di when they performed at Tony's
        coffeehouse at the University of Winnipeg from 1966 to 1968. She

then became lead singer in Rin Tin Iron, whose original members also included Ken Koblun, Bill Hamilton (Lynne Hamilton's brother), Doug Mackenzie, Fraser Lindsey and Chuck McCandless. They performed at Kelvin High, the Fireplace, local coffeehouses and community clubs from 1969 to 1970. Diana continues to pursue her many musical interests. Several of her photos taken of the Squires in March 1965 appear in the Archives Book of *The Neil Young Archives (Volume 1)*.

134 Burton Cummings has been a part-owner of the Salisbury House restaurant chain since 2001, when local investors bought out the previous owners from Montreal. The majority owners are Earl and Cheryl Barish.

135 Smith, "A ballad of Winnipeg's musical past: New documentary 'Drop the Nickel' chronicles the quest for a Manitoba-made musical and cultural treasure." (The Rock-Ola jukeboxes were named after David C. Rockola, an entrepreneur from Virden, Manitoba.)

136 Einarson, *Four Strong Winds: Ian & Sylvia*, 104.

137 Ibid., 6.

138 Neil Young, *Waging Heavy Peace*, 10.

139 Ibid., 263.

140 Ibid., 264.

141 Ibid., 263.

142 Mickey's name at birth was Modest William Theodore Sklepowich and Bunny's birth name was Orissia Ewanchuk. Mickey and Bunny used the anglicized stage surname Sheppard when performing.

143 Neil included a version of "This Land Is Your Land" on *Americana*, released in 2012. Mickey and Bunny released a single of the song, retitled "This Land Is Our Land," on V Records not long after the Squires' single was released.

144 Böllhoff, "'Neil Young and The Squires' — Die ukrainischen Wurzeln."

145 McDonough, *Shakey*, 108.

146 Ibid.

147 A November release date is noted at the Museum of Canadian Music website: www.mocm.ca/Music/Title.aspx?TitleId=302065.

148 Neil Young, *Waging Heavy Peace*, 264.

149 Neil was filmed opening the sealed letters more than 40 years

later. These video clips were included in *The Neil Young Archives (Volume 1)*.

150  Undated letter held in the Trent University Archives, Scott Young fonds. The date — late December 1963 — can be inferred from the letter's contents (90-003/26/2).

### 10: Kelvin High School (Year Three)

151  Neil gave an ironic shout-out to Coach Kachmar during his sold-out October 28, 1996, concert at the Winnipeg Arena. During the intro to "F*!#in' Up," Neil recalled his torture in gym class and used colourful language to describe his memories of the coach. The chorus of the song includes *Why do I keep fuckin' up?* repeated numerous times.

152  Roger Currie, "Rock 'n' Roll High School!," 32-33.

153  McDonough, *Shakey*, 86.

154  *Neil Young: Don't Be Denied*, documentary directed by Ben Whalley.

155  Roger Currie, "Rock 'n' Roll High School!," 32.

156  Einarson, *Don't Be Denied*, 91.

157  According to information included in the Archives Book of *The Neil Young Archives (Volume 1)*. A recording date of September 15, 1963, is given.

158  Neil Young Archives *Post Informer (Vol. 1, No. 3)*, "Mustang," January 21, 2010.

159  Information sent via e-mail from Ralf Böllhoff on May 15, 2012.

160  "The Loner," *UNCUT*, March 2009, 32-45. Complete transcript of Allan Bates's interview by Rob Hughes — "Neil Young: The Squires' Years by Allan Bates" — published online at www.uncut.co.uk/neil-young/neil-young-the-squires-years-by-allan-bates-interview.

161  Ibid.

162  The guitar itself was apparently not at fault. Neil's long-time guitar tech, Larry Cragg, recently weighed in on the subject (in an email dated January 13, 2012): "On all electric guitars the strings are grounded. The problem was with the ac electricity. The PA must not have been grounded at all. Or the polarity was wrong at the ac plug. The bottom line is it had nothing to do with the guitar

itself. Any guitar would have done that." (DIY basement rehearsal rooms and small venues at that time were notorious for electrical problems. The two-wire AC cords common in the 1960s were ungrounded, compounding the problem.)

163   Neil Young, *Waging Heavy Peace*, 58.

164   There is conflicting information regarding the year of Randy Bachman's first Gretsch. Photos from 1962 with Chad Allan and the Reflections show him playing a late 1958/1959 model. In photos from the early 1970s, he is playing a 1957 model. At his bookstore signing in Toronto for *Vinyl Tap Stories* in fall 2011, Randy indicated that there was a knothole in the natural grain on the 1957 model. (He pointed to a photo of a 1957 model included in pages of Grestch models from 1956 to 1961.) Randy claims he played his first Gretsch on "Shakin' All Over" by the Guess Who and also on "Takin' Care of Business" by BTO. He has been searching for his first Gretsch guitar ever since it was stolen from his car in a hotel parking lot in Toronto in 1976 while mixing BTO's *Freeways*, their last studio album. Randy believes Tom Bailey of the Thompson Twins is now the owner of his first Gretsch. He has been spotted playing a 1957 Gretsch on videos posted to YouTube. Randy attempted to connect with the band when the Thompson Twins played GM Place in Vancouver some years ago. A friend who worked backstage approached one of their guitar techs who reported that the Gretsch wasn't brought on tour since it's too valuable. Therefore, the exact model year of Randy Bachman's first Gretsch remains a mystery.

165   Neil was technically not yet 18. In September 1963 he was still a few months' shy of his 18th birthday.

166   McDonough, *Shakey*, 88.

167   Letter dated May 5, 1964 held in the Trent University Archives, Scott Young fonds (90-003/26/2).

168   Böllhoff, "Neil Youngs 'Orange Period' — Die Gretsch 6120."

169   It's unclear whether Neil purchased a Martin D-18 or Gibson 12-string acoustic guitar. Richard Bienstock interviewed Neil in December 2005 and asked, "So you started out as an electric player. How did you come to the acoustic?" Neil replied, "I got into the acoustic when I moved to Toronto, around 1964 [sic].

I started doing the coffeehouse thing. I think I had a [Martin] D-18." Neil added, "I may have borrowed a guitar, a Gibson, from a local guy named David Rea." Neil remarked to Jimmy McDonough that he sold — or pawned, according to some of his friends — his Gretsch in Toronto in the fall of 1965 because he planned to purchase a Gibson 12-string (*Shakey*, 123).

170   Neil Young, *Waging Heavy Peace*, 71.

171   Neil purchased a replacement for his beloved 1960 orange Gretsch 6120 "Chet Atkins" during his time with the Buffalo Springfield. He purchased folksinger Steve Gillette's Gretsch 6120 during the summer of 1966. The guitar is similar to his original Gretsch and has the distinguishing V-cut Bigsby. However, there are a few slight differences from Neil's original Gretsch, so it may be a late 1959 model.

172   Neil Young, *Waging Heavy Peace*, 47.

173   Einarson, *Don't Be Denied*, 73.

174   *Ibid.*

175   Neil Young, *Waging Heavy Peace*, 57.

176   The door to the Cellar was one of the 1960s music artefacts on display at the "Shakin' All Over: The Manitoba Music Experience" exhibit held July 1–September 6, 2010, in Alloway Hall in Winnipeg.

177   The Loner," *UNCUT*, March 2009, pp. 32-45. Complete transcript of Allan Bates's interview by Rob Hughes — "Neil Young: The Squires' Years by Allan Bates" — published online at www.uncut. co.uk/neil-young/neil-young-the-squires-years-by-allan-bates-interview.

178   Roger Currie, "Rock 'n' Roll High School!," 32.

179   Ibid., 34.

180   Kraft Dinner is known in the U.S. as Kraft Macaroni and Cheese — and more affectionately by Canadians as KD. In 1996 Canadians purchased 75 million boxes of KD, ranking them as the top worldwide consumer of the product. archives.cbc.ca/lifestyle/food/clips/8427/. Canadians eat 3.2 boxes per capita in an average year, about 55 per cent more than Americans. Canadians are also the only people to refer to Kraft Dinner as a generic term for instant mac and cheese. (See "Manufacturing Taste: The

(un)natural history of Kraft Dinner — a dish that has shaped not only what we eat, but also who we are" by Sasha Chapman, *The Walrus*, September 2012, 28.)

181 Chickering Square grand pianos were manufactured by the Chickering Company in Boston from about 1850 to 1875. These Victorian-style pianos were mainly used in parlour situations for entertaining and for decorative purposes. They were a mainstay in many American homes during the late 19th century.

182 The Beatles made their American debut, and only live onstage appearance, on *The Ed Sullivan Show* on February 9, 1964. They would appear on the show eight more times via either live telecast from other locations, tape or music video.

183 McDonough, *Shakey*, 94.

184 The Loner," *UNCUT*, March 2009, 32-45. Complete transcript of Allan Bates's interview by Rob Hughes — "Neil Young: The Squires' Years by Allan Bates" — published online at www.uncut .co.uk/neil-young/neil-young-the-squires-years-by-allan-bates-interview.

185 McDonough, *Shakey*, 93.

186 Crowe, "So Hard to Make Arrangements for Yourself."

187 Einarson, *Don't Be Denied*, 76.

188 McDonough, *Shakey*, 94.

189 Lewis, "Paul McCartney gets his star on the Hollywood Walk of Fame."

190 At a benefit gala the next evening where Paul was feted, Neil and Crazy Horse paid tribute by performing "I Saw Her Standing There." This was the first time Neil had played with Crazy Horse since the Greendale tour in 2003/4, and their blistering performance crackled with excitement and energy.

191 Squires' list of songs (circa 1964) from Ken Koblun's private collection.

192 Long, *Ghosts On The Road*, 8.

193 Neil Young, *Waging Heavy Peace*, 125.

194 Ibid., 123.

195 McDonough, *Shakey*, 98

196 *Neil Young: Don't Be Denied*, documentary directed by Ben Whalley.

197  Tyrangiel, "The Resurrection of Neil Young."

198  Neil Young, *Waging Heavy Peace*, 10.

199  Ibid.

200  Cohen, "Bob Dylan: Not Like a Rolling Stone."

201  Neil Young, *Waging Heavy Peace*, 124.

202  Ibid.

203  "Dylan turns up at Neil Young's childhood home for a tour," CBC News/Manitoba, November 10, 2008. www.cbc.ca/news/canada/manitoba/story/2008/11/10/dylan-young.html.

204  Ibid.

205  After the 4-D closed in March 1966, Charlie Clements opened Tubby's Pizza at Stafford Street and Grosvenor Avenue, right beside Stan's Drugstore in Crescentwood. He added the Lounge of Charlie O and Friends four years later. It became a Winnipeg institution and a favourite hangout for rock musicians. It was also a performance venue for young and up-and-coming bands. Neil visited when he was in town. Charlie recalls advising Neil, "Why don't you go to Toronto because big promoter Bernie Fiedler is there." Before Neil left Winnipeg for Fort William in April 1965, Charlie loaned him $40 for gas. It was never repaid, but Charlie didn't care. He valued Neil's friendship most. Tubby's Pizza closed in April 2010, a victim of the slow economy.

206  Charlie Clements booked the Squires for their first gig at the 4-D in Fort William on November 15, 1964. The band wasn't paid anything but was fed. They were paid $15 per night for two additional gigs on November 20 and 21.

207  McDonough, *Shakey*, 97.

208  Charlie Clements revealed that Terry Koreen was the fourth person in Neil's hearse Mort during the drive to Fort William in April 1965. It had been previously written that only three people were in the hearse — Neil, Ken Koblun and Bob Clark. Ken recalls that their additional passenger disappeared for "parts unknown" shortly after they arrived in Fort William.

209  Neil Young, *Waging Heavy Peace*, 278.

210  The Down to Earthenware Jug Band morphed into the Electric Jug and Blues Band by the fall of 1964.

211  Bernie Barsky was earlier the leader of Bernie and the Vampires,

a Grant Park High School band. (Allan Bates was also a member.) After the Brambles dissolved, Bernie formed rock band Expedition to Earth in the late '60s.

212   Einarson, "Folk 'n' Roll."

213   Ibid.

214   Schneider, *Whispering Pines,* 180.

215   Neil Young, *Waging Heavy Peace,* 278.

216   An audio clip of Neil singing "Sweet Joni" at the Civic Auditorium in Bakersfield, CA, on March 11, 1973 is posted at www.youtube.com/watch?v=_9PcDfjkzN0.

217   Einarson, *Don't Be Denied,* 85.

218   Posner, "A Beautiful Position."

219   Einarson, *Don't Be Denied,* 93.

220   McDonough, *Shakey,* 104.

221   Ibid., 113.

222   Einarson, *Don't Be Denied,* 93.

223   Previously unreleased, "Hello Lonely Woman" is included on Disc 0 of *The Neil Young Archives (Volume 1).*

224   Fussman, "What I've Learned: Neil Young."

225   Einarson, *Don't Be Denied,* 95.

226   An entry on p. 184 of the Archives Book, part of *The Neil Young Archives (Volume 1),* shows the date it was written as March 15, 1964, with a question mark after it; this date is obviously a "best guess" since the song was never recorded.

227   Wiebe, "From Kelvin to Princeton University."

228   Roger Currie, "Rock 'n' Roll High School!," 33.

229   Neil Young, *Waging Heavy Peace,* 52.

230   Neil remembered J. O. Blick's Caddy in years to come. In 1974 Neil purchased a 1959 Cadillac Eldorado Biarritz, a car similar to Blick's 1959 Cadillac Series 62 Convertible. Neil's long-time producer and friend David Briggs formally christened Neil's car "Nanu the Lovesick Moose."

231   Jurgensen, "Neil Young: It Was Only a Change in Plan."

232   Einarson, "Whatever happened to . . . Lucille Emond."

233   Lorne Saifer later became Burton Cummings' manager and is employed in the same capacity to this day. In 2001 he joined Cummings and a small group of local investors when they

purchased the Salisbury House restaurant chain from its Montreal owners.

234 Bachman, *Vinyl Tap Stories*, 43.

235 Aloi, "Randy Bachman on Neil Young."

236 "The Loner," *UNCUT*, March 2009, 32-45. Complete transcript of Randy Bachman's interview by Rob Hughes — "Part 4: Randy Bachman" — published online at www.uncut.co.uk/neil-young/part-4-randy-bachman-interview.

237 North, "City DJ finds early Neil Young tape." When this article was originally published, a telephone number was included that the public could call to listen to an audio excerpt from "I Wonder." Members of the online Neil Young community knew of its existence and called the number repeatedly. Mike Cordova had the foresight to tape the clip and subsequently include it on the fan compilation *Archives Be Damned 2000* (ABD2K). Only this short excerpt had been heard by some prior to Randy Bachman debuting the entire song on his *Vinyl Tap* show on Neil's 60th birthday. ("Mustang" received its debut on Randy's show at the same time.)

238 Ibid.

239 Ibid.

240 Also included in *The Neil Young Archives (Volume 1)* is a *second* version of "I Wonder," recorded on November 23, 1964, at CJLX in Fort William by deejay Ray Dee. In material accompanying the Blu-ray Live (a.k.a. BD-Live) Update of a *third* version of "I Wonder" (recorded in Mickey and Bunny Sklepowich's basement studio on March 15, 1965), Neil says the Ray Dee version is his favourite. Author John Einarson discovered the existence of this Fort William tape and contacted Neil, who then flew Ray Dee to the ranch in California so he could hand-deliver the tape. Ray was interviewed at the ranch and this was included in *The Neil Young Archives (Volume 1)*. The Ray Dee version of "I Wonder" can be found hidden behind the roach clip on "I'll Love You Forever," also recorded by Ray on the same date. This matchup was made because the Ray Dee version of "I Wonder" was supposed to be the B-side of "I'll Love You Forever," as he reveals on the audio clip "That Was Gonna Be Our B Side," included in *The Neil Young Archives (Volume 1)*.

241    Einarson, *Don't Be Denied*, 89-91.

242    McDonough, *Shakey*, 93.

243    North, "City DJ finds early Neil Young tape."

244    Letter dated May 5, 1964, held in the Trent University Archives, Scott Young fonds (90-003/26/2).

245    Neil Young, *Waging Heavy Peace*, 60.

246    Einarson, "Neil Young & the Squires."

247    Letter dated April 28, 1964, held in the Trent University Archives, Scott Young fonds (90-003/26/2).

248    Letter dated May 5, 1964, held in the Trent University Archives, Scott Young fonds (90-003/26/2).

249    There is no reference to the Squires playing a school dance anytime in April 1964 on Ken Koblun's "List of Shows." Ken may not have included the school dance because the show was not completed due to Neil blowing his amp.

250    This is the first documented reference of Neil expressing an interest in dividing his time between teaching and music. Most likely he is just trying to appease his father. It's interesting to note, however, that the subject Neil thought he might teach is English, exhibiting that English was the subject where he felt most competent.

251    Letter dated May 5, 1964, held in the Trent University Archives, Scott Young fonds (90-003/26/2).

252    Letter dated May 9, 1964, held in the Trent University Archives, Scott Young fonds (90-003/26/2).

253    Letter dated May 9, 1964, held in the Trent University Archives, Scott Young fonds (90-003/26/2).

254    McDonough, *Shakey*, 100.

255    Letter dated May 11, 1964, held in the Trent University Archives, Scott Young fonds (90-003/26/2).

256    Letter dated May 16, 1964, held in the Trent University Archives, Scott Young fonds (90-003/26/2).

257    Scott expressed his concern regarding Neil taking five years to complete three years of high school. In Ontario, where Scott lived at the time, high school started in Grade 9. Neil had failed Grade 9 at Lawrence Park Collegiate in Toronto and had to repeat his year at Earl Grey School in Winnipeg. He then failed his first attempt at Grade 10 at Kelvin Technical High School and had to repeat his

year, and then was finally placed in Grade 11 at Kelvin for a total of five years, as noted by Scott.

258 Letter dated May 21, 1964, held in the Trent University Archives, Scott Young fonds (90-003/26/2).

259 McDonough, *Shakey*, 102.

260 Brian Klym's son Zev now owns this guitar. George sold it to Zev for $1,000.

**11: Get Gone**

261 The August 6 date for the Town 'n' Country gig is also noted in the Archives Book of *The Neil Young Archives (Volume 1)*. A scan of the advertisement appears on p. 23. The date may have been taken from Ken Koblun's "List of Shows" and not cross-referenced with the July 27 ad that appeared in the *Winnipeg Free Press*. A few other discrepancies in Ken Koblun's "List of Shows" are apparent. A three-night engagement at the Twilight Zone for December 18-20, 1964 — as advertised in the December 18 *Winnipeg Free Press* — is listed as December 15-20 in Ken's "List of Shows." The Squires' recording session in Mickey and Bunny Sklepowich's basement studio on March 15, 1965, is not listed. (Ken has admitted he missed listing this date.) In the March 20, 1965, edition of the *Winnipeg Free Press* the Squires are advertised as appearing at the Twilight Zone on March 23, 24 and 25. This engagement is not listed on Ken's "List of Shows."

262 From "A Brief History of The Squires" (with Ken Smyth), included in *Here We Are In the Years: Neil Young's Music Box*, DVD (Studio: Sexy Intellectual), released June 21, 2001. www.youtube .com/watch?feature=player_embedded&v=HzttcZOg42U.

263 These photos, which appear in the Archives Book of *The Neil Young Archives (Volume 1)*, were originally published in *Broken Arrow 23* (May 1986) in an issue devoted to the Squires and written by John Einarson. Pam Smith is identified merely as "a friend," while she is identified by name in the Archives Book in the notes on p. 226.

264 McDonough, *Shakey*, 89.

265 Ibid.

266   Neil Young, *Waging Heavy Peace*, 49.

267   Ibid., 64.

268   Ibid.

269   McDonough, *Shakey*, 102.

270   From "A Brief History of the Squires" (with Ken Smyth).

271   Ibid.

272   Ibid.

273   Ibid.

274   Ibid.

275   Neil Young, *Waging Heavy Peace*, 37-38.

276   Neil would perform both numbers at the Squires' Reunion at the Blue Note Café in Winnipeg on June 27, 1987. The Jimmy Reed song was included on *Broken Arrow* (1996) and performed at a selection of gigs from 1981 to 1996, while "Hi-Heel Sneakers" was included on the regular set list during the U.S. Club Tour with the Bluenotes in 1987-88. ("Ain't It the Truth" was also a regular item on the set list during this time.) Neil wrote "Find Another Shoulder" and "Hello Lonely Woman" at the Victoria Hotel in Fort William while playing at the Flamingo Club. "Find Another Shoulder" remains unreleased but was included on the regular set list during the 1987 Club Tour (through California), and 1988 U.S. Club Tour with the Bluenotes. "Hello Lonely Woman" was eventually recorded with Comrie Smith in the attic of his parents' house at 46 Golfdale Road in Toronto during fall 1965. This number would also become a regular on Neil's set list during his 1987 Club Tour with the Bluenotes, as well as the 1988 Fall Tour with Ten Men Workin'.

277   Neil Young, *Waging Heavy Peace*, 5.

278   McDonough, *Shakey*, 104.

279   The Labour Day weekend occurred on September 5, 6 and 7, 1964.

280   Neil joked with interviewer Pierre Robert that Mortimer Hearseburg was "a Jewish hearse." From a 93.3 WMMR Rocks! podcast posted November 30, 2012 at www.wmmr.com/music/mmarchives/blogentry.aspx?BlogEntryID=10473296.

281   Böllhoff, "Neil Youngs Leichenwagen restauriert — Mort 3 als Mietwagen."

282   McDonough, *Shakey*, 116.

283 *Don't Be Denied*, documentary directed by Ben Whalley.

284 Neil Young, *Waging Heavy Peace*, 49.

285 Ibid.

286 Ibid., 48.

287 Böllhoff, "Neil Youngs Leichenwagen restauriert — Mort 3 als Mietwagen."

288 Neil Young, *Waging Heavy Peace*, 50.

289 Mike Currie, "An Interview with Ken Koblun," 45.

290 In the lyrics to "Long May You Run," Neil notes 1962 as the year Mort's transmission dropped out. But June 1965 has been thoroughly documented as the correct period. It is not known why Neil decided to use 1962 instead of 1965.

291 Mike Currie, "An Interview with Ken Koblun," 45.

292 Oddly, Brian reports never having taken a ride in the hearse.

293 Neil Young, *Waging Heavy Peace*, 49.

294 Einarson, *Don't Be Denied*, 88.

295 Neil Young, *Waging Heavy Peace*, 49.

296 McDonough, 103.

297 Ibid.

298 Einarson, *Don't Be Denied*, 92.

299 Letter dated September 22, 1964, held in the Trent University Archives, Scott Young fonds (90-003/26/2).

300 Letter dated September 29, 1964, held in the Trent University Archives, Scott Young fonds (90-003/26/2).

301 Letter dated September 30, 1964, held in the Trent University Archives, Scott Young fonds (90-003/26/2).

**PART THREE**

**12: Oh Canada**

1 Part of the original handwritten lyrics for "Don't Be Denied," included on a large fold-up lyrics sheet inserted with the original vinyl release of *Time Fades Away* (1973). Joel Bernstein, Neil's long-time photographer and archivist, took the front album-sleeve photo of the audience at the Philadelphia Spectrum before a show in January 1973 during the Time Fades Away tour with the Stray

Gators. The "Oh Canada" verse does not appear on the version
of "Don't Be Denied" included on the album — recorded live on
March 28, 1973, at the Arizona Veterans Memorial Coliseum in
Phoenix. (There are two additional lines in the "Oh Canada" verse
— *Down in Hollywood / We played so good.*) Mysteriously, Neil
appears to have included this verse at only a handful of shows near
the beginning of the tour. It can be confirmed through the existence
of audience-taped recordings that Neil sang the "Oh Canada"
verse in Detroit on January 8 and 9, in Chicago on January 10 and
11, in Buffalo on January 14 and in Toronto on November 15,
1973. The set list for the tour opener in Madison, Wisconsin, on
January 4 is still unknown. "Don't Be Denied" was not performed
the next night in Milwaukee and the set list for the January 7
show in Bloomington, Minnesota, is unknown. The set list for the
third show played in Chicago on January 12 is unknown, as is the
set list for the January 16 show in Ottawa. "Don't Be Denied"
was included in the set list in Montreal on January 18, but a
confirmation regarding the inclusion of the "Oh Canada" verse is
still needed. Starting with the Baltimore show on January 19, and
continuing to the end of the tour, the verse was not included at
any of the shows and was never sung again live in concert, except
for a surprising one-off return during a performance in Linz,
Austria, on April 5, 2003, during the Greendale (acoustic and solo)
European Tour. This information is included in "Time Fades Away
(Oh Canada!)" by Scott Sandie and Giovanni Pompili, *Broken
Arrow 96* (November 2004), 56-7. An update was provided in a
more recent article in *Broken Arrow,* also by Sandie and Pompili.
(See "Errors & Omissions Excepted (Part 1)," *Broken Arrow 128*
(November 2012). Also see Long, *Ghosts On The Road,* 74-85,
and *Sugar Mountain: Neil Young Set Lists* — 1973 Time Fades
Away Tour with the Stray Gators, www.sugarmtn.org/year
.php?year=1973.

2    The Bonnvilles, who became the Plague a few years later, released a
cover of "High Flyin' Bird" as a single on the Reo label in Canada.
(They used Neil's arrangement of the song.) By 1968 the band had
changed their name to Lexington Avenue and included a version of
"Farmer John" on one of their releases from 1968. (Another nod

to Neil's influence from Fort William.)

3 Both songs remained unreleased until they were included on Disc 0 of *The Neil Young Archives (Volume 1)*.

4 A listing at the back of the Archives Book of *The Neil Young Archives (Volume 1)* indicates that the tape for "Together Alone" is lost.

5 Neil Young Archives *Post Informer (Vol. 1, No. 1)*, "*I Wonder*," June 2, 2009.

6 A copy of "I Wonder," recorded in Mickey and Bunny's basement on March 15, 1965, was sent as an audio track BD-Live Update on July 3, 2009, to owners of the Blu-Ray edition of *The Neil Young Archives (Volume 1)*.

7 Although *The Neil Young Archives (Volume 1)* describes them as "Recorded in a basement (unknown location), Winnipeg," Bunny Sklepowich has confirmed that "I Wonder" and "(I'm a Man and) I Can't Cry" were recorded in the basement of her old home and that Mickey was the recording engineer. Bunny stored the master tape from the time of its recording until it was picked up for use in *The Neil Young Archives (Volume 1)*; the tape was subsequently returned to her.

8 *Don't Be Denied*, documentary directed by Ben Whalley.

9 Archives Book, *The Neil Young Archives (Volume 1)*, 31.

10 Neil later used the melody of "Casting Me Away from You" for "The Emperor of Wyoming" on *Neil Young* (1968).

11 All three of these songs are included on Disc 0 of *The Neil Young Archives (Volume 1)*. The recording date is uncertain but is shown as October 15, 1965, in the Archives Book. Some additional songs were also recorded — six Neil originals ("Casting Me Away from You," "Hello Lonely Woman," "There Goes My Babe," "Betty Ann," "Don't Tell My Friends," "My Room Is Dark ('Cepting for the Light of My Cigarette)" and one cover ("Hi-Heel Sneakers"). Comrie also remembers playing the following songs with Neil during the late fall of 1965: "Runaround Babe," "Stranger in Town" and "Brougham Town" (all original Neil compositions), as well as some of Comrie's songs — "Yesterday's Tomorrows," "Someday," "Your Fooling Heart" and "I'll Be Your Lover, Not Your Friend."

12    A photo of 46 Golfdale Road can be seen in the official video for "Born in Ontario." www.youtube.com/watch?v=1woTG_DaTuw.

13    Neil relates a humorous tale about working at Coles in "Bookstore Rap" on *Live at Canterbury House 1968*.

14    McDonough, *Shakey*, 137.

15    Long, *Ghosts On The Road*, 13.

16    Known as "Don't Pity Me Babe" on a bootleg recording in circulation among fans from Neil's Elektra demo session in New York City in December 1965. "The Ballad of Peggy Grover" — previously unreleased — is included on Disc 0 of *The Neil Young Archives (Volume 1)*. Neil revealed that he wrote this song while living at 88 Isabella Street in Toronto during the fall of 1965 and that "'Peggy Grover' was a play on words for Grover pegs, which were the best tuning pegs you could buy for a guitar." (*Waging Heavy Peace*, 276.)

17    A second version of "The Rent Is Always Due," recorded in August 1967 as a Gold Star Solo Demo and previously released on the *Buffalo Springfield Box Set*, was sent as an audio track BD-Live Update on November 2, 2009, to owners of the Blu-ray edition of *The Neil Young Archives (Volume 1)*.

18    An audio track of "I Ain't Got the Blues" from the Elektra demo session was sent as a BD-Live Update on March 29, 2010, to owners of the Blu-ray edition of *The Neil Young Archives (Volume 1)*.

19    The Elektra demo recording of "Nowadays Clancy Can't Even Sing" is included on Disc 0 of *The Neil Young Archives (Volume 1)*. A second version is included as a hidden track in the Blu-ray edition of *The Neil Young Archives (Volume 1)*. It was recorded at Gold Star Recording Studios in Hollywood on July 18, 1966, and is the track used on the Atco Records recording of *Buffalo Springfield* (1966). Richie Furay sings lead vocal on the track.

20    The tracks from Neil's recording session at Elektra Records are included on Disc 0 of *The Neil Young Archives (Volume 1)*. The recording date is not certain and is shown as "12/15/65?" in the Archives Book.

21    Two tracks from the Mynah Birds' recording sessions in Motown — "It's My Time" and "Go On and Cry" — were released on

November 24, 2006, as part of Hip-O Select's *The Complete Motown Singles (Volume 6)*. These same tracks were sent as BD-Live Updates on February 26, 2010, to owners of the Blu-ray edition of *The Neil Young Archives (Volume 1)*. "It's My Time" b/w "Go On and Cry" by the Mynah Birds was released as a special single on Record Store Day — April 21, 2012. Two of the Mynah Birds' songs were composed by Neil and Rick James — "I'll Wait Forever" and "It's My Time." Neil's vocals do not appear on any of the Motown sessions with the Mynah Birds and his guitar work is mixed down so low that it is barely discernable.

22   The four other passengers in Mort II were Jeanine Hollingshead, Tannis Neiman, Judy Mack and Mike Gallagher.

23   *Neil Young: Shakin' All Over Reunion 28/06/87*, Bootleg DVD, interview with Neil from one of a number of backstage interviews at the Shakin' All Over Sixties Winnipeg Bands Reunion held at the Winnipeg Convention Centre on June 28, 1987, the Squires Reunion at the Blue Note Café in Winnipeg, and a dinner also held at the Winnipeg Convention Centre.

24   Ibid.

25   The Loner," *UNCUT*, March 2009, 32-45. Complete transcript of Randy Bachman's interview by Rob Hughes — "Part 4: Randy Bachman" — published online at www.uncut.co.uk/neil-young/part-4-randy-bachman-interview.

26   Brautigan, "Author, rock star dad Scott Young remembered."

27   Friedman, "10,000 Photos of Neil Young."

28   McDonough, *Shakey*, 115.

29   Neil Young, *Waging Heavy Peace*, 5.

30   *Don't Be Denied*, documentary directed by Ben Whalley.

31   Patton, "For Neil Young, a Journey Through Rock and Rust."

32   Astrid Young, *Being Young*, 47.

33   Brautigan, "Author, rock star dad Scott Young remembered."

34   Sims, "Neil Young Profile."

35   Neil Young, *Waging Heavy Peace*, 140.

36   From a post-show interview with Neil and Jonathan Demme at the screening of *Neil Young Journeys* at the Princess of Wales Theatre in Toronto on September 12, 2011, during the Toronto International Film Festival.

37    Neil Young, *Waging Heavy Peace*, 370.

38    Gross, "In Memoir, Neil Young Wages Heavy Peace."

39    Gibson, *An Interview with Daniel Lanois*.

40    Simpson, "Astrid Young basks in own artistic glow."

41    Tyrangiel, "The Resurrection of Neil Young (Continued)."

42    Appleford, "Q&A: Jonatham Demme on the making of *Neil Young Journeys*."

43    DeVito, "Neil Young and Jonathan Demme."

44    Appleford, "Q&A: Jonatham Demme on the making of *Neil Young Journeys*."

45    Tyrangiel, "The Resurrection of Neil Young (Continued)."

46    Neil Young, *Waging Heavy Peace*, 433.

47    Ibid., 272.

48    Nineteen years later a glimmering of "Oh Susannah" appeared in a snippet of the song Neil played on harmonica just before launching into the debut of "California Sunset" (performed on banjo) during a performance at the Civic Auditorium in Santa Cruz on January 5, 1983, during the Solo Trans Tour. Twenty-eight years later he would perform "Oh Susannah" with Dave Matthews and Tim Reynolds at the Bridge School Benefit Concert at the Shoreline Amphitheatre in Mountain View, CA, on October 22 and 23, 2011. Ken Koblun later watched a clip of this performance and commented, "He beefed up the front end. Otherwise the basic chord structure is the same as the arrangement we played in Fort William." Less than a year later Neil included his version of "Oh Susannah" on *Americana*, recorded with Crazy Horse and released in June 2012. Neil confirmed in the liner notes that the arrangement by Tim Rose and the Thorns is the one Crazy Horse used.

49    Einarson, *For What It's Worth*, 49-50.

50    Neil added an additional Canadian twist to this song when he sang it as part of R.E.M.'s performance at the 12th annual Bridge School Benefit concert at the Shoreline Amphitheatre in Mountain View, CA, on October 17 and 18, 1998. Neil inserted a distinctive "eh?" after the line "I'm up in T.O. keepin' jive alive." R.E.M. distributed the October 18 live recording of this song as the B-side of their 12th annual Christmas Fan Club Single in 1999. "Country

Feedback," also recorded live at the Bridge School Benefit concert on the same day — but not featuring Neil — was selected as the A-side.

51   "Hitchhiker" was written by Neil in the mid-to-late-1970s. The lyrics were updated slightly in 2010 for the recording of *Le Noise*.

52   Neil is referencing Tinker Bell, a 1947 Buick convertible he owned for a short time in Toronto during summer and fall 1965. It's not known why Neil states the year of the car as 1948 in "Hitchhiker."

53   Neil Young, *Waging Heavy Peace*, 139.

54   Fulford, "Neil Young didn't come back for you either."

55   Uhelszki, "Neil Young and Daniel Lanois: Love and War."

# ✯ BIBLIOGRAPHY ✯

"A Brief History of the Squires (with Ken Smyth)." In *Here We Are in the Years: Neil Young's Music Box*, DVD released June 21, 2001, by Sexy Intellectual.

Aloi, Daniel. "Randy Bachman on Neil Young." *Broken Arrow #60*, August 1995.

Appleford, Steve. "Q&A: Jonathan Demme on the making of Neil Young Journeys." *Rolling Stone* (website), June 27, 2012.

Bachman, Randy. Neil Young tribute in honour of his 60th birthday. *Vinyl Tap*, CBC Radio One, November 12, 2005.

────── *Vinyl Tap Stories*. Toronto: Viking Canada, 2011.

Bienstock, Richard. "Rider on the Storm." *Guitar Legends (Issue #118)*, reprint from *Guitar World Acoustic*, December 2005.

Böllhoff, Ralf. "Neil Young and The Squires' — Die ukrainischen Wurzeln." Under the Rusted Moon (blogsite), May 18, 2012. www.rusted-moon.com/2012/05/neil-young-and-squires-die-ukrainischen.html.

────── "Neil Youngs 'Orange Period' — Die Gretsch 6120." Under the Rusted Moon (blog), June 7, 2011. www.rusted-moon .com/2011/06/neil-youngs-orange-periode-die-gretsch.html.

────── "Neil Youngs Leichenwagen restauriert — Mort 3 als Mietwagen." Under the Rusted Moon (blog), July 6, 2012. www.rusted-moon.com/2012/07/neil-youngs-leichenwagen-restauriert.html#more.

Brautigan, Tara. "Author, rock star dad Scott Young remembered." *Winnipeg Free Press*, June 17, 2005.

Bunte, Jim. "Railroading Together." *Classic Toy Trains*, March 1993.

Burcher, Mary L. "The Largest Single Hospital, Medical, Educational Unit on the Continent." *Canadian Hospital*, May 1930.

Chong, Kevin. *Neil Young Nation: A Quest, An Obsession (and a True Story)*. Vancouver/Toronto/Berkeley: Greystone Books, 2005.

Cohen, Scott. "Bob Dylan: Not Like a Rolling Stone." *Spin (Vol. 1, No. 8)*, December 1985.

Connor, J. T. H. *Doing Good: The Life of Toronto's General Hospital.*
Toronto/Buffalo/London: University of Toronto Press, 2000.
Crowe, Cameron. "Neil Young: Still Expecting to Fly." *Musician,*
November 1982.
———— "So Hard to Make Arrangements for Yourself: The Rolling Stone
Interview with Neil Young." *Rolling Stone (Issue 193)*, August 14,
1975.
———— "Neil Young: The Last American Hero." *Rolling Stone
(Issue 284)*, February 8, 1979.
Currie, Mike. "An Interview with Ken Koblun." *Broken Arrow #101*,
February 2006.
Currie, Roger. "Rock 'n' Roll High School," *Broken Arrow #103*, August
2006. (Originally published as "My Famous Classmate" in the
*Winnipeg Free Press*, March 22, 2005.)


Demme Jonathan, *Neil Young Journeys*, Shakey Pictures/Clinica Estetico,
2011.
———— *Neil Young: Heart of Gold*, Shakey Pictures/Clinica Estetico/
Playtone (in association with)/Shangri-La Entertainment, 2006.
Denberg, Jody. "Music just takes you wherever you want to go."
*No Depression (Issue #60)*, November/December 2005.
Devito, Darren. "Neil Young and Jonathan Demme: Words and Music
2012." WFUV interview recorded on June 7, 2012. Posted online
June 26, 2012. www.wfuv.org/audio/archives/words-and-music-
studio/neil-young-and-jonathan-demme-words-and-music-2012.
"Dylan turns up at Neil Young's childhood home for a tour." CBC News/
Manitoba (website), November 10, 2008.


Echard, William. *Neil Young and the Poetics of Energy.* Bloomington/
Indianapolis: Indiana University Press, 2005.
Einarson, John. "Folk 'n' Roll." *Broken Arrow #112*, November 2008.
———— *Neil Young: Don't Be Denied — "The Canadian Years."*
Kingston: Quarry Press, 1992.
———— "Neil Young & the Squires." *Broken Arrow #23*, May 1986.
———— "Shakin' All Over: The Winnipeg Sixties Rock Scene," Variety
Club of Manitoba, 1987.

——— "Whatever happened to . . . Lucille Emond." *Winnipeg Free Press*, March 17, 2011.

Einarson, John (with Ian Tyson & Sylvia Tyson). *Four Strong Winds: Ian & Sylvia*. Toronto: McClelland and Stewart, 2011.

Einarson, John (with Richie Furay). *For What It's Worth: The Story of the Buffalo Springfield*. New York: Cooper Square Press, 2004.

Fisher-Heasman, Marlyne. *A Walker's Guide to Omemee: The Pigeon Town*. Peterborough: Trent Valley Archives, 2008.

Friedman, Jon. "10,000 Photos of Neil Young." *Wall Street Journal* (website), June 21, 2011.

Fulford, Robert. "Neil Young didn't come back for you either." *National Post*, April 2, 2012.

Fussman, Cal. "What I've Learned: Neil Young." *Esquire*, December 31, 2005.

Gibson, Donald. "An Interview with Daniel Lanois." BC blogcritics (website), posted December 27, 2010. blogcritics.org/music/article/an-interview-with-daniel-lanois/.

Goddard, John. "Neil Young's childhood friend walks down memory lane." *Toronto Star*, May 30, 2009.

Goddard, John, and Richard Crouse. *Rock and Roll Toronto: From Alanis to Zeppelin*. Toronto: Doubleday Canada, 1997.

Gross, Terry. "In Memoir, Neil Young Wages 'Heavy Peace.'" NPR *Fresh Air* program, October 1, 2012. www.npr.org/2012/10/01/162082545/in-memoir-neil-young-wages-heavy-peace.

Gzowski, Peter. "Pierre Berton, fresh from a 47th book tour, still calls me Pete." *The Globe and Mail*, November 24, 2001.

Henderson, Stuart. *Making the Scene: Yorkville and Hip Toronto in the 1960s*. University of Toronto Press, Scholarly Publishing Division, 2011.

Jennings, Nicholas. *Before the Gold Rush: Flashbacks to the Dawn of the Canadian Sound*. Toronto: Viking, 1997.

Jurgensen, John. "Neil Young: It Was Only a Change in Plan." *Wall Street Journal*, June 16, 2011.

Kent, Nick. "I Build Something Up, I Tear It Right Down: Neil Young at 50." *Mojo*, December 1995.
—— "Neil Young: This Young Will Run and Run." *Vox*, November 1990.

Lewis, Randy. "Paul McCartney gets his star on the Hollywood Walk of Fame." *Los Angeles Times*, February 9, 2012.
Long, Pete. *Ghosts On The Road: Neil Young in Concert, 1961-2006.* Winchester, U.K.: The Old Homestead Press, 2007 (revised edition). First published in 1996.

McDonough, Jimmy. *Shakey: Neil Young's Biography.* New York: Random House, 2002.
McKay, Alastair. "Neil Young — London Hammersmith Apollo." *Uncut*, March 2008.

"Neil Young: the Loner," *Uncut*, March 2009. Interviews by Michael Bonner, John Einarson, Nick Hasted, Rob Hughes and John Lewis. Complete transcripts available online.
North, Peter. "City DJ finds early Neil Young tape. Box in basement yields '64 recording of up-and-coming rock superstar." *Edmonton Journal*, February 23, 2000.

O'Connor, Sean. "Rock star gets honorary degree." *The Chronicle-Journal*, May 24, 1992.

Patton, Phil. "For Neil Young, a Journey Through Rock and Rust." *New York Times*, June 11, 2011.
Posner, Michael. "A Beautiful Position." *The Globe and Mail*, June 24, 2006.

Rogan, Johnny. *Neil Young: Zero to Sixty — A Critical Biography.* London: Calidore Books, 2001 (revised edition). First published in 2000.

Rutty, Chris. "Helpless: The 1951 Ontario Polio Outbreak; the Neil Young Case." *Broken Arrow #36*, August 1989.

Sandie, Scott. "The Original Lyric Manuscript: 'Nowadays Clancy Can't Even Sing.'" *Broken Arrow #102*, May 2006.

Schneider, Jason. *Whispering Pines: The Northern Roots of American Music . . . From Hank Snow to The Band.* Toronto: ECW Press, 2009.

Simmons, Sylvie. "Crazy Horse: Ralph, Billy, Poncho . . . and Neil." *Mojo*, July 1997.

Simpson, Barbara. "Astrid Young basks in artistic glow." *Simcoe Reformer*, August 6, 2010.

Sims, Judith. "Neil Young Profile." *Teen Set*, April 1968.

Smith, Kenton. "A ballad of Winnipeg's musical past: New documentary 'Drop the Nickel' chronicles the quest for a Manitoba-made musical and cultural treasure." *Uptown* (website), October 2010.

Tyrangiel, Josh. "The Resurrection of Neil Young." *Time*, September 2005.

Uhelszki, Jann. "Neil Young and Daniel Lanois: Love and War." *American Songwriter*, January/February 2010.

Verlinde, Jason. "Photo Outtakes: Guitar Tech Larry Cragg." Photos posted online from an article by Brian Fisher in *Fretboard Journal #23* (Fall 2011).

Whalley, Ben. *Neil Young: Don't Be Denied*, documentary originally screened on American Masters, BBC Four, October 31– November 2, 2008.

Wheeler, Brad. "Lanois' Neil Young project proceeds with caution." *The Globe and Mail*, July 22, 2010.

"Who Was Clancy?" KSAN radio transcript, November 12, 1969. *The Neil Young Archives (Volume 1)*.

Wiebe, Lindsey. "From Kelvin to Princeton University: First female prez once walked halls of city school." *Winnipeg Free Press*, February 27, 2011.

Wilkinson, Alec. "The Open Man — Inside Neil Young's private world." *Rolling Stone (Issue 992)*, January 26, 2006.

Williamson, C. Hillier, and John Gilbert Jones. *Omemee*. Peterborough/Lindsay: Pigin Publishing, 2000 (2nd edition).

Young, Astrid. *Being Young*. Toronto: Insomniac Press, 2007.

Young, Neil. *Waging Heavy Peace: A Hippie Dream*. New York: Blue Rider Press, 2012.

Young, Scott. "$100 a month — 'You-All Should Be in Florida Too.'" *Saturday Night*, February 23, 1952.

—— "Company Report: Neil's Chicken Business." *The Globe and Mail*, May 2, 1957.

—— "Company Report: Veritable Business Cyclone." *The Globe and Mail*, May 3, 1957.

—— "Cutups All, Grass Type, That Is." *The Globe and Mail*, June 9, 1958.

—— "Dr. Young Says Penny Ante Psychology Backfires." *The Globe and Mail*, March 15, 1957.

—— "Family Journey Problems." *The Globe and Mail*, July 8, 1957.

—— "The Foundling Budgie." *Winnipeg Free Press*, September 22, 1956.

—— "Long may you run. Neil and me: a father's memories of his famous son." *Toronto Life*, December 1980.

—— *Neil and Me*. Toronto: McClelland and Stewart, 1984.

—— "Polio Recalled: Sickness A Time To Think." *The Globe and Mail*, November 27, 1957.

—— "Presents Not Easy to Choose." *The Globe and Mail*, December 9, 1957.

—— *A Writer's Life*. Toronto: Doubleday Canada, 1994.

Zimmer, Dave. "Blue Notes for a Restless Loner." *BAM* magazine, April 22, 1988.

# ✭ OTHER SOURCES ✭

Archives of Ontario at York University, Scott Young fonds
City of Toronto Archives
Hot Rods & Jalopies (blogsite)
John Wanless Alumni Association
Legislative Library of Manitoba
Manitoba Music Museum (website)
Neil Young Appreciation Society (NYAS) and *Broken Arrow* magazine
"Neil Young (Legends on Twitter)," October 24, 2012
Neil Young Online Community (Rust list, Human Highway list,
    Bad News Beat, various Neil Young Facebook groups)
"Neil Young – Waging Heavy Peace," Twitter Q&A event sponsored by
    Blue Rider Press, December 2, 2012
Omemee Historical Society
Pickering-Ajax Digital Archives
Pickering Public Library
Pickering Township Historical Society
Sugar Mountain: Neil Young Set Lists (website)
The Globe and Mail Archives
*The Neil Young Archives (Volume 1)*
Thrasher's Wheat (blogsite)
Town of Ajax Archives
Trent University Archives, Scott Young fonds
Under the Rusted Moon (blogsite)
Winnipeg Free Press Archives
Yearbooks from Lawrence Park Collegiate Institute in Toronto, Earl Grey
    Junior High School, Kelvin High School, Grant Park High School
    and Churchill High School in Winnipeg
Youngtown Museum

# ⭑ INDEX ⭑

Page numbers in italics refer to photographs. The abbreviation "NY" refers to "Neil Young."

# * ACKNOWLEDGEMENTS *

THE WRITING OF THIS BOOK was truly an epic journey for me, and it would not have been possible without the help and support of many people. All of these individuals have my heartfelt thanks, but there is unfortunately room to mention only some of them.

Scott Sandie supported my research from the start, providing advice, encouragement and a forum in which to publish early versions of some sections of this book. He was enormously helpful when we made an initial trip to the Trent University Archives to explore the Scott Young fonds, and his guidance and suggestions as my research evolved were invaluable.

I spoke with Ken Koblun, bass player for the Classics and the Squires, by phone on countless occasions, and he provided a wealth of information and material. I am indebted to him for his remarkable patience and goodwill. His detailed accounts of his early years with Neil proved indispensable.

I was privileged to participate in an ongoing dialogue with Allan Bates, rhythm guitarist for the Squires, until the time of his passing in December 2011, and I remain indebted to him for his help. Ken Smyth, drummer for the Squires, also contributed greatly with an account of his experience in the band.

Don Marshall, Richard Koreen and Linda Fowler shared memories of their time playing with Neil, and their stories helped fill in and give structure to the account of Neil's music career prior to his formation of the Squires. Jim Kale, bass player in the Guess Who, was also kind enough to speak at length about his early years in Winnipeg.

I received a magnificent education in guitars and amplifiers from Ralf Böllhoff, whose encyclopedic knowledge helped unlock a number of mysteries.

A solid grounding in history and geography was also crucial to the success of this book, and many people gave me far more of their time and attention than I could ever have expected. John Sabean, president of the Pickering Township Historical Society, was instrumental in providing relevant material and research information. Marlyne Fisher-Heasman, John Gilbert Jones and Joan Rehill of the Omemee Historical Society were also most generous with their time. Other individuals who provided useful historical and geographical detail include Sandra (Ezell) Blackmer, Shirley (Cargill) Cloar, John Flower, Lynne "Hammy" Hamilton, Susan (Wilson) Hill, Rob McConnell, Peter "Cinnamon Boy" McMurtrie, Bain Myers, Martha (Cleland) Ross, Jim Sowerby and Elvin Wingay.

Over the course of my research I interviewed more than 150 individuals. Their firsthand information was a tremendous asset to this project and I am indebted to all of them. Principal participants, in addition to those already mentioned, were: *(Earliest Toronto years/Lake of Bays/Jackson's Point)* Pamela Berton, Penny Berton, Beryl Braithwaite, Anne MacPherson, Chris Rutty; *(Omemee)* the late Edna Carew, David Finney, Morag Gray, Trevor Hosier, Henry Mason, Don Weir, David Whitmore, Garfield "Goof" Whitney; *(New Smyrna Beach)* the late Rick Ahlgren, S. Jane Allen, Jim Pearsall, Katherine F. Shepard, Shalaine (Crain) Solomon; *(Brock Road/Pickering)* Beverly Boys, Brian Boys, Ian Buttars, Clayton Cary, Marlene (Bath) Coulby, Richard Doble, Ruth Doble, Bob Hunter, Carol (Shanley) Irvine, Ross D. James, Murray Maurer, Dennis Murray, Jan (Carter) Nimmo, Wilson Paterson, Mike Shanley, Doug Summers, Gwen Summers, Doug Suter;

# ACKNOWLEDGEMENTS

*(Toronto)* Mary Ellen Blanch, David Bradley, Peter Broderick, Owen Charlesworth, Keith Cowan, Sheila (Smith) Edgar, Mike Foulds, Harold Greer, Eric Hennessey, Marilyn Mutch, Forbes Pritchard, Gary Renzetti, Carol Susko, Rick Wardell; *(Winnipeg/Fort William)* Joe Barnsley, Charles "Chic" Bell, Brian Blick, Garry Bowles, Barry Brazier, Katharine Bruce, Barry Carther, Glenn Church, Charlie Clements, John Michael Copsey, Roger Currie, Peter Edmondson, Terry Erickson, Fran Gebhard, Jack Gowenlock, David Gregg, Diana Halter, Tim Henry, William Hoogstraten, Ken Johnson, Susan Kelso, Brian Klym, Jean (Truman) Ko, Carmine La Rosa, Bill and Lauren Laing, Patrick Liss, Robert Liss, Shirley Lord, Sharon McCrae, Bonnie (Bater) McMullen, Clive Morrison, Mari-Jean (Liss) Naghtigall, Bill Pawlyk, Randy Peterson, Erwin Ploner, Natalie Pollock, Heather (Tozeland) Powell, Maureen (Goldberg) Rabin, Garry and Yvonne Reid, Dave Romanyshyn, Mike Sambork, Bunny Sklepowich, Ross F. "Clancy" Smith, Wayne Smith, Jim Sweeney, John Teskey, Larry Wah, Harold Westdal, Jan (Booth) Williamson, George Wolak, Jeffrey Dack Wuckert. The thousands of members of the online Neil Young community provided information and moral support that made the writing of this book feel almost like a collaborative effort. I thank them all.

I want to extend my sincere thanks to the staff at ECW Press, especially Jack David, who took an early interest in my work and encouraged its progress. The editing process was made easier by Stuart Ross, my sure-handed copy editor.

And as a first-time writer I am grateful for the assistance, advice and support I received from my husband, Robert Charles Wilson. His guidance and experience made the journey from initial concept to finished book much less stressful and daunting than it would otherwise have been.

# GET THE EBOOK FREE! ✳ ✳ ✳ ✳ ✳ ✳ ✳ ✳ ✳ ✳ ✳

At ECW Press, we want you to enjoy this book in whatever format you like,
whenever you like. Leave your print book at home and take the eBook to
go! Purchase the print edition and receive the eBook free. Just send an email
to ebook@ecwpress.com and include:

- the book title
- the name of the store where you purchased it
- your receipt number
- your preference of file type: PDF or ePub?

A real person will respond to your email with your eBook attached. Thank
you for supporting an independently owned Canadian publisher with your
purchase!